Dawson 26/07/01

£55.00

ENTREPRENEURSHIP EDUCATION

The articles in this book were mostly selected from the papers presented at the Internationalizing Entrepreneurship Education and Training Conference (IntEnt$_{97}$), held in Monterey, California, USA.

(www.intent-conference.de)

Production of this volume is supported by
Foerderkreis Gruendungs-Forschung e.V.
Entrepreneurship Research
www.fgf-ev.de
c/o EUROPEAN BUSINESS SCHOOL
Schloss Reichartshausen
65375 Oestrich-Winkel, Germany

Entrepreneurship Education
A global view

Edited by

ROBERT H. BROCKHAUS
Saint Louis University, USA

GERALD E. HILLS
University of Illinois, Chicago, USA

HEINZ KLANDT
European Business School, Schloss Reichartshausen, Germany

HAROLD P. WELSCH
DePaul University, Chicago, USA

Ashgate
Aldershot • Burlington USA • Singapore • Sydney

Published by
Ashgate Publishing Limited
Gower House
Croft Road
Aldershot
Hants GU11 3HR
England

Ashgate Publishing Company
131 Main Street
Burlington, VT 05401-5600 USA

Ashgate website: http://www.ashgate.com

British Library Cataloguing in Publication Data
Entrepreneurship education : a global view
   1.Entrepreneurship - Study and teaching
   I.Brockhaus, Robert H.
   338'.04'071

Library of Congress Control Number: 2001088788

ISBN 0 7546 1224 4

Printed in Great Britain by
Antony Rowe Ltd, Chippenham, Wiltshire

Contents

PART D: NETWORKS IN ENTREPRENEURSHIP EDUCATION

PART E: VARIOUS ASPECTS OF ENTREPRENEURSHIP EDUCATION

List of Contributors

Alcaraz, Rafael, Dean of Entrepreneurial Program, Monterrey Institute of Technology System (ITESM), Mexico

Armer, Michael, Professor in the Department of Sociology, Florida State University, USA

Bellini, Emilio, Doctoral Student in Managerial Engineering ODISSEO, Dept. of Computer Science and Systems, University of Naples Federico II, Napoli, Italy

Bodie, Dusty, College of Business and Economics, Boise State University, Idaho, USA

Brockhaus, Robert H., Holder of the Coleman Chair of Entrepreneurship, director of the Jefferson Smurfit Center for Entrepreneurial Studies, St. Louis University, Missouri, USA

Capaldo, Guido, Researcher in Managerial Engineering at the Faculty of Engineering of the Second University of Naples, Napoli, Italy

Carland, James W., Dr., Professor of Entrepreneurship, Western Carolina University, USA

Carland, JoAnn C., Dr., Professor of Entrepreneurship, Western Carolina University, USA

Crijns, Hans, Professor, De Vlerick School voor Management, University of Ghent, Belgium

De Clercq, Dirk, De Vlerick School voor Management, University of Ghent, Belgium

Deschoolmeester, Dirk, Prof. dr. ir., Head of the Center of SMEs, De Vlerick School voor Management, University of Gent, Ledeberg-Gent, Belgium

Duchéneaut, Bertrand, EURO PME, Groupe ESC, Rennes, France

Fiet, James O., Professor, PhD., University of the Pacific, Eberhardt School of Business, Stockton CA., USA

Gillin, L. Murray., Chair of Innovation and Entrepreneurship Swinburne University of Technology, Melbourne, Australia

Guedalla, Martin, University of Westminster, UK

Halvarsson, Dan, Scandinavian Institute for Research in Entrepreneurship (SIRE), Växjö University, Sweden

Henry, Colette, Dundalk Regional Technical College, Dundalk, Ireland

Herlau, Henrik, Professor, Copenhagen Business School, Denmark

IX

Hills, Gerald E., Executive Director, Institute for Entrepreneurial Studies, University of Illinois at Chicago, Chicago, Illinois, USA

Hjorth, Daniel, Scandinavian Institute for Research in Entrepreneurship (SIRE), Växjö University/Lund University, Sweden

Hornsby, Jeffrey S., Institute for Entrepreneurship, Ball State University, Muncie, IN, USA

Huang, Xueli, PhD, Faculty of Business and Economics, Monash University, Victoria, Australia

Hurley, Kelli M., Institute for Entrepreneurship, Ball State University, Muncie, IN, USA

Johannisson, Bengt, Professor, Scandinavian Institute for Research in Entrepreneurship (SIRE), Växjö University/Lund University, Sweden

Kickul, Jill R., De Paul University, Department of Management, Chicago, Illinois, USA

Klandt, Heinz, Holder of the DtA Chair for Entrepreneurship, European Business School, Oestrich-Winkel, Germany

Koen, Peter A., Associate Professor, PhD., Wesley J. Howe School of Technology Management, Stevens Institute of Technology, Hoboken, NJ, USA

Kuratko, Donald F., Institute for Entrepreneurship, Ball State University, Muncie, IN, USA

Learned, Kevin, Dr., College of Business and Economics, Boise State University, Idaho, USA

Ledezma, Jorge, Assistant of Entrepreneurial Program, Monterrey Institute of Technology System (ITESM), Mexico

Lövstal, Eva, Scandinavian Institute for Research in Entrepreneurship (SIRE), Växjö University, Sweden

McMullan, W.E., Faculty of Management, University of Calgary, Calgary, Canada

Mohan-Neill, Sumaria, MBA, PhD., College of Business Administration, Roosevelt University, Schaumburg, IL, USA

Morrison, Alison, Dr., The Scottish Hotel School, University of Strathclyde, Glasgow, UK

Napier, Nancy K., College of Business and Economics, Boise State University, Idaho, USA

Nieuwenhuizen, Cecile, Senior Lecturer, Technikon Southern Africa, Republic of South Africa

Ooghe, Hubert, De Vlerick School voor Management, University of Ghent, Belgium

Qaiser, Shazeen, University of Westminster, UK

Raffa, Mario, Scientific Director of ODISSEO and Professor of Business Economics and Organization, ODISSEO (Centre for Organization and Technological Innovation), Dept. of Computer Science and Systems, University of Naples Federico II, Napoli, Italy

Romano, Claudio, PhD, Faculty of Business and Economics, Monash University, Victoria, Australia

Schamp, Tom, Academic Staff at the Center of SMEs, De Vlerick School voor Management, University of Gent, Ledeberg-Gent, Belgium

Smyrnios, Kosmas, PhD, Faculty of Business and Economics, Monash University, Victoria, Australia

Tanewski, George, Dr., PhD, David Syme Faculty of Business, Monash University, Victoria, Australia

Titterington, Albert, Division of Information Management, Queens University, Belfast, Northern Ireland

Ulrich, Thomas A., Sellinger School of Business and Management, Loyola College, Baltimore, Maryland, USA

van Niekerk, Albert, Dr., Springbok Dental c/o Hoechst AG Kalle-Albert, Wiesbaden, Germany

Vandenbroucke, Anne-Maria, Academic Staff at the Center of SMEs, De Vlerick School voor Management, University of Gent, Ledeberg-Gent, Belgium

Vesper, Karl H., Professor of Management, University of Washington, USA

Watson, C. Howard, Dr., Centre for Entrepreneurship, Technikon Pretoria, Pretoria, Republic of South Africa

Welsch, Harold P., De Paul University, Dep. of Management, Chicago, Illinois, USA

Yendell, Mike, Dr., Director Strathclyde Entrepreneurship Initiative, University of Strathclyde, Scotland

Zollo, Guiseppe, Associate Professor of Business Management, ODISSEO, Dept. of Computer Science and Systems, University of Naples Federico II, Napoli, Italy

Foreword

Robert H. Brockhaus, Sr.

Coleman Foundation Chairholder in Entrepreneurship
and Director of the Jefferson Smurfit Center for Entrepreneurial
Studies, Saint Louis University, St. Louis, Missouri

Introduction

The important role of entrepreneurs has in recent years been known to most of the world. Individuals who have never touched a keyboard or who have no idea exactly what an email is have heard of Steven Jobs and Bill Gates. They are known throughout the world as entrepreneurs who have changed the world through their innovations.

Despite the renown of these, other entrepreneurs collectively have had an even larger impact. In the United States over 20 million business tax returns are filed each year and another 20 million of unreported micro entrepreneurs are believed to exist. That total of 40 million represents approximately one in seven living Americans. If you subtract the number of very young and very old, perhaps as high as one in four or five adult Americans have some form of business. There are five million businesses with more than one employee. Ninety-eight per cent have fewer than 100 employees. Fifty-four per cent of the work force is employed by businesses with fewer than 500 employees and approximately half of the GNP is provided by small business. Since 1980 the 100,000 businesses with more than 500 employees have decreased their number of employees. At the same time the number of new employees in small businesses has increased by over two million. Similar trends are reported in almost every major industrialized country.

Failure rates are reported from as low as one per cent to as high as 80 per cent depending on the criteria used for measurement. The losses are not just financial but also include psychological effects to the entrepreneur and his or her family. Moreover, there are economic and social losses to the community. It is generally agreed that the survival rate can be improved with a greater awareness of entrepreneurial management skills.

Entrepreneurship has been important for thousands of years as providers of needed services to the general population and as a source of innovation. However, it has only been in the last two decades that the general public and the academic world have come to realize the important contribution to the economy and standard of living that entrepreneurs make.

Before then, there were very few universities that offered courses in entrepreneurship or small business. One of the first courses was offered at the Harvard Business School in 1947. Peter Drucker taught another early course at New York University in 1953. As the academic world has come to recognize the importance of entrepreneurship and the value of entrepreneurship education, there has been increasing attention given to the teaching of entrepreneurship. The first conference on small business was held at St. Gallen University in Switzerland in 1948. In recent years, there have been many educational conferences that attempt to disseminate information about the teaching of entrepreneurship and small business. Nevertheless, very little is still known about effective teaching techniques for entrepreneurial educators. And even less have been demonstrated in well-constructed research studies.

The diversity of the "students" range from primary school students to owners and employees of well-established and sometimes huge businesses; from those with doctorate degrees to those who are illiterate; from countries that have a well-established tradition of entrepreneurship to those from Third World or socialistic countries. The educational setting varies from university graduate classes to television shows to books and pamphlets. The length of the educational program can be years in degree granting institutions to a few hours in one evening for a lecture. Given this diversity of audiences, settings and purposes, it is no wonder that the research and knowledge about how to teach entrepreneurship is so underdeveloped.

This book is a major step toward addressing the needs of entrepreneurship educators. Leading experts from throughout the world have contributed their knowledge and experience so that others can benefit and that the field of entrepreneurship education can advance.

Overview of Content

In the initial section of the book, Karl Vesper, one of the pioneers in entrepreneurship education, provides an overview of research questions that entrepreneurship educators should consider. His suggestions of these missing links in entrepreneurship are both thought provoking and deserving of careful investigation. Howard Watson presents research findings that urge that a definition of entrepreneurship is important for the future of entrepreneurship research. Although this suggestion might seem very self evident, entrepreneurship researchers have spent the last two decades debating what is the correct definition. To date, they have been unable to reach a consensus. Watson suggests that there are certain variables that can differentiate small business and entrepreneurship. Because he involved hundreds of entrepreneurship educators from throughout the world in his study, the findings bear careful consideration by all entrepreneurship educators and researchers.

In the early years of entrepreneurship education, faculty members independently tried to teach the course in the best way possible. Over the years, a body of knowledge has been developed that provides the beginnings of a theoretical framework for the teaching of entrepreneurship. The second section of the book contains theoretical concepts that have been developed from a combination of experience in teaching entrepreneurship courses and learning theories developed by others outside of the field of entrepreneurship. Each of the authors supports their thoughts with actual application of their theoretical approaches.

Jim Fiet argues that the learning process is enhanced when the students are involved in activities rather than simply listening to lectures i.e., "being taught". He believes that these activities need to be based on theoretical learning frameworks. Recognizing that the current theories are not completely adequate, he urges that entrepreneurship educators should be engaged in the process of generating theory-based knowledge about the entrepreneurship education. He concludes by proposing a strategy for implementing this approach. Similarly, Ed Leach and Basil Mortley propose that with careful consideration to effective learning principles entrepreneurs can be deliberately developed rather than simply 'happen'.

JoAnn and Jim Carland describe a series of courses that lead to a degree with a major in entrepreneurship. The curriculum features experiential learning as student teams develop a business idea into a venture complete with growth, expansion and diversification. The courses are taught by a faculty team and include half of the classroom hours devoted to team centered learning.

The importance of team centered learning is becoming increasingly important as more and more of new business formations require more resources (both financial and knowledge) than the typical individual possess. Henrik Herlau describes the KUBUS model that he has developed. It is based on leadership, team development, networking, market research and project management. The initial results in terms of employment and export sales are most encouraging.

Bertrand Ducheneau recognizes the increasing importance that governmental authorities are placing on programs designed to influence students to consider entrepreneurial careers. He reviews the contextual elements that effect the teaching of entrepreneurship and then suggests specific pedagogical approaches for these courses. The final author of this section, Thomas Ulrich, links the psychological characteristics of entrepreneurs and Kolb's research on learning styles. His research finds that there is a preferred style. He concludes with suggestions for implementing these findings in training programs for the development of entrepreneurs.

In the third section of this book, the authors consider nontraditional audiences that could benefit from entrepreneurship education. The overall impression that the reader receives is that there are many appropriate audiences that can benefit from exposure to entrepreneurial education. Sumaria Mohan-Neill using focus group discussions and in-depth interviews answers three important questions from a marketing perspective about entrepreneurship education. Who would be interested in entrepreneurship education programs? What benefits are perceived to result from such programs? And what content and process would satisfy the needs of these target markets? It is this type of approach that should allow entrepreneurship education to be more meaningful to the recipients.

Corporate entrepreneurship or intrapreneurship has been a topic of interest since the mid 1980s. The successes of small entrepreneurial businesses have led some large corporations to try to instill innovation behavior and entrepreneurial thinking into its workforce and mid level managers. These attempts to infuse entrepreneurship into large corporations have had mixed results. Kuratko, Hurley and Hornsby review the literature related to intrapreneurship and then offer a model for a corporate entrepreneurship training program based on their experiences. Peter Koen describes a successful corporate entrepreneurship course and reports that the key criteria for success in obtaining corporate funds to implement the new ventures were corporate strategic fit, understanding of the business, the market and the product and the ability to develop a comprehensive business plan.

Family businesses have been a long neglected aspect of entrepreneurship education. However, in the last decade their importance to the economy has finally become apparent to both government officials as well as to many entrepreneurship educators. Tanewski, Romano, Huang and Smyrnios developed an international profile of family business programs through a literature search and the Internet. They also conducted a national survey of 5000 Australian family businesses. The results identified several key educational needs. These findings as well as the theoretical rationale for developing educational training programs for family businesses are presented.

Nieuwenhuizen and Niekerk address another neglected but very important audience for entrepreneurship education, professionally qualified persons. Lawyers, medical doctors, insurance agents, dentists, accountants and many others are actually entrepreneurs but they often have never received any training in entrepreneurship. This lack of knowledge handicaps their professional practices. It also limits their ability to make well informed business recommendations to entrepreneurs who are clients. Moreover, their own investments in other businesses may be less well evaluated and managed. They conclude by making several suggestions for entrepreneurship education of the professionals.

Entrepreneurs often report the value of networking to the success of their businesses. Entrepreneurship educators can similarly benefit by including others in their planning and execution of programs and courses. There are many examples of universities that provide students with the opportunity to interact in some manner with entrepreneurs. Bodie, Learned and Napier offer insight into the matching of students with businesses in the global economy. Johannisson, Halvarsson and Lovstal report an undergraduate course in which 90 students provided consultation to 30 new firms. They found that the interaction with the entrepreneurs gave the students an increased level of self-confidence and increased interest in entrepreneurial careers.

Morrison describes a collaboration between an entrepreneur and an educator that resulted in a learning package for students. It consists of a video, student workbook, case study and tutors' guide. The process that led to this package is described.

Almost all entrepreneurship courses are offered in business schools with a few engineering schools also offering some form of entrepreneurship. Until recently there have been relatively few university-based courses in entrepreneurship for students who were not in business or engineering schools. An interactive computer-based entrepreneurship class and a creativity class, both open to non-business students, are described by Yendell. Also discussed are issues such as alumni and entrepreneurs involvement and interactions with academic colleagues across the university.

Universities often act as if walls exist that prevent them from interacting with other organizations that have a similar vision and mission. This attitude can limit the ability to form alliances that would be beneficial to everyone. Hurley and Kuratko describe an alliance that eventually resulted in the outside organization being integrated into the university's entrepreneurial program. The new structure provides even more services and programs than the two separate programs did previously.

The final section of the book is a collection of insightful reports of entrepreneurship education that stood separate from any other grouping. Henry and Titterington report the results of a program that attempts to determine entrepreneurial suitability, developing entrepreneurial talent through training and predicting entrepreneurial success.

Many of the research efforts in the field of entrepreneurship education research are descriptive. Unfortunately, it is rare to have a research study that is comparative. Deschoolmeester, Schamp and Vandenbroucke have undertaken such a study in which they compare entrepreneurs who have participated in a training program and those who have not been in the program. The program is for starting SME-business owners. The results provide insight not only of the impact of the training program but into the relationship between entrepreneurial characteristics and managerial techniques, planning skills and the business growth patterns.

Historically, universities have sought new knowledge and historically, they have sought new and increased funding. More recently, these two efforts have come together as universities seek to obtain new funding from the sale or licensing of new knowledge. One of the ways in which that occurs is through academic research that leads to new discoveries that in turn lead to new companies that spin-off from the university. Bellini, Capaldo, Raffa and Zollo describe this process and the resulting relationships between the university and the small firms.

Most entrepreneurship educators continually seek ways to improve and expand the entrepreneurship offerings at their institution. DeClercq, Crijns and Ooghe provide an in-depth view of entrepreneurship education at the university level and issues associated with the introduction of new courses and programs at the graduate level.

Hjorth and Johannisson examined the Swedish educational system and found a number of activities that promote entrepreneurial behavior in both high schools and universities. They suggest a language-game framework for entrepreneurship.

In the concluding chapter, Ledezma and Alcaraz describe the application of technology to the development of a business plan.

Summary

This collection of articles is diverse in terms of nationality of the authors, the specific content and the populations that are studied. However, the strong and consistent central core in each of them is the importance and complexity of entrepreneurial education. As you read and study each one, I strongly encourage you to not simply accept the suggestions and findings as the conclusion but instead to consider the information contained in them as another step in the continual effort to better understand entrepreneurship education. And I hope that these articles will motivate you to share your own insights with others through academic journals, professional meetings and proceedings or in future editions of this series on entrepreneurship education.

Acknowledgements

The compilation of this volume involved many people, without whom this book could not have been created.

First and foremost, we are indebted to all of the authors whose contributions are found here.

The editors would especially like to thank Dipl.-Kff. Tanja Helen Finke-Schürmann in her previous role as academic assistant to the Deutsche Ausgleichsbank Chair for Business Administration and Start-up Management and Entrepreneurship at the European Business School, Schloß Reichartshausen for her dedication in accomplishing various organisational tasks, in the selection of the material and in correspondence with the authors.

Our thanks also go to cand. rer. pol. Elke Strebe for coordinating the technical side, particularly for the research done in her role as student assistant to the Chair. The formatting and layouting of the preliminary version were done by stud. rer. pol. Anne Freund and the final version by Nicole Barth, Secretary to the Chair.

We are grateful to Julia Waldner who, as a native speaker, was frequently on hand to give linguistic advice.

Finally we would like to thank Kirstin Howgate of Ashgate Publishers for her patience during the project.

The Editors

PART A

ENTREPRENEURSHIP RESEARCH: DEFINITIONS AND PERSPECTIVES

1 Missing Links in Entrepreneurship Research[*]

Karl H. Vesper

Introduction

Among the questions that might be used to guide research on entrepreneurship, two that this discussion seeks to explore are (1) what topical areas seem to have received the least treatment to date, and (2) what topics within those areas might yield information of utility to practicing entrepreneurs.

Certainly, these are not the only questions that might be used for guidance. Others could include many combinations of the following:

1. where are data easiest to obtain,
2. to what questions do the lenses used in prior studies most readily apply,
3. where can a large 'n' most readily be obtained,
4. what builds on a prior study of particular interest to me,
5. what study is most likely to be supported by a financing source,
6. what do I happen to be curious about,
7. what have 'significant others' asked me about,
8. what would yield greatest visibility,
9. which would be eligible for the most academically admired journal,
10. which would most often be cited,
11. what would an available graduate student most like to work on or be best able to work on with minimal supervision, and
12. what have other people said should be investigated, and

13. what can be explored by working off of some existing theory or combination of theories?

No doubt there could be any number of additional guiding questions, and it is also likely that sometimes two or more such guiding questions might point to the same topics. This by no means a complete list, but it serves to illustrate that there are many criteria among which arbitrary choices could be justified. The two noted in the first paragraph above comprise one such arbitrary choice. Others will necessarily follow in application of the methodology. The proposed test of utility here is not elegance but rather whether it suggests directions and research topics that seem interesting and likely to lead eventually to insights or information of interest to practicing entrepreneurs. That is for readers to decide.

Method

Identification of areas relatively less explored required choice of a way to sort existing research of the field and measure coverage. The method chosen here was to set up a more or less arbitrary topical listing and then count articles for each topic. That approach can be faulted for treating all articles as equally deserving to be counted at all and then counting them equally. It also presumes that each article fits exactly into one topical area and only one, which can readily be demonstrated to be an oversimplification. For example, an article on applying for a bank loan might be classified under forecasting, planning or financing. It might also fall under categories having to do with how entrepreneurs think or how bankers think.

The formulation of any particular list of categories for sorting, and how finely to break each category down into further subcategories is also open to valid criticism. It inevitably requires debatable choices. Presumably, this could be remedied statistically by impaneling enough judges to generate acceptable interrater reliability with an overwhelmingly large 'n,' but that seems neither feasible nor justifiable.

The saving element, given these methodological weaknesses, would seem to be that once the claim, by any method including the one used here is applied and identifies certain topical research areas as being lightly treated, any critic is free to consider the literature and form an opinion about whether that claim can be refuted. If it cannot, then the claim of light

4

treatment about a particular topic would seem to be supported and researchers can move in to investigate the topic, thereby rendering the claim not wrong, but simply obsolete. That, then, can move the field ahead and this effort will have served its purpose.

Sorting Articles

The framework chosen for sorting articles in this study was based on the table of contents in one of the author's books, *New Venture Experience*, made up of ten general topical areas, which in turn were subdivided and further elaborated to produce a finer overall listing of between two and four sub-areas within each of the ten, or 29 sub areas in total. These are listed in Table 1, with a brief characterization of each.

Other sorting systems appear both in textbooks and in the way conference proceedings are organized. For example, different headings under which papers have been grouped over time in *Frontiers of Entrepreneurship Research* can be seen in Table 2. One observation from this table is that of the 19 headings used for the first volume, only two were used in later volumes. By the fifth year, only 13 headings were used, but nearly half of them had not been used before. So there was considerable change over time.

Table 1: Topics List

Chapter	Sub-Chapter	Topic
1	a	Economics and Occurrence of Entrepreneurship
	b	Entrepreneur's Job
	c	Entrepreneur's Mentality and Thinking
2	a	Breaking loose to seek ideas for possible ventures
	b	Focusing the search
3	a	Screening ideas for physical and market feasibility
	b	Screening ideas for financial attractiveness and founder fit
	c	Strategic formulation of the business
4	a	Forecasting venture results
	b	Business plan formulation
5	a	Personal equity sources
	b	Borrowing
	c	Venture capital sources
	d	Going Public
6	a	Protecting ideas
	b	Legal formation of the business and government compliance
	c	Facilities for the venture
	d	Location for the venture
7	a	Creating a founder team
	b	Obtaining outside help
8	a	Starting sales
	b	Starting operations
	c	Controlling operations and cash flow
	d	Updating the venture
9	a	Finding an acquisition
	b	Dealing with a company seller
	c	Franchise entry
10	a	Purusing growth
	b	Coping with growth
	c	Exiting the venture

Table 2: Frontiers of Entrepreneurship Research

	SECTION HEADINGS	1996	1995	1994	1993	1992
1	E'ship in the not for profit sector	x				
2	Personal characteristics of the 'er	x				
3	Women and e'ship	x				
4	Personal experiences and e'rial behavior	x				
5	Managerial characteristics and behavior of e'rs	x				x
6	Competitive strategies	x				
7	Geographic expansion	x				
8	Franchising	x				
9	Business angels	x				x
10	Investment, vc decisions	x				
11	Financing: traditional sources	x				
12	Market value and firm growth	x				
13	Firm growth	x				
14	Management and growth	x				
15	Firm ownership and performance	x				
16	High technology product development	x				
17	High technology firms and strategy	x				
18	Gov't policy, programs and e'ship	x				
19	Miscellaneous topics	x				
20	Demographics		x			
21	E'rial process		x	x		
22	Entrepreneurs of the entrepreneur		x	x	x	
23	Technology		x			
24	Social issues		x			
25	Finance or financing		x	x	x	
26	Formal and informal venture capital		x			
27	Leaders and teams		x			
28	Growth		x			x
29	Alliances, cooperatives and franchises		x	x		
30	Advisers and consultants		x			
31	Entrepreneurial corporations		x			
32	Public policy and public sector		x	x		
33	Training and education		x	x		
34	Organizational factors			x		
35	Strategy			x		
36	Global			x	x	
37	Franchising			x		

38	University related (or university role)	x	x	x
39	Innovation and growth		x	
40	Startups		x	x
41	Survival, failure, buyouts & harvest		x	x
42	Corporate entrepreneurship		x	x
43	High technology and cross - cultural studies		x	
44	Case studies, ethnic and minority e'ship		x	
45	Methodology and other		x	
46	Cognitive process characteristics			x
47	Opportunity recognition			x
48	Venture capital			x
49	International and cross - functional studies			x
50	E'ship in east. and cent. Europe and emerging countries			x
51	Methodology in education and research			x

Articles for sorting into this framework were chosen from four sources, three of them academic and the fourth, commercial. The academic sources were (1) *Frontiers of Entrepreneurship Research*, the last 621 articles up to the 1996 issue, (2) *Marketing at the Entrepreneurship Interface*, the last 236 articles up to the 1995 issue, (3) the *Journal of Business Venturing*, the last 323 articles up to the last issue in 1997, and (4) *Inc. Magazine*, the last 499 articles up to the last issue of 1997. This made a total of 1679 articles sorted.

The method of sorting was basically inspection by the author. Certainly, another person doing the sorting would have produced a different result, and re-sorting by the same person would also have produced a different result. How much different is not known, and might be worth doing if the time and budget were available. But it will be argued here that mainly the same conclusions would be reached; namely that there is substantial imbalance in the attention given to different topics, that it is easier to defend the view that there should be a closer balance, and that some specific topics deserving more study can be identified.

Topic Loadings Found

What the loadings turned out to be, both overall and in the different publications reviewed here, can be seen in tables beginning with number three. Chart 1 shows that the especially high densities of articles are in the categories at the 'front end' of the spectrum dealing with broad topics such as occurrence of entrepreneurship, what entrepreneurs are like and how they think. Particularly the occurrence, macroeconomics and sociology of entrepreneurship (topic number 1a) is heavily populated, there being 219 articles in that category.

The only category with more articles than that was at the other end of the classification scheme, the one concerned with management of ongoing companies (number 10b), particularly growing enterprises and corporate venturing, which had 238 articles. Thus it appears that the most researched topics in the entrepreneurship literature are those of macroeconomics and management of going concerns.

Aside from those two, the most populated topics were those associated with venture capital (number 5c), those dealing with strategy of the venture (number 3c) and those dealing with marketing in new ventures (number 8a).

Chart 1 - Article Quantity by Topic Area

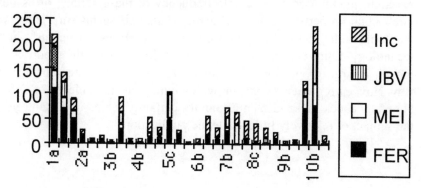

Chart 2 displays the densities in terms of percentages of the articles for each of the periodicals. Essentially it shows the same pattern as do the quantities in Chart 1. In both of these first two charts it can also be seen that the proportions of articles among different topic areas in Inc.

Magazine are quite different at times than the academic serials. For instance, Inc. tends to have a smaller proportion of articles on the economics and occurrence of entrepreneurship (1a) and substantially more on 'nuts and bolts' topics such as facilities and location (6c), operations (8b) and control (8c).

Chart 2 - Article Quantities in Three Academic Serials

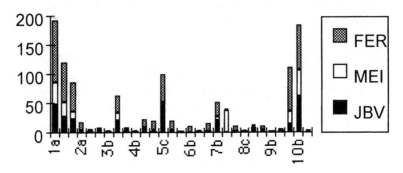

Chart 3 shows which topics are heavily treated and which are less treated by the three academic serials. Of particular interest may be the subjects where treatment is light. for instance, there is almost no academic research, judging from the article frequency of these serials, on issues of intellectual property in entrepreneurship (6a). This seems surprising, since that topic is the focus of dispute for so many ventures, particularly in high technology. Entry via acquisition (9a, 9b) seems to get little attention, even though a large proportion of entrepreneurs appear to enter business that way. How entrepreneurs come up with winning business ideas (2a, 2b), and how they check those ideas out (3a, 3b) certainly seems important, yet are the subject of relatively little academic publication.

Chart 3 - Article Quantity by Topic om FER + MEI + JBV (n 0 1,180)

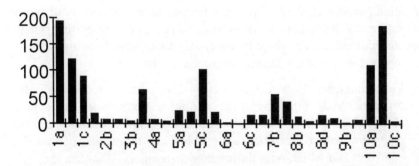

It can be argued as odd that there are so many articles dealing with venture capital as a money source for entrepreneurs (5c) and so few about how entrepreneurs get money from banks (5b) or go public (5d).

Such oddities appear with all three of the academic serials reviewed, as can be seen in Chart 4, although there are differences in relative emphasis among them. It is not surprising that *Marketing at the Entrepreneurship Interface* has a relatively large proportion of its articles focused on how entrepreneurs get their sales (8a). But it could be seen as surprising that the subject accounts for less than a third of the articles in that particular serial and that the other two serials contain almost no articles on that subject at all.

For readers who might wish to perform their own search for potential disparities of attention among the periodicals, a tabulation of the article counts appears in Table 3.

Chart 4 - Article Quantities by Topic in Three Academic Serials

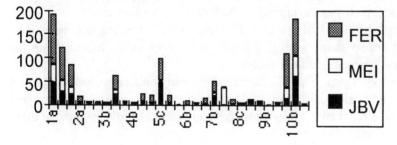

Some Topics inviting more Investigation

The main purpose of these displays, however, is not to identify disparities but rather to highlight areas where there may be useful research opportunities. Based on where treatment seems to have been lightest, here are some subjects that might bear further research.

1. Legal angles - How entrepreneurs deal with protection of ideas, organizational form angles to minimize taxes, such as separate corporations to hold assets, enforcement of nondisclosure agreements, managing patent protection are problems entrepreneurs must and do confront. But which ones do it better than others, what can they learn from each others' experiences, and are still better methods possible? The current research literature apparently says nothing about it.
    Example - Southwest Airlines had to fight all sorts of legal battles, particularly against Braniff and Texas International Airlines, to get started and later against the airport authority that wanted it not to use Love Field.
2. Insurance - An agent or broker could probably say a lot. The research says nothing.
3. Philanthropy of entrepreneurs. Particularly schools, as well as entrepreneurs, should be interested in this.
4. Using job shops. Fabricating prototypes. This is an area of technological change in itself, which both serves entrepreneurs and provides opportunity for new start-ups.
5. Starting service versus product companies. Some academic studies notice SIC loadings, but many fail to make industrial distinctions.
6. Operating virtually.
7. Contrasts between start-up types: Software, vs. service, vs. tangible products (toys or avionics) vs. biotech - very different.
8. Starting with SBIR - there is a billion a year in funding out there now.
9. Setting up shop - getting good deals on equipment, watching out for lease terms and hidden liabilities.
10. Business plans, either in formulation or in application, are almost not treated at all, which seems funny, since most entrepreneurship courses make a big deal out of writing them and some schools even make them a competitive sport.
11. The term harvesting, to characterize what happened when an entrepreneur cashes in, may be misleading because it may connote

stripping assets off a business and leaving it naked to grow back replacements. The term cashing in may be better. Anyway, clearly it is an important point in the history of a venture, and on that point there are almost no research publications, whether the entrepreneur's withdrawal be by stripping assets, selling out, going through bankruptcy or converting ownership through an IPO.

12. Inadequate control and mismanagement of cash flow is alleged to be a bugaboo of startups, but there are almost no studies of what entrepreneurs should do to initiate and grow an effective control system. (The Stevenson and Sahlman book has more chapters on control than on any other topic. But the research literature has almost nothing on it at all.)

13

Table 3: Article Quantities by Topic in Four Serials Reviewed

K.H. Vesper

Number of articles counted

Code	Topic	JBV	MEI	FER	Inc	All
1a	Occurrence of venturing and opportunities	48	38	108	25	219
1b	Entrepreneurs' characteristics and careers	29	23	70	20	142
1c	Thinking about entrepreneurship	23	15	50	4	92
2a	Mental departure in quest of opportunity and ideas	1	5	13	9	28
2b	Guiding the search for successful ideas	1	1	5	4	11
3a	Assessing physical and market feasibility	1	4	4	8	17
3b	Assessing personal fit	2	2	2	2	8
3c	Strategic vision, design and refinement	22	12	30	30	94
4a	Forecasting sales, expenses and cash needs	2	6	1	4	13
4b	Writing and presenting business plans	2	3	0	6	11
5a	Equity sources early on, including angels	9	0	15	31	55
5b	Borrowing and banks	4	1	16	15	36
5c	Formal venture capital	49	3	49	5	106
5d	Capital from going public (IPO's)	5	0	16	8	29
6a	Protecting ideas	0	1	1	5	7
6b	Designing the business legal form	1	0	11	11	23
6c	Physical location and facilities	4	0	2	42	48
7a	Partnering	2	1	13	20	36
7b	Help from outsiders	20	7	27	21	75
8a	Getting sales	0	40	2	24	66
8b	Initiating physical operations and quality	1	2	10	35	48
8c	Controlling cash	2	1	3	38	44
8d	Continuing advance of the venture's tech	10	1	4	21	36
9a	Finding and checking out acquisitions	6	0	6	15	27
9b	Acquisition dealing	1	0	1	7	9
9c	Entry through becoming a franchisee	1	1	6	3	11
10a	Trajectories of growth	15	23	73	17	128
10b	Managing growth and corporate venturing	61	46	78	53	238
10c	Exits from ventures	1	0	5	16	22
	Total	**323**	**236**	**621**	**499**	**1679**

13. Business management best-sellers, such as *In Search of Excellence* and those that have followed it over the years, set forth characteristics that distinguish between winners and losers. A closer look suggests that those characteristics that make companies long-term winners seem to have been present from the companies' beginnings. How do they get there? Is it by conscious decisions of the entrepreneur or not? Studies exploring or answering such questions seemed to be absent, although there were some that started in that direction by exploring 'success versus failure' causes.

14. Where should TQM, whether by that name or not, get introduced in the life of a business? There has been little in the way of studies about setting up plants or getting production operations started, as an approach to answering that question.

15. Is there such a thing as adequate or inadequate fit between the particular entrepreneur and the particular venture? No studies seem to treat that subject, although there are many about psychological characteristics of entrepreneurs generally.

16. What should be learned about acquisition as a mode of entry? Anecdotal experience suggests that entrepreneurs do vastly better with acquisitions than corporations do. Is that true, and if so, why? Do some entrepreneurs accomplish it better than others? Is its failure rate lower as an entry mode than that of start-up? The subject appears not to have been investigated or even to have been the topic of more than a very few case studies.

17. Implicit specifications for the company's initial product offering and how it gets shaped and refined is not treated in the research literature. It is clear historically that 'specs' have been crucial to the success of products such as helicopters (the Army's LOH) and fighters (Japanese Zero). How true is that in start-ups? The subject appears not to have been explored.

18. Most venture capitalists believe 'the jockey is more important than the horse' or 'pick the grade A team over the grade A product.' Just how does the mechanisms behind that belief work? What fraction of the time is it wrong versus right, and why? What can a would-be entrepreneur do to make the most of it?

19. How important are the selection and operating rule choices in working with bankers, lawyers and other professionals. What tactics will get the most out of them for the least money. Is that important? Are there

things that can be learned about it through systematic study? We don't know.

20. Just what is it that schooling transmits of utility to starters? There are currently some studies underway on this topic by the author and others. But they barely scratch the surface. Broadly, the answer is that different students get different benefits from different schooling elements. But what the patterns are and how schooling should be shaped based on that is unknown. It is, moreover, continually changed by the education disseminated about entrepreneurship by general media.

More Questions

These are clearly only a very few of the arguably under-treated topics. Any number of others further could be suggested. What are the start-up origins of longer term corporate culture? Do firms really often go through the growth stages alleged in the academic literature? How do starters become runners, is it a manageable choice and if so, how can it best be done? How are business plans actually used by start-ups and to what effect? What opportunities do start-ups miss, or which do they hit upon later than they should, why, and what can be done about it?

What priorities should be assigned to these and other possible research questions, and how the academic establishment might be most economically given incentives to explore them is probably worth some thought and perhaps discussion at a conference. Other viewers would likely have contrasting views of even the questions that should be listed here.

One way to proceed is simply to let things run on their present path. Another would be to reflect on the claims made here, consider the future topics suggested here plus some others and then map a new strategy that would display different areas of relative emphasis in the future, one that might be easier to defend.

Note

*Based on Keynote Address for the IntEnt Conference, Monterey, CA, August, 1997.

2 Small Business versus Entrepreneurship Revisited

C. Howard Watson

Abstract

Entrepreneurship research has been criticized for lack of a generally accepted definition for entrepreneurship. Clarification the distinction between entrepreneurship and small business would improve the validity and reliability of entrepreneurship research. This paper investigates fundamental questions, namely, should there be a distinction and, if so, which direction should carry the emphasis of future research to facilitate the study of the phenomenon of entrepreneurship. On what basis should this distinction be made. Data were obtained by a survey questionnaire which was sent to an international sample of 647 academics which were knowledgeable in the field of entrepreneurship. A total of 132 responses were received. Data were statistically analyzed using descriptive statistics, Chi Square test, MANOVA and Analysis of Variance. Results indicated the necessity to clarify definitional issues and that a definition of entrepreneurship seems important to .future entrepreneurship research. Variables that differentiate small business and entrepreneurship seem to have been identified.

The motivation and need for the study arises from the importance of entrepreneurship as an economic phenomena, as an important area of research and from the need for generally accepted definitions. Arising from this need is the debate on the distinction between small business and entrepreneurship which seems to be adjourned rather than completed.

Entrepreneurship is an important area of study. Entrepreneurship research, from an economic point of view, is important because, as Timmons (1990) states; *There is a growing realization internationally that*

17

entrepreneurs are the fuel, engine and throttle that drive the economic engine of the country.

Entrepreneurship is of particular importance as regards South Africa which is currently at a critical juncture of its political, economic and social history (Rupert, 1994). It is again entering global markets and will experience the effects of international competition from a very low base of economic activity and large scale unemployment. South Africa is therefor in need of wise strategies to promote economic growth and yet little is known about South African entrepreneurs (Boshoff, Bennet and Owusu, 1992).

Entrepreneurship is a young field of study and consequently presents scholars several problems and challenges. It is one of the newest and most promising research fields in management as most of the empirical research has occurred within the past two decades (Wortman, 1987). It is therefor a young paradigm (Bygrave, 1989), still in its infancy (Perryman, 1982; Churchill and Lewis, 1986; Ireland and Van Auken, 1987) and consequently, many problems arising from its nouveaux research state are becoming evident.

Typically, such problems relate to the lack of a common set of agreed upon conceptual frameworks and definitions (Köllermeier, 1992; Perryman, 1982; Churchill and Hatten, 1987) for the paradigm and are the result of unsystematic entrepreneurial research (Bygrave, 1989), a large diversification of contributing disciplines, a lack of theory (Carsrud, Olm and Eddy, 1986; Wortman, 1987) and that the nature and direction of research was undefined (Ireland et al. 1987) and fragmented (Sexton and Bouwman - Upton, 1988; Köllermeier, 1992).

Commentaries on the state of entrepreneurship in respect of the quality of the research in the paradigm (Hornaday and Churchill, 1987; Bygrave, 1989; Gartner, 1989; Smith, Gannon and Sapienza, 1989, Boshoff, et al. 1992) also indicate that a theoretical problem exists.

Literature relates some specific theory problems and dilemmas in entrepreneurship research such as definitional issues (Gartner, 1988), the distinction between entrepreneurship and small business (Carland, Hoy, Boulton and Carland,1984) and the approaches that should be used in future entrepreneurship research (Gartner, 1988; Robinson, Stimpton, Huefner, and Hunt, 1992). Specifically, two problems should be attended to: Firstly, the insufficiency of constructs; the lack of a common set of agreed-upon frameworks and definitions (Köllermeier, 1992), and, secondly, the lack of agreement on the directions for future entrepreneurship research in terms of topics for research. This study focuses on the first problem.

Background

A brief review of the historical progression of entrepreneurship research and the demands of what constitutes good entrepreneurial research would serve to indicate the need for definitional clarification.

By the early 1980s, the field had expanded but was still in its infancy, in the exploratory stage and quite fragmented. Some scholars thought the development of a total research framework or model for future research, and clarity on a generally accepted definition, were needed (Sexton, 1982; Paulin, Coffey and Spaulding, 1982) and other thought frameworks were premature (Perryman, 1982).It seems that in the early 1980s, although a great deal of disagreement existed among authors, a certain degree of consensus had been achieved.

Authors still differed on whether the paradigm was mature enough for effective development or application of a unifying framework or model for investigation (Perryman, 1982 ; Sexton, 1982; Aldrich, 1992). They also differed on a definition of entrepreneurship and whether it was needed (Sexton, 1982; Paulin, et al, 1982).

Churchill et al. (1986) assumed, at the outset, that the field of entrepreneurship research was young, at a formative stage, still in its infancy and that the definition of entrepreneurship was neither agreed upon nor static. It is a field involving considerable discovery oriented research and consequently they expected to find that its research directions are fragmented, creative, and diverse. His summative critical comment was that most studies still used a combination of questionnaire and interview techniques. Carsrud et al. (1986) were more specific than Wortman (1986) (who only expressed the need for such a framework) and presented an integrating framework to interface entrepreneurship and small business (Aldrich, 1992).

Between 1980 and 1985 some progress was made in the area of entrepreneurship and small business: The factor of 'growth' was recognized as the distinguishing factor separating small businesses from entrepreneurial firms (Churchill, 1992: Wortman 1986).

In summary, few breakthroughs had been made by 1985. The issues of *characteristics of entrepreneurs* and *the relationship between entrepreneurship and small business* had been to some extent resolved. A paucity of public data bases existed and non - systematic methods of data collection were still being applied (Aldrich, 1992). No generally accepted definition or unified framework had evolved.

As regards those issues on which agreement had been reached by 1985 Churchill (1992), in his review of entrepreneurship research issues maintains that considerable progress was achieved in many areas of research. He states:

> The atmosphere in 1990, as reflected by the chapters within this volume, was less one of excitement about what was going to happen than a guarded ebullience about what had been accomplished, an awed perception of the enormity of the entrepreneurial field, a dawning recognition of the breadth and nature of the research methodologies required, and a mature optimism of what work in the next few years would achieve.

Churchill (1992) found that, by 1990, increased understanding and consensus seems to have been achieved regarding three issues. Firstly, the issue regarding the economic effects of small and growing firms in job creation and innovation (Churchill, 1992: Acs and Audretsch, 1992). Secondly, there seemed to be general agreement among the authors of contributing articles to Sexton and Kasarda (1992) on the conceptualization of entrepreneurship as *the process of uncovering or developing an opportunity to create value through innovation and seizing that opportunity without regard to either resources (human and capital) or the location of the entrepreneur - in a new or existing company* (Churchill, 1992: 586), and thirdly, the greater availability of databases and the application of new theoretical tools to the data, such as population ecology, had made possible the expansion of research at both the macro-level and micro-level. The macro-level comprised issues of firm start-ups, survival and growth, job creation, industry turbulence and firm failure rates. Micro-level comprised information accumulated on entrepreneurs, their support groups and entrepreneurial organizations from start-up, through growth, to death or harvest (Churchill, 1992).

As regards areas where agreement had not yet been achieved Churchill (1992) felt that there still existed a lack of well-developed theories based on generalizable studies of causal relationships and that

20

'...we are just now beginning to comprehend what we do not know and what we must understand in the future...' (Churchill, 1992: 586).

In summary, by 1980, researchers were relating similarities and differences and it was recognized that the entrepreneur was different to non - entrepreneurs. By 1985 some general dimensions of the field were becoming more clear, issues relating to psychological characteristics of entrepreneurs and the relationship between entrepreneurship and small business were in the process of resolution, entrepreneurship was at this stage being recognized as a new area of research and education (Churchill, 1992), agreement could still not be reached as to the dimensions /magnitude/extent of the subject of entrepreneurship, the interrelationship of its parts, what processes were involved in entrepreneurship itself and what it was, e.g. definition. By 1992, research had increased substantially, better instruments had been acquired, developed and applied, the enormity of the paradigm was realized and the scope of research had broadened significantly, and the entrepreneurship research community began to realize what it did not know, structure its research more effectively and to do more careful research so that results were extendible and not confounded by uncontrolled and unknown variables Clarification of definitional issues and the various components of what we call entrepreneurship seem to need more attention.

During the early 1990s the entrepreneurship research community began to realize what it did not know, structure its research more effectively and to do more careful research so that results were extendible and not confounded by uncontrolled and unknown variables.

The Quality of Entrepreneurship Research

The demands of what constitutes good entrepreneurial research would serve to substantiate indicate the need for definitional clarification. In order to evaluate the state of entrepreneurship research, from a positivistic research perspective, it is necessary to present a framework of what constitutes good research. Such a framework of characteristics of positivistic research can then serve as a criterion against which to evaluate the quality of entrepreneurship research.

According to Berelson and Steiner (1964), as reported by Luthans (1981), behavioral scientists strive to attain the following hallmarks of any science: the procedures are public, the definitions are precise, the data-collecting is objective, the findings are replicable, the approach is systematic and cumulative, the purposes are explanation, understanding, and prediction.

According to Kerlinger (1986), the basic and ultimate aim of science is theory. He gives the definition of theory as: A theory is a set of interrelated constructs (concepts), definitions, and propositions that present a systematic view of phenomena by specifying relations among variables, with the purpose of explaining and predicting the phenomena (Kerlinger, 1986: 9) and attempts to define scientific research as: scientific research is systematic, controlled, empirical, and critical investigation of natural phenomena guided by theory and hypotheses about the presumed relationships among such phenomena (Kerlinger, 1986: 10).

The criterial framework applied in this study, to evaluate the quality of entrepreneurship research, is drawn from a combination of the criteria stated by Berelson and Emory and will include criteria implied by the aim and definition of theory and scientific research given by Kerlinger. The resultant criteria are as follows:

1. Theory criteria.

   a) The aim of science is creation and expansion of theory (Kerlinger, 1986).
   b) Scientific research is guided by theory (Kerlinger, 1986).
   c) A theory should specify relations among variables (Kerlinger, 1986).

2. The procedures are public and open.
3. The definitions are precise.
4. The approach is systematic and cumulative.
5. The findings are replicable.
6. The purposes are explanation, understanding, and prediction of phenomena
7. The purpose, or problem, of the research should be as unambiguous as possible
8. The data-collecting and sampling are objective.
9. Analysis of the data should be sufficiently adequate to reveal its significance; and the methods of analysis should be appropriate.
10. The procedural design should be carefully planned to yield results that are as objective as possible.

11. The researcher should report, with complete frankness, flaws in procedural design and estimate their effects on the findings.
12. Conclusions should be confined to those justified by the data of the research and limited to those for which the data provide an adequate basis.

The following criteria indicate the need for definitional clarification :

1a The aim of science is theory (Kerlinger, 1986).

Kerlinger's (1986) view that theory is the ultimate aim of science, the explanation of natural phenomena, and that all else flows from theory seems to present a challenging problem with the theory development in the field.

Various views have, during the past decade, been expressed by scholars regarding this *theory* problem in entrepreneurship research. Carsrud, et al. (1986) indicated that a lack of theory exists in entrepreneurship research and Hornaday et al. (1987) concluded that there was inadequate application of theory from related fields. Bygrave (1989) felt that there were inadequacies within the paradigms used. He further stated that there was an absence of a paradigm specifically developed for entrepreneurship research and suggests that the entrepreneurship paradigm should develop its own distinct methods and theories and compares the paradigm with older paradigms such as that of physics. He felt that entrepreneurship is yet to develop its own methods and theories. It currently borrows its methods and theories from other sciences and this may not be appropriate because, firstly, entrepreneurship research is disjointed, discontinuous and non-linear in nature and, secondly, as a science it is in its infancy, researchers should not force sophisticated methods on it.

Some scholars even question whether there is an entrepreneurship paradigm because of the utilization of so many different concepts from so many diverse disciplines (Bygrave, 1989). Bygrave (1989) further felt that the assumption that good research follows a fixed sequence of theory selection, deducing a model from which testable hypotheses can be developed, instrument development to test these hypotheses on a database with static tools, presents a problem in an infant paradigm such as entrepreneurship.

It seems that the quality of entrepreneurship research is still affected by the lack of theory in the field and the lack of consensus with respect to which models, level of statistical sophistication and types of research are appropriate to effective progress of entrepreneurship research.

1b Scientific research is guided by theory (Kerlinger, 1986).

Effective research should be guided by theory. Research should be theory driven (Low and MacMillan, 1988). Gartner (1989), while addressing traits and characteristic research, felt that researchers were not basing their studies on theory. He recognized various shortcoming in entrepreneurship research and called for studies to have a theory which explains and predicts, and offers a model of the phenomenon as well as a definition of all of the variables.

Consensus among researchers regarding the degree of unification and convergence of the field has not been reached. Some call for convergence (Wortman, 1986), while others suggest that the large diversity of approaches and method should be encouraged provided the range of research methods match the complexity of the phenomena under study. Additional theoretical perspectives should be explored, while future research should examine and clearly state theoretical assumptions (Low et al. 1988). Hofer and Bygrave (1992) feel that the basic characteristics of the entrepreneurial process cannot be adequately captured by the current conceptual frameworks, models and theories found in the field and which place serious limitations on the application of many theories and models.

1c A theory should specify relations among variables and phenomena (Kerlinger, 1986).

Besides listing hypotheses a manuscript should also present a model showing the links between variables. Studies should articulate a theory and specify its relationship to the entrepreneur. They should construct theories of entrepreneurship based on contingency type models that specify the influence of certain entrepreneurial characteristics on certain types of entrepreneurs in certain types of environments (Gartner, 1989). According to Low et al. (1988), there is a need to pursue causality more aggressively and the fields ability to generate theory will be severely circumscribed unless progress is made in the development of rigorous models of the

24

entrepreneurship process. They feel that as the paradigm develops the quality and usefulness of the theory that developments will be tied to the ability of researchers to identify patterns of causality and that descriptive studies or cross-sectional studies should be followed by more systematic studies and be subjected to formal testing to work towards the development of theory. Entrepreneurship research seems to have reached a stage of development where its theory should specify relations among variables and phenomena but consensus does not seem to exist among scholars on how best to achieve this objective.

2. The procedures are public and open.

Research reports should reveal with candor the sources of data and the means by which they were obtained. Omission of significant procedural details makes it difficult or impossible to estimate the validity and reliability of the data and justifiably weakens the confidence of the reader in the research (Emory, 1985: 10). The introduction of various research journals specializing in the field of entrepreneurship, such as Entrepreneurship: Theory and Practice and Journal of Business Venturing, and conference proceedings, such as Frontiers of Entrepreneurship Research, have contributed significantly to the transparency of research procedures in the field of entrepreneurship. No serious criticisms of the degree of openness of research reports were encountered in the literature reviewed for the current study.

3. The definitions are precise.

Theory articulation requires that key variables and ideas be defined with precision to provide a clear sense of the study's research focus. Effective comparisons among studies can be made if reviewers are not confused by 'fuzzy' definitions. As Gartner (1989: 32) states:
    Definition of key variables are a bridge between what often seems to be vague ideas presented in a theory and the actuality of conducting research on a specific group of individuals. A problem situation is brought about by the diversity of entrepreneurship research and the multifaceted phenomena involved (Low et al. 1989). No definition captures, for instance, the whole picture of entrepreneurship in terms of the varied disciplines involved. An analogy with leadership research was drawn by

25

Pfeffer (1977) who felt that the term entrepreneurship was too imprecise to be useful to researchers.

A central problem with entrepreneurship research is that for many concepts no generic definitions exists and consequently each study must produce its own definitions. Some studies do not even state definitions. Many and often vague definitions have been used to define entrepreneurship and in many studies it is never defined, few studies employ the same definition and lack of basic agreement (Gartner, 1988). Moore (1990), in examining present research on women entrepreneurs, for example, found that of the 21 studies she reviewed, only 2 attempted to define what made the business under study an entrepreneurial undertaking.

A problem seems to exists in entrepreneurship research due to the lack of a generally accepted definition for entrepreneurship. Scholars have stated that the high variation, and sometimes imprecision, of definitions create a problem for entrepreneurship research and affects the quality of research negatively. If definitions are imprecise the validity and reliability of the research may be in question and the quality affected. The purpose, or problem, of the research may be obscured, data-collecting and selected samples inaccurate and not clearly focussed, and finding may not be replicable. By these criteria entrepreneurship research seems to have a major problem as key ideas and variables are not precisely defined.

4. The approach is systematic and cumulative.

Good quality research demands that studies be performed in a logical, systematic and cumulative way. Because of a lack of an acceptable conceptual framework, a wide variety of topics and its complexity entrepreneurship is characterized by an unsystematic approach to research. Research tends to be peripheral to the core of entrepreneurship, the sum of which is neither moving researchers to the center of the subject matter nor expanding their ability to understand and predict (Churchill et al. 1987).

In order to achieve quality and usefulness of the theory, earlier successful efforts using exploratory case studies or cross sectional statistical studies should be followed '...by more systematic studies that subject a priori hypotheses to formal testing and work towards the development of theory...' (Low et al. 1988; 154). Progress towards priori hypothesis testing has been slow but there has been some progress toward

26

building upon previous research and designing more rigorous studies (Low et al. 988).

Gartner (1989) felt that some researchers do not ground their studies in the context of previous research. They do not read the literature and even seem to reinvent the wheel and do not seem to be familiar with the literature, resulting in some research not being cumulative. He felt scholars should link their work to current research in other disciplines and ground their studies in the context of previous research. The fragmented nature of research also makes accumulation on a very wide front slow and difficult. Carsrud et al. (1986) ask that those researchers engaged in studies using psychological or sociological characteristics be familiar with contemporary research in those areas. Although individual studies seem to have been largely systematic the fragmented nature of the paradigm has resulted in non-systematic and non-cumulative research.

5. The findings are replicable.

This criteria calls for researchers to report their procedure and should reveal their sources of data, and the means by which they were obtained with candor. Omission of significant procedural details makes it difficult or impossible to estimate the validity and reliability of the data and justifiably weakens the confidence of the reader in the research (Emory, 1985; 10). Samples should also be consistent to allow replication. A difficulty with entrepreneurship research seems to be that because definitions are imprecise, data collection becomes imprecise, samples vary, and studies cannot be repeated because the samples can in some cases not be replicated. The lack of basic agreement on definition has resulted in selection of samples which are not homogeneous across samples and within single samples (Gartner, 1988). The problem is exacerbated when samples of convenience are used.

Other scholars disagree with this view. No immediate attempts at defining the field will provide the guidance which the field needs for comparability of research. In other fields of study progress was made without a consensus definition. (Van der Werf and Brush, 1989). Inconsistencies in research methods seem to also result in replication difficulties within the field, making results contradictory (Van der Werf et al. 1989).

Sexton and Bouman (1985) showed that scholars used different instruments for measuring personality characteristics of entrepreneurs and that some of the instruments are potentially invalid and that is why contradictory results occur. They suggest that the solution was to make studies comparable by using comparable instruments.

6. The purposes are explanation, understanding, and prediction of phenomena.

Low et al. (1988) seems to feel that entrepreneurship research lacked clarity of purpose, or purpose was of little consequence. They further suggest that entrepreneurship research should go beyond descriptive studies to pursue causal inference. The emphasis should be on explanation and prediction of phenomena to achieve quality research (Kerlinger, 1986). Gartner (1988) felt that certain approaches do not lead to adequate prediction, such as the use of demographic variables to predict entrepreneurship. It seems that there is a need for an overall common purpose that will forge some unity among researchers.

7. The purpose, or problem, of the research should be as unambiguous as possible.

The statement of the problem should include analysis into its smallest elements and should specify the meaning of all the words significant to the research (Emory, 1985; 10). Entrepreneurship scholars do not always seem to comply with this criterion of good research. According to Low et al. (1988), the failure to clarify purpose and the lack of common ground for synthesizing findings has hampered advancement of the field. The specific purpose of studies should be explicitly stated and linked to suggested overall purpose.

Gartner (1988) emphasized that theory articulation requires that key variables and ideas be defined with precision to provide a clear sense of the study's research focus and that scholars do not always define key variables adequately. There is a need for future entrepreneurship research programs to include a clear statement of purpose, as unambiguously as possible.

8. The data - collecting and sampling are objective.

Bygrave (1989) states that too many databases were produced by collecting data with self-reporting subjective questionnaires or generated by others and used for the wrong purpose. Aldrich (1992) felt that, in some cases, research is hampered by lack of investigator imagination when it comes to data collection and showed that the field still relied heavily on survey data. He further states that data collection methods have not changed very much since the 1980s and that entrepreneurship research is still a mono-method field despite calls for the field to free itself from its dependence on mail surveys and questionnaire based methods.

The unique nature of the entrepreneurship process suggests that data gathering methods such as direct observation, verbal protocols, archives, and focus groups are more effective than questionnaires for the study of entrepreneurship. Multiple data-gathering methods are needed to provide 'triangulation', to generate more accurate and complete descriptions of what has occurred (Hofer et al. 1992). As Gartner (1989) observed, the sample of entrepreneurs selected by researchers is also their operational definition of the entrepreneur. He states that most show a general lack of concern about selecting appropriate samples and that scholars often do not describe what variables specifically characterize the entrepreneur. In many instances groups are not specified, which implies that the characteristics of the sample become both the definitions and the results. The careful selection of research samples of entrepreneurs and non entrepreneurs would help to identify and control for variation. It is therefor critical to devote a great deal of effort to identify what sample of individuals most appropriately represent the kind of individuals the study seeks to analyze. Past studies usually made broad generalizations in defining entrepreneurs, and the sample, therefor, included executives, managers, salespersons, and small business persons. This lack of consistency in defining the entrepreneur also affects the quality of results obtained. The sampling of subjects from very different populations creates empirical inconsistency across empirical entrepreneurship studies (Van der Werf et al. 1989) and this causes contradictory results because populations under 'entrepreneur' can differ significantly in characteristics and behavior. (Begley and Boyd, 1987; Cooper and Dunkelburg, 1987). The lack of basic agreement on definition has resulted in selection of samples which are not homogeneous among various samples and within single samples (Gartner, 1988) and this in turn effects the objectivity of the data being collected.

The quality of entrepreneurship research seems to be affected negatively by various issues relating to objectivity of data collection such as the definition problem, sample specification and definition of key variables and groups.

9. Analysis of the data should be sufficiently adequate to reveal its significance; and the methods of analysis should be appropriate.

The validity and reliability of data should be checked carefully. The data should be classified in ways that assist the researcher to research pertinent conclusions. Bygrave (1989) feels that some researchers think that regression analysis puts us on a par with physicists and he cautions against interpreting R^2 approaches 1 as a causal law of nature. He feels we should avoid a reductionist approach and that there is an over-reliance on statistical sophistication. Other researchers say that there is an underutilization of statistical methods (Wortman, 1987).Cooper et al. (1987) warned that analytical methods have not been very sophisticated and the field is complex and that narrowly based studies must be interpreted with care. Hofer et al. (1992) call for more extensive use of qualitative techniques and that those using them do not use them rigorously enough.

10. The procedural design should be carefully planned to yield results that are as objective as possible.

Hofer et al. (1992) point out that the entrepreneurial process involves change of state and discontinuities, is a holistic and dynamic process. This unique nature of the field effects research design to the extent that traditional methods currently used may be rendered inadequate and will not continue to be used productively in the field in future. They suggest that these traditional methods now being used are supplemented by other approaches that better fit the unique characteristics of the entrepreneurship process. They argue for multi-stage designs and suggest that pilot studies are essential in entrepreneurship research.

The uniqueness of the field also suggests that studies should be longitudinal in character to capture all aspects of the start-up process.

Carsrud et al. (1986) suggested the need for longitudinal studies to evaluate the impact of decisions or changing dimensions over time. Van de Ven (1992) suggests that scholars have become more interested in the process of entrepreneurship as opposed to trait research and consequently a need has developed for a new set of methods for conducting longitudinal procedures. It seems that field studies/longitudinal studies are needed (Bygrave, 1989).

Although Bygrave (1989) suggested that the field of entrepreneurship is an infant paradigm and that scholars should not aspire to what he calls 'physics envy' it nevertheless seems that entrepreneurship research, in order to develop effectively, must support the notion that all types of research are needed for effective development of knowledge. Research must progress from exploratory studies in the field, though formal theory development, to testing in the laboratory and finally back to the field for verification (Paulin et al. 1982). There seems to be a need for experimental and quasi-experimental studies resulting in a gain in predictability.

The quality of entrepreneurship research seems to have been hampered by its reliance on survey research and by the fact that various theoretical perspectives exist within the paradigm.

11. The researcher should report, with complete frankness, flaws in procedural design and estimate their effects on the findings.

A sensitive researcher should be sensitive to the effects of imperfect design and his experience in analyzing the data should give him a basis for estimating their influence (Emory, 1985). This criterion is often not complied with, as inspection of the research reveals, probably because some researchers may often be unaware of the shortcomings in their procedural design. Several new entrepreneurship research journals have adopted rigorous reviewing standards which should constitute a source of guidance for researchers.

12. Conclusions should be confined to those justified by the data of the research and limited to those for which the data provide an adequate basis.

'...Researchers should not be tempted to broaden the basis of induction beyond the controls under which the data were gathered...' Low et al. 1988, warns practitioners to look out for some inappropriate generalization and misleading assumptions about '...causality. This tends to decrease the objectivity of the findings and weakens confidence in the findings...' (Emory, 1985; 11). Diversity within the field implies that care should be taken in noting the nature of the sample and that samples should be broadly based if generalizations are to be made (Cooper et al. 1987). Conclusions should not be drawn from a limited population and applied universally. '...Good researchers specify the conditions under which their conclusions seem to be invalid. Failure to do so justifiably weakens confidence in the research...' (Emory, 1985).

Currently researchers tend not to report negative findings adequately. Negative findings make a positive contribution to the field and should by reported and should be published as they indicate which concepts and theories have not proved worthy of further use (Hofer et al. 1992).

Researchers also do not discuss the implications of the findings for the conceptual models or theories on which the hypotheses were based but only discuss the specific hypotheses. Their discussion should also extend to the discussion of findings which address the assumptions and concepts on which the research has been based (Hofer et al. 1992).

In summary, although scholars do not agree on this, the primary criticisms of entrepreneurship research seem to be the problems caused by the absence of an accepted definition, inadequacies of the paradigms used, lack of theory, the absence of a paradigm specifically developed for entrepreneurship research, inadequate application of theory from related fields, underutilization of statistical methods and over reliance on statistical sophistication, or on the other hand, underutilization of statistical analysis techniques.

Boshoff et al. (1992) concluded that future studies should undertake better research with a stronger frame of reference, better defined constructs, more clarity on theory building, building on others work, and appropriate data gathering and analytical methods.

It seems that specific theory problems exist in the field of entrepreneurship research. These problems relate to issues such as definitional issues (Gartner, 1988), the distinction between entrepreneurship and small business (Carland et al. 1984), the topic that should be researched to facilitate the unification of research in the field (Paulin et al. 1982; Wortman, 1985: Slevin and Covin 1992), the approaches that should be used in future entrepreneurship research (Gartner, 1988; Robinson,

Stimpton, Huefner and Hunt 1992) and the goals of research (Brockhaus, 1987; Ireland et al. 1987).

Distinctions between Small Business and Entrepreneurship

Carland et al. (1984) tried to use the logic of Schumpeter (1934), Glueck (1980) and Vesper (1980) to conceptually distinguish between the two groups in terms of innovative behavior and strategic management practices. Empirically, they found that a distinction could be made on innovative behavior and cognitive style and presented definitions for Entrepreneur, Small business owner, Entrepreneurial venture and Small business venture.

Wortman (1985) seems to accept this dichotomy, as his separated research typologies indicate. However, Gartner (1988) was highly critical of both the research approach and the distinguishing definitions. He felt that Carland et al. argument would have been more fruitful had they looked at the behavioural perspective of entrepreneurship ending. He strongly debated that the definitions raised more questions than they answered and increased the ambiguity of the definitional dilemma. He further argued that an innovation/entrepreneurship correlation implies that almost all firms which sell to similar customer groups would be considered small business (Gartner, 1988). He based his argument on the difficulty of defining innovative products or companies.

Attempts at making a distinction between entrepreneurs and non-entrepreneurs, particularly the distinctions between small business and entrepreneurship has presented researchers of future directions of study with a fundamental question, namely, should there be a distinction and, if so, which direction should carry the emphasis of future research to facilitate the study of the phenomenon of entrepreneurship? On what basis should this distinction be made?

A great deal of confusion seems to exist with regard to the clarification of this distinction (Boshoff and Van Vuuren, 1992) and it still seems to presents a conceptual problem for future entrepreneurship researchers.

The Problems of Definition

In this section no temporal development of a definition, or definitional types and trends, is discussed. The intention here is merely to show that a theory problem exists in entrepreneurship research and to review some of the problems caused by the lack of a generally accepted definition.

Literature seems to support the argument that there is no generic accepted definition, working or otherwise, of the terms 'entrepreneur' or 'entrepreneurship' (Hornaday 1992), or if there is we do not have the psychological instruments to discover it at the time (Brockhaus 1987, Gartner, 1988; Carland, Hoy, and Carland, 1988). Most of the attempts to distinguish between entrepreneurs and small business owners or managers have discovered no significant differentiating features (Gartner, 1988).

Entrepreneurship research seems to be experiencing difficulties in establishing a generally accepted definition. Since Schumpeter's (1934) seminal work on entrepreneurs scholars have been unable to agree on a definition of an entrepreneur (Bygrave and Hofer, 1991), although many attempts at establishing such a definition are found in the literature (Cunningham and Lischeron, 1991; Gartner, 1990). Other scholars have concurred that a common definition of the entrepreneur remains elusive (Carsrud et al. 1985; Sexton et al. 1985; Wortman, 1986) and is yet to emerge (Gartner, 1990).

Gartner (1990) concluded that in many studies entrepreneurship is never defined and that many, and sometimes vague, definitions are used in entrepreneurship research, few studies employ the same definition, samples of 'entrepreneurs' are consequently not homogeneous, that the startling number of traits attributed to entrepreneurs are contradictory and describes a sort of 'Everyman.' The acceptance of a definition seems elusive, as Bygrave et al (1991) commented that all researchers recognize the importance of definitions, but we entrepreneurship scholars have been embroiled in a never-ending debate over the definition of an entrepreneur (Bygrave et al. 1991: 13).

A large number of definitions of entrepreneurship exist and have been used (Boshoff, et al 1992) and this diversity created inconsistency across empirical entrepreneurship studies (Van der Werf et al. 1989). Further inconsistencies are also caused by the application of a sampling of subjects from different populations (Low et al. 1988) loosely defined as 'entrepreneurial' but which differ significantly in character and behavior (Cooper et al. 1986; Van der Werf et al. 1989).

Some scholars view a consensus definition as imperative to meaningful future entrepreneurship research and called for a unifying definition of the field of entrepreneurship (Low et al. 1988). In 1987, Brockhaus argued that, if theory in the field of entrepreneurship research is to develop, commonality will have to be found so that cross study comparisons can be made.

The constant revision in the description of entrepreneurship results in a situation where any candidate definition faces extreme difficulty in gaining acceptance by the majority of researchers. The solution to the problem appears to be the attainment of a consensus definition for the field (Wortman, 1987).

Other scholars do not regard this as a priority to future entrepreneurship research. Some argue that the desire to invent a better definition is miss directed and that priorities should be reversed. The priority focus, they maintain, should be on developing a useful theory of entrepreneurship which might resolve the definitional issue or render it somewhat irrelevant. The search for the best definition may have impeded the development of theory and robust theoretical models and be hampering progress towards developing a theory (Bygrave, 1989a; Bull and Willard, 1993).

The definitional dilemma seems to be a challenging problem for future entrepreneurship scholars (Cunningham et al. 1991). Some scholars have declared that every researcher ought to establish his or her definitions in order to legitimize research findings (Carland et al. 1988). Bull et al. (1993) stated that researchers, teachers and policy makers need a commonly accepted definition that distinguishes an entrepreneur from a non - entrepreneur and suggests that Schumpeter's definition is adequately descriptive and discriminatory for academic purposes and precise enough for policy making purposes.

In conclusion, it appears that some scholars have argued that a consensus definition is an imperative for meaningful future entrepreneurship research and others have argued that a definition should not be a priority and may be unnecessary to make research progress. Some scholars suggest that the search for a definition, and the difficulties involved, may even be hampering progress towards developing a theory of entrepreneurship and some suggest solutions to the dilemma.

Further clarification regarding the distinction between entrepreneurship and small business (Carland et al. 1984) still appears necessary. The lack of agreement on a definition of entrepreneurship and of an entrepreneur, and whether such definitions are a prerequisite for meaningful entrepreneurship research (Low et al. 1988; Köllermeier, 1992).

Research Strategy

In order to answer the research questions a survey research strategy was implemented. A content analysis was undertaken to develop a topic framework for future research, referred to as the Entrepreneurship Life-cycle framework, which was used to develop a survey questionnaire. The questionnaire, which was referred to as the FER questionnaire, was sent to an international sample of academics which were knowledgeable in the field of entrepreneurship.

The Research Questions

Question 1:
The distinction between entrepreneurship and small business still seems to presents a conceptual problem for future entrepreneurship researchers. The first question to be answered is therefore: 'is it important, for research purposes, to make a distinction between entrepreneurship and small business?'

Question 2:
If a distinction is made between entrepreneurship and small business, on which definitional constructs can such a distinction be made? In view of the definitional problems the following question is asked; 'which terms in relation to the degree in which an individual's activities correspond to either small businessmen or entrepreneurs should be researched?'

Question 3:
In view of the lack of consensus among scholars regarding the importance of a definition to meaningful future entrepreneurship research the

following question is asked; 'how important is the clarification of a definition of entrepreneurship to future entrepreneurship research?'

Methodology and Data Collection

The initial intention was to identify individuals who were active in the field of entrepreneurship research to act as respondents to the questionnaire. The research group was defined as those persons who are members of the Entrepreneurship Professional Division (Number 17) of The Academy of Management. This group, consisting of 742 persons as listed in the 1992 Membership Directory, served as the population for this study.

The Academy of Management is a professional institute whose members are primarily academics specializing in various management related disciplines. Members of Division 17 specialize in Entrepreneurship and was therefore seen to constitute a suitably knowledgeable group which best meets the purposes of the study and satisfies the primary selection criterion of persons who are active in, and who have knowledge of, the field of entrepreneurship research.

The names and addresses of all the members of this Division were obtained from the 1992 Membership Directory of The Academy of Management, which was the latest available Directory when the study was undertaken.

Sample

The 130 individuals whose usable questionnaire responses were processed served as the sample (respondent group) for this study. Not all the respondents answered all the questions. The sample will be described in terms of biographic (age, sex), educational, career and geographic variables. This information was obtained by means of the questionnaire (Part B) used in this study.

Non - Participation of Respondents

In mail surveys the receivers of the questionnaire decide for themselves on the extent of their participation or non-participation (Emory, 1985). In this study a possible main reason for non-participation seems to be that questionnaires had to be returned by a certain due date, placing a time constraint on respondents of only two to three weeks. This time limit may have deterred some persons from responding. Other possible reasons for non-participation may have been that letters of introduction enquiring about willingness to participate and follow-up questionnaires could not be sent due to cost constraints and that no stamp/franking of the return envelope was possible. Although an offer was made to reimburse respondents for their postage expenses, on request, none of the respondents made use of this offer.

Various reasons for non-participation were corresponded in isolated cases, for example, 4 respondents were out of town when the questionnaire was received, one could not understand the questionnaire, one wrote that he found the questionnaire too long and 12 requested another copy of the questionnaire. One apologized that he was too old and one potential respondent had died.

Biographical Variables of Subjects

Sex and age

The sample consisted of 108 (83.7 per cent) males and 21(16.3 per cent) females. One respondent did not answer the question on sex. Almost three-quarters of the respondents (72.23 per cent) were between the ages of 40 and 59 years of age. 14.28 per cent were below 40 years of age and 13.49 per cent were 60 years and above. The mean age of respondents was 48.71 years with a Standard Deviation of 9.62 years.

Highest academic degree

It was important to use a sample containing subjects with a high academic involvement with entrepreneurship research in order to improve the quality and validity of the responses regarding future entrepreneurship research.

The division of the sample into those respondents who held a doctoral degree and those who did not is shown in Table 2. The distribution of highest academic degree as indicated in Table 2. shows that the great majority (80.77 per cent) of the sample held doctoral degrees. The information on age and qualifications of the sample presented thus far seems to indicate that the sample consists of an academically mature group largely aged in their 40's and 50's.

Academic status

The distribution of current academic status is shown in Table 3. and indicates that approximately 84.4 per cent of the sample held positions from Assistant Professor to full Professor. Less than 10 per cent of the respondents were not academics.

Number of publications

The profile of publications regarding small business/entrepreneurship authored/co-authored by respondents is as follows:
Proceedings papers: Only 19.5 per cent of respondents had not published any proceedings papers whereas 80.5 per cent had published proceedings papers.
Articles in refereed journals: Only 26 per cent of respondents had not published in refereed journals whereas 74 per cent had published in refereed journals.
Articles in non-refereed journals: 54.5 per cent of respondents had not published in non-refereed journals whereas 45.5 per cent had done so.
In newspapers and trade journals: 53.7 per cent of respondents had published in newspapers and trade journals whilst 46.3 per cent had not done so.
Textbooks: Although 69.9 per cent of respondents had not published a textbook 20.3 per cent of respondents had published one or two textbooks and 9.8 per cent of respondents had published three or more textbooks.
Popular books: Only 11.4 per cent of respondents had published popular books.

Time involved in research

As Table 4 displays, the majority of respondents (97.62 per cent) have had some research experience.

Time involved in teaching

Table 5 shows that the majority of respondents (98.5 per cent) have had some teaching experience, 5 of the respondents did not answer the question, 84 per cent of the respondents have had more than 5 years of teaching experience and 65.6 per cent of the respondents have had more than 10 years of teaching involvement.

Teaching and research emphasis

As indicated in Table 6, only 17.83 per cent of respondents taught entrepreneurship as a principal subject and only 10.94 per cent of respondents did only entrepreneurship research; 82.17 per cent of respondents had some entrepreneurship teaching experience and 89.84 per cent had some entrepreneurship research experience.

Geographic distribution

The majority of respondents were found in the United States of America (80 per cent) and Canada (7.69 per cent) as intended at research group selection. Only 12.31 per cent of the group were therefor not found in the U.S.A. or in Canada. These respondents were found in Belgium (1; 0.77 per cent), England (2; 1.52 per cent), Finland (3; 2.31 per cent), Germany (2; 1.52 per cent), Korea (1; 0.77 per cent), Mexico (1; 0.77 per cent), Netherlands (1; 0.77 per cent), Norway (1; 0.77 per cent), Spain (2; 1.52 per cent) and South Africa (2; 1.52 per cent).

The allocations to countries was made firstly from the optional address facility on the questionnaire. If this address was not supplied by the respondent the address on the returned covering letter, which most respondents returned attached to the completed questionnaire, was used. If both these addresses were not given the location of the institution where the respondent was employed was used.

Country educated

The majority of the respondents were educated in the United States of America as shown in Table 8.

Country born

Table 9 indicates that almost three-quarters of the respondents were born in the United States of America. Over two-thirds of the respondents have owned, managed or started a business.

The Research Instrument

This research project is the result of discussions which started at the 1992 International Conference on Internationalizing Entrepreneurship held in Cambridge, England where it was decided to determine the views of individuals who attended the conference on directions for entrepreneurship research. Emanating from this decision a survey questionnaire was produced by a working party established during the conference. The supervisor of the present study was a member of this working party.

This survey questionnaire served as a foundation document for the development of the survey questionnaire used in this study and referred to as the FER questionnaire (future entrepreneurship research).

Development of the Survey Instrument

The main study focussed on future research topics in entrepreneurship and not on both entrepreneurship and small business research as does the base document developed in 1992. Therefor the only questions concerning small business that were retained in the FER questionnaire relate to macro directional and definitional entrepreneurship and small business issues. Three questions, namely A1, A5, A6, were extracted from this questionnaire and uses in this study. Biographical variables were revised and also incorporate into the questionnaire which was then referred to as the FER questionnaire (Future Entrepreneurship Research Questionnaire).

41

The Pilot Study

Six individuals were identified at the Technikon Pretoria to serve as a sample for the pilot study. Two of these academics hold doctorates in management, two hold doctorates in the social sciences, one holds an M.B.A. and one a B.Sc. degree. A pilot study questionnaire was specifically draw up to elicit responses, from these six individuals, relating to their experience while completing the FER questionnaire and to test the eight issues mentioned above. Each individual was given a blank FER questionnaire and a pilot study questionnaire and requested to complete both questionnaires. On collection of the completed questionnaires respondents were interviewed by the researcher. All partially or incomplete questions on the pilot study questionnaire were clarified and completed including those which required that the respondents be verbally tested by the interviewer.

Two of the respondents also provided additional comments, criticisms and suggestions on various aspects of the FER questionnaire. These comments together with the information on the completed pilot study and FER questionnaires were analyzed, synthesized, evaluated and incorporated into the final FER questionnaire as used in this study.

Measurement of Variables

Variables in question A6: Viewpoints of respondents regarding the importance of the clarification of a definition for future entrepreneurship research, were measured using a one to eight point interval (1 to 8) Likert Type Scale with 1 being 'very unimportant' and 8 being 'very important'. A one to eight scale was selected to reduce the incidence of neutral selection and to facilitate division into halves and quartiles.

Variables in question A1 were measured by multiple choice single response question. Variables in question B28 were measured by a multiple choice multiple response question. Variables in questions A5 were measured on a 1 to eight continuum scale ranging from Small businessmen to Entrepreneurs. Biographical variables were measured by a multiple choice multiple response question.

Collection of Data

Data was collected by means of a postal questionnaire (FER) as developed for this purpose. The questionnaire, accompanied by a covering letter and a return-addressed envelope, was sent to each of the 742 members of the Entrepreneurship Professional Division (Number 17) of The Academy of Management by airmail. After receiving 129 responses a follow-up letter was sent out to non-respondents which resulted in the receipt of a further 3 completed questionnaires by the cut-off date for the study.

Of the 742 questionnaires sent out, 132 were returned of which 130 could be used in the research thus yielding a response rate of 17,52 per cent. The 2 unusable questionnaires were discarded because they were inadequately completed by the respondents and yielded insufficient data for processing.

The cut-off point for inclusion of questionnaires in this study was established at two months after the date indicated on the covering letter as the final return date for responses and one month after sending the follow-up letters. At this point sufficient returns had been received to start analyzing the data. A total of 30 (4.04 per cent of the total addresses) envelopes marked 'return to sender' were received, indicating an acceptable level of accuracy of the addresses in the 1992 Membership Directory.

Statistical Treatment of Data

The computer software utilized to analyze the data consisted of the Statistical Analysis System (SAS/STAT - Release 6.03) package as loaded into the computer at the University of Pretoria and was accessed via the terminal at the Bureau of Financial Analysis. The raw response data on the questionnaires were prepared for analysis by a process of editing, coding and tabulation. After coding the data were captured on computer and various procedures in the SAS/STAT system were applied to the data.

Descriptive statistics (means, standard deviations, tendency analysis, skewness coefficient, kurtosis and frequency analysis) were calculated to demonstrate and describe the basic tendencies in the data and to summarize the data. Single-classification Chi Square test, as suggested by Kerlinger (1986: 155) and Dixon and Massey (1983: 273), was applied to find answers to question 1 to establish if a significant difference existed between scores. The Coefficient of Contingency (C) was calculated to index the strength of the relationship between the variables. The GLM procedure in SAS was used to execute MANOVA and Analysis of Variance. Correlation coefficients were calculated by means of the Correlation Procedure in SAS.

Question 1: 'Is it important, for research purposes, to make a distinction between entrepreneurship and small business?'

In earlier formulation of the directions for future research the question arose whether a distinction should be made between entrepreneurship research and small business research to indicate the main stream direction for future research.

To answer this question a single-classification Chi square test, as suggested by Kerlinger (1986: 155) and Dixon and Massey (1983: 273), was applied to the responses to establish if a significant difference existed between the number of respondents answering Question 1 positively and those answering negatively. The coefficient of contingency (C) was then calculated, as suggested by Kerlinger (1986: 158), to index the strength or magnitude of the association between the variables. The frequencies obtained were: 'Yes' = 118; 'No' = 8 and 'Don't Know' = 1. The 'Don't Know' frequency was omitted from the test.

As regards the importance of a distinction between entrepreneurship and small business in future research the results of the Chi square test (Chi Square = 96.03, d.f. = 1, p = 0.005) indicated that respondents evidently tended to think that a distinction should be made between entrepreneurship and small business for the purposes of future research in entrepreneurship. According to the results of the measure of association, the coefficient of contingency © = 0.66) seems to indicate that the tendency revealed (i.e. that respondents thought that a difference should be made) was quite strong.

Question 2: 'To what degree do certain terms relating to an individual's activities correspond to either small businessmen or entrepreneurs?'

This question was posed to contribute to the definitional clarification and as a further indication of which topics are important for future research in entrepreneurship, as opposed to small business. The terms were scored on small businessmen (1) - entrepreneurs (8) continuum, converted to a percentage scale and tested for significant differences between the two groups by means of One-way ANOVA, and the Tukey Ranges Test. The results are shown in Table 1. Table 1 shows that several significant differences were obtained between the mean scores of the terms. The Tukey standardized range test indicated the following results in respect of mean scores:

1. Innovation is significantly higher than all other terms.
2. Opportunist is significantly higher than Promotion/Promoter, Artisan/Craftsman, Administrative/Manager and Security/Family but not significantly higher than Independence/Growth.
3. Independence/Growth is significantly higher than Promotion/Promoter, Artisan/Craftsman, Administrative/Manager and Security/Family.
4. Promotion/Promoter is significantly higher than Artisan/Craftsman, Administrative/Manager and Security/Family.
5. Artisan/Craftsman is significantly higher than Security/Family but not significantly different from Administrative/Manager.
6. Administrative/Manager is significantly different from Security/Family.

The $100R^2$-value indicates a very strong conviction by the respondents that at least some of the terms were more closely related to either small businessmen or entrepreneurs.

The scale applied to $100R^2$ was as follows:

If the value of $100R^2$; is greater than 0 per cent less than 6 per cent the value is regarded as very low,
is greater than 6 per cent less than 10 per cent the value is regarded as low,
is greater than 10 per cent less than 20 per cent the value is regarded as moderate,
is greater than 20 per cent less than 30 per cent the value is regarded as moderately high,
is greater than 30 per cent less than 50 per cent the value is regarded as high,
is greater than 50 per cent the value is regarded as very high.

Question 3: 'How important is the clarification of a definition of entrepreneurship to future entrepreneurship research?'

In earlier formulation of the research questions the proposition was made that the definition of entrepreneurship is important to future entrepreneurship research.

To answer this question responses were reduced to two categories, Unimportant (f = 38) and Important (f = 91). A single-classification Chi square test, as suggested by Kerlinger (1986: 155) and Dixon et al. (1983), was then applied to the obtained frequencies to establish if a significant difference existed between the number of responses in the Unimportant and Important categories. The coefficient of contingency (C) was then calculated, as suggested by Kerlinger (1986: 158), to index the strength or magnitude of the association between the variables.

The results of the Chi square test (Chi square = 21.78, d.f. = 1, p = 0.005) indicated that a significant majority of the respondents evidently felt that it is important for a definition of entrepreneurship to be clarified for the purposes of future research in entrepreneurship.

The results of the measure of association, the coefficient of contingency C = 0.38), seems to indicate that the tendency for respondents to regard clarification of the definition of entrepreneurship as important rather than unimportant, is therefor moderately strong.

Discussion of Results

Results pertaining to the importance, for research purposes, of making a distinction between entrepreneurship and small business (Q1). The rationale for this question arises from the need to identify the main stream of future entrepreneurship research as this distinction seems to present a conceptual problem for future research. It was decided to perform a single-classification Chi square test on the data to establish whether a significant difference existed between the number of respondents answering this question.

The results indicated that significant differences were found to exist between the number of respondents who answered this question positively and those that answered it negatively. The respondents therefore tended to think that a distinction should be made between entrepreneurship and small business for purposes of future research. This result seems to highlight the necessity to clarify definitional issues relating to research in the entrepreneurship field.

The findings seem to support the views of Carland et al. (1984). It can be speculated that the reason respondents are strongly in favor of a distinction is that the influence of Carland et al. (1984) and the logic of Schumpeter (1934), Glueck (1980) and Vesper (1980) to conceptually distinguish between the two kinds of endeavor has had a significant impact and is an indication of the degree to which the idea that the two kinds of endeavor are different has been accepted by academics.

The measure of association (C) was interpreted as an indication of the strength of the conviction of the respondent regarding their response to the question. A high strength of conviction that a distinction should be made is evident from the obtained value of C. Results pertaining to: The Terms in relation to the degree in which an individual's activities correspond to either small businessmen or entrepreneurs should be researched (Q2). This question was posed as a further attempt clarify the distinction between small businessmen and entrepreneurs and to determine which topics are important for future research.

With regard to the research question whether significant differences exist between means of responses obtained for the individual's activities the One-way ANOVA and Tukey Ranges Test indicated results as shown in Table 1. Significant differences were obtained between the mean scores on several of the terms.

Innovation was found to be significantly higher than all the other terms, indicating that respondents viewed this term as the individual activity corresponding most to entrepreneurs rather than to small businessmen. It seems that Innovation is an important area for future entrepreneurship research, being seen by the respondents in the current study as typical of entrepreneurial behavior.

Opportunist and Independence/Growth were found to be significantly higher than Promotion/Promoter, Artisan/Craftsman, Administrative/ Manager and Security/Family. Opportunist and Independence/Growth are therefor viewed by respondents as individual activities corresponding to entrepreneurs rather than to small businessmen.

Promotion/Promoter had a significantly higher score than Artisan/ Craftsman, Administrative/Manager and Security/Family. Promotion/ Promoter seems to numerically correspond slightly less to small business-

47

men (40.6 per cent) than to entrepreneurs (59.4 per cent). It appears that this term is important for both research on the small businessmen and entrepreneurs.

Artisan/Craftsman had a significantly higher score than Security/ Family but was not significantly different from Administrative/Manager. Artisan/Craftsman and Administrative/ Manager seem to be activities corresponding to small businessmen rather than to entrepreneurs and consequently possibly less important to future entrepreneurship research.

Security/Family is indicated as the individual activity that correspond the most to small businessmen and the least to entrepreneurship. It consequently appears to be the least important term for future entrepreneurship research.

The 100R^2-value indicated a very high percentage of common variance between the variables compared and was interpreted as an indication of the strength of conviction of respondents about the degree to which an individual's activities correspond to that of either small businessmen or of entrepreneurs.

The findings therefor show a high degree of conviction of respondents regarding the correspondence of the terms to either entrepreneur or small businessmen.

These findings are important when formulating differences between, and when defining, entrepreneurs and small businessmen and indicate that Innovation, Opportunist and Independence/Growth are important topics for future entrepreneurship research.

The finding that the term Innovation is the individual activity associated most strongly with entrepreneurs rather than with the behavior of small businessmen supports the logic of Carland et al. (1984), Schumpeter (1934), Glueck (1980) and Vesper (1980) to conceptually distinguish between the two groups in terms of innovative behavior. The findings also support the empirical findings of Carland et al. (1984) that a distinction could be made on innovative behavior and cognitive style. It seems that Innovation is possibly an important area for future entrepreneurship research.

The findings also support the view of Hoy, McDougall and Dsouza (1992) that Opportunity recognition and Growth are variables distinguishing entrepreneurship from small business and that these variables should be researched further.

48

Results pertaining to the importance of clarifying a definition of entrepreneurship to future entrepreneurship research (Q3).

The rationale for this question arises from the lack of consensus among scholars regarding the importance of a definition to meaningful future entrepreneurship research. It was decided to perform a single-classification Chi square test on the data to establish whether a tendency existed for the respondents to see the classification of the definition as either important or not important.

The results indicated that a significant tendency was found to exist for respondents to answer this question positively. The respondents therefor tended to think that a definition is important to future entrepreneurship research.

These findings are consistent with the views of those scholars advocating a consensus definition for the field (Van der Werf et al. 1989; Low et al. 1988; Wortman, 1987) but not necessarily in agreement with those scholars who do not regard a consensus definition as a priority to future entrepreneurship research (Bygrave, 1989a; Bull et al. 1993). The measure of association (C) was interpreted as an indication of the strength of the conviction of the respondent regarding their response to the question. A medium strength of conviction that a distinction should be made is evident from the findings.

A shortcoming of the study is that the sample did not include practitioners.

Conclusions and Implications

Distinguishing between entrepreneurship and small business

A fundamental decision that researchers have to make is whether to research entrepreneurship or small business, i.e. to distinguish between entrepreneurship and small business. This issue contributes to the solution of the directions for research problem by indicating the direction that should be taken in terms of the two main research streams in the field. The results of this study indicated that academics feel strongly that a distinction should be made. The implication here is that future research in this field will develop into two distinct but overlapping areas or paradigms of study. The implication of this distinction implies that future research can be more focussed and this awareness could lead to better developed theories and frameworks, and scholars should specify clearly on which area their research is concentrated.

A further implication seems to be that a research agenda for entrepreneurship could be developed separate to that of small business and that clarification of definitions may now be a priority to facilitate the development of the entrepreneurship research paradigm. It seems that the interface, such as that proposed by Wortman (1986), between the two fields then also becomes a research priority and should demand further attention. There seems to be a need for comprehensive frameworks to provide impetus for systematic research on all parts of both fields (Churchill et al. 1986).

The theoretical implications are that researchers recognize and clarify the distinction in terms of models, definitions and unifying frameworks by extending the work of scholars such as Carland et al. (1984) and Wortman (1986). It seems that the distinguishing factors present an opportunity for future research and could lead to more focussed research in both fields of study.

Activities corresponding to entrepreneurs rather than to owners of small business

Regarding the distinguishing factors the results in this study indicate that Innovation is the activity most strongly corresponding to entrepreneurs, followed by Opportunism and Independent growth. It seems that research should follow the current trend of growing consensus that the economic impact of entrepreneurship is the result of a small number of growing firms and that entrepreneurship is 'a process of opportunity recognition and pursuit that leads to growth' (Sexton et al. 1992: xix).

The results of the study support this view, which distinguish between the activities of small businessmen and entrepreneurs, and suggest innovation, opportunity exploitation and independent growth are typical entrepreneurial phenomena that are important in defining entrepreneurs. Similarly, the activities of Artisan/craftsman, administration/manager and security/family are indicated as being important areas of study in small business research and as characteristic of small business ownership.

The clarification of a definition

The results of the present study essentially showed that respondents viewed it as important to clarify a definition of entrepreneurship for future entrepreneurship research.

The implication of this result is that greater effort needs to be made to achieve a consensus or unifying definition of each of the two phenomena (entrepreneurship and small business). It seems unlikely that intellectual order will be created unless researchers in future decide on whether they are studying entrepreneurship or small business endeavors.

It is, nevertheless, evident from the findings of this study relating to the activities pertaining to either entrepreneurship or small business that a certain degree of consensus is developing among scholars regarding which entrepreneurial activities pertaining to entrepreneurship. It seems that few scholars would dispute the inclusion of such variables as Innovation, Opportunism and Growth in a definition of entrepreneurship.

These findings seem to reflect the natural desire of scholars for systematic research in the field rather than the logic arising from the practicality of actually developing a consensus definition. However the need to produce such a definition is apparent and researchers should regard the necessity of developing a consensus and unifying definition for entrepreneurship as an important area of future entrepreneurship research, provided the difficulties involved do not hamper progress towards developing a theory of entrepreneurship, as some scholars suggest it might.

References

Aldrich, H. E. (1990, Spring). Using an ecological perspective to study organizational founding rates. *Entrepreneurship: theory and practice. 14*(3), 7 - 24.

Aldrich, H. E. (1992). Method in our madness? trends in entrepreneurship research. In D. L. Sexton and J. D. Kasarda (Eds), *The state of the art of entrepreneurship* (pp 191 - 213). Boston, MA: PWS - Kent Publishing Company.

Begley, T. M., and Boyd, D. P. (1987a). A comparison of entrepreneurs and managers of small business firms. *Journal of Management, 13*, 99 - 108.

Berelson, B., and Steiner, G. A. (1964). *Human behavior.* New York, NY: Harcourt, Brace and World.

Boshoff, A. B., Bennett, H. F., and Owusu, A. A. (1992, February). Entrepreneurship research: where are we and where are we going? *Development Southern Africa. 9*(1), 47 - 63.

Boshoff, A. B., and Van Vuuren, J. J. J. (1992). Distinguishing successful and less successful entrepreneurs from bankers and state employees by means of personality traits, fields of interest and biographical variables. Paper presented at Int Ent Conference, Dortmund, July (6 - 8).

Brockhaus, R. H. Sr. (1987). Entrepreneurship research: Are we playing the correct game? *American Journal of Small business, 11*(3), 43 - 49.

Bull, I., and Willard, G. E. (1993). Towards a theory of entrepreneurship. *Journal of Business Venturing 8,* 183 - 195.

Bygrave, W. D. (1987) Syndicated investments by venture capital firms. *Journal of Business Venturing, 2*(2), 138 - 154.

Bygrave, W. D. (1989, Fall). The Entrepreneurship Paradigm (I): A Philosophical Look at its Research Methodologies. *Entrepreneurship: theory and practice, 14*(1) , 7 - 26.

Bygrave, W. D., and Hofer, C. W. (1991, Winter). Theorizing about entrepreneurship. *Entrepreneurship: theory and practice, 16*(2), 13 - 22.

Bygrave, W. D. (1993). Theory building in the entrepreneurship paradigm. *Journal of Business Venturing, 8*, 255 - 280.

Carland, J. W., Hoy, F., Boulton, W. R., and Carland, J. A. (1984). Differentiating entrepreneurs from small business owners: a conceptualization. *Academy of Management Review, 9*(2), 354 - 359.

Carland, J. W., Hoy, F., and Carland, J. A. (1988, Spring). 'Who is an entrepreneur?' is a question worth asking. *American Journal of Small Business, 12*(4), 33 - 39.

Carsrud, A. L., Olm, K. W., and Eddy, G. G. (1986). Entrepreneurship; in quest of a paradigm. In D. L. Sexton and R. W. Smilor (Eds). *The art and science of entrepreneurship* (pp. 367 - 378). Cambridge, MA: Ballinger Publishing Company.

Churchill, N. C. (1992). Research issues in entrepreneurship. In D. L. Sexton and J. D. Kasarda (Eds). *The state of the art of entrepreneurship.* Boston, MA: PWS - Kent Publishing Company.

Churchill, N. C., and Hatten, K. J. (1987). Non - market based transfers of wealth and power: a research framework for family businesses. *American Journal of Small Business, 11*(3), 51 - 64.

Churchill, N. C., and Lewis, V. L. (1986). Entrepreneurship reseach: directions and methods. In D. L. Sexton and R. W. Smilor (Eds). *The art and science of entrepreneurship* (pp. 333 - 365). Cambridge, MA: Ballinger Publishing Company.

Cooper, A. C., and Dunkelburg, W. C. (1987). Entrepreneurship research: old questions, new answers, and methodological issues. *American Journal of Small Business, 11*(3), 11 - 24.

Cunningham, J. B., and Lischeron, J. (1991, January). Defining entrepreneurship. *Journal of Small Business Management, 29*(1), 45 - 61.

Curran, J., Stanworth, J., Watkins, D. (1986). *The Economics of Survival and Entrepreneurship: The Survival of the Small Firm 1.* Aldershot: Gower

Dixon, W. J., and Massey, F. J. (1983) *Introduction to statistical analysis.* (3rd ed.). Tokyo: McGraw Hill.

Emory, C. W. (1985). *Business research methods.* (3rd ed.). Homewood, Il: Irwin.

Emory, C. W., and Cooper, D. (1991) *Business research methods* (4th ed.). Homewood: Richard D. Erwin.

Filley, Alan C., *The Compleat Manager: what works when.* Illinois, Research Press Company.

Filley, Alan C., House, Robert J., Kerr, Steven. *Managerial process and organizational behaviour.* (2nd ed.). Illinois, Scott, Foresman and Company.

Gartner, W. B. (1988). 'Who is an entrepreneur?' is the wrong question. *American Journal of Small Business, 12*(4), 11 - 32.

Gartner, W. B. (1989). Some suggestions for research on entrepreneurial traits and characteristics. *Entrepreneurship: theory and practice, 14*(1), 27 - 37.

Gartner, W. B. (1990). What are we talking about when we talk about entrepreneurship. *Journal of Business Venturing, 5*, 15 - 28.

Glueck, W. F. (1980). *Business policy and strategic management.* New York: McGraw - Hill.

Hornaday, R. W. (1992). Thinking about entrepreneurship: a fuzzy set approach. *Journal of Small Business Management, 30*(4),12 - 23.

Hornaday, R. W. , and Churchill, N. C. (1987). Current trends in entrepreneurship research . In N.C Churchill, J.A. Hornaday, B.A. Kirchhoff, O.J. Krasner, and K.H. Vesper (Eds), *Frontiers of entrepreneurship reseach* (pp 1 - 21). Wellesley, MA: Babson College.

Hoy, F., McDougall, P. P., and Dsouza, D. E. (1992). Strategies and environments of high - growth firms. In D. L. Sexton and J. D. Kasarda (Eds), *The state of the art of entrepreneurship* (pp 341 - 357). Boston, MA: PWS - Kent Publishing Company.

Ireland, R. D., and Van Auken, P. M. (1987, Spring). Entrepreneurship and small business research: an historical typology and directions for future research. *American Journal of Small Business, 11*(1), 9 - 20.

Kerlinger, F. N. (1986). *Foundations of behavioral research.* (3rd ed.). New York, NY: Holt, Rinehart and Winston, Inc.

Köllermeier, T. (1992). Entrepreneurship in an economy in transition: perspectives of the situation in the ex GDR. In S. Birley, I.C. MacMillan, and S. Subramony (Eds), *International perspectives on entrepreneurship research: Vol. 18. Advanced series in management.* (pp. 32 - 36). Amsterdam: North - Holland.

Lau, T. (1992). The incident method - an alternative way of studying entrepreneurial behaviour. Paper presented at the Int Ent Conference, Dortmund, July.

Low, M. B., and MacMillan, I. C. (1988). Entrepreneurship: Past research and future challenges. *Journal of Management, 14*(2).

Moore, P. D. (1990). An examination of present research on the female entrepreneur - suggested research strategy for the 1990's. *Journal of Business Ethics, 9(*4 - 5), 275 - 281.

Paulin, W. L., Coffey, R. E., and Spaulding, M. E. (1982). Entrepreneurship research: methods and directions. In C. A. Kent, D. L. Sexton, and K. H. Vesper (Eds), *Encyclopedia of Entrepreneurship* (pp. 353 - 373). Englewood Cliffs, NJ: Prentice Hall Inc.

Perryman, R. (1982). Commentary on research methodology in entrepreneurship. In C. A. Kent, D. L. Sexton, and K. H. Vesper (Eds), *Encyclopedia of Entrepreneurship* (pp. 377 - 379). Englewood Cliffs, NJ: Prentice Hall Inc.

Pfeffer, J. (1977). The ambiguity of leadership. *Academy of Management Review, 2*(1), 104 - 112.

Robinson, P. B., Stimpton, D. V., Huefner, J. C., and Hunt, H. K. (1992, Summer). An attitude approach to the prediction of entrepreneurs. *Entrepreneurship: theory and practice, 15*(4), 13 - 31.

Rupert, A. E. (1994). Foreword. In W. B. Vosloo (Ed.), *Entrepreneurship and economic growth*. Pretoria: HSRC Publishers.

Schumpeter, J. A. (1934). *The theory of economic development*. Cambridge, MA: Harvard University Press.

Sexton, D. L., and Bouwman, N. (1985). The entrepreneur: a capable executive and more. *Journal of Business Venturing*, 1(1), 129 - 140.

Sexton, D. L., and Bouwman - Upton, N. (1988). Validation of an innovative teaching approach for entrepreneurship courses. *American Journal of Small Business, 12*(3), 11 - 22.

Sexton, D. L., and Kasarda, J. D. (Eds). (1992). *The state of the art of entrepreneurship*. Boston, MA: PWS - Kent Publishing Company.

Sexton, D. L., and Smilor, R. W. (Eds). (1986). *The art and science of entrepreneurship* Cambridge, MA: Ballinger Publishing Company.

Sexton, D. L. (1982). Research needs and issues in entrepreneurship. In C. A. Kent, D. L. Sexton, and K. H. Vesper (Eds), *Encyclopedia of Entrepreneurship* (pp. 383 - 389). Englewood Cliffs, NJ: Prentice Hall Inc.

Slevin, D. P., and Covin, J. G. (1992). Creating and maintaining high performance teams. In D. L. Sexton and J. D. Kasarda (Eds), *The state of the art of entrepreneurship* (pp. 358 - 386). Boston, MA: PWS - Kent Publishing Company.

Smith, K. G., Gannon, M. J., and Sapienza, H. g. (1989). Selecting methodologies for entrepreneurship research: Trade - offs and guidelines. *Entrepreneurship: theory and practice, 14*(1), 39 - 49.

Stanworth, M. J. K., and Curran, J., *Management Motivation in the Smaller Business*. Aldershot: Gower.

Timmons, J. A. (1990). *New venture creation*. (3rd ed.). Homewood, Ill; Erwin.

Timmons, J. A. (1994). *New venture creation*. (4th ed.). Homewood, Ill; Erwin.

Van der Werf, P. A., and Brush, C. G. (1989). Achieving empirical progress in an undefined field. *Entrepreneurship: theory and practice, 14*(2), 45 - 58.

Vesper, K. L. (1988). Entrepreneurial academics - how can we tell when the field is getting somewhere? *Journal of Business Venturing, 3*, 1 - 10.

Vesper, K. H. (1980). *New venture strategies*. Engelwood Cliffs, NJ: Prentice Hall.

Wortman, M. S., Jr., (1986b). A Unified Framework, Research Typologies, and Research Prospectuses for the Interface Between Entrepreneurship and Small Business. In D. L. Sexton and R. W. Smilor (Eds). *The art and science of entrepreneurship* (pp. 272 - 33). Cambridge, MA: Ballinger. Publishing Company.

Wortman, M. S. (1987). Entrepreneurship: an integrated typology and an evaluation of the empirical research in the field. *Journal of Management, 12*(2), 159 - 280.

PART B

THEORETICAL CONCEPTS IN ENTREPRENEURSHIP EDUCATION

3   Entrepreneurship Education in the Nineties: Revisited[*]

W.E. McMullan
L.M.Gillin[1]

Abstract

Although universities have been offering courses in entrepreneurship education for over thirty years, graduate level degree programs are only seven years old. In 1986 the Journal of Business Venturing printed an article, which provided the architecture for a graduate degree program in entrepreneurship which was subsequently adopted in 1987 for the design of a program offered through Swinburne University of Technology in Melbourne, Australia. Over the next eight years several hundred students have passed through the three graduate levels of programming now offered in six cites in Australia, Singapore and Indonesia. Plans are underway to extend the program to two more Australian cites and to Israel in 1997.

This paper discusses the implementation of the program design, the results from two surveys tracking the activities and performance of graduates, and some of the implications of this type of program offering. Since 87 per cent of those surveyed started ventures, either independently or under the auspices of a corporation, and since the average number of employees in firms with sales was at approximately six quite high, this type of programming shows signs not only of helping people begin meaningful entrepreneurial careers but also of providing governments with an effective micro-economic response for job creation.

The *Journal of Business Venturing* printed an article by McMullan and Long in 1987 entitled 'Entrepreneurship education in the nineties' in which the authors speculated about the future of entrepreneurship education (McMullan and Long, 1987). First, the authors envisaged the field moving from courses in the seventies to concentrations and majors in the eighties and finally to programs in the nineties. Second, the authors imagined degree programs changing in fundamental ways from conventional business education with different types of goals, professors, students, course contents, teaching methods and support programming. The 1987 article provided the intellectual architecture for a then two-year-old program which was accordingly restructured at Swinburne University of Technology in 1988. This article is a follow-up on the results and implications of implementing this new design for entrepreneurship education.

Evaluating Performance

Evaluating the performance of an education program is not easy at the best of times. Education by its nature is set up for medium or longer-term outcomes. However, program designers can't typically afford to wait for long-term effects and even if they could, such effects would be confounded by many intervening variables. Since success has many fathers, what outcomes become attributed to what preceding events? It was difficult enough to produce convincing evidence that smoking produces lung cancer within the human body. In the social world, it is much more difficult still to find out whether MBA education, for instance, has a positive measurable benefit on a regional or national economy or for graduates on an individual basis. In the case of entrepreneurship education one may get an early indication of success for the economy based upon: (1) the likelihood of graduates starting a business; (2) early indications of business size in terms of employment, sales and perhaps even choice of industries; and (3) indications of growth and success over time. This article presents some preliminary results on the first two of these measures.

For the individual, success might be measured in terms of earnings, capital gains and non-tangible bend such as enhanced job satisfaction. Ideally there would be evidence available to distinguish what people do with the benefit of the program from what similar people do without. Ideally, when comparing the results of different programs, adjustments could be made for the favorableness of student backgrounds for starting ventures. For example, all things being equal one would expect a higher rate of start-up and ultimate success from Harvard or Babson graduates than from Calgary or Swinburne graduates simply because the former two groups are favored with parents with more connections, money, and appropriate knowledge and skills. The three different schools on which data is presented in this report are middle socioeconomic class institutions with student bodies without special advantages and therefore roughly comparable despite the fact that one is in Canada and two are in Australia.

A third measure of success is program success. Are entrepreneurship programs growing in terms of the number of graduates, international recognition and financial success. Is new knowledge being generated? Has there been any diffusion of ideas or programs elsewhere.

From Concentrations and Majors

The movement from concentrations and majors in entrepreneurship education to degree programs has not been an easy transition. Since entrepreneurship educators were housed primarily within established business school programs they were likely to have been institutionally constrained by the business school paradigm. The first school to break the mold might very well have been Stirling, a new university in Scotland, which started a Masters in Entrepreneurship program in 1985 at the same time that it started its business education program. The Stirling program was set up to educate, not entrepreneurs, but rather the people in the various businesses and social institutions that support entrepreneurs. According to Frank Martin, a former director of the Stirling program it still struggles to get enough students in 1996. To cover its somewhat higher operating costs the Stirling program is still primarily aimed at foreign students that pay higher out-of-country fees thereby undermining any impact it might have had upon Scotland. The Swinburne University of Technology in Melbourne set up a Master's of Enterprise Innovation in 1989 (likely the second graduate degree program departure) but this time within the Faculty of Engineering with the purpose of educating entrepreneurs who would develop more new technology growth ventures both as independents and through corporations. Since then, both Babson College and the University of Calgary (MBA in Enterprise Management in 1993) have set up hybrid MBA programs of traditional management mixed

59

with entrepreneurship; not entirely the type of new degree program envisaged within McMullan and Long's 1987 article. Otherwise, the authors are unaware of other degree programs primarily dedicated to entrepreneurship education. The standard practice at this time, at least in North America, is still the concentration or major in entrepreneurship. Case Western Reserve in Cleveland may become one more exception to the norm in the next couple of years.

Program Design

In 1979 the Australian Government initiated in Australia the 'Enterprise Workshop Program' based on ideas from Wayne Brown, then Dean of Engineering at the University of Utah, founder of the Utah Innovation Center and two time successful high technology entrepreneur. From 1981 the then Swinburne Institute of Technology hosted the Victorian Enterprise Workshop with Murray Gillin as the Director. By 1984 it was clear to Murray that the business planning model for developing new business ventures was flawed. The six month part-time program provided an excellent basis to develop a business plan which in the 80's could attract venture finance. However, the program provided little training and development in the skills necessary to manage an on-going and growing business. It was this awareness that led to the development of an integrated two year part-time graduate diploma in entrepreneurial studies, first offered in 1986.

The new program at Swinburne, when extended to a graduate degree program in 1989, was designed to be a three-year half-time program fully dedicated to the creation of new growth businesses either as independent operations or as new ventures within a corporation. The program allowed the students to exit with a formal university-recognized credential at the end of each of the three years; from certificate to diploma to master's degree, one year at a time. The flexibility contained in this design allowed program administrators to alter entrance standards to attract people whose apparent entrepreneurial ability might have exceeded their earlier academic achievements. The progressive ordering of credentials has also allowed students multiple exit points thereby facilitating relatively more emphasis on ventures than degrees. However the program is still a graduate degree program with the responsibility of providing higher education while simultaneously directing students towards entrepreneurial careers.

Exhibit 1: Profile of Melbourne Teaching Faculty

Highest Degree	Academics	Academic Practitioners	Practitioner Academics	Practitioners
PhD		4[a]	2[c]	
Master	1	1[b]	4[c]	
Bachelor of Engeneering				2[c]

a One professor ½ time appointment
b ½ time appointment
c Single Course appointment

The core academic (tenured) faculty is equivalent to five full-time professors. This core group operates as a team with qualifications in marketing, finance, manufacturing, organizational behavior and strategy. Four have had entrepreneurial experience in business creation, They are to varying degrees experienced practitioners in their own rights and may be usefully thought of as academic-practitioners. All are committed to developing an integrated set of courses. This core group is joined by an equal number of successful business practitioners with acceptable academic credentials who are called the practitioner-academic group. Five of the six members of this latter group have first degrees in engineering. In summary the preponderance of the teaching faculty is composed of academic-practitioners and practitioner-academics. A smaller number of academics that have limited new venture experience and practitioners with only a single university degree round out the teaching team.

From the second year on all the courses are team taught typically between one academic practitioner and one practitioner academic. Although such team teaching is relatively more expensive it has been seen as a very important part of the education program. The additional pay-off that comes from teaming academic-practitioners with practitioner academics in the classroom might be described as providing the student with more intellectual space for their own creative thinking. The teaching partners will inevitably find themselves at odds on various points which forces the student to find his or her own resolutions. Moreover, the practitioner-academic may bring an experience bias, which is based on venture specific knowledge while the academic-practitioner may bring a theoretical bias which is based more on formal study. Programming and course design is firstmost the responsibility of the core teaching group, although it is done with the active involvement of the practitioner-academics who are, however, paid a competitive fee based on student contact hours.

The students have been increasingly selected, by interview, for their entrepreneurial potential. They are selected on the basis of three criteria: (1) level of responsibility attained in their career to date, (2) their apparent commitment to entrepreneurship and (3) displayed evidence of creative and/or lateral thinking ability. It is significant to add that it is people who are being selected and not new business ideas being screened. Although students with engineering and science degrees may have composed approximately 80 per cent of the pre-1 990 classes, the proportion of engineers and scientists has progressively shrunk to 40 per cent of current classes. A significant proportion of entering students switch to part time employment when they go back to school but financial sponsoring by companies is still uncommon. Students typically range from 28 to 40 years of age and have 8 or more years of experience prior to entry into the program. About 75 per cent of those applying to the certificate program are accepted. To be accepted directly into the Masters Degree program at the outset students will typically have an Honors Degree when applying. Of those having the general pre-qualifications to apply to the Masters Degree about 85 per cent are accepted.

As shown in Exhibit 2 the course content has been organized around issues facing an entrepreneur as a venture evolves through time, integrating the more traditional concerns of the business disciplines within a venture development framework and offered in 39 contact hour courses (McMullan and Long, 1990):

Exhibit 2: Program Course Structure at Swinburne

YR 1 : THE GRADUATE CERTIFICATE
Semester 1:   The Entrepreneurial Organization
                Opportunity Evaluation Techniques
Semester 2:   New Venture Marketing
                Commercializing Innovation

YR 2: THE GRADUATE DIPLOMA
Semester 3:   Innovation, Creativity and Leadership
                Managing the Growing Business
Semester 4:   New Venture Financial Planning
                The Business Plan

YR 3: THE MASTER'S YEAR
Semester 5:   Growth Venture Evaluation
                Advanced Business Plan 1 (1/2 course)
                Entrepreneurial Research Project 1 (1/2 course)
Semester 6:   Strategic Intent and Corporations
                Advanced Business Plan 2 (1/2 course)
                Entrepreneurial Research Project 2 (1/2 course)

The design of the curriculum is based on the integration of Master's level academic materials and applied experiential learning. The academic learning is provided through experienced professors using Harvard style case studies, case research, readings from research journals and books together with an entrepreneurial research project.

The students are directed to begin searching for opportunities early in the first term. In particular students are encouraged to seek opportunities based on innovations. Innovation is defined as 'the process that endows a recognized opportunity with the capacity to add value to an already existent invention, product, process or service and at a price a customer will pay'. Informal observation from insiders would suggest that about 80 per cent of the students develop opportunities based on innovations over the duration of their exposure to the program. It is this early emphasis upon innovative opportunities that is felt to be fundamental to the subsequent formation of growth companies, both independent and corporate. Whereas the program began with independent venturing predominating pre-1990, the shift since has been to about 50 per cent of students pursuing corporate ventures as their first venture upon graduation.

Although the program is applied and experiential it is also academic. Experiential learning is achieved through active participation. of students in 'live' and relevant growth ventures in conjunction with appropriate readings. Increasingly the. students are also encouraged to be involved in consulting relationships as part of their program. The academic character of the program is attested to, in part, by the fact that over the last few years about 10 per cent of the graduating Master's class has been enrolling in PhD programs.

Support programming to facilitate effective opportunity identification, teaming and/or venture financing has been primarily provided through the established network of contacts of the practitioner-academic team. About 15 to 20 per cent of the students have their ventures formally showcased through the program to members of the investment community. Further networking support is available through Ernst Young, Swinburne's joint venture partner in this project whose training facilities constitute the location for about 90 per cent of the teaching.

Findings

From 1988 to 1992 there were 109 graduates from the original Swinburne program in Melbourne, from which a responding sample of surveyed graduates reported the results presented in Exhibit 3. Since 1993 there have been a further 159 graduates from Melbourne from which a responding sample of surveyed graduates reported the results presented in Exhibit 4. Although results are not in a form that allows a straightforward comparison between the two tables, both the absolute size of the start-up numbers and the patterns of findings are interesting. When percentage start-ups are compared from certificate through degree levels of education the percentages start high and become higher with level of education obtained in both samples. Secondly, the per cent with sales tends to increase with level of education obtained although this observation appears to be at least partially confounded by length of time since graduation. For new businesses the absolute level of both sales and employees is high relative to country norms. More time still may be required to sort out the effects of education levels upon employment and sales given that a high proportion of the companies are technology companies many of which may take several years to mature.

Obviously, both additional data and analysis is needed. Data is needed on the longer-term performance of ventures created by graduates. Analysis is needed to partition out the relative impacts of independent variables such as education level obtained, years developing businesses beyond graduation, pre-program education and experience, and type of venture format chosen (eg. independent or corporate) upon dependent variables at both the individual and the economic level. Of interest at the individual level are such outcomes as salaries, capital gains and job satisfaction. Of interest at the level of the economy are such things as number of jobs created, types of jobs generated, sales and exports, profits, innovations, and additional taxes paid. The data presented here is intended more to draw attention to the general significance of a social innovation in education than to explore the range of inter-relationships involved.

Exhibit 3: Student Performance by Education Level attained and by Number of Years since Graduation (1988 - 1992 grads)[2]

Awarded degree (time since award)	Sample Number	Total Graduates	per cent Sample in New Ventures	per cent Sample with Sales	Average Sales for Ventures with Sales ($Aus.000)
Grad Certificates 1992 (8 mos.)	12	16	60	38	286
Grad Diploma 1988 - 1992 (8 mos. - 6 yrs.)	31	68	75	68	1130
Masters 1991 - 1992 (8 mos. - 2 yrs.)	23	25	85	73	1090*

* One company grew from $3M to $20M in sales revenue or turnover.

Exhibit 4: Student Performance by Education Level Attained and by Number of Years since Graduation*[3] (1993 - 1995 grads)

	Sample Number	Total Graduates	per cent Sample in New Ventures	per cent Sample with Sales	Mean No. Employed in Ventures with Sales	Average Sales for Ventures with Sales ($000)
Certificate						
- after two months	19	25	74%	21%	11[4]	780[5]
- after one year	1	5	100%	0%	0	0
- after two years	8	17	88%	75%	2.5	211
Diploma						
- after two months	20	25	75%	40%	5.5	1100[6]
- after one year	14	22	100%	64%	2.4	490
- after two years	8	20	88%	63%	7.8	1400
Degree[7]						
- after two months	10	15	90%	60%	2.4	100
- after one year	6	15	100%	66%	1.0	100
- after two years	7	15	100%	71%	6.0	400

* each row represents a different graduating class

Exhibits 5, 6 and 7 provide more detail on the ventures created: the number of jobs created, the volume of sales generated and the types of industries involved. Overall there were 47 new business with sales identified from the January, 1996 survey of 159 graduates from post 1993 graduating classes from the Melbourne program. Those business collectively generated 268 jobs or an average of 5.7 jobs per business within a weighted average time since graduation of 9.2 months (Exhibit 5). In that same time annual sales levels reached $29,610,000 for the entire sample (Exhibit 6) of which $xxxxx was in export sales. The average level of sales for the sample was therefore at the $630,000 level by the time of the survey.

In terms of the types of businesses developed (Exhibit 7), 30 of the 47 reporting (64 per cent) were in manufacturing and another 15 (32 per cent) were in business services. The remaining two businesses (4 per cent) were in retailing. The high proportion of in-company starts is likely explained by the fact that a number of students discovered their best opportunities at their job and felt that those opportunities were more easily accessed through their employer's organization than independently. Typically, graduates develop arrangements with their employers that provide them with additional financial incentive to justify their entrepreneurial initiatives.

With regard to the type of start-up sponsorship 22 of the 47 new businesses (47 per cent) were in-company starts. Those 22 firms were responsible for: 132 of the 268 new jobs (49 per cent), $21,670,000 of the $29,610,000 of total annual revenues produced (73 per cent) but only for 5 of the 17 service businesses started (29 per cent). Therefore, in-company start-ups represent proportionally more of the new revenue as might be expected of entities that normally should have greater access to both capital and markets. Finally the heavier representation of independent starts in the service sector may be, on some occasions, a result of graduates seeing opportunities to become consultants in business growth based directly on re-teaching the learning experience from the program.

Exhibit 5: Full-time Equivalent Employment of Graduate Ventures

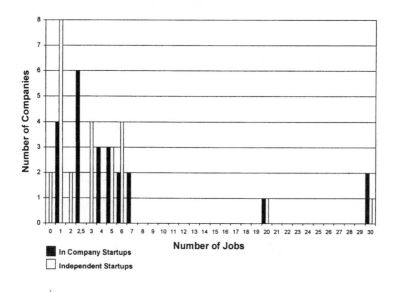

Exhibit 6: Annual Sales Performance of Graduate Ventures

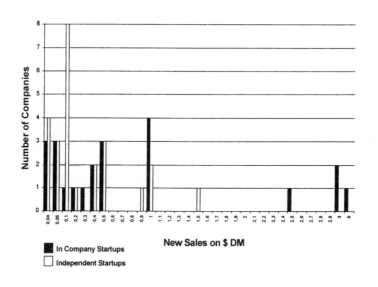

Exhibit 7: Industries chosen by Graduates

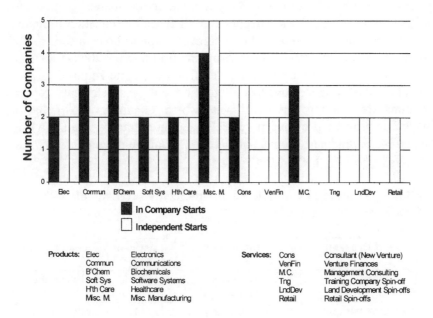

Products: Elec   Electronics   Services: Cons   Consultant (New Venture)
           Commun   Communications   VenFin   Venture Finances
           B'Chem   Biochemicals   M.C.   Management Consulting
           Soft Sys   Software Systems   Tng   Training Company Spin-off
           H'th Care   Healthcare   LndDev   Land Development Spin-offs
           Misc. M   Misc. Manufacturing   Retail   Retail Spin-offs

Exhibit 8 provides a comparison of the relative impact of four different programs in producing graduates that start businesses. The comparison between Calgary before and after the introduction of the new Enterprise MBA is particularly interesting. Although for eighteen years Calgary had an MBA, and for thirteen years a concentration in entrepreneurship, it wasn't until the introduction of the new Enterprise Management MBA program that the entrepreneurial activity of graduates exceeded Canadian norms for the population, i.e., fourteen per cent of the working population of which only fifty per cent have employees.[8] Those who had businesses with employees had not infrequently brought the business with them into the program. The change in start-up rates was sudden and dramatic corresponding directly with the introduction of the Enterprise Management MBA, despite the facts that students were not selected much differently than in earlier years and that the faculty remained relatively constant. This change in outcome suggests that entrepreneurial programs can encourage entrepreneurial activity.

69

It is also possible that causation is confounded in part by self-selection with more entrepreneurial students choosing more entrepreneurial programs. Such self-selection it should be remembered is not only desirable but typical of what happens in all types of education programs. Over time though it should be incumbent upon those offering such programs to provide evidence of program usefulness although to some degree this is a function performed for free by the marketplace. Student self-report data might prove useful to find out what elements of such programs are working better and what worse. Graduates report that the Swinburne program provides more useful and more transferable knowledge than do MBA graduates from a competing Melbourne program.

Exhibit 8: Graduate Economic Performance by Intensity of Entrepreneurship Education

Type of Program	Institution	per cent Starts	Time Frame
MBA (no E'ship courses)	Australian University (unnamed)	18%	1 year after
MBA Concentration in E'ship	U. Calgary	14%	follow-up after 18 years of grads
MBA Hybrid E'ship Program	U. Calgary (class starting in 1993	37%	8 mo. after
MEI E'ship Degree Program	Swinburne	87%	2 mo. to 2 years after

The program at Swinburne University of Technology is not only interesting because of the results being generated at the Melbourne campus but also because of its demonstrated ability to expeditiously set up satellite programs in other places. In 1996, Swinburne offers its entrepreneurship programs and graduate level certification in the following cities to the following numbers of students: Melbourne (140), Singapore (20), Sydney (35) and Brisbane (20). Jakarta (60) and Surabaya (80) are set to begin in July of 1996. In 1997, plans are in place to launch programs in the following additional places with the following enrolments at launch: Israel (30), Adelaide (20) and Perth (20). Singapore is the only other university –

apart from Melbourne – who's programs are developed far enough to evaluate the graduates and outcomes.

Some Case Examples

Although there are many interesting stories of high potential start-ups there is only room to provide a select few for illustrative purposes:

19xx Grad Diploma graduate, Bruce Dwyer recognized an opportunity to develop the Smart Lamp from an innovation that improved the operating efficiency of light bulbs. In two years he expanded the company from $2 million to $20 million sales. Having done that he saw another opportunity for exploiting the strong demand for emu oils, feathers, meat and leather. Bruce created the successful cosmetic product company Mt Romance Cosmetics, which has captured a large niche market for cosmetics using emu oil as a base and providing effective skin care.

Digital Media Pty Ltd is a film and television post-production facility that brings the power of supercomputing to the field of audio-visual technology. This computer based manipulative power thrusts the film and television industry into the twenty-first century. After the initial success of this small start-up business. And a break-even cash flow in four months to April 1995, 19xx Grad Diploma grad Judy Grant, the Managing Director, has projected the growth of the business to have sales in 1999 of $6.5 million and a profit of $4.5 million, thus highlighting the large financial returns for innovation in knowledge-based, industries.

One of Victoria's most exciting small businesses is VME Systems Pty Ltd. By 1994 the founder and Managing Director, 19xx Master's grad Michael Hornsby had developed the company in seven years to achieve a sales volume in excess of $7 million and be the market leader in VME bus systems. As an example, these systems are currently used to control car engine testing and many manufacturing robot control systems both in Australia and especially in Asia. The company is committed to a 100 per cent client retention rate, quality, customer service and value for money. The company has won the Victoria and National Small Business Awards and the Victorian Premier's Gold Medal for the most enterprising business.

A 1989 winner of the National Enterprise Workshop Business Plan competition, 19xx Master's grad Valerie McDougall established her company Skye Pty Ltd in Shepparton, Victoria. The company manufactures air-conditioning gas cleaning systems so that the freon gas is never vented to the atmosphere. Because the market in Australia is small the company established an assembly plant in Dallas, Texas. Due to the growth of the market and the need to increase market share Valerie has now moved to Texas to manage this new growth phase. The company is now earning 80 per cent of its income from the U.S.market.

Discussion

From formally and informally collected observations from both Swinburne and Calgary we have reached some conclusions.

(1) People can be educated to start businesses with growth potential. Even students who were not initially intending to develop new businesses or become members of the entrepreneurial team of small growing firms find themselves so directed, perhaps by the norms and expectations of the group or perhaps by the content of their studies. More importantly, the evidence is in the results; students in entrepreneurship degree programs start new companies or initiate corporate ventures at much greater rates than comparison groups of students without entrepreneurship courses or students with only a few courses as part of an MBA (Gillin et. al., 1996). For would-be entrepreneurs then, the choice between a program dedicated to entrepreneurship and one with only a major should be easy. The idea that providing a little education may make little difference with respect to subsequent entrepreneurial initiatives is not likely to be a popular one with business schools since almost all of today's business schools have chosen a limited commitment approach to entrepreneurship education.

(2) Despite a high level of interest in entrepreneurship programs by students, established entrepreneurs and governments, there is reason to be concerned about the pace with which new degree programs in entrepreneurship education will be developed and diffused.[9] Over a hundred years has passed since business school education was first developed at the Wharton School at the University of Pennsylvania in 1890 with the intent of professionalizing middle management for large US corporations. Business academics have become confident in the general usefulness of the business school model. Any new entrepreneurship program offered within a business school will usually have to fight against

well-entrenched traditions, vested interests and established cannons of required knowledge. In some cases even some entrepreneurship educators who have spent their careers operating within a traditional business school may resist new models of education. Obviously courses within the functional areas of business are potentially useful to would-be entrepreneurs. So also are courses in the social sciences, engineering, the sciences, languages, mathematics and so on. In consequence it may be a fact of life that it is more efficient to develop entrepreneurship programs outside business schools than within them. Contrast the developments at Swinburne over eight years outside a business school with those at Calgary over eighteen within a business school. Although there is no way to directly compare the effort that went into each, teams at both schools were dedicated to much the same goals and worked diligently and consistently over time to see them realized. Only the results were different.

(3) In order to be able to structure education programs from scratch around new paradigms we may need new institutional frameworks. It is interesting to note that the educational innovations that have come forward to date have largely come from rather new or obscure institutions. Stirling was a small, new, regional school when it founded its program. Swinburne, as an Institute of Technology (to 1992) was obscure even in Australia. Calgary was not only quite new but also the least known and most poorly funded of the thirteen major universities within Canada. Babson College, without entrepreneurship, would only be a little regional business school for the children of well to do parents. What is more the program at Swinburne was started by a Dean of Engineering and the only year which the program spent within the business school resulted in a decline in enrolment. At this time the Swinburne program is in actuality a joint venture between the University and Ernst Young. The Ernst Young teaching facilities around Australia provide additional campuses for Swinburne. The fact that the practitioner academic is likely to be one of the continuing hallmarks of entrepreneurship education in the future should create even more problems for fitting such programs within business schools since they are so firmly based on the academic model, especially in North America.

(4) The evidence for an international demand for entrepreneurship education at the graduate level is mixed. On the one hand there is some reason for optimism. First, there is the experience of Swinburne itself with a demonstrated ability to charge from $18,000 Aus. to $25,000 Aus. in a

variety of southeast Asian markets and Australia. Second, there is an oftentimes reported demand for entrepreneurship courses especially in the US (Vesper and McMullan, 1989). Third, in 1989 McMullan conducted an unpublished market survey of existing MBA students for degree programs in entrepreneurship education at four universities in Canada and four universities in Europe. The survey revealed that of those currently enrolled in MBA programs about one third were primarily doing their degrees to prepare for future entrepreneurial initiatives as opposed to preparing for corporate careers. Those with entrepreneurial aspirations generally reported a strong preference for an education program dedicated solely to entrepreneurship in preference to their current program of study. On the other hand though, there is ad hoc evidence to suggest that graduate entrepreneurship education may be a tougher sell than it might first appear in some parts of the world. Frank Martin from Stirling commented that those Scots preparing to do graduate education in business want the security of a job while those inclined to start a business neither had the time nor the money for graduate education. The Calgary experience over an 18 year period prior to the introduction of the Enterprise Management MBA demonstrated a moderate rather than a strong demand for individual entrepreneurship courses.[10] UBC's new specialization in entrepreneurship drew only 6 of 75 students in its first offering of its new $8500 fifteen month MBA program although individual courses tended to fill up.[11] Babson College's 1996 promotional literature reports only 3 per cent of its MBA graduating with a specialization in entrepreneurship and this despite the fact that Babson College has been ranked the top entrepreneurship program in the U.S. The marketability of new entrepreneurship programs will likely be location specific and change with the continuing maturation of the field.[12] In different regions the relative degree of subsidization of competing programs such as MBA programs - is likely to influence demand.

(5) Particularly outside the US, working models for effectively educating entrepreneurs should be particularly interesting to governments faced with continuing high unemployment and underemployment. Entrepreneurship education may be one of the few unexploited, cost-effective, micro-economic tools governments have for intelligently developing local economies. Any program that produces continuing wealth creating jobs at a full cost of $7000Aus. a job or at a public cost of $1400Aus. per job, 12 months beyond the normal time of graduation

should be taken very seriously (Gillin et. al.). However, our experience within Canada has shown it can be difficult to find a place on the public agenda for graduate entrepreneurship education even if it promises to be a new and better method of job creation.

(6) There are still many unknowns despite the apparent success of Swinburne to date. As a potentially important strategic departure from the traditional business school model the Swinburne approach is still an early stage model with lots of room for improvement. With some years for further refinement, graduate level entrepreneurship education could become not only a major tool for personal career development but also a better tool for economic development. Now is the time for international financial commitment to underwrite the pilot programming for the twenty-first century to begin answering the many questions such an innovation raises:

(a) How well do professionally trained entrepreneurs perform over time?

(b) How well do these programs transfer to satellite campuses?

(c) What is the relative influence of different program features upon program effectiveness?

(d) Can business schools be motivated to provide program level entrepreneurship education? If so, with what relative effectiveness?

(e) How can the Swinburne model be improved?

(f) Can professionally educated entrepreneurs be systematically married to high tech venture opportunities?

(g) Will these programs work well in smaller communities? In less developed countries and regions?

(h) How well will professionally educated entrepreneurs perform in corporate positions? How much demand will there be for their services within established firms? How will their performance compare with traditional MBAs on the job?

(i) What proportion of entrepreneurial activity will occur where students went to school as opposed to where they lived prior to school? Can programs be created to effectively move economic activity into relatively depressed economic regions?

(j)Under what conditions are students generally better off to do independent starts? Corporate starts? Or to join executive teams of small growing firms in equity positions?

(k) Who makes more money and/or enjoys their work more, entrepreneurship education graduates or traditional MBAs?

Notes

* Prize winning paper: 1st Rank of the Best Paper Award at the IntEnt 97 Conference in Monterey (Internationalizing Entrepreneurship Education and Training).

1 The authors would like to thank Profs. Jim Chrisman and Karl Vesper for their helpful comments.

2 Reconstructed from Gillin and Powe, 1994.

3 One reason for high rate of launches even two months beyond graduation is because students have been working on their business ideas throughout the program and as a result many leave the program running.

4 One successful corporate venture was in the Salvation Army. Three new recycling businesses were started as a result of the certificate training program. They employed some thirty new people-basically long term unemployed.

5 Includes a new corporate venture that signed an order for $6M to be delivered over 1996 and 1997.

6 Includes a new corporate venture in manufacturing with $2.5M in sales.

7 Our data shows that Masters graduates are involved in proportionately more independent than corporate starts in comparison with Certificate and Degree graduates. Perhaps Masters graduates are trying to maximize personal gains through higher levels of equity ownership or perhaps there is a higher threshold for involvement by professionally trained people in independent ventures.

8 Many of the 50 per cent without employees expressed a preference for a job over being a consultant.

9 University of British Columbia has developed an interesting MBA specialisation in entrepreneurship which, beyond a three month common multidisciplinary core, allows not only for a heavy concentration in the subject but also for open competition with other business fields for students.

10 However, when Calgary introduced its Enterprise MBA in 1993 its enrolments nearly doubled within a 2 year period despite a precipitous decline in student assistance over the same period.

11 Personal communication with Raffi Amit who believes that students prefer not to take on the entrepreneurship designation in case it negatively affects their marketability as employees which is their fall-back position.

12 It is possible that most students in a position to make a partial commitment to entrepreneurship education will do in order to hedge their bets even when they are drawn to programs because of their reputations for entrepreneurial education. It is also possible that by so compromising their commitment to entrepreneurship students dramatically reduce the likelihood of becoming entrepreneurial. It might not be unreasonable to speculate that the commitment threshold required to both launch and successfully develop a growth venture might be quite high.

References

Gillin, L. M. and Powe, M. (Sept. 1994). Added value from teaching entrepreneurship and innovation. *Innovation Papers*, Swinburne University of Technology.

Gillin, L.M.; Powe, M.; Dews, A.L. and McMullan, W.E. (March, 1996). An empirical assessment of the returns to entrepreneurial education, presented at the *Babson Conference on Entrepreneurship Research*, Seattle.

McMullan, W.E. and Long, W.A. (1987, Summer). Entrepreneurship education in the nineties, *Journal of Business Venturing*.

McMullan, W.E. and Long, W.A. (1990). *Developing New Ventures: The Entrepreneurial Option*, Harcourt, Brace, Jovanovich, San Diego.

4 Education for Entrepreneurial Competency: a Theory-based Activity Approach

James O. Fiet

Abstract

If our objective is to teach aspiring entrepreneurs how to master requisite competencies, this paper argues that the most effective method is to engage them in theory-based activities. Entrepreneurial educators may want to ask, 'What am I going to have my students do today?', rather than 'What am I going to teach my students today?' This paper also argues that it is essential to ground learning activities in theoretical frameworks and that educators ought to be engaged in the process of generating theory-based knowledge. The paper concludes by proposing a strategy for implementing the approach.

A New Entrepreneurial Era

The United States is entering an important new era of entrepreneurship, which has increased student interest in the field. A surprising demand for information about how to launch a business has resulted in an explosive growth in the number of classes and programs. In 1971, there were only 16 colleges and universities teaching entrepreneurship. Today, there are over 800 colleges and universities with entrepreneurship classes, programs and initiatives. This new interest is more than just a fad and accurately reflects an emerging economic environment created by a confluence of changes in the corporate world, new technology and emerging world markets (Venkatraman, 1996). As educators, we will undoubtedly have increased opportunities to influence aspiring entrepreneurs, as well as positively impact economic development, but are we ready to meet the challenge?

A 1994 national Gallup poll showed that 70 per cent of high school students want to start their own companies some time in the future. At the same time it indicated that colleges and universities throughout the United States have reported tremendous growth in their students' interest in learning about entrepreneurship and ultimately becoming entrepreneurs. For example, Northwestern University's Kellogg School of Business reported that a record 45 per cent of incoming first-year students in 1996 expressed an interest in entrepreneurship as a major compared with 30 per cent in 1995, 12 per cent in 1994 and 7 per cent in 1993.

Another example shows that whereas 3 per cent to 4 per cent of the country's population actually starts a businesses annually, Stanford University's Career Center reported that the percentage of their MBA's starting businesses right out of school increased from 3 per cent in 1994 to 10 per cent in 1995. In addition, approximately 40 per cent of Harvard's current class of graduating MBA students is planning to pursue a career in the venture capital industry (Bygrave, 1997). This desire to work at evaluating prospective deals is in contrast to previous MBA classes at Harvard that aspired to land top paying jobs on Wall Street. Whereas previous Harvard MBA students aspired to work in the top echelons of corporate America, increasing numbers of current students desire to participate in the birthing process of new ventures (Bygrave, 1997). Students are not the only ones interested in becoming associated with entrepreneurship programs.

Donors from many quarters demonstrate their willingness to financially support the establishment of entrepreneurship centers and underwrite endowed faculty positions (c.f., Jerry Katz's E-Web site at St. Louis University). We also see more students participating in business plan competitions nationwide and greater interest from foundations that are willing to help make entrepreneurial education available to ever widening audiences.

Deans and department heads also see the need to ensure that their units are not left behind this gathering wave of interest in entrepreneurial education. Their interest is partially in response to indications from the American Assembly of Collegiate Schools of Business (AACSB) that entrepreneurship will play a future role in the accreditation of academic programs. The AACSB recently concluded a gathering for member institutions titled, 'AACSB Workshop on Business Schools and Entrepreneurship.' One of the things that made this workshop noteworthy was that the invitation to attend it was not just extended to entrepreneurship educators, but specifically to entire faculty teams from participating institutions. Its stated purpose was to provide programmatic guidance on how to better integrate entrepreneurship issues into the mission and strategic focus of their activities. Lastly, during November, 1996, in Cambridge, MA, seven of the top business schools in the country convened a meeting of their deputy deans and heads of their entrepreneurship program to discuss how they ought to respond collectively and individually to the new market for entrepreneurship education (Low, 1997). Although these institutional leaders espoused different approaches for responding to the new need for entrepreneurship educators at their institutions, they were all paying close attention to the rising interest in this area.

Can there be any question about the importance and timeliness of the topic of entrepreneurship education? As Jerry Brown, a former California governor stated when approached by the legislature to increase funding for education, 'I am in favor of education, but education for what?' The answer to his question as it relates to entrepreneurial education ought to be education for theory-based, entrepreneurial competencies that are taught using activity-based approaches to learning. This paper begins by arguing that entrepreneurship educators must link research with teaching in the classroom if they are to succeed in honing student competencies to make judgments about the consequences of present decisions.[1] Next, it examines pedagogical problems associated with teaching theory-based concepts. Third, it introduces a strategy for developing a theory-based activity (TBA) approach for teaching entrepreneurial competencies.

The Link between Research and Teaching in Entrepreneurship Education

In 1974, I graduated from the first Masters level program in entrepreneurship. Our curriculum consisted largely of listening to very successful entrepreneurs recount how they had launched their ventures. It was enjoyable, motivational, and very entertaining - what some might refer to today as 'edutainment'. However, by the end of the semester I was beginning to ask myself what I had learned. As I thought back on my graduate school experience, I could only identify a few lessons that I had been taught that would help me actually start a business of my own. Of greater concern, however, was that after having started 6 different businesses, and having endured varying degrees of success with each of them, it occurred to me that there was very little in my entrepreneurship courses that could help me to explain these different outcomes. Finally, I was not certain about what I had learned that would help me to improve my future chances of success.

During the time since my MBA studies, researchers have deepened our understanding of entrepreneurial outcomes and provided us with powerful frameworks to interpret what entrepreneurs do, as well as predict their success. Although most entrepreneurship theory does not have a distinctive origin in entrepreneurship, it nevertheless helps us to better understand how wealth is created. For example, agency theory (Fama and Jensen, 1983; Jensen, 1994; Jensen and Meckling, 1976), procedural justice theory (Linda, Kulik, Ambrose and de Vera Park, 1993; Fiet, Busenitz, Moesel and Barney, in press) and transaction cost economics (Williamson, 1979; 1985) help us to understand how entrepreneurs without resources can marshal the means to launch an entirely new business; informational economics (Fiet, 1995; Gifford, 1992, in press) and decision making theory (Busenitz and Barney, 1997) help us to understand why some entrepreneurs are able to recognize an economically lucrative opportunity that others miss; industrial organization economics (Porter, 1985), game theory and competitive dynamics (Barney, 1997) provide insights into why some industries are simply more attractive than others; the resource based theory of the firm (Barney, 1997) helps us to understand the sustainability of competitive advantage; Austrian economics (Jacobson, 1992) and the theories of hypercompetition (D'Aveni, 1994) and the new competitive landscape (Hitt, 1997) help us to understand the necessity of continually reinventing a company's offerings if it hopes to avoid obsolescence and oblivion. These theories, among others, provide cogent intellectual premises that students can utilize to examine and analyze immensely complex scenarios.[2] Most of these areas of inquiry were either not developed until recently or not applied to the study of entrepreneurs.[3]

In spite of how far we have come in our understanding of entrepreneurs, previous work has still provided us with only a partial understanding. More to the point, if we are to improve the substance of what we teach to entrepreneurship students, in my view, we need to do two things. First, entrepreneurship scholars must pursue theory-driven research agendas. And second, entrepreneurship teachers must ensure that their students understand that there are different theoretical explanations of why some entrepreneurs succeed and others fail.[4]

The Importance of Theory-driven Research Agendas

Colin Camerer (1985) observed that many research findings tend to 'accumulate rather than cumulate.' This accumulation of factoids occurs because too much research is exploratory rather than confirmatory. Many of us have tended to report interesting bits of data without answering the 'so what' question, which is - 'Why should we care about this new bit of data?' The difference between data and information is that information signals the observer that a response from the observer is appropriate, whereas data must be interpreted and is often interpreted differently by those who receive it. Too much of our research provides us with data only and fails to answer the 'so what' question. The inevitable result is that it makes little or no theoretical contribution to what we know about entrepreneurs. Many entrepreneurship research findings are accumulations of data that do very little to build a theory of entrepreneurship. We should not be satisfied with this type of research because '... it is insufficient to transmit and apply present knowledge. It is the function of higher education to advance the state of knowledge as well' (Barney, 1997).

If our research is to pass the 'so what' test, in my view it should satisfy two criteria. First, much more of it should be theory-driven rather than descriptive, because after all, we have been reporting descriptive research findings for most of the last twenty-five years. This descriptive research has done little to help us predict why some entrepreneurs succeed and others fail. Second, we should integrate research findings and theory in a way that can be understood and applied by students.

The Role of Theory in an Entrepreneurship Course

As Bill Bygrave, the Director of Entrepreneurial Studies at Babson College noted, 'there are two ways to ruin an entrepreneurship course. The first way is to have it consist entirely of the practical application and analysis of cases. (A course consisting only of practical applications and cases provides us with no basis for assisting students to act on the basis of their decisions.) The second way is to have it be entirely theory' (1993). (A course consisting only of theory could be an arid wasteland where only the most intellectually curious students would succeed. Most of the rest of the students would become bored and would simply not listen for understanding.) Clearly, Kuhn was correct when he noted, 'there really isn't anything quite as practical as a good theory' (1970). Ideally, good theory will help us to make predictions about the consequences of our decisions. A good course requires the practical application of theory but we must take some responsibility for the application.

Pedagogical Problems Associated with Teaching Theory-based Concepts

'Theory is boring! Lectures are boring! School is boring!' All three of these - theory, lectures, and school can also be irrelevant. We as teachers can also be boring and irrelevant![5]

We become boring when our classroom style becomes predictable. Predictability means that our students are never surprised. When we utilize approaches that are predictable, students become bored. Some negative consequences that can result are students who daydream, less cooperation in the classroom, and students who substitute previously learned skills for those that they were supposed to have learned in class because they were not listening when new concepts were introduced. Taken to the extreme individual boredom can translate into collective boredom that can even infect us as teachers.

We become irrelevant as teachers when we fail to apply theory as a tool to answer student questions. This can occur in three ways. First, when we are teaching weak theory that was not generated in the search for practical solutions to entrepreneurial problems. Second, when we resort solely to recounting war stories and anecdotes that lack generalizability.

Students can discern between education and entertainment.[6] The former exposes them to principles that enable them to make predictions about the consequences of their decisions. The second way provides short-term satisfaction through its entertainment component, but students can discern the difference. The third way that teachers can become irrelevant is when they fail to apply theory to resolve situations that students can reasonably expect to encounter in their own careers. Thus, good theory can always pass the test of applicability and if we fail to apply it for our students, it is we who are at fault, not the theory.

Generally speaking, our textbooks contribute to the boredom problem because they consist largely of discussions of the functional areas of business - mostly reworked discussions of corporate approaches. Where is the theory in these treatments? What do these books contribute that will help aspirants to recognize the future ramifications of their entrepreneurial decisions. There are few surprises for students in these approaches. In fact, students have already learned about these functional approaches in their introductory courses. So not only are these functional level treatments repetitious, they are also shop worn. Because functional material tends to change very slowly, professors can make it appear even more shop worn by lecturing from old notes. Revisions and the notion of continuous improvement can become distractions and be overshadowed by claims that the course is already good enough. Even instructors who are assigned the responsibility of teaching these concepts can find it difficult to become excited about them because they too can become bored - bored with the material and bored with students who are bored with the material.

A Strategy for Developing a TBA Approach for Teaching

Entrepreneurial competencies

If our strategy as educators in entrepreneurship is to assist students to acquire skills in theory-based competencies, the most effective method for accomplishing this objective is to establish a student-approved system for class meetings that requires students to practice specific skills until they become competencies. I argue for theory-based competencies so that we as educators can always answer the 'so what' question for our students.

I argue for a student-approved system because almost any system of learning will work better if the students feel good about it.[7] In contrast, if students have reservations about the appropriateness or fairness of the approach, even the most thoroughly reasoned and well-intended approach will not work as well as it could. As a consequence, one of the most important class sessions is the one where we initially gauge the extent of student acceptance of the approach.[8] If we do not secure student acceptance, our approach will fail in the sense that students will be less willing to take responsibility for their own learning. On the surface, it may appear that they are complying with classroom requirements, but during class their reservations are likely to distract them from concentrating on the key concepts under discussion, and away from class they will not be dreaming and scheming about how they can use them to launch their own venture. If we substitute fear tactics for student approval, we will probably secure compliance, but over the long-term, when students have a choice about whether to consider starting their own businesses, they may be inclined to avoid it based on the unpleasantness of their earlier entrepreneurship class.

My approach is also based on the assumption that to the extent that a teacher is the initiator of knowledge transfer, students tend to practice less and acquire fewer competencies, if for no other reason than it is the teacher who is the most engaged, not the students, which is the reverse of what would be optimal. It is the students who are most in need of learning. Worse, as argued previously, students tend to become bored with predictable class routines in which they play a limited role, which further inhibits their learning and mastery of skills.[9]

The teacher's role in using a TBA approach

The teacher's primary role is to achieve student approval of the learning contract and to identify the competencies to be mastered.[10] Thus, the question for educators faced with ensuring student mastery of competencies is not, 'What am I going to teach today?'[11] but 'What am I going to have my students do today?' Moreover, the question of 'What am I going to have my students do today' can be delegated to students and there are some advantages to doing so. Delegating responsibility for the selection of specific learning activities to students can introduce more variety and surprises into the classroom, each of which can alleviate boredom.

85

At the beginning of each class, the teacher introduces the concept to be mastered and the associated learning activities. These activities should be extensions of previously assigned reading material that provides the theoretical basis for the competency to be mastered. During the activities that follow it is imperative that students understand that the activity is only one application of the underlying theoretical concept from the assigned readings. The theoretical application can also be productively related to why some entrepreneurs succeed and others fail. I do not recommend reviewing the assigned reading materials in class unless they are widely misunderstood. Normally the theoretical issues can be exposed as students engage in the assigned activities.

The responsibility for deciding which activities are most appropriate for teaching a competency may be assigned to groups of students, to a single student, or it may be retained by the instructor.[12] The activities should be ones that assist students to understand and apply underlying course concepts. A common characteristic of each of these activities is that they must involve every student. This enables students to receive immediate feedback from those in the class. In this setting, the teacher may move around the classroom as a coach, rather than an evaluator of student performance.

During student-led activities, the teacher participates by initiating discussion and facilitating learning by individual students as they participate in the activities. Teachers should also feel free to participate in the activities. Judgment about the appropriateness of teacher participation is required, however, when the activities become competitions among student teams. Sometimes teacher participation stimulates the competition, and at other times, particularly if the opposition feels overwhelmed, it diminishes it.

I find that the most stimulating activities are those that arouse competitive discussion among students about the appropriateness of competing analyses. The discussion of these analyses frequently becomes very animated, but seldom becomes rancorous because students have previously accepted the format for the class and realize that they will have their turn to 'win' with their particular activity, if they choose.

Advantages of a TBA Approach

There are several advantages of using a TBA approach. For example, it avoids boredom by inviting student-generated surprises to a play a role in the learning environment. It is also easier to enlist the entire class as mentors in a theory-based learning approach, which facilitates class-wide learning. In addition, if the learning activities are part of a clearly outlined set of procedures for succeeding as an entrepreneur, focusing on specific skills avoids students asking the 'so what' question, which is really an issue of relevance. A TBA approach positions the instructor as a coach and mentor rather than a lecturer who delivers information from a textbook or a lesson in a boring predictable manner. And finally, a TBA approach can potentially involve every student in the learning process.

Obstacles to the Implementation of a TBA Approach

Switching from a traditional lecture format to a TBA approach can be quite difficult, especially for someone who enjoys exercising professorial control. We feel responsible for what our students learn and we want to control how the learning occurs. We may secretly harbor fears that the students will learn less and that we will be responsible for allowing that to occur.[13] When we feel this way we forget that we are deluding ourselves if we believe that we can control everything that our students think or learn. We forget that most of what captures the attention of our students during class is controlled by the students themselves, and not by us, which is the reason that it is fundamentally important for our students to accept the change.

The loss of predictability during class can be threatening to professors who would prefer to more closely control the process themselves. Surprisingly, it can be threatening to students also because they think that the evaluation of their work and learning could be adversely affected by their perception of less classroom structure.[14] Many of these students expect us to tell them what is most important to learn. What they do not realize is that we are freer to do so without structure because we can intervene at any time. Because this is a legitimate student concern, it is critical at the end of class that we summarize what has been learned. In essence, we have to answer the 'so what' question for them. If we ritualistically tell students what they have learned at the end of class, they will soon relax and join with us in the fun of learning that precedes our summary.

Suppose that a student were making an oral presentation of her understanding of a concept that she misconstrued. Under a more rigid system, courtesy could dictate that the instructor either not provide feedback during the presentation or at least wait until after the student had finished. However, using an TBA format, an instructor can explain to students that acceptable classroom protocol is a free wheeling exchange of ideas that does not allow for 'a wait until you are finished' protocol. Instead, class members and the instructor may interject questions that are directed at both the class and the presenter. For example, any listener might say, 'Class, given Sally's argument, what conditions would have to hold for her to be correct?' Also, the listener might follow up with, 'What evidence is there for Sally's conditions?' And finally, the listener might add, 'What alternative conditions might also explain her conclusions?' Such a series of questions could expose her logic, which could normally be true, so long as we understand her conditions and evidence.

Another obstacle to the implementation of a TBA approach is that it seemingly requires preparation for multiple class scenarios. The fallacy in this concern is that it presupposes that all preparation for these scenarios occurs right before class. This fallacy is well illustrated by the wag who claimed that, 'The secret to good teaching is to act as if you have known all your life the things that you have prepared just before class.' However, if we were limited in the learning that we could bring with us to class, we would probably be less successful than we would wish with a TBA approach.

Lastly, instructors who undertake a TBA instructional approach will quickly learn that it requires a major time commitment when done correctly with few institutional rewards. Thus, we often find that instructors rely more upon passive lecture approaches because they can be accomplished within acceptable evaluative tolerances, particularly when the institution is dependent upon grants to support its research agendas.

The Discovery of Theory-based Learning Activities

After reviewing the advantages of theory-based learning activities, the reader could expect that this paper would list a variety of these activities with instructions about how to utilize them in class. Specific activities are usually discovered one at a time through the process of trying things, some that work and others that do not work. My experience is that the most effective activities for teaching theory are related to specific people, places, timing, relationships, and special circumstances (*c.f.,* Hayek, 1945). These activities often have ephemeral results, because otherwise, as students, we would be expecting them and we would be less surprised. Someone has referred to them as 'silver bullets.' When the class seems to be getting bored, he fires a 'silver bullet' to liven things up. Sharon Gifford at Rutgers University refers to 'lobbing grenades' to shake things up. The most effective teachers are able to shake things up in their own way by making students do things that generate surprising, theory-based results. The most stimulating classes are those in which the members of the class are constantly on the alert for a 'silver bullet' or are ducking a 'grenade.'

The list of activities is also fundamentally elusive, because as the activities on such a list become known they cease to be surprising to students. This may not be a short-range problem, but repetition of the same techniques can become as well known to students as our test banks, if we use them. When the activities cease to be surprising to students, they no longer say to themselves, 'ah ha.' Losing the 'ah ha' factor also means that it has lost most of its pedagogical benefits. Worse, if the list became well known, it could become trivialized and an obstacle to learning.

If we cannot think of one theory-based activity, we may want to do the following: Assign a group of students the responsibility to present a particular theory-based topic. Explain to them that they can present it any way that they wish except that originality will be rewarded and boredom will be penalized. Plead with them to not bore the class. In this way, we share the responsibility for creating the activity with our students. We do not have to worry that our students will not be able to create an interesting activity because we can and should review their activities with them before class. Our students will develop everything from TV games shows, to invited role-playing, to in-class calisthenics. I suspect that our own enjoyment of teaching and learning will increase as we participate more in the process.

Notes

[1] Entrepreneurship as a field is in the process of creating a body of theory-based knowledge, much of it the product of the diverse backgrounds of those who are attracted to the field from other disciplines.

[2] A related issue is that many of those researchers who do test theory driven questions tend to utilize single perspectives in doing so, which may limit their fields of vision. Some researchers justify single perspective approaches on the basis of the internal consistency of the arguments. However, these approaches are not necessarily contradictory, could in fact be complementary, and could lead us to a more sophisticated level of understanding. (*c.f.*, Fiet, Busenitz, Moesel and Barney, in press) A worthwhile discussion would be to examine the merits of multi-disciplinary approaches to doing research. Unfortunately, this important topic is beyond the scope of this paper.

[3] There is some debate about whether each of these areas of inquiry has actually matured into a full fledged theory. Because they originate from different disciplines, it is more difficult to arrive at a consensus about what constitutes a theory. This paper utilizes a Daftian approach that assumes that theory is nothing more than 'story telling" about how certain factors may influence future events.

[4] This paper makes a distinction between entrepreneurial theories and the indicated competencies for starting a business. In most cases, students can assume the major responsibility for learning these theories from assigned readings before they come to class. Class time is used better for the application of these theories to specific problems faced by entrepreneurs. Ideally, these applications would be activity-based exercises.

[5] A potentially challenging issue for entrepreneurship educators is that students know that most entrepreneurs have succeeded without formal training in entrepreneurship. So not only do we have to avoid being boring—we have to convince them that we can provide them with tools and information that will increase their prospects of success as entrepreneurs.

[6] Examples are important as applications of theory, but the overreliance on anecdotes without placing them in a theoretical context is inappropriate because by themselves they lack generalizability.

[7] I argue that there is much that can be learned from the Hawthorne studies about participants feeling good about group processes. Even though the Hawthorne studies did not examine student subjects, these studies suggest that teachers should be sensitive to achieving the proper mood in class as a part of achieving their learning objectives.

[8] The most memorable session for gaining approval of my activity-based approach happened by accident before I knew of its effectiveness. I had been using a lecture-based approach laced with a voluminous number of overheads. I had just completed a contract for producing overheads for a textbook. As I was walked confidently to my first class with my folder of twenty-five overheads, the following question occurred to me: 'If I were a student, would I want to see any of these overheads?' The answer that came to me was a resounding 'No!' So when I arrived at class, I handed the folder of overheads to a student on the first row, and asked him to describe its contents to the class. He said that it contained 'a bunch of overheads.' I then mentioned to the class that I had a similar folder of overheads for every session scheduled during that semester. They were quite surprised when I asked them, 'How many of you want to see them?' The hisses and boos were so loud that it took a while to hear their collective pleas for mercy. 'Anything, but the overheads' - that part was unanimous. I said that I would make a deal with them that they would not have to see the overheads if

everyone of them agreed to become involved in the class activities that we would substitute for the overheads. All of this was spontaneous, and the most successful teaching experience that I had ever had. Needless to say, I have never gone back to my lecture-based approach.

[9] It is certainly true that any material could be taught in a boring predictable fashion, so this particular argument is not about course content; it is about how to make the teaching of entrepreneurship concepts and competencies more inviting to students.

[10] 'The contract is a two-way street, and the teacher must be willing to more than meet the students' commitments. On the instructor's side, the professional nature of the contract and its surrounding relationship will be shown by: (1) careful and complete preparation for the classroom experience, (2) concern and devotion to the students in all dealings, including those in the classroom and in the office, and (3) striving to make the course a satisfying development experience. By and large, the more the teacher does, the more the students will do' (Harvard Business School Publishing).

[11] Some advocates of active learning approaches from educational psychology would argue that a more relevant question is, 'What should students learn through self-discovery today" (Miles, 1997). It is true that a lot of what we call learning is self-discovery. I prefer the emphasis on 'doing," however, because it provides teachers with an observable way of gauging student learning outcomes. Personally, I am less confident that a teacher can guide the learning process without observable outcomes.

[12] If the instructor decides to delegate the selection of learning activities to students, it is normally beneficial to have them explain the activity to the instructor before class. By checking with them prior to class, the instructor can be assured that they will effectively facilitate the achievement of the learning objectives by class members. An advantage of using students to organize the activities is that they often develop unique approaches, which are fun for students, and which introduce more variety into the classroom. Nevertheless, delegating to students will fail to achieve its learning objectives if the teacher views it as a way of avoiding work. The teacher is always responsible for what occurs in class. In some ways, delegating to students requires more work because it requires more out-of-class preparation by the instructor than simply delivering a lecture or organizing the learning activity by him or herself.

[13] My own limited experience refutes concerns that students will learn less. Using examinations of comparable difficulty, my average scores increased by 20 per cent by switching to a TBA approach. This improvement has remained stable since making the change. I should also add that my teacher evaluation scores have also improved by more than 20 per cent on a five-point scale. Not only are my students learning more, but they think that I am doing a better job by allowing them to become active participants.

[14] A TBA approach follows a clear pedagogical structure and the more alert students who have understood the theory presented in their readings will perceive it without assistance. Most students who have had difficulty with the theory will probably understand it during class as it is applied in specific exercises. Once this latter group understands the theory, it will probably also see the structure. At the end of each class, the instructors summarizes the concepts that have been taught and applied in class. At that point, the majority of students who have not learned the theory through classroom activities should understand them. Those who are still unclear about what has been taught should be invited to visit privately with the instructor.

References

Barney, J.B. (1997). *Gaining and Sustaining Competitive Advantage*. Reading, MA: Addison-Wesley.

Busenitz, L.W., and Barney, J.B. (1997). Differences1 between entrepreneurs and managers in large organizations: Biases and heuristics in strategic decision-making. *Journal of Business Venturing*, 12, 1: 9-30.

Bygraves, W.D. (1993). *Personal conversation*.

Bygraves, W.D. (1997). Address given at the *Kaufman/Babson Entrepreneurship Research Conference*.

Camerer, C. (1985). Redirecting research in business policy and strategy. *Strategic Management Journal*, 6: 1-15.

D'Aveni, R.A. (1994). *Hypercompetition*. New York: Free Press.

Fama, E.F., and Jensen, M.C. Agency problems and residual claims. *Journal of Law and Economics*, 26, 327-349.

Fiet, J.O. (1996). The informational basis of entrepreneurial discovery. *Small Business Economics* 8: 419-430.

Fiet, J.O., Busenitz, L.W., Moesel, D.D., and Barney, J.B. In press. Complementary theoretical perspectives on the dismissal of new venture team members. *Journal of Business Venturing*.

Gifford, S. (1992). Innovation, firm size and growth in a centralized organization. RAND *Journal of Economics*, 23, 2, Summer, 284-298.

Gifford, S. in press. Limited entrepreneurial attention. *Small Business Economics*.

Harvard Business School Publishing. (1994). Hints for case teaching. Boston, MA: *Harvard Business School Publishing*.

Hayek, F.A. (1945). The use of knowledge in society. *American Economic Review*, 35, 519-530.

Hitt, M. (1997). Personal discussion at *the Kaufman/Babson Entrepreneurial Research Conference*.

Jacobson, R. (1992). The 'Austrian' school of strategy. *Academy of Management Review*, 17, 782-807.

Jensen, M.C. (1994). Self-interest, altruism, and agency theory. *Journal of Applied Corporate Finance*, 7, 2: 40-45.

Jensen, M.C., and Meckling, W.H. (1976). Theory of the firm: Managerial behavior, agency costs and ownership structure. *Journal of Financial Economics*, 3, 305-360.

Kuhn, T. 1970. *The Structure of Scientific Revolutions*. Chicago: University of Chicago Press.

Lind, E.A., Kulik, C.T., Ambrose, M., and de Vera Park, M.V. (1993). Individual and corporate dispute resolution: Using procedural justice as a decision heuristic. *Administrative Science Quarterly* 38: 224-251.

Low, M. (1997). Special report presented at the 1997 Lennox Retreat for Young Faculty Scholars hosted by *Rennselaer Polytechnic Institute*.

Miles, J. (1997). Personal communication.

Small Business Administration, Office of Advocacy. (1995*)*. *The third millennium: Small business and entrepreneurship in the 21st Century*. A special publication prepared for delegate so the 1995 White House Conference on Small Business.

Venkataraman, S. (1997). Personal correspondence.

Williamson, O.E. (1979). Transaction cost economics: The governance of contractual relations. *Journal of Law and Economics* 22: 233-261.

Williamson. O.E. (1985). *The Economic Institutions of Capitalism*. New York: Free Press.

5 Entrepreneurship Education: an Integrated Approach Using an Experiential Learning Paradigm

JoAnn C. Carland
James W. Carland

Abstract

We have established a major in entrepreneurship which incorporates experiential learning, follows an integrated format, and focuses on team centered learning. The curriculum includes three sequential six hour courses. We employ an experiential, hands on format, featuring a project which takes student teams from the inception of an idea to the initiation of a business venture, through the establishment of that venture and into the growth, expansion and diversification of that venture. The course is taught by a faculty team and half of the class hours are devoted to instructor centered learning and half to team centered learning. In each week, we learn, then do, then, evaluate, critique, and re-do. Further, each team repeatedly employs each of the skills after the initial introduction in the on going management and operation of the business.

Introduction

It is nothing short of a miracle that modern methods of instruction have not yet entirely strangled the holy curiosity of inquiry, Albert Einstein (Dearing, 1965, p. 49).

Experiential learning has been a concept of interest for many years to educators in a variety of disciplines. Its advocates and its critics are many and varied (i.e., Hutchings and Wutzdorff, 1988; Henry, 1989; Boud, 1989; Wildemeersch, 1989; Nelson, 1989; Peterson, 1989; Walter and Marks, 1981; Kolb, 1984). Experiential learning is defined as a sequence of events which require active involvement by the student at various points (Walter and Marks, 1981). There may be multiple learning objectives but the central tenet is always that one learns best by active involvement. Astin (1984) was deeply concerned by the motivation required for success in learning. He argues that merely exposing the student to a particular set of courses may or may not work. Coleman (1976) believes that experiential learning has a strong advantage in that it depends upon intrinsic motivation. More importantly, Coleman believes that learning through experiential concepts is less easily forgotten than learning through the information assimilation of the traditional classroom. It is well established that two of the four primary learning styles exhibited by students, the divergent and accommodation learning styles, function better with concrete experience (Kolb, 1984), and most business students are accommodation learners (Kolb, 1984). Clearly, there is strong support for the validity and value of a teaching paradigm which emphasizes experiential learning concepts.

We have established a new major in entrepreneurship which incorporates experiential learning, follows an integrated format with respect to subject material, and focuses on team centered learning. The curriculum includes three sequential six hour courses. To establish an integrated understanding of business and entrepreneurship principles, we employ an experiential, hands on format, featuring a single project which takes student teams from the inception of an idea to the initiation of a business venture, through the establishment of that venture and into the growth, expansion and diversification of that venture. The course is taught by a faculty team and learning is centered in the student teams. Half of the class hours are devoted to instructor centered learning and half to team centered learning. In each week, we learn, then do. Then, we evaluate, critique, and re-do. Each of the tools, each of the skills, each of the knowledge areas is presented as an integral part of the business establishment, growth and management. Further, each team repeatedly employs each of the skills after the initial introduction in the on going management and operation of the business.

The new program offers a vehicle for the introduction, justification, and application of each of the concepts in business and entrepreneurship. These concepts are brought to bear as their needs become manifested in the on going process. As we begin to evaluate ideas for the business venture, we must master and employ cost-volume-profit concepts to support that evaluation. We must understand the competitive environment and the target market for our venture. We must learn to market our products and services. We employ these and other concepts continuously throughout the remainder of the three semesters, but the introduction of each concept is heralded by student recognition of the need for such skills and the role they play in the business environment. This paper describes the program and the process which we employed in its development.

Historic Perspective of Curriculum Development

In 1926, a professor of education at Columbia University, New York City, stated '...American life being what it is - complicated, difficult to understand, highly dynamic; the school constituted as it is - large classes, relatively uninformed teachers, early elimination of pupils - only one conclusion can be drawn. That is that the greatest hope for improvement by our generation lies in the construction of a curriculum which shall as fully as possible overcome the handicaps of the present school situation, and which shall lead the great body of pupils to an understanding and appreciation of the conditions and problems of our complex civilization' (Rugg, 1926, p. 6). That attitude persists in the U.S. to this day. The great body of educators and citizens seem to think that the solution to the ills of society rests in education and that the solution to the problems in education rests in the construction of a curriculum. That reasoning explains why criticisms of the education system focus on curricula. They represent the most visible aspect of education. And yet, curriculum development is perceived as a highly simplistic process. Clearly, the highly educated specialists in education which make up the faculties of institutions of higher learning should be able to accomplish the task. Parents, legislators, teachers and citizens have every right to ask why so many graduates seem to be unable to read, speak, comprehend simple mathematics, or understand the most basic of business and economic principles. Why, indeed?

To design a strong curriculum, the popular perspective is that one must first determine the desired outcomes. At that point, designing the inputs is straight forward. This has long been an established approach to curriculum design in the U.S. (Rugg, 1926; Bloom, 1956; Monroe, 1988). The inputs become courses, activities, programs, cores, assignments, etc. In short, the inputs become a curriculum. That paradigm closely follows the description of curriculum design espoused in 1926 (Rugg, 1926) and used by many professional groups today (Longenecker and Feinstein, 1991; Tucker, 1991). Like any dynamic system, curriculum design is an on-going process. The curriculum is continuously evolving and has done so since the earliest days of American education (Rugg and Counts, 1926), but fundamental change is extremely difficult because the curriculum paradigm itself has not changed.

Problems with the System

In 1926, critics of the process observed that the interests, skills, and abilities of teachers and administrative officers, the lobbying effect of textbook publishers, the needs and interests of certifying and examining boards, the entrance requirement of higher institutions, the desires of legislative bodies, and the concerns of a host of other interested parties combine to entrench content and academic organization, resist change and continue the status-quo (Rugg and Counts, 1926). The limits to effectiveness with which we must all deal today are summarized as follows.

1. Vested interests of a host of parties interact during design so that the resulting program is as much the result of exchange, concession and compromise as it is the result of outcomes assessment. It is a political process.
2. Courses tend to become ends in themselves rather than means to an end because they serve a diverse student population and support multiple programs, and because they tend to exist in isolation with few faculty involved.
3. Curriculum design frequently fails to take into consideration the learning styles of students.
4. The problems in curriculum design are exacerbated by uncooperative faculty and/or administrators.
5. Highly specialized faculty are not qualified to build interdisciplinary programs.

6. Goal congruence among faculty is not usually established which tends to prevent effective implementation of a curriculum, even if it is effectively designed.

The Effects of Learning Styles

Traditionally, business is taught passively by lecture and illustration of problem and solutions. That paradigm and its historic and persistent role permeate the university system in the United States. The traditional view is that business programs are rigorous and many students are not sufficiently motivated to perform well. Traditionally, the expectation is that those students who succeed are those who are achievement oriented and highly motivated, or, those students who work hard. Further, such students will succeed regardless of the approach used to teach the course.

The corollary is that those students who do not do well are uninterested, not highly motivated or not achievement driven, or, not willing to devote long hours outside of class. Such students will not do not do well, regardless of the approach used. Modern researchers in business education are increasingly recognizing that learning is different from academic performance and that the structure of the teaching paradigm needs to change in order to increase the learning rate of all students.

Karl Jung's (1921/71) theory of personality types forms the foundation for much of the field of cognitive psychology. Kolb (1976, 1984), building on Jung's theory of personality typology, identified four types of learning styles which people employ. These are described as follows:

- The **Convergent Style** relies on conceptualization and active experimentation, and has as its major strength problem solving, decision making and practical application of ideas.
- The **Divergent Style** emphasizes concrete experience and reflective observation, and has as its major strength imaginative ability and awareness of meaning and values.
- The **Assimilation Style** emphasizes abstract conceptualization and reflective observation, and has as its major strength inductive reasoning and an ability to create theoretical models.
- The **Accommodation Style** emphasizes concrete experience and active experimentation, and has as its major strength doing things, carrying out plans and tasks and getting involved in new experiences.

Keirsey and Bates (1984) developed four dominant types of temperaments from the work of Jung, Kretschmer, Freud, Adler, Sullivan, Maslow, Myers and Briggs. The four groups which result, labeled SP, SJ, NF, or NT, are called temperaments. Extrapolation of Kolb's learning styles to the temperaments elucidated by Keirsey and Bates would result in groups with the characteristics displayed as follows.

Keirsey and Bates Temperaments　　　　**Kolb's Learning Styles**

The SJ Temperament　　　　　　　　　　Convergent Learning Style
　　The SJ is decisive, a traditionalist, likes policies, rules, schedules, standards and is resistant to change, but can be pessimistic and critical and can preserve useless rules.

The SP Temperament　　　　　　　　　Accommodation Learning Style
　　The SP goes into everything full speed ahead, is practical, flexible, open-minded, excited, enthusiastic, a risk taker, but dislikes theory or routine and lives for the moment.

The NT Temperament　　　　　　　　　Assimilation Learning Style
　　The NT is a visionary and architect of change who enjoys complexity, hungers for competency, knowledge, and mastery, but loses interest in a task before completion

The NF Temperament　　　　　　　　　　Divergent Learning Style
　　The NF is personable, idealistic, empathic, and charismatic, focuses on individuals, and is participative, but makes decisions based on personal likes and dislikes.

As the above description shows, two of Kolb's four learning styles, the Divergent and the Accommodation, would clearly benefit from a shift in the teaching paradigm away from lectures and problem illustrations because of their strong preference for concrete experience. In a survey of Business Administration students, Kolb (1984) found that students of management or business administration tended to display the accommodation learning style, a style at odds with the traditional approach to business instruction.

Experiential learning has been a concept of interest for many years to educators in a variety of disciplines. Its advocates and its critics are many educators in a variety of disciplines. Its advocates and its critics are many and varied. The central tenet is always that one learns best by active involvement. Jerome Coleman (1976) presents an excellent differentiation between experiential and classroom learning. He focuses on the sequence of steps in the learning process employed in the classroom and in experiential processes. Coleman describes the steps in learning under the two systems as follows.

The Classroom Learning System

1. receiving information through a symbolic medium such as a book or lecture;
2. assimilating and organizing information so that the general principle is understood;
3. being able to infer a particular application from the general principle; and,
4. moving from the cognitive and symbol-processing sphere to the sphere of action.

The Experiential Learning System

5. carrying out an action in a particular instance and seeing the effects of the action;
6. understanding the effects in a particular instance;
7. understanding the general principle under which the particular instance falls; and,
8. applying the concept through action in a new circumstance within the range of generalization.

The advantages of the classroom method include a reduction of the time and effort required to learn something new. Its disadvantages are that it depends heavily on the symbolic medium, which is usually language, and it depends upon extrinsic motivation. On the other hand, experiential learning is time consuming; however, it has a strong advantage in that it depends upon intrinsic motivation. More importantly, learning through the experiential concepts is less easily forgotten than learning through the information assimilation of the traditional classroom.

Astin (1984) was deeply concerned by the motivation required for success in learning. He posits a theory of student involvement in which he maintains that, '...a particular curriculum, to achieve the effects intended, must elicit sufficient student effort and investment of energy to bring about the desired learning and development' (p. 301). Astin's work supports a belief that experiential learning could be a superior approach to education, at least for those students who require a stronger involvement in order for their investment of physical and psychological energy to result in learning.

Both the divergent and accommodation learning styles function better with concrete experience (Kolb, 1984). Most business students are accommodation learners and would be better served with a paradigm which emphasized experiential learning concepts.

A New Paradigm

If the desired outcome of an entrepreneurship major is an integrated understanding of business principles and the desired approach is an experiential, hands on format, we reason that the logical structure is to employ a single project which would take students from the inception of an idea to initiate a business venture, through the establishment of that venture and into the growth, expansion and diversification of that venture. This would require a multiple semester course and an interdisciplinary team of professors. To ensure that the experiential method is the key vehicle, it would require more classroom hours and intensive involvement by students.

To that end, we propose a single, multi semester course which would meet for at least six hours each week in three hour blocks of time. The course would be team taught, but more importantly, the learning would be team based. The key, we feel, is the transfer of responsibility for learning from the instructor to the student. We propose student teams to work together across semesters. The teams would be responsible for developing, presenting and defending plans, analyses and strategies that would take their ventures from idea conceptualization to international competitiveness. Half of the class hours would be devoted to instructor centered learning and half to team centered learning. In each week, we would learn, then do. Then, we would evaluate, critique, and re-do. Each of the tools, each of the skills, each of the knowledge areas would be presented as an integral part of the business establishment, growth and management. Further, each team would repeatedly employ each skill after the initial introduction.

We think that such an approach offers a vehicle for the introduction, justification, and application of each of the concepts in entrepreneurship.

These concepts will be brought to bear as their needs become manifested in the on going process. At every turn and every juncture, the knowledge which we will present will be clearly linked to the on going business venture that each team is managing. We will show the students each layer of bricks from the foundation to the roof, but we will also require each team to lay those bricks in their weekly works. This continuous, experiential approach, coupled with the clear cut need for the knowledge and the repeated applications of the knowledge over the three semesters will, we believe, produce our desired outcome: students who demonstrate an integrated mastery of the key concepts in entrepreneurship.

Conclusion

We must hold fast to the idea that we are educators. Consider the inaugural address of John Stuart Mill in 1867 as Rector of St. Andrew's University in Scotland. Mill (1874, p. 333) stated that education included not only:

> ...whatever we do for ourselves, and whatever is done for us by others, for the express purpose of bringing us somewhat nearer to the perfection of our nature; it does more: in its largest acceptation, it comprehends even the indirect effects produced on character and on the human faculties, by things of which the direct purposes are quite different; by laws, by forms of government, by the industrial arts, by modes of social life; nay, even by physical facts not dependent on human will; by climate, soil, and local position. Whatever helps to shape the human being--to make the individual what he is, or hinder him from being what he is not--is part of his education.

We are, each of us, changing the lives of our students forever. Given that weighty responsibility, it is incumbent upon us to do everything within our power to ensure that we change those lives for the better.

References

Astin, A.S. (1984). Student involvement: A Developmental Theory for Higher Education. *Journal of College Student Personnel*, July, 297-307.

Bloom, B.S. (1956). *The Taxonomy of Educational Objectives: Classification of Educational Goals, Handbook 1: The Cognitive Domain*. New York, NY: McKay Press.

Boud, D. (1989). Some Competing Traditions in Experiential Learning. *Making Sense of*

Experiential Learning: Diversity in Theory and Practice, Weil and McGill (Eds), Philadelphia: Open University Press, 38-49.

Coleman, J.S. (1976). Differences between Experiential and Classroom Learning. *Experiential Learning*, Washington: Jossey-Bass Publishers, 1976, 49-61.

Dearing, B. (1965). The Student on his Own: Independent Study, in S. Baskin (Ed.), *Higher Education: Some Newer Developments*. New York, NY: McGraw-Hill Book Company, 49-77.

Henry, J. (1989). Meaning and Practice in Experiential Learning, *Making Sense of Experiential Learning: Diversity in Theory and Practice*, Weil and McGill (Eds), Philadelphia: Open University Press, 25-37.

Hutchings, P. and A. Wutzdorff. (1988) Experiential Learning Across the Curriculum: Assumptions and Principles. *Knowing and Doing: Learning Through Experience*, San Francisco: Jossey-Bass Publishers, 5-19.

Jung, K.G. (1921/71). *Psychological Types*. R.F.C. Hull, trans., Collected Works of K.G. Jung, Vol. 6, Bollingen Series XX, Princeton, NJ: Princeton University Press. (Original work published in 1921).

Keirsey, D. and M. Bates. (1984). *Please Understand Me: Character and Temperament Types*. Del Mar, CA: Prometheus Nemesis Book Company.

Kolb, D.A. (1976). Management in the learning process, *California Management Review*, Spring, 21-31.

Kolb, D.A. (1984). *Experiential Learning*. Englewood Cliffs: Prentice-Hall.

Longenecker, H.E. and D.L. Feinstein (1991). (Eds). *Information Systems: The DPMA Model Curriculum for a Four Year Undergraduate Degree*. Park Ridge, IL: Data Processing Management Association.

Nelson, J.K.S. (1989). Generating Integration and Involvement in Learning. *Making Sense of Experiential Learning: Diversity in Theory and Practice*, Weil and McGill (Eds), Philadelphia: Open University Press, 101-113.

Peterson, S.L. (1989). Reducing Student Attrition: Towards a More Successful Learning Environment. *Making Sense of Experiential Learning: Diversity in Theory and Practice*, Weil and McGill (Eds), Philadelphia: Open University Press, 170-178.

Rugg, H. (1926). A Century of Curriculum-Construction in American Schools, in G.M. Whipple (Ed), *The Twenty-Sixth Yearbook of the National Society for the Study of Education*, Bloomington, IL: Public School Publishing Company. 3-118.

Rugg, H. and G.S. Counts (1926). A Critical Appraisal of Current Methods of Curriculum-Making, in G.M. Whipple (Ed), *The Twenty-Sixth Yearbook of the National Society for the Study of Education*, Bloomington, IL: Public School Publishing Company. 425-447.

Tucker, A.B. (1991). (Ed.) A Summary of the ACM/IEEE Joint Curriculum Task Force Report, Computing Curricula, *CACM*, 34(6), June, 68-84.

Walter, G.A. and Marks, S.E (1981) *Experiential Learning and Change*. New York: John Wiley and Sons.

Wildemeersch, D. (1989). The Principal Meaning of Dialogue for the Construction and Transformation of Reality. *Making Sense of Experiential Learning: Diversity in Theory and Practice*, Weil and McGill (Eds), Philadelphia: Open University Press, 60-69.

6 The KUBUS® System - an Holistic Approach to Enterprise and Entrepreneurship

Martin Guedalla
Henrik Herlau
Michael Armer
Shazeen Qaiser

Abstract

KUBUS® is a dynamic process model of leadership used in an entrepreneurial environment. This covers both the profit making as well as the non-profit making sectors of the economy. It is a skeleton that walks which has embedded within it a number of tools and concepts that allow participants to add their own relevant culture (flesh) to it using Action Learning techniques.

The **KUBUS®** model is the invention of Professor Henrik Herlau of Copenhagen Business School and was originally designed to alleviate the 7 per cent unemployment rate north of Copenhagen amongst knowledge workers in 1990. He has had over 100 per cent success rate in that new jobs have been created for more than the number of participants on the courses. Over £24 million of new exports were created in a four year period.[1]

In the Angle Saxon world the concept of the Entrepreneur is somewhat different. Here it is usually based on a notion of 'Market Forces' and de-regulation as opposed to 'The Social Market' and a more regulated system in much of Europe. However, we have evidence that similar outcomes are possible in the UK although the question of raising finance is very different. The model rests on a number of holistic but discrete elements which can be summarized as follows, Leadership, team development, networking, market research and project management.

The **KUBUS®** model is now also being piloted in the context of 'Intrapreneurship' with companies seeking to project manage potential new products or services.

Introduction

There has been important theoretical and research work done on the semantics of 'Entrepreneurship' and its suitability as a taught subject in the formal educational process. Work done by Professor Gibb[2] covering European issues and his later work putting forward a powerful overview for Enterprise education in the UK[3] has had a profound impact on this debate at all levels of the educational system. For the purposes of this paper we will take these as our foundation to make a few critical remarks and then put forward for discussion a model for developing Enterprise Education both within formal educational structures as well as in the world of work.

It is interesting that the concept 'Enterprise' has sometimes been used in contra-distinction to the term Entrepreneurship. At other times these terms are used interchangeably. Following Professor Gibb's distinction we will use the term Enterprise - in the context of education - as challenging the educator as well as those being educated and as having a structure and declared outcomes but contextual delivery methods. This allows us to look at all levels and all formal subject areas of education and training by focusing on, in this context, specific outcomes as well as modes of delivery. After a brief overview we will then concentrate on the application of one model of Enterprise which is located in the field of Entrepreneurship.

Firstly we will take a look at some philosophical questions. Secondly we look at the role of Critical Analysis as a potential unifying force in the field of Entrepreneurship. Thirdly, linked with business strategy we suggest a model of leadership Fourthly, we suggest that the **KUBUS®** dynamic model will assist us to progress towards the new environments facing us all in the 90s and beyond. It embodies all the major strands of Entrepreneurial theory, psychology, sociology and economics in a process model that is itself based on a philosophy of 'becoming'. Finally we look at what needs to be done.

Philosophy and Methodology

In Europe we still have fundamental difficulties in bridging the divide between the British Empiricists and the European Rationalists. Many and varied developments have emerged since their originators first opened the debate in the 17th century. It is still sometimes impossible for us in the UK to accept the 'metaphysics' of dialectics, of continuous change and development, of 'the individual in society', of 'the community', et al. Although there still remains an echo of some sort of predetermination embedded in much dialectical philosophy there are also many who use the theory as another skeleton to provide a developing framework to hang their 'gestalts' on. Apart from a host of other contextual matters this is one fundamental reason why we do not perceive of Gibb's concept of Enterprise in a similar manner to our European colleagues. Nor for that matter, but for different reasons, as the Pragmatists of the US.

We would like to suggest a scenario based on a European model which has its philosophical underpinning not in Locke, Hume and Berkeley and their later developments but rather upon the European Rationalist approaches and the dialectics of Hegel. To give some solidity to this approach it is relevant to point out that quantum physics, since the 20s, has been able to incorporate such concepts as 'the same phenomena' being both a wave and a particle, Heisenberg probability Theory and the influence of the experimenter on the experiment. These ideas, transferred to the social sciences whose practitioners often attempt to mirror the supposed rigour of the natural sciences appear to produce Pavlovian responses of anger and dismissal by the empirical number crunches. For those interested see the work of Einstein, Planck, Blor and Heisenberg and their work on quantum theory.[4]

If we now turn to the concept of Entrepreneurship we immediately face some similar dilemmas. A good example of this is the work of Churchill (1989) who attempts to put forward a paradigm that takes account of the subjective and the objective within the dynamics of change when analyzing the issues of Entrepreneurship in the micro as well as the macro environment.

> The mathematics revolution, it seems to me, is affecting science and philosophy as profoundly as the two greatest scientific revolutions of this century, relativity and quantum mechanics. .... Catastrophe and chaos are two very entrancing theories of the new golden age. They provide a

mathematics for systems in which tiny changes in inputs make a large difference to outcomes. To some Entrepreneurship scholars that appears to be a good metaphor for the startup of a new venture'.[5] He looks at the start up, which for these purposes are equated with Entrepreneurship, as changes of the existing state. 'Starting a new venture is not a smooth, continuous, ordinary process. Rather it is a disjointed, discontinuous, unique event, no matter whether it is a mega or a micro venture.[6]

He offers a model of the Entrepreneurial Process which is described as follows:

It is discontinuous. This discontinuity ranges in size from a quantum jump to a tiny increment. The variables which 'cause' new events are many, varied and complex. The actual changes are usually tiny in isolation and are unique in their own context. This process is inherently unstable and holistic. However, although standard mathematics cannot make sense of these events he suggests that Catastrophe theory, introduced in 1972, can. It allows for jumps from one stable state to another stable state. Although never able to embrace the whole, it does allow for simplistic models of Entrepreneurship. It can also be used to support Schumpeter (1939) and his model of the heroic Entrepreneur who moves the macro economic framework forward from one point of stability to another. A major problem with this view is limiting and isolating the important variables to a usable number. However, Chaos theory, which is also non-linear, works on the model of tiny changes in initial conditions that produce big and unexpected changes in what is deemed to be the final outcome Although neither of these methodologies can as yet give us predictable, testable, hypothesis generating science he claims they are the prerequisites to this goal.

The social sciences are not distinct from the natural sciences simply because the human element somehow contaminates the purity of the former. Auguste Compte (1798 - 1857) the French founder of the social sciences suggested that abstract sciences could be viewed in a hierarchical form. The most precise was Mathematics followed by physics, chemistry, biology, psychology and then last, sociology. This is based on a view of classical determinism or predicative powers as viewed from a linear and Human causal prescription. Churchill (1989) offers a paradigm which includes what he terms the Applied as well as the Basic sciences listed above. The Applied would have the following order; Engineering, medicine, economics, business entrepreneurship.[7] Whereas Physics could be said to originate in the 5th century BC (Democritus and Plato), Entrepreneurship could be said to have originated in the 18th (Smith). Empirical research for the former is therefore at least 2000 years old whereas the latter is around 40 years old. Teaching the subject is similarly staggered with the former also over 2000 years old and the later around 30 years old. The point is that we are nowhere near having agreed methods, concepts, data or even agreed peer understanding of the issues with the work being done on Entrepreneurship. We are certainly not suggesting we seek refuge in the Post Modernist concept of relativity with all gestalts being of equal value. All we are pleading for is a stark realization that there are many and varied routes to new knowledge and the one we are proposing here, which does have credible antecedents in the natural sciences, be given a small place in the sun for the time being.

We are still at the stage of defining our variables which are fuzzy, unlike the apparently 'solid' variables of mass, length, time etc. in physics. Our instruments, (Questionnaires, Likert scales, psychometrics), have a dubious solidity supporting them unlike the rulers, scales and clocks of physics. The populations we investigate can be individuals, firms, or industries which are somewhat nebulous in their definition unlike the particles, atoms, liquids and solids (in their acceptance even if not in their actuality) of physics. We are also faced with the underlying cultural fuzziness which lay behind our assumptions of the world we are investigating. this applies to both physics as well as Entrepreneurship but is mediated in the former by the longevity and 'discoveries' of the former. This, by definition has not yet taken place with the latter. It is suggested that Entrepreneurship is a process of becoming (dialectics) rather than a steady state. It changes in quantum leaps which cannot be understood by regression analysis. Rather, the concepts of Tectonic plate theory would hold where small incremental changes which are not noticeable produce startling catastrophic change on the surface as the mounting pressure seeks release.

In the accepted empirical standard of the UK the concept that Innovation was umbilically linked to Entrepreneurship in the small business sector was spelled out by Curran and Stanworth (1989) 'Entrepreneurship, rigorously defined, refers to the creation of a new economic entity centered on a novel product or service or, at the very least, one which differs significantly from products or services offered elsewhere in the market.'[8]

This view embodies part of Drucker's concept of Innovation in it as expounded with his seven sources of innovation. His seminal work 'Innovation and Entrepreneurship' (first published in 1985) is still one of the most important theoretical frameworks for looking at these concepts. He says 'Entrepreneurs innovate. Innovation is the specific instrument of Entrepreneurship. It is the act that endows resources with a new capacity to create wealth. Innovation, indeed creates a resource. There is no such thing as a 'resource' until man finds a use for something in nature and thus endows it with an economic value'.[9] Somewhat surprisingly this concept echoes the political economists of the last century as formalized by the Marxist's concept of exchange and use values. It is clearly based on the interconnection of psychological, economical and cultural elements and so brings all three strands together. Certainly his seven sources for innovative opportunity[10] embrace these three legs of Entrepreneurship. However, in his later work, particularly 'Managing in the Non-profit Organization' he looks at some of the criticism of his previous concepts which were addressing the profit making core of the US economy and often the larger or growing company.

About the only consensus of the meaning that should be embedded in the concept of Entrepreneurship in the sphere of economics is that, 'the greater the conditions of uncertainty and change the more this actor becomes illuminated and at center stage'.[11]

Staying with the economists' approach to Entrepreneurship we could look at the long wave theory.[12] It does not matter for these purposes whether or not this view is accurate or predictive, Rather, the theory is illustrated as one that embraces an historical perspective which centers on technological innovation to explain developments in Entrepreneurship. It can be quickly summed up in terms of the British experience as follows: 1) 1780-1840 innovation in production specifically iron; the mechanization of cotton and development of steam power. This activity was concentrated in Lancashire, Shropshire and the Black Country. 2) 1850-1890. innovation in transport, particularly the railways, steel production, coal mining and further developments in steam power. It was concentrated in S Wales, NE England and central Scotland. 3) 1890-1930 innovation in electricity, chemicals, synthetic materials and the internal combustion engine. It was concentrated in the West Midlands and Greater London. 4) 1940, to 1980. Electrical and light engineering, petrochemicals, and the motor industry. Again, concentrated in West Midlands and Greater London. 5) 1980's to the present day based on innovations in microelectronics, information and communication technologies largely concentrated in the South East and M4 corridor.[13] We too, using the **KUBUS®** model, look at how we got where we are not just who we are now.

Turning to business strategy the work of Stacey comes to mind.[14] Here the concept of chaos is used in the correct mathematical context. It involves us immediately in the problems of dynamics, spontaneous change, self organization, and feedback. 'With this new frame of reference we can see that it is impossible for managers to plan or envision the long term future of an innovative organization. Instead they must create and discover an unfolding future, using their ability to learn together in groups and to interact politically in a spontaneous self-organizing manner'.[15] As he discovered, this way of analysis has aroused controversy amongst his peers. We are not suggesting his work is always right but he does represent a move away from the attempt to model a social science on a representation of the natural sciences whose methodology is sometimes perceived to rest on 19th century thinking. (Mechanical determinism.)

Although he focused on corporate strategy we would like to take some of his comments out of context and use them whilst referring to group dynamics and **KUBUS®** teams. For example, his view is that all organizations are constantly and dynamically always pulled in two directions - disintegration and ossification. 'Success lies at the border between these states'. This concept is born out in our work with **KUBUS®** teams in their initial forming mode. We look at the Project, that is the stage before the project is formulated, delimited and goal orientated. The point is that this instability which we have sometimes referred to in the past as 'turmoil' is *always* present. It becomes more refined and burdened with cultural paraphernalia the more self reflecting the team and the more critical analysis we bring to bear on the present situation.

The information - the immediate and unsophisticated meanings that we transmit to others becomes exformation - the pyramid of knowledge and experience we carry with us unseen and highly ambiguous, as we apply this critical analysis to the process as well as the product, but always on a spiral of development. The 'always' here is itself ambiguous. It is being suggested that even if the **KUBUS®** team disintegrates those remaining as well as those leaving will have learnt something through the use of the tools and the interaction with their environment which would include the coaches/facilitators. One golden lesson might well be that not everyone at all times is best suited to work in teams and that teams are not necessarily the best or only method for solving problems. The point that a camel is really a horse designed by a team is important to remember!

Stacey says the following about organizations '..This means that the long-term future of a creative organization is absolutely unknowable and that no one can intend its future direction over the long-term or be in control of it..'.[16] With the qualification that the concept 'long-term' is itself ambiguous and contextual the same can also be said of teams. However, it is our view that the concept of a dynamic skeleton, one that walks, runs sits and lies down, that has the flesh put on it by the owners of the problem squares the circle of the dilemma of seeking something solid, learnable, productive and fun that can assist us when we think team work is appropriate in a given situation. This is before we focus on the issue of leadership.

The issue is one of enormously increased complexity as investigators continuously struggle to objectify their work. Mathematical and behaviorist models have resulted which have the allure of certainty yet continuously fail to match up to their own rules of testability, repeatability and hypothesis testing. The only advance is one of obscurity and jargon soaked 'non sense'. What we are suggesting is that it is possible to use this **KUBUS®** process model, isolating a range of variables, and test it out in society based on certain outcome tests stated in advance and used by other researchers and businesses. It is not complete as a model yet but our numerous pilot studies have got us to an advanced Beta version.

The essential point that we would like to focus on is that of Critical Analysis. The suggestion is that critical analysis is the unifying force here.

Critical Analysis

Critical analysis is essentially the attempt to analyze 'objectively' the theory and practice of being engaged in the world which one is both part of and distinct from at the same time. This analysis is both theoretical as well as practical. It involves a range of practices such as comparing hypotheses, suggesting new ones, criticizing existing ones based on various forms of evidence. It requires an open and questioning outlook based on what is socially accepted as evidence. Most of all perhaps it requires a constant attempt to seek a form of objectivity based initially on peer review but ultimately on consciously demonstrating a closer working relationship with perceived reality over a period of time. Big scientific theories this century as already referred to such as Relativity Theory, Probability Theory, Quantum Theory, Genetic Theory, Tectonic Plate Theory, even Gia Theory, are only possible when the social conditions allow for such development in terms of technology, culture, politics and economics (long wave theory). What they

111

have in common is the use of dialectics (becoming). They all show that small incremental changes, often unseen or unseeable, produce explosions of change at a critical point. They show the relativeness of context which can explain the absoluteness of the particular. They show how Critical Analysis was the underpinning that allowed huge (non linear) steps forward in our limited understanding of the world around us. They show that 'facts' are not just pure Human Facts but influenced by and influencing each other in a constantly changing dynamic.

It is our hypothesis that holistic concepts of Entrepreneurship, that consciously bring together the process as well as the practice, that develop critical analysis and focus on the group as a reference point rather than the individual, are a way forward for economic as well as educational development in the next millennium. The system we expound which is itself directed specifically towards the world of work, nevertheless covers psychological, social, economical, cultural, political, organizational, environmental and financial issues in a way that draws out their constant influence on one another.

Many studies have shown how the role of the manager, (in all working environments), has structurally changed in Western society. Other centralized systems have collapsed or changed out of all recognition. These enormous shifts, conceptually similar to Tectonic plate movements, have the corollary that new methods of teaching are being developed to bring out the need for 'continuous learning' and project managing our working environment. The thing about Enterprise education (Gibb 1988) in the field of Entrepreneurship - in whatever context we are taking about - is that it requires judgements and answers to be given based on probability and a form of risk reward analysis. If these concepts can be consciously harnessed and systematized as a skeleton - for flesh to be added in any particular context - then we might be onto something very powerful. That is where the **KUBUS®** model comes into play.

KUBUS® - Background

It was invented by Professor Henrik Herlau of Copenhagen Business School as a methodology to change the situation that had arisen just north of Copenhagen in the early 90s where there was 7 per cent 'knowledge worker' unemployment.[17]

It has a number of facets but the ones we shall look at here are those that develop the skills and knowledge of participants seeking to make small initial developments so that they can make their own jobs as well as seek them. The same model applies in a different format to larger organizations seeking to develop team leadership and project management. We suggest that it should be used for bringing new ideas to the market place. Anecdotal evidence that we have gained from some pilot studies supports our view that this is indeed a methodology to vastly increase the precision and productivity of this process.

An underlying theme which has emerged is one of building confidence in a non-hierarchical situation and cutting out the typical diversions that we know exhaust us in typical unstructured meetings. **KUBUS®** is based on the concept of Social Entrepreneurship. This is not meant to describe Non Profit Making Entrepreneurship (NPME) as in the UK context but rather Entrepreneurship based on the notion of being embedded in local and national needs. It also embodies a fundamental training programme for group participation and leadership. (Big ears little mouth).

We will describe later some aspects of the **KUBUS®** model. However, the important point to make here is that it is based on our concept of Action Learning. (AL).

What is Action Learning? Is it learning to learn by doing? There are no quick small definitions of what A L actually is and the initiator of the concept in terms of Management Training, Reg Revans, says himself, 'In practice we find small groups are more effective at learning than simple pairs, provided that every member can describe his need to learn with and from each other in his set. The explanation of our paradox - that the learning dynamic is the recognition of a common ignorance rather than of some collective superfluity of tradable knowledge - is both simple and elusive.'[18] He goes on to say (p6), '...But the true leader must always be more interested in what he cannot see in front of him, and this is the mark of the wise man; ...'

The **KUBUS®** model starts with the premise that we have to spend time working out what the real problem is that we need to focus on. This might sound strange but we find in most areas of life we obscure the reality by subjective unstated agendas so that we often finish up actively pursuing issues and resolving problems that were not the ones at the heart of the matter. This links totally with Revans's idea that, 'Action Learning ensures that, before skills and other resources are brought to bear in conditions of ignorance, risk and confusion, some of the more fertile questions necessary to exploring those conditions have been identified: there is nothing so terrible in all human experience as a bad plan efficiently carried out, when immense technical resources are concentrated in solving the wrong problems.[19]

Often this search for new ways of proceeding from a strong analytical starting point can cause great confusion especially when the goals (*products*) to be achieved have not been, (and should not be), proscribed from the outset. We are all, particularly in the West, expected to state the problem to be resolved at the beginning of the discussion and are often expected to provide solutions very quickly. With **KUBUS®** we spend time discussing what the problem is and clarifying its basis BEFORE seeking to resolve it. This can lead to confusion, impatience, fear and anger.

This can come to the fore if participants have not been made aware - in advance - that the model is not based on didactic delivery methods but AL delivery methods. It is true to say that the facilitator - who is sometimes a coach - cannot tell EXACTLY how the sessions will evolve though they will have clear outcomes that they wish to achieve. The Absolute of the stated outcomes is contained within the Relative of the process. Thus, the whole educational experience is based on a certain risk/reward system which, like Entrepreneurship in general, is based on consciously seeking to lower the risk element whilst always looking to increase the reward element.

In epistemological terms, there is more to it than that. Participants are both acting and acted upon. (Dialectics). They bring their history with them which sometimes has to be unpacked and looked at consciously. Or it might have to be re-interpreted so that the same becomes different. It also involves consciously working with the world at large both in terms of people as well as the resources available. Finally, the point is also made that the participants are not neutral but are changed by the 'experiment' as they change the matter that is being experimented on. (This is clearly contrary to Belbin's analysis of groups).[20]

With AL - and with **KUBUS®** in particular - the object is to make these issues conscious in the minds of the participants so that new knowledge of both the process as well as the product is carried forward independently of the specific project at hand and can be used by the newly formed **KUBUS®** experts at later stages in their lives. (Critical Analysis). Thus, at this time we have trained knowledge workers in the field of making jobs as well as seeking them located in the context of Social Entrepreneurship whilst working in teams. Leadership skills are vital to this development. **KUBUS®** is the skeleton that allows the systematization to take place. Participants are learning a language and methodology to carry them forward throughout their lives and are not simply repositories of particular academic knowledge or professional skills. We like to call the system 'Taylorism of the mind' to emphasize the increased productivity that stems from utilizing the techniques learnt. Workshop techniques are the chosen methods for making this ongoing development possible. Feedback is often done by the use of video and the log books (Critical Analysis), certainly for Higher Education (HE) and knowledge workers. Participants are required to read widely and crystallize past knowledge into them.

In the world of work it is more difficult to ask the participants to commit themselves to this level of activity. However, they too are asked to produce log books at least relating to their subjective experiences. They are requested to fill out and discuss the feedback forms in training sessions and to watch video of their group's work with the facilitators. Again and again the experience is that this video feedback produces the biggest and most profound 'Ah Ha's'. Participants who we have spoken to many months later still remember those scenes vividly and indicate how that feedback has changed their perception of themselves and others.

KUBUS® - The Model

KUBUS® teaches you to consciously assimilate skills and knowledge within a shared set of values and expectations. Critical analysis is the foundation and reference point for this. The whole becomes far greater than the individual parts. We ask participants to work with a six sided figure (a Cube) so that it is possible for all participants to focus sequentially on specific topics without being diverted or confused as so often happens in meetings and with project teams. These boxes are not absolute but are simply ways of seeing the world in such a way so as to facilitate the group to make decisions after discussion in a systematic way.

We can begin to show measurable evidence of the success of this methodology in providing participants with the skills and knowledge required in the world of 'The Empty Raincoat'[21] both in Denmark and through work carried out in the UK in HE and for Women Returners courses matched funded through European Union Employment Now programme. In Denmark more work has been done in the corporate sector than in the UK but here too initial feedback is very favorable. The skeleton looks like this:

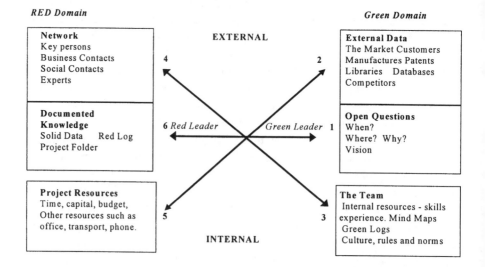

Network	EXTERNAL	External Data
Key persons		The Market Customers
Business Contacts	4 2	Manufactures Patents
Social Contacts		Libraries Databases
Experts		Competitors

6 *Red Leader*   *Green Leader* 1

Do not be confused with the concepts of RED and GREEN leadership. We could have called them Cold/Hot, or anything else. The color does not signify anything. What matters is the role these two extremities of leadership play in this context.

All participants in **KUBUS®** courses have a shared language usable across national boundaries. The contents will be different for each group (the flesh), but the model (skeleton) will remain the same. It embodies a concept of leadership that needs to be carefully absorbed for the whole system to make sense. Unfortunately there is not enough space here to fully unpack the skeleton for you.

Please note the following very carefully as it often causes confusion. The six boxes are task or subject areas. They are NOT individual team members. However, when we talk about Red and Green leaders we also refer to their specific tasks in boxes 1 and 6. Please remember, this is a training model and reflects a dynamic situation where we are seeking understanding. That means it might well be that other team members can and do take on these responsibilities at times to facilitate the meeting. The fundamental issue is always one of raising the conscious understanding of the process. It is not necessarily about being right or wrong! A unique aspect of KUBUS® teams is that ALL participants have to take responsibility for their teams development (both process and product) and not just the designated leaders. *The perspective is for all to be training each other all the time.* [22]

This is clearly not the formal hierarchical system or 'Major-General' style that some of us have been used to in the past. It is the 'quality circle' facilitator model that is being used extensively in large companies today as well as non-profit making organizations. Small businesses have not always been strong on staff issues with a charismatic leader who controls the whole. Rather, they *think* they control the whole. In fact, on analysis, they too use outside experts and network and need all the skills outlined in the boxes. Over time, it is suggested that they do better when engaged in the social development of their work than as a 'tiger in jungle' typified in the 'market forces' scenario.

The model has been used for large and small company work, under and post graduate students, community development and other non-profit making sectors of the economy. The conceptual overview of a course is as follows:

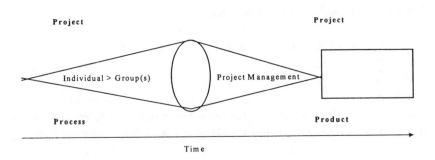

We have proposed a model which is still being developed This is not being done in isolation. Part of the process is to use standardized log sheets - templates - that have been designed to assist with the systemization of the process as well as the product outcomes. Green Logs are essentially what we call 'Fuzzy Data' logs. Examples would be mindmaps, pathfinder ideas not yet researched, (Moonbeams), and group feedback logs. Red logs are essentially what we call 'Hard Data'. Examples would be minutes of meetings, tasks allocated, network contacts in use, cash flow and models.

These templates, available in English as the most internationally used business language, are being used on the back of Internet mailing systems. With the correct permissions and password access it allows different groups nationally and internationally to work with comparable groups. At its lowest level it makes it possible to see the cultural influences involved in different national settings. It also gives **KUBUS®** groups the opportunity to network market their projects at virtually no cost working with highly motivated and supportive knowledge workers in their own specific locality. In addition, this allows for the potential of 'virtual projects' owned by two or more groups but sharing their teams' knowledge and skills.

Finally, it allows for an audit trail to be followed. It is here we can effectively work on the productivity of the group or what we term the 'Taylorism of the mind'. To quote a senior marketing executive in a multi national US company 'This is Innovation with crunch'. It is not only possible to check carefully what was done but - sometimes more importantly - what was NOT done. It allows for analysis and discussion of the process by the team and outside coaches or senior management.

Facilitator, Coach, Lecturer or Mentor

Who coaches, facilitates, and mentors this form of education? Is it possible for one person to do this? It is suggested that the answer is definitely NO and that it requires **KUBUS®** teams. This raises large questions of resources. It requires a critical mass of sales or participants to make it possible to build up **KUBUS®** teams of facilitators. To date, we have spent many weeks training staff, the majority of whom have been recruited from their participation in **KUBUS®** courses. This might not always be possible in the future and we are developing a CD to cut down on the human resource input where possible.

In the Reg Revans mode of operation we would all be facilitators using what is known as the Socratic method of discovery. That is, extracting from an individual what they knew all along but did not appear to know when faced with a specific task. It is not telling, it is not lecturing, and it is not exhorting. By means of logic (deduction in this case), questions are put that are meant to allow the other to make their own new leaps of knowledge or 'Ah ha's!' This is the classical role of a facilitator. It also means that when taking on the role of a facilitator (or as we shall see later - a coach), the

118

outcome of any session is not known in advance. This situation is very dangerous, stimulating, and full of potential mine-fields. It is also very exhausting for all participants and requires goodwill all round for it to be successful in producing new Ah ha's!

The best way to describe the role of a coach is to look at what a football manager or a gym instructor does. They praise, exhort, criticize, and substitute team players so that the individual and the team get the best out of their collective action. There is intervention, instruction and even 'sending off' at times which is at variance to the classical facilitator mode of operation. Both these roles are used in **KUBUS®** team building though most AL is described when facilitators are in use.[23] *The point is that whatever method is used the participants become self aware, self driven and able to us the model, its jargon and tools, independently and in new situations.*

A lecturer uses what is called Program Learning techniques. They speak and others make notes, or, more frequently, day dream. There is much evidence from psychologists that the maximum span of attention for the listener is 20 min and there is rarely a congruence between what is spoken and what is noted. A mentor is usually someone who has got certain life experiences or has acquired certain skills and is prepared, even eager, to show a colleague how to do the same. They are often older and wish to encourage a younger person. They have discovered that the time and effort it took them to discover certain truths is so long that by the time they are known they are unusable.[24]

It has been found on KUBUS® courses that roles change very rapidly and are not always confined to the 'staff'. Often the participant will have greater skills or knowledge in certain areas than the staff. At this point, if there is a genuine desire to learn, the formal roles of 'staff' and 'student' are reversed. This is quite proper and an immensely useful way of making self and group developments based on the sharing of informed knowledge.

Leadership

There has been volumes of published work on leadership mostly emanating from the discipline of psychology. Such themes as power and influence, intelligence and creativity, personality, values, attitudes, behavior and skills are all in the literature. Models of charismatic, transformational and managerial leadership styles are many and varied. We appear to be in the middle of the 'team leadership' period. Here we are referring to the investigation of the conductor type of leadership as opposed to the major-general style. Now we look at relationships,[25] delegating,[26] setting goals, interpersonal skills,[27] managing conflict and cross cultural perspectives.[28]

What we have tried to do in **KUBUS®** is to unpack some of the skills that are required in our entrepreneurial teams and assign them to what we have designated Red (solid data) and Green (fuzzy date) leaders. (Again, these two characters might well be a single person in reality. What we are doing here is unpacking the Yin and Yang using leadership for Critical Analysis). There needs to be a constant 'becoming' dynamic not just between these two characters but with the whole team. The important new factor that we have emphasized above is that leadership is a process of empowerment. It can be removed by those that did the empowering. It is also, with upside down thinking, the equal responsibility of the led to train their leaders. This is a key issue as responsibility is never owned by the others - it is always yours.

If we link the concept of improving leadership of the team as it changes from a facilitating mode to a coaching mode as we move from process to product we can also link it to the Stacey model of strategy stated above. The model would look as follows:

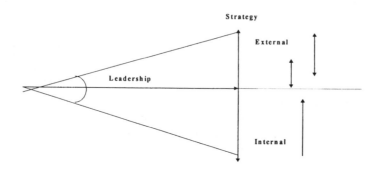

The suggestion is that the horizontal line is describing the learning development of the leadership in any particular team. Although it is described in a linear fashion here it is in practice a spiral which is not always going forward and is characterized by many 'quantum leaps'.

The vertical line is similarly non-linear in practice and at each extremity (external and internal) is in a constant state of movement. We suggest that **KUBUS®** teams succeed in bringing these vertical movements closer and closer to the horizontal center point over time which in turn increases the speed of leadership development (left to right). The faster the speed from left to right the closer the Internal and External strategy extremities come. This is how such teams can enormously raise their productivity. The ideal would be for them to be in unison in one spot but in reality that can never happen. The arrows on the right indicate the non-linear waves as the tides come in and out in the strategic sphere.

Research

We have been looking at both Belbin (1981) as well as Bales (1979) psychometric tests when looking for management attributes that could be tested through **KUBUS®**. Neither of these have proved entirely satisfactory. Similarly with correlation studies though we have used Introvert/Extrovert, Problem solver, Self esteem and Depression grounded tests. We are now seeking to develop our own model of what constitutes a **KUBUS®** leader and measuring, where possible, this model against participants at the beginning, middle and end of their particular course against others engaged in Entrepreneurial courses not using the **KUBUS®**. methodology. Fiedler (1987) has offered valuable insights here.

There are additional cultural variables at stake which do not appear to have been thoroughly investigated. (Pascale RT and Athos AG. 1986). Some of these appear to have come full circle, eg the concept of quality as first recorded in Chinese texts of the last millenium (Wei Jiang 1994). We have also concentrated some of our work on looking at Women in Management match funded by European Union Social Funds. This has brought to the fore various gender issues. See our forthcoming paper 'From home work to paid work via the **KUBUS®**. system: A preliminary report on Women Returners' to be given next month.[29]

Conclusion

We suggest that Critical Analysis is the Unifying Force of Enterprise learning in both the formal educational system as well as work based training. This can be assessed at all levels from schools to Higher Education including job creation, Entrepreneurship as well as offering huge productivity gains for organizations looking to pare down and reduce the lead time of gestation to action. Project Management abilities rest, in our view, on the constant application of Critical Analysis. There is a constant need to accept upside thinking in the learning process as well as outside it to come to terms with and enjoy looking behind immediate appearance. Critical Analysis, it is suggested, is the Gestalt that thrives in the world of dilemmas.

In the current climate in many areas of paid work it is difficult to see ourselves as anything else but individuals who have to compete with each other for survival. We have either lost many of the social reference points older generations were accustomed to or they have been deliberately dismantled. It is accepted by many that there will be no return to the 'job for life' career in the UK and this idea is rapidly spreading across Europe and globally. (Handy 1994). We all have to develop transferable social skills to learn to work in small teams, often project led, and relying on the specific expertise and knowledge of the participants who may have never met before and may never meet again after the project is completed.

> We have to learn how to be knowledge workers in this entrepreneurial and innovative environment. We have to learn what are the component parts of leadership, how to be led and how to train the appointed leaders. We have to learn as quickly as possible how to objectify the discussion, listen to others, support solid ideas and use our networks to make leaps in understanding We have to learn how to work in a fast changing environment by having a dynamic model (Skeleton) to hang our coats on.[30]

The **KUBUS®** methodology is based on an upward positive spiral of reinforcement of good practice which can be specified and learnt by all and can therefore be practiced in different circumstances and in different contexts. It can be described as a skeleton which is duplicated methodologically though each time it swings into action the flesh that is built upon it is different from previous incarnations. There can never be an exact replica of another **KUBUS®** group. Self reflection, particularly with the use of log books, feedback and analyzing videos of the team work is an essential element in this process as are the specific business skills of project management based on real world constraints and opportunities.

We have to learn what we are good at objectively at specific times and places and to grasp what others around us are best at in order to get the maximum out of every team. We have to decide whether or not we understand what we are doing, why we are doing it, and whether we want to be committed to it or perhaps just act as a semi-detached assistant. We have to learn how best to use the teams knowledge and experience and their network contacts. We have to look at and learn about the complex issues of leadership and make decisions as to our role in directly taking on a leadership role at any particular time and whether or not we are prepared to assist a leader for the greater good of the team and the project, rather than withdraw from the problems and become an observer.

We have to test whether the first very positive results of the KUBUS® methodology is what might be termed a 'Hawthorn effect' or something that can be claimed credibly as unique to this model and we have to test it out in the context of Intrapreneurship. A first study of this is being researched in Denmark and two pilot projects are being discussed with large organizations in the UK. We have to develop a methodology that is both usable as well as incorporating fuzzy data and is acceptable to the market place. Can we, in the social sciences emulate our colleagues in the natural sciences and make a break through in our knowledge acquisition and general theory of becoming? Certainly that is our long term task.

Appendix 1.
From the MBA **KUBUS®** course handbook at the University of Westminster.

Achievements

We hope that you will acquire the following skills from this course:

- The ability to critically analyze
- The ability to research
- The ability to use the English language appropriately

- An understanding of the possibilities you have to re-join the paid labor market
- An understanding of the macro economic environment
- An understanding of leadership in teams
- Confidence in your abilities to gain satisfying paid work.

In addition, on this course you will be expected to demonstrate a number of skills such as, working with others, delegation, leadership, communicating with peers as well as outside contacts and employers, using IT as appropriate, and managing a project.

You are not expected to do everything! You will be shown how to achieve a good result in these areas but you must understand that much of the work will be developed from your own initiatives and analysis of the process that you are involved in. To remind you, this course embodies both Action Learning and Action Research and it is vital that you work within this context and the culture that it implies.

Activities that flow from this perspective are:

- The keeping of personal log books
- Sharing information and networks
- An openness to new ideas
- A willingness to discuss your and team members work objectively
- A willingness to accept the 'good faith' of the other participants
- The confidence to work in a 'safe' environment with tutoring staff
- Taking up a problem solving self motivated attitude to the work
- Using and keeping up-to-date the appropriate templates
- Completing designated tasks as agreed
- Using your own initiative
- Working in your time as necessary
- To assist other team members achieve the most that they can in these circumstances
- Consciously learn how to lead even if this is not your designated role.

Many of these concepts are new in some areas of paid work and might be difficult to grasp initially. That is understood by the tutors but we will constantly be encouraging you to make these developments at your own speed as your confidence in the process develops.

Notes

[1] Herlau H. and Tetzschener H. (1996) 'Entrepreneurship: The KUBUS® Model: Action Learning and Team-building. Some Methodological Reflections on Training. P. 51-53. Department of Management, Politics and Philosophy. Copenhagen Business School.

[2] Allan A. Gibb. 1988 'Stimulating Entrepreneurship and new business development' INTERMAN programme for promoting Entrepreneurship and new enterprise creation (UNDP/ILO project INT/87/029). International Labour Office, Management Training Branch. Geneva.

[3] Allan A. Gibb. 1993 'The Enterprise Culture and Education' International Small Business Journal Vol. 11, Nos 3 April - June.

[4] Horz et al. 1980 'Philosophical Problems in physical science' published in English by Marxist Educational Press ISBN. 093065613X pp. 70 -71, 83,106-112 and 141 - 144).

[5] Churchill, Neil. 1989 ' The Entrepreneurship Paradigm(11): Chaos and Catastrophes among Quantum Jumps? Entrepreneurship Theory and Practice 14 (Fall) pp. 7 - 26.

[6] Ibid.

[7] Ibid.

[8] Curran J. and Stanworth J. (1989) 'Education and Training for Enterprise: Some problems of Classification, Evaluation, Policy and Research'. International Small Business Journal. Vol. 7, no 2 pp. 11-12.

[9] Drucker P. (1995) 'Innovation and Entrepreneurship' p 27 Butterworth Heinemann.

[10] Ibid Chapter 1.

[11] Deakin D. (1996) p. 14.

[12] Kondratieff N. ' The long wave of economic life' Review of Economic Studies 1935 Vol. 17 No 6, Schumpeter J. 'Business Cycles: A Theoretical, Historical and Statistical Analysis of the Capitalist process' London: McGraw Hill 1939.

[13] Burrows R. 'The Enterprise Culture and restructuring of Britain' p23 chapter in Paths of Enterprise edited by Curran J. and Blackburn R. Routledge 1991.

[14] Stacey Ralph. 1993 'Strategy as Order Emerging from Chaos' Long Range Planning Vol 26 No 1 pp. 10 - 17. Pergamon Press.

[15] Ibid.

[16] Ibid.

[17] For more information on this pioneering work see Herlau H. and Tetzschner 'The Cube Model: A Human Software' IntEnt 1994 conference on Internationalizing Entrepreneurship, Education and Training at Stirling University. Also Herlau and Guedalla 'Systematic Entrepreneurship; investigating the third wave'. 18th National Small Firms Conference November 1997 ISBA. ISBN 0-904391-21-3.

[18] Pedlar M. Ed 1991 'Action Learning in Practice' 2nd Gower. Chapter one Pp1 -15. Chapter written by Reg Revans.

[19] Ibid P5.

[20] Belbin RM. 1981 ' Management of Teams: Why they succeed or fail' Heinemann.

[21] Handy. C. 1995 'The Empty Raincoat' Arrow.

[22] Course handbook for MBA students at The University of Westminster written by Martin Guedalla 1996.

[23] Blanchard K: 'The one Minute Manager... builds high performing teams' Harper Collins 1993.

[24] Clark, Neil: 'Team-building: a practical guide for trainers' McGraw Hill 1992.

[25] Yukl, G.A. 1989 'Leadership in Organisations' 2nd ed. Prentice Hall.

[26] Bass, 1990 'Bass and Stoghill's Handbook of Leadership' 3rd ed. New York Free Press.

[27] Kanter, R.M. 1982 'Dilemmas of managing participation' Organizational Dynamics 11, No 1 pp. 5-27.

[28] Adler, N.J. and Graham, JL. 1989 'Cross-cultural interaction: the international comparison fallacy'. Journal of International Business Studies, 20. Bartlett, C.A and Ghoshal S. 1995 'Transnational Management', 2nd ed. Irwin Chicago.

[29] Leech. N., Guedalla M, Hooper J, Armer M, 1997 'From home work to paid work via the KUBUS®. system: A preliminary report on Women Returners' 3rd European Feminist Research Conference University of Coimbra, Portugal 8 - 12th July.

[30] Course handbook for MBA students at The University of Westminster written by Martin Guedalla, 1996.

References

Adler, N.J. and Graham, J.L. (1989) 'Cross-cultural interaction: the international comparison fallacy'. Journal of International Business Studies, 20.

Bales, R.F. and Cohen, S.P. (1979) 'SYMLOG: a System for multiple level observation of Groups' The Free Press (Macmillan).

Bank, J. (1992) 'The Essence of Total Quality Management' Prentice Hall.

Bartlett, C.A. and Ghoshal, S. (1995) 'Transnational Management', 2nd ed. Irwin Chicago.

Bass, (1990) 'Bass and Stoghill's Handbook of Leadership' 3rd ed. New York Free Press.

Belbin, M. (1985) 'Management Teams: why they succeed or fail' Butterworth Heinemann.

Belbin, Meredith (1981) 'Team roles at work' Butterworth Heinemann.

Blanchard, K. (1993) 'The one Minute Manager... builds high performing teams' Harper Collins.

Boot, Lawrence and Morris (1994) 'Managing the unknown' McGraw Hill.

Braverman, H. (1974). 'Labour and Monopoly Capital'. Monthly Review Press.

Buzan, Tony (1993) 'The Mind-Map book' BBC books.

Chel, E. et al. (1991) 'The Entrepreneurial personality' Routledge.

Churchill, Neil (1989) 'The Entrepreneurship Paradigm(11): Chaos and Catastrophes among Quantum Jumps?' Entrepreneurship Theory and Practice 14 (Fall).

Clark, Neil (1992) 'Team-building: a practical guide for trainers' McGraw Hill.

Crainer, Stuart (1996) 'Key Management Ideas' FT Pitman.

Deakins, D. (1996) 'Entrepreneurship and Small Firms' McGraw-Hill.

Drucker, P.F. (1985) 'Innovation and Entrepreneurship'. Butterworth Hienmann.

Drucker, P.F. (1995) 'Management: tasks, responsibilities, practices', Butterworth Heinemann reprinted.

Drucker, Peter (1990) 'Managing the non-profit Organisation'. Butterworth Heinemann.

European Management Journal. (1990) 'High rates of Innovation. The Japanese Culture shock to Europe'. Pp 31-39.

Fiedler, F.E. and Garcia, J.E. (1987) 'New approaches to Leadership: Cognitive Resources and Organizational Performance' New York, Wiley.

Gibb, A. (1993) *'The Enterprise Culture and Education*' International Journal of Small Business April - June Vol. 11 No 3.

Gibb, A. (1988) *'Stimulating Entrepreneurship and new business development*' INTERMAN programme for promoting Entrepreneurship and new enterprise creation (UNDP/ILO project INT/87/029). International Labour Office, Management Training Branch. Geneva.

Handy, Charles (1977) *'Understanding Organisations*' Basic Books.

Handy, Charles (1994) *'The Empty Raincoat*', Random House, UK.

Henry and Walker (1992) *'Managing Innovation*'. Sage.

Herlau, H. and Guedalla, M. (1995) *'Systematic Entrepreneurship; investigating the third wave*'. Paper given to the 18th ISBA National Small Firms Conference in Paisly. November.

Herlau, H. and Tetzschener, H. (1994) *'The Cube Model: A Human Software*' IntEnt Conference on Internationalizing Entrepreneurship, Education and Training at Stirling University.

Herlau, H. and Tetzschener, H. (1996) *'Entrepreneurship:* **KUBUS**® *Model: Action Learning and Team-building. Some Methodological Reflections on Training.*' Department of Management, Politics and Philosophy. Copenhagen Business School.

Horz et al. (1980) *'Philosophical Problems in physical science*' published in English by Marxist Educational Press ISBN. 093065613X pp. 70 -71, 83,106-112 and 141 - 144).

Huczynski, A.A. (1996) *'Management Gurus*' Routlege.

Hutton, W. (1995) *'The State We're In*'. Jonathan Cape.

Kanter, R.M. (1982) 'Dilemmas of managing participation' Organizational Dynamics 11, No 1 pp. 5-27.

Kuhn, T.S. (1970) *'The Structure of Scientific Development*' (2nd Ed) University of Chicargo Press.

Kuratko, D. and Hodgetts, R. (1995) *'Entrepreneurship - a contemporary approach*' Drydon Press.

Leightom, R. and Felstead, R. (1992) *'Entrepreneurship in the 90s*' Pitman.

Leech, N., Guedalla, M., Hooper, J., Armer, M., (1997) *'From home work to paid work via the* **KUBUS**®. *system: A preliminary report on Women Returners*' 3rd European Feminist Research Conference University of Coimbra, Portugal 8 - 12th July. (Unpublished at this time).

McGill, I. and Beaty, L. (1995) *'Action Learning*' Kogan Page. 2nd Edition.

Pascale, R.T. and Athos, A.G. (1986) *'The Art of Japanese Management*'. Penguin.

Pedler, M. Editor. (1991) *'Action Learning in Practice'*, 2nd Edition Gower.

Peters, Tom (1994) *'Liberation Management*'. MacMillan.

Peters, Tom and Waterman, R. (1993) *'In search of Excellence*' Harper Collins.

Reeves, T. (1994) *'Managing Effectively*' Butterworth Heinmann.

Schumpeter, J. (1939) *'Business Cycles*' McGraw Hill.

Storey, D.J. (1994) *'Understanding the small business sector*'. Routledge. London.

Toffler, Alvin (1980) *'The Third Wave*', Bantam Books, USA.

Yukl, G.A. (1989) 'Leadership in Organisations' 2nd ed. Prentice Hall.

Wei Jiang (1994) *'Chinese Business Strategies*' A siapic Books (ISBN 981-3029-48-X).

Weinstein, K. (1995) *'Action Learning*' The successful Small Manager Series Harper Collins.

7 Entrepreneurship and Higher Education from Real-life Context to Pedagogical Challenge

Bertrand Duchéneaut

Introduction

Entrepreneurship is a permanent concern in most industrialized countries. Economic difficulties, the general tendency towards trade liberalization and the resultant competition all amplify the essential role of the entrepreneur. At the same time, the rise of the SME is in line with the pre-eminent role of the company chief, and it is clear that the image of the entrepreneur is more closely associated with the head of an SME than with a manager within a large company.

Public authorities and economic leaders of the industrialized nations insist on the importance of promoting the entrepreneurial spirit in young people in order to encourage the setting up of businesses. This often leads to a questioning of the role of the education system and the assertion that teaching methods are insufficiently developed or even non-existent, due to lack of motivation. The present study will attempt to contribute to the debate, firstly by reviewing some of the contextual elements without which the issues facing teachers cannot be grasped, then secondly by tackling the specific theme of pedagogy.

The Context of Entrepreneurship

Creating a business is a complex process involving different elements, in particular the different factors, which constitute the profile of the entrepreneur.

In their review of a number of studies, Yvon Gasse et al. present an abridged model of the entrepreneurial process leading to the setting up of a new business:

Table 1

Antecedents	Pre-dispositions	Behavior	Triggers
Family	Motivations	Emotional	Negative
Extra-curricular	Attitudes	Cognitive	Positive
Professional	Aptitudes	Action	
Environmental	Interests		

From Yvon Gasse et al (1985)

Drawing a parallel with Fayolle's (1994) analysis, simply put it can be said that the entrepreneurial process involves two types of context. The first is the sociocultural environment of the future business creator, the second is his/her specific personal motivations. These combine to lead one day to the decision to create a business, as in the following diagram:

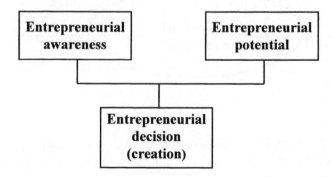

Figure 1

This diagram illustrates the structure of the first part of this study.

129

Entrepreneurial Awareness

Entrepreneurial awareness refers to the birth of an 'entrepreneurial spirit' in an individual that may one day lead them to decide to create a business. In this respect researchers and experts are divided into two camps (Berger, 1991): on the one hand, there are the economists, who tend to see entrepreneurship as a variable dependent on economic factors, little affected by culture; on the other hand, researchers from other disciplines see it as a variable inseparable from culture, produced by and producing the latter.

While its economic context cannot be ignored, the analysis of entrepreneurial awareness must necessarily take important psychosocial and cultural dimensions into account. Drawing an analogy with computer programming, Geert Hofstede (1991) refers to 'mental programming' of individuals. This programming is akin to what is often included in the notoriously difficult-to-define term 'culture'. To simplify, most studies in this field distinguish three major areas: models, national socioculture and the educational system.

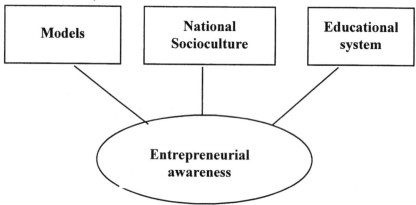

Figure 2

The theory of models belongs to the 'social apprenticeship' school of thought, the context of which has been defined by Bandura (1997). In this analysis, apprenticeship and motivation arise from the observation of the behavior of others considered as models. This pattern is abundantly illustrated in the family model.

In France, for example, Paul Rasse and Denis Parisot (1989, 1992) have shown that 66 per cent of company creators have at least one non-salaried near relative (from their own, their parents' or their children's generation). These observations were confirmed in 1994 by Jacques Bonneau and Dominique Francoz, who found that most of such creators are close to another person who also runs their own business; often a family member (41 per cent of cases), a friend (21 per cent) or both (10 per cent) (Bonneau and Francoz, 1996). In Great Britain, studies on this theme have reached identical conclusions: the family is an essential element of the 'model' which inspires creators (Curran and Burrows, (1988); Hakim (1988)). To take this further, a recent study indicates that 'close friends' have an even more determining influence (Stanworth et al, 1989); the authors conclude that the social context is pre-eminent in forming the psychological model. The same observation has been made in the United States, where Shapero has indicated that starting a new business requires an 'imaginable act', where the potential entrepreneur can refer to a model who has already made the attempt. The model is usually a parent, most often the father (Shapero, 1975). Studies carried out by Frederick T. Waddel, Charles H. Matthews and Steven B. Moser confirm that company owners, be they male or female, have been very strongly influenced by the parental model. (Waddell (1983); Matthews and Moser, 1996).

Since time spent with one or several company chiefs during childhood is a strong motivating factor, one of the challenges for societies wishing to develop entrepreneurship is certainly to be able to offer models to young people other than their parents, in order to progress beyond simple family development. Getting young people into contact with SME managers is clearly a first necessity. Training institutes have a role to play here, by facilitating closer contact between the world of education and company directors.

National socioculture has many components, one of which is fundamental to the promotion of entrepreneurship. It can be summarized as the positioning of initiative: is it individual or collective? At the risk of oversimplification, it can be ventured that in countries with a strong State and strong institutions, where initiative is situated 'at the top' and the individual becomes a seeker of protection, entrepreneurial awareness is lowest. Conversely, in countries where initiative is in the hands of the individual, given a State and institutions which simply determine the rules of the game and act as a referee, entrepreneurial awareness is highest.

Moreover, entrepreneurial awareness is highest in societies with a 'masculine' culture as defined in Geert Hofstede's study (1991).

The teaching system takes as a cultural reference the preparation for salaried employment. In this context, educational methods are essentially adapted to preparing future workers for all levels of companies or administrations, but not entrepreneurs. In fact, the educational system can play a prime role in promoting the two essentialcomponents of entrepreneurship: initiative/taking responsibility and risk-taking. Allan A. Gibb (1992) reveals two extreme pedagogical models: one 'didactic', the other 'entrepreneurial'.

Table 2: Teaching Methods: Characteristics of 'didactic' and 'entrepreneurial' Models

Teaching methods	
Didactic model	**Enterprising model**
Learning from teacher alone	Learning from each other
Passive role as listener	Learning by doing
Learning from written texts	Learning from personal exchange and debate
Learning from 'expert' frameworks of teacher	Learning by discovering (under guidance)
Learning from feedback from one key person (the teacher)	Learning from reactions of many people
Learning in well organised, timetabled environment	Learning in flexible, informal environment
Learning without pressure of immediate goals	Learning under pressure to achieve goals
Copying from others discouraged	Learning by borrowing from others
Mistakes feared	Mistakes learned from
Learning by notes	Learning by problem solving

Allan A. Gibb, 'The enterprise culture and education'
International Small Business Journal, 11,3, 1992, p. 24

The didactic model is widely used in most countries. The entrepreneurial model does not exist anywhere in a pure form, but its components are more or less present in different countries.

As a summary of this first stage, a kind of scale of an individual's entrepreneurial awareness can be represented as follows:

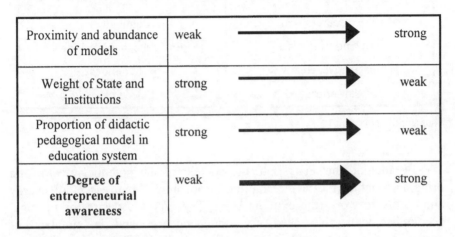

Proximity and abundance of models	weak ⟶ strong
Weight of State and institutions	strong ⟶ weak
Proportion of didactic pedagogical model in education system	strong ⟶ weak
Degree of entrepreneurial awareness	weak ⟶ strong

Figure 3: A Scale of Entrepreneurial Awareness

Entrepreneurial Potential

Each individual has a number of personal attributes which make up a specific profile. For entrepreneurship, various essential elements have been distinguished in entrepreneurs. Referring to the studies of Timmons (1978), Hornaday (1982), Brockhaus and Horwitz (1986), Hisrich (1986), Louis-Jacques Filion produces the following summary (Filion, 1994):

Table 3: Characteristics Most Often Attributed to Entrepreneurs

Tenacious	Detect opportunities
Able to handle ambiguity and uncertainty	Concrete, practical , realistic
Use resources well	Committed
Take moderate risks	Energetic, hardworking
Imaginative, creative	Self-confident
Result-orientated	Independent

Source: Filion (1994)

Broadening the analysis to the context of the potential creator and bringing together the themes outlined, four areas seem essential: energy and ability to work (the extreme being Type A), the desire for personal accomplishment, the need for independence and a number of characteristics which can be summarized as 'the taste for enterprise'. These elements are to a large extent transnational, as shown by the study done by Roger A. Blais and Jean-Marie Toulouse using 2278 company creators in fourteen countries (1991).

Table 4: Entrepreneurial Potential

Energy/ Capacity to work/ Type A	Desire for personal accomplishment/ Need for social recognition	Need for independence/ Power	Taste for enterprise

Energy and a large capacity for work are regularly quoted as fundamental attributes for potential creators. In the extreme they lead to the Type A Behavior Pattern, defined by Meyer Friedman and Ray H. Rosenman (1974) as a set of actions and emotions found in people who constantly and aggressively conduct a personal battle to achieve more and more things in less and less time. For Thomas M. Begley and David P. Boyd, the TABP is that of an extreme response to challenge. Its visible signs are impatience, instability, urgency, ambition, feverish activity and permanent competition (Begley and Boyd, 1987). Studies carried out by these authors in the United States show that founders of businesses have a Type A score which is markedly higher than for the rest of the population. The image often used to describe such active people is that of the 'workaholic' (Flamholtz, 1990).

The desire for personal accomplishment has been a blue-chip stock in enterprise culture since the studies of McClelland (1951, 1953, 1969). Tests allow the degree of need for personal accomplishment to be defined in individuals of all origins. Their application leads to strong conclusions as to the relevance of the model (Palmer, 1987). Studies carried out in the United States show that the need for personal accomplishment is not strong in the general population, since only 5 per cent of Americans feel this as a very strong need. However, such motivation is very strong in most successful entrepreneurs (Hellriegel and Slocum, 1992). The desire for personal accomplishment can be analyzed in relation to the image the future company chief wishes to give himself, as well as in relation to the social recognition being an entrepreneur brings him in his environment.

The very strong motivation generally expressed by creators is 'to be my own boss'. Most studies carried out on creation of businesses confirm that the desire not to depend on anyone is a powerful factor in setting up one's own business. This desire is not unconnected with a certain taste for power, even if business leaders themselves rarely make a show of this (Jacob-Duvernet, 1994).

The 'taste for enterprise' is made up of many criteria, including leadership, the power to control and risk-taking. It is mainly a product of entrepreneurial awareness. If leadership appears as more important in the post-creation phase, when the entrepreneur has to lead a group of workers, it is also important in the pre-creation phase inasmuch as it encourages confidence in those who are in contact with the potential creator.

The power of internal control relates to the individual's perception of his control of his environment. Simply put, a strong power of internal control leads its possessor to believe he can influence his environment, while a weak power of internal control, corresponding to a strong external power, will result in his being guided and formed by this environment (Brokhaus and Horwitz, 1986; Mitton, 1989). Yvon Gasse and Camille Carrier write that 'For the typical entrepreneur, the events of day-to-day life are mostly determined and highly conditioned by the action of individuals themselves' (Gasse and Carrier, 1992, p. 12). The power of internal control is also linked to the recent notion of pro-activeness, which has been the target of many studies, particularly in the United States (Bateman and Grant, 1993). The pro-active type person is less limited by situations and the pressure of the environment. A pro-active people identify opportunities; they show initiative, act, and persevere until they achieve the expected changes.

The ability to take risks is certainly a personality trait which strongly determines the career of entrepreneurs. While it is true that entrepreneurs are risk-takers, they are above all risk-calculators. An entrepreneur will decide to take the plunge consciously, knowing the estimated possibility of failure. Strictly in terms of company creation, four types of risk can be distinguished: the financial risk arising from the fact that the creators invest their own funds and those of their creditors; the career risk, which can result in entrepreneurs who fail having difficulty finding a job; the family risk, due to the fact that a wife and children may suffer from the psychological distance and stress involved in creation; and finally the psychic risk taken by the entrepreneur who may identify himself totally with his business and consider a failure as his own (Longenecker and Moore, 1991).

Entrepreneurship and Higher Education

In the phenomenon of creation and development of companies, the 'dosage' of technical skills/motivational and behavioral aspects is progressively inverted as illustrated in the following diagram:

136

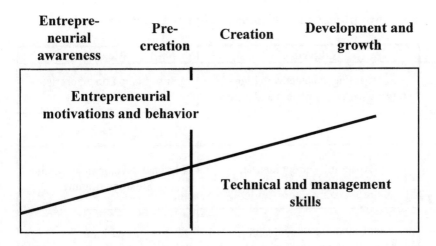

Figure 4: Progression of Motivations and Behavior/Technical Skills through Phases Surrounding Company Creation

It is widely recognized that behavioral skills are mainly acquired during childhood and that they develop relatively little thereafter. While motivations for creation may develop (at least they can 'mature'), entrepreneurial awareness as discussed previously is fundamentally rooted in the life period preceding entry into higher education. What can a university education in entrepreneurship hope to add?

Two main objectives may be retained: i) detect students with a high degree of entrepreneurial awareness and potential and ii) give training which reveals these characteristics, consolidates them and completes them through the acquisition of technical skills which reinforce the chances of successful creation and, subsequently, the successful development of businesses.

Table 5: Entrepreneurial Training in Higher Education

	Objective	Means
1	Detecting students with high entrepreneurial awareness and potential	Information on enterprise culture
		Tests
2	Expanding entrepreneurial potential	Personal development training Situation training
	Communicating on skills	Teaching

Objective 1 may be achieved by offering short entrepreneurship awareness courses in which students are informed about the context of creation, hear entrepreneurs tell their story, and become aware of their own potentialities. In this respect the use of tests should, it seems, be encouraged.

Objective 2 requires in-depth work, mainly through partially or totally integrated courses. The objective of totally integrated courses is the creation of companies in the short term, at the end of the course. Partially integrated courses aim rather to enable a future opportunity to be grasped effectively. In this case creation of a business is one of a number of professional possibilities that may be envisaged by the student.

Detecting Candidates

There has been an ongoing debate for many yeas in business schools between those in favor of presenting modules of entrepreneurship as mandatory course requirements and those who prefer to create a special track reserved for selected highly motivated students. In a study by Sandra Honig-Haftel (1995), 700 Deans of universities were questioned on this theme (35 per cent response rate). While many universities offer some entrepreneurship classes, they were rather reluctant to develop or systematize them, for three reasons: firstly, lack of resources in teachers in this area; secondly, (in the case of American universities) the entrepreneurship classes are not required by the AACSB; thirdly, the demand for entrepreneurship classes is great enough that there seems no need to make them mandatory.

What can mandatory teaching on entrepreneurship give to students enrolled in a university management course? As we have just seen, the acquisition of specific entrepreneurship skills must, at the risk of being useless, be supported by the entrepreneurial potential of the students concerned. 'He who does more can do less'. Therefore making such a module mandatory would make it possible to include those students not yet aware of their potential. Mandatory classes would be a means of revelation for the student, thereby accomplishing the goal of detection of potential creators. However this (expensive) option can be achieved at lower cost by tests.

On the other hand, in the case of optional courses, it must be noted that the sole fact of a student signing up is already proof of motivation and thus an informal element of selection/detection.

The success of entrepreneurial courses in the United States is a perfect illustration of the fact that in some form or other a formal or informal selection is made on entry. The study by Nancy B. Upton, Donald L. Sexton and Carlos Moore (1995), shows that amongst 150 entrepreneur 'major' graduates of BBA level between 1991 and 1994, 40 per cent have set up their own business, 30 per cent have joined the family company, and 30 per cent are working in a large company. While the proportion joining family businesses is high, it is remarkable that 70 per cent of graduates from such programs are placed in entrepreneurial situations or contexts. These figures are quite impressive, and are much higher than those recorded in France, for example, where 'majors' or entrepreneurship courses lead to a relatively small rate of business creation (an article in the review Le Moci estimates that between 1 and 2 per cent of ESC Business School 'entrepreneur' course graduates immediately set up their own business-Le Moci, 1997). In this context, the reassurance offered is that the entrepreneurial outlook of these graduates will lead to business creation in the long term, and business creation immediately following the course is not considered a prime objective.

If it is assumed that pre-entry tests can be a determining measure of 'yield' of entrepreneurial courses, it would be interesting to gather data on methods used by the relevant institutions. Tools are available to measure the need for personal accomplishment, pro-activeness, and an individual's psychological profile. Are they used and if so, how? One very interesting example of defining an individual's entrepreneurial potential has been developed by the GRPME (ICE, Inventory of Characteristics of Entrepreneurs) (Gasse et al., 1995). Is there any other experimental work being done?

Entrepreneurial Training

In his summary of the relevant literature, Jean-Pierre Béchard (1994) shows that researchers are divided between those who think that entrepreneurship can give rise to formal teaching (by giving the initiative to teachers or asking the advice of successful entrepreneurs, or even by asking students), and those who emphasize learning by experiment and doing. For example Johannisson (1991), presents a taxonomic approach to entrepreneurship skills in the following model:

Table 6

Level of learning	Individual skills
'Know-why' ⇘ attitudes, values, motivations	Self-confidence Motivation to achieve Perseverance, risk acceptance
'Know-how' ⇘ skills	Technical skills
'Know-who' ⇘ social skills	Ability to develop networks
'Know-what' ⇘ knowledge	Encyclopedism Institutional facts

Extract from B. Johannisson (1991)-Presented by J-P. Béchard (1994)

As Jean-Pierre Béchard indicates, '...this figure clearly illustrates that the traditional approach to the teaching of entrepreneurship (know-what) has little impact on the development of entrepreneurial skills. Programmes of entrepreneurial development should emphasize skills linked to vision and concrete action...' (Béchard, 1994, p. 17). This leads us to conclude that 'two-pronged' courses should be promoted: behavioral and development of entrepreneurial potential on the one hand, acquisition of knowledge on the other hand.

Development of Entrepreneurial Potential

Whether in the case of totally or partially integrated courses, training can definitely develop the entrepreneurial potential of the student, by taking two complementary axes: personal development and learning by doing. Personal development consists in promoting all interactive training which enables the student to progress in his skills in terms of self-awareness, awareness of others, or stress limitation. Learning by doing is an experience-acquisition accelerator, an opportunity for the student to be confronted with reality whilst allowing for the possibility of failure without major and definitive consequences. Two fundamental elements should be taken into account: projects and tutorials.

In general, students must be given the opportunity to carry out concrete projects from start to finish, wherever possible starting with a student's idea, in any field: economic, cultural, the humanities... The main thing is to have to convince 'suppliers', 'clients', and 'sponsors/financers'. In this context, organizing a drama festival, a sporting event or sending medicine by container to a country in need, all provide the same challenges and lead to the same acquisition of experience: ability to take initiative and to undertake an enterprise is required.

The pedagogical process inherent in this type of activity requires assistance in the form of regular debriefing, comparison between objectives and achievements, and finally intellectual capitalization from the experience. Can this tutorial assistance be achieved by a teacher? This is not easy to answer, because there are two dimensions to the question. Firstly, motivation: if the teacher prefers to give classes, or take on other activities such as research, and if he himself does not have the experience or even a taste for entrepreneurship, it seems clear that tutorials will be confined to a sort of 'gentleman's agreement', a development which is to be avoided. Tutoring in the pedagogy of experience can only be carried out by teachers motivated for this type of approach.

What is the state of higher education establishments with respect to the development of the entrepreneurial potential of their students? Are there forms of 'doing' pedagogy and tutorials other than those just described? It would be particularly interesting here too to compare experiences, methodologies and results.

Imparting Knowledge

Over and above the behavioral elements just cited, the future entrepreneur should - ideally - have a basic knowledge of management skills, as well as being able to handle the environment and techniques linked to the sector and the product or service offered by the business. Since higher education establishments which dispense basic training are dealing, 'ex ante', with potential creators whose project is rarely defined as yet, it is logical that the 'trade' of the future business is hardly taken into account, and learning in this field is passed on to prior, parallel, or later courses (different issues are raised in the case of post-experience courses).

To consider just initial education, the need to provide students with basic management skills leads schools to offer programs the 'density' of which varies between business schools and other institutions, in particular for technical graduates. For the former, the idea should be to develop areas which have not been studied in depth and which are specifically geared to business creation (business plan, social, fiscal, legal frameworks...), whereas in the latter case, before coming to this kind of content, it is necessary to offer the sort of basic classes which are similar to those found in the catalogues of all business schools.

This difference in approach may raise the question of both any overlap or omission which exist in the case of end-of-study or integrated postgraduate entrepreneurial courses offered to students from a variety of disciplines (management and engineers for example).

Finally, here again, even if the issue is imparting knowledge, more than any other the entrepreneurial model requires an interactive pedagogy, leaving the initiative to the student. Group work, problem-solving, case studies, documentary research and methodology are certainly fundamental

142

ingredients in a personalized pedagogy of assuming responsibility and taking action, leading again to the need for individual tutorship. What approaches are taken by the relevant establishments?

In general it can clearly be seen that the types of pedagogy suited to the entrepreneurial context necessitate far-reaching development of the traditional role of the teacher. However it does seem that entrepreneurial courses are simply the catalysts for a phenomenon which will affect teachers across all faculties. As Gérard Verna points out, in his summary of a joint study of the future by a group of teachers, the 21st century teacher 'will no longer be a lone individual advancing knowledge (researcher), nor a lone individual imparting it (communicator), nor even the organizer of all this (executive director); instead, no matter what the future holds, he will keep his role as a source of motivation and as a facilitator of exchange' (Verna, 1994, p. 3). With respect to entrepreneurial syllabuses, the specific profile of students leads here more than elsewhere to certain types of approach by the teacher, and this must be taken into account. The fact that these students should in theory be more independent-minded, self-confident and have more power of internal control should naturally be taken into account (Sexton and Bowman Upton, 1987). Gardner and Vesper (1994) have highlighted some recent experiments: concentration on 'basics', inviting people from business to give lectures, giving tutorials and using case studies. Successes and failures have been reported. Can an optimum pedagogy be defined based on these conclusions?

Conclusion

The development in an individual of an entrepreneurial perspective is not just the prerogative of the higher education system. Rather it should be considered as being the final phase of a process of awareness and training, in which the sociocultural dimension is pre-eminent.

The degree of a nation's enterprise culture, the types of model known in childhood and the pedagogical methods encountered are strong influences on 'entrepreneurial awareness'. The desire to create a business is certainly not very conscious until a business opportunity appears, or sooner while following a program of higher education, but the characteristics of the environment up to that time will have already highlighted two essential qualities: initiative and risk-taking.

These two components of the entrepreneurial spirit appear to be sine qua non conditions for the creation of a business. In addition a specific potential is required, of which the main elements are energy and a capacity for work, the desire for personal accomplishment and the desire for independence or even to exercise power over others rather than be subjected to someone else's power. Finally, the taste for enterprise, a synthesis of leadership, power of control and risk-taking ability, is the sum of an individual's potential at the junction between intrinsic personal attributes and entrepreneurial awareness, which is conditioned principally by the environment.

Anyone interested in entrepreneurship in higher education will inevitably recognize that the decisive moments are mostly in the past, and that each student does not have the same potential. Therefore it is probably not useful, for most programs, to provide mandatory in-depth teaching on entrepreneurship which has little chance of attracting a response on the part of the majority - unless, that is, such classes are considered as a means of spotting the most highly motivated students. Nevertheless, in order to have the greatest impact, the potential entrepreneur must be detected somehow or other. This may be achieved through awareness modules and/or the use of tests including elements of behavioral and psychological profiling which are the determining factors in company creation. An international comparison of experiences in this field would be welcome.

Beyond this, courses specializing in entrepreneurship should structure their contents around two major axes: behavioral and experience acquisition on the one hand, importation of knowledge on the other hand. In our view, the first dimension is the most important; in this case, students must be given the opportunity to experience in the real world the implementation of projects for which they themselves are responsible, with the benefit of a tutorial accompaniment. The role of the latter is both fundamental and ambiguous, characterizing a major shift in the traditional profession of teaching. How are establishments offering entrepreneurial courses responding to these issues?

Finally, while this paper has considered the role that higher education can play in entrepreneurship, it should also be remembered that given that most awareness regarding business creation is imparted in primary and secondary education, the implementation of appropriate teaching methods is a vital challenge for primary and secondary educational structures that wish to participate in the development of the entrepreneurial potentialities of their society. A better knowledge of the realizations and experiments carried out so far would enable thinking and action to progress.

References

Anyansi-Archibong Chi. R. (1994) '*Enhancing entrepreneurship and small business education through case development and application*' - 39th ICSB World Conference, Strasbourg, p. 16 - 16.

Bateman Thomas S. and J. Michael Grant (1993) '*The proactive component of organizational behavior*' - Journal of Organizational Behavior, 14(2), p. 103 - 118.

Béchard Jean-Pierre (Novembre 1994) '*Les grandes questions de recherche en entrepreneurship et éducation*'- Université de Laval, Québec - Cahiers de Recherche n° 94 - 11 - 02, 43 pages.

Begley Thomas M. and David P. Boyd (Winter 1987) '*Psychological characteristics associated with performance in entrepreneurial firms and smaller business*' - Journal of Business Venturing, vol. 2, n° 1, p. 73 - 93.

Berger Brigitte (1991) '*The culture of entrepreneurship*' - San Francisco, ICS Press.

Bowman Upton Nancy, Donald L. Sexton, Carlos Moore, '*Have we made a difference? An examination of career activity of entrepreneurship majors since 1981*' - Baylor University, Waco - Résumé dans 'Frontiers of Entrepreneurship Research 1995', William D. BYGRAVE and al., Babson College.

Brockhaus R. H. and P. S. Horwitz (1986) '*The psychology of the entrepreneur*' in '*The art and science of entrepreneurship*', D. L. SEXTON and R. W. SMILOR (Eds) - Cambridge, Mass., Bellinger.

Fayolle Alain (Juin 1994) '*De l'ingénieur à l'entrepreneur : une contribution essentielle et un parcours sous influences multiples*' - Actes de la 39e Conférence mondiale de l'ICSB, Strasbourg, p. 95 - 106.

Filion Louis-Jacques (Octobre 1993) '*Le développement d'activités de formation en entrepreneuriat : une approche intégrée*' - Cahier de Recherche n° 94 - 02 - 01, HEC Montréal, Février 1994 - 10e colloque annuel du CCPME, Moncton, NB, 28 - 30.

Flamholtz Eric (1990) '*Growing pains*' - San Francisco, Jossey - Bass inc. Publishers.

Friedman Meyer and Ray H. Rosenman (1974) '*Type A behaviour and your heart*' - Knopf.

Garavan Thomas N. and Barra O'Cinneide (1994) '*Entrepreneurship education and training programmes : a review and evaluation*' - Part 1, Journal of European Industrial Training, vol. 18, n° 8, 1994, p. 3 - 12 - Part 2, Journal of European Industrial Training, vol. 18, n° 11, p. 13 - 21.

Gardner William B. and Karl H. Vesper (1994) '*Experiments in entrepreneurship education: successes and failures*' - Journal of Small Business Venturing, 9, p. 179 - 187.

Gasse Yvon et Camille Carrier (1992) '*Gérer la croissance de sa PME*'- Montréal, Les Editions de l'Entrepreneur.

Gasse Yvon, Jean - Jacques Bernier, Nathalie Daigle, Aline d'Amours (Octobre 1995) '*L'inventaire du potentiel entrepreneurial : validation empirique d'un modèle d'appréciation du profil entrepreneurial*' - GRPME, Université de Laval, Québec - Document de travail n° 95 - 51 - 12e conférence annuelle CCSBE, 25 - 27, Thunder Bay, 13 pages.

Gibb Allan (1992) '*The enterprise culture and education*' - International Small Business Journal, 11, 3.

Hellriegel Don and John W. Slocum (1992) '*Management*' - Addison Weshley Publishing Company Inc., - 6th edition.

Hisrich R. D. (1986) '*The woman entrepreneur: characteristics, skills, problems and prescriptions for success*' in '*The art and science of entrepreneurship*' - D. L. SEXTON and R. W. SMILOR (Eds) - Cambridge, Mass., Bellinger, p. 61 - 81.

Hofstede Geert (1991) '*Cultures and organizations - Software of the mind*' - Mac Graw Hill.

Honig - Haftel Sandra (1995) '*Entrepreneurship at the core: toward advocating entrepreneurship as a requirement*' - Center of Entrepreneurship, Wichita State University, Wichita - Résumé dans 'Frontiers of entrepreneurship Research '.

Hornaday J. A. (1982) '*Research about living entrepreneurs*' in '*Encyclopedia of Entrepreneurship*' - KENT et al. (Eds), Englewood Cliffs, N. J. Prentice Hall, p. 20 - 34.

Jacob - Duvernet Luc (1994) '*Le miroir des princes - Essai sur la culture stratégique des élites qui nous gouvernent*'- Editions du Seuil.

Le MOCI (Valérie Collet) (15 Mai 1997) '*A l'école de la création d'entreprise*' - n° 1285, p. 89 - 90.

Longenecker Justin G. and Carlos W. Moore (1991), '*Small business management: an entre - preneurial emphasis*' - South Western Publishing Co.

McClelland David, '*The achievement motive*' - Appleton Century Crofts, 1953. '*Personality*' - New York, Dryden Press, 1951.

Mitton D. G. (Spring 1989), '*The complete entrepreneur*' - Entrepreneurship Theory and Practice, vol. 13, n° 3.

Palmer Michael (1987) '*The application of psychological testing to entrepreneurial potential*' in '*Entrepreneurship and venture management*' - Clifford M. BAUMBACK and Joseph R. MANCUSO - Prentice Hall, second edition.

Rasse Paul et Denis Parisot (Novembre 1989) '*Faire le pas - Recherche sur les créateurs d'entreprises*' - Concept SHSA - Commissariat Général du Plan.

Sexton D. L. and Nancy Bowman Upton (January 1987) '*Evaluation of an innovative approach to teaching entrepreneurship*' - Journal of Small Business Management, p. 35-43.

Timmons J. A., '*Characteristics and role demands of entrepreneurship*' - American Journal of Small Business, 3 - 1, p. 5 - 17.

Verna Gérard (Novembre 1994) '*Le rôle des professeurs d'université au siècle prochain*' - Travail collectif réalisé sous la direction de Gérard VERNA - Document spécial 94 - 118, Université de Laval, Québec, 9 pages.

Vesper Karl H. (1985) '*Entrepreneurship education*' - Wellesley, MA, Babson College.

8 An Empirical Approach to Entrepreneurial-learning Styles

Thomas A. Ulrich

Abstract

Research concerned with the psychological characteristics of entrepreneurs and Kolb's research on the learning style is reviewed, towards linking individual learning styles with entrepreneurial abilities. A 'preferred' learning style for entrepreneurs is proposed and empirically tested. Suggestions are presented for improving programs concerned with the training and development of potential entrepreneurs.

Introduction

The importance of entrepreneurial education is derived from the importance of the entrepreneur to our economic system. Cole (1959) writes that economic systems set the stage for their own survival to the extent that they provide both an opportunity for entrepreneurs to exist and an opportunity for those entrepreneurial individuals to respond to the needs of society. Since formal education is an important asset in the entrepreneurial process (Hornaday and Aboud, 1971; Cooper, 1975; Mancuso, 1975; Douglas, 1976), it is vital that our educational systems provide an educational environment that is conducive for that purpose. Responding to this challenge, colleges and universities have been leaders in developing and working with entrepreneurs through the establishment of courses and programs in entrepreneurship and small business. Zeithmal and Rice

147

(1987) found that 92 per cent of the colleges and universities surveyed engaged in some type of entrepreneurship program. In general, it may be stated that society has a vested interest in providing for the development, nurturing, and growth of entrepreneurial individuals, encouraging such individuals to stay the course. However, the question remains whether the educational programs in place are as efficient and effective as they can be?

The purpose of this paper is to review the research concerned with the psychological characteristics of entrepreneurs and Kolb's research on the learning style with the objective of linking individual learning styles with entrepreneurial abilities. The overall goal is to establish a 'preferred' learning style for entrepreneurs which can be used to guide those involved in training and developing entrepreneurs. The first part of the paper focuses on the psychological and organizational behavior literature which provides a framework for understanding entrepreneurial behavior. Specific reference is made to research which examines characteristics of: a need for achievement; the locus of control; risk-taking, of itself; and a tolerance of ambiguity. Recognizing the growth of academic programs concerned with entrepreneurship, research concerned with learning style theory is presented next. The third section links the entrepreneurial characteristics with aspects of learning styles to develop a 'preferred' learning style for the entrepreneur. This is followed by an empirical testing of the 'preferred' learning style. Finally, based on the result of the analyses suggestions for improving the education of potential entrepreneurs are presented.

Behavioral Characteristics

A substantial body of literature exists which indicates that entrepreneurs exhibit certain personality traits, more so than others. The research has led to the belief that entrepreneurs share common personality traits which partially account for entrepreneurial behavior. From the literature, four primary, distinguishing, characteristics are identified.

Need for achievement

Entrepreneurs have been characterized as individuals with a high need for achievement (McClelland 1961, 1965; McClelland and Winter 1969). Such individuals demonstrate a desire for setting goals, achieving those goals through their own efforts, solving problems, and receiving feedback on how well they accomplished their tasks. McClelland concluded that the characteristic of a high need for achievement was an important factor in an individual becoming an entrepreneur. McClelland's conclusions have been confirmed in numerous subsequent studies (Schrage 1965; Roberts 1968; Warner and Rubin 1969; Hornaday and Bunker 1970; Hornaday and Aboud 1971; Komives 1972; Lachman 1980; and Vesper 1980).

Locus of control

Another attribute which is associated with entrepreneurs is internal locus of control. An individual's belief about one's locus of control reveals that person's perception about the origin of forces which control one's actions. An internal locus of control is associated with the belief that, within limits, an individual can determine one's own fate. An external locus of control is associated with the belief that outside forces determine the fate of an individual.

A close relationship between a high need for achievement and an internal locus of control is reported in the work of Rotter and Mulry (1965). Subsequent research with entrepreneurs found them to have both a high need for achievement and an internal locus of control (Borland 1975; Pandey and Tewary 1979). Moreover, a study of successful entrepreneurs found them to have a high internal locus of control (Hornaday and Aboud 1971). In addition, it has been demonstrated that individuals with entrepreneurial intentions have an internal locus of control (Borland 1975; Brockhaus 1975; and Rupkey 1978).

Risk-taking

The willingness to take risks is noted in one of the earliest works concerned with the entrepreneur (Mill 1848). In Atkinson's (1957) model of risk taking, it is theorized that persons with a high need to achieve also prefer intermediate levels of risk. The hypothesis is that entrepreneurs prefer intermediate levels of risk is supported in the work of Meyer, Walker, and Litwin (1961). Notably, they found that those who were in jobs with definite entrepreneurial aspects showed a greater preference for intermediate levels of risk than did others.

While popular thought, with some research backing, might associate a tendency toward risk-taking with entrepreneurial actions, such may not necessarily be a characteristic which is found only in entrepreneurs. While Brockhaus (1980) reports that entrepreneurs prefer an intermediate level of risk, it must be noted that he also found such a preference to exist in a comparative group of managers, as well as in the general public.

Tolerance of ambiguity

The importance of innovation, for entrepreneurship, with its attendant need for tolerance of ambiguity is emphasized in the work of Schumpeter (1954). He did not place an emphasis on the risk-taking factor, because he believed that both managers and entrepreneurs must deal with risk. Palmer (1971) noted that since an entrepreneur must make decisions under uncertainty, a distinguishing characteristic, and an appropriate measure for entrepreneurial potential, would be the willingness to deal with uncertainty. Subsequently Schere (1982) posited that the uncertainty bearing role of the entrepreneur may be viewed as an ambiguity bearing role, and that tolerance of ambiguity is a distinguishing psychological trait. One which underlies the ability to fulfill the entrepreneurial role of uncertainty bearing. Using Budner's (1962) Tolerance/Intolerance of Ambiguity Scale, Schere found entrepreneurs to have a higher tolerance for ambiguity than did non-entrepreneurs.

Seeking additional insight into the difference between entrepreneurs and managers, with reference to a tolerance of ambiguity, Schere examined the basic dimensions of Budner' scale. The largest difference between the entrepreneurial group and the managerial group was on the dimension of 'novelty', with entrepreneurs having a greater tolerance of novelty. Such a finding tends to support the level of importance which Schumpeter (1954) placed on innovation as a defining characteristic of an entrepreneur. Clearly, the ability to deal successfully with novelty, or situations of change, provides the entrepreneur with an additional psychological impetus to innovate. Regarding those who express an intention to become entrepreneurs, Sexton and Bowman (1984a, 1984b) found entrepreneurial students to be significantly more tolerant of ambiguity than were other students. Again, a high tolerance of ambiguity appears to be a distinguishing psychological characteristic, both for the entrepreneur and for those who wish to be entrepreneurs.

Other characteristics

There are other psychological traits which have been found to be characteristic of entrepreneurs. In most instances, the other traits tend to be related to and supportive of the traits which have already been specifically noted. The other traits include: a high need for autonomy (Collins et al. 1964; Hornaday and Bunker 1970); dominance (Sexton and Bowman 1983); endurance (Mescon and Montanari 1981); and independence (DeCarlo and Lyons 1979; Hornaday and Aboud 1971). Additionally, entrepreneurs tend to have a low need for either conformity (Komives 1972; Sexton and Bowman 1983) or support (Litzinger 1965; Hornaday and Aboud 1971).

Learning Style Theory

An individual's learning style describes the way in which one acquires and uses information in developing an understanding of and in solving problems. Given the basic entrepreneurial traits presented thus far, it is worthwhile to examine Kolb's (1978) research concerned with learning style.

Kolb's learning model

Psychologists have identified two primary dimensions of cognitive growth and learning (Harvey, Hunt, and Schroeder 1961; Flavell 1963). The first dimension ranges from concrete experience (CE) to abstract conceptualization (AC); the second dimension ranges from active experimentation (AE) to reflective observation (RO); Kolb (1978) incorporated the two bipolar dimensions into a learning style model.

An understanding of the learning process may be gained by examining Kolb's learning model, as presented in Figure 1. Conceptually. Kolb's learning model is a four-stage cycle. Stage I begins with a concrete experience, which is the basis for observation and reflection in Stage II. In Stage III, the observations are resolved into a generalized theory. Stage IV draws hypotheses or implications from the generalized theory of Stage III to serve as a guide for the development of new experiences. All learning moves through the four stages, and all four abilities are required in

151

learning. But, the abilities are polar opposites in this two-dimensional model. Therefore, one must continually decide which learning abilities to apply in a given learning situation.

As one grows and develops, one must resolve the conflicts between being active or reflective, and between being concrete or analytical. Through socialization, past experiences, and demands of the current environment, the conflicts are resolved. In time, the individual develops a learning style preference.

Kolb's learning styles

As shown in Figure 1, four distinct learning styles are possible. On the basis of extensive research, Kolb (1978) is able to characterize each of the four learning styles. A converger's greatest strength is in the practical application of ideas. Through hypothetical-deductive reasoning, the converger focuses knowledge on specific problems. Convergers tend to be good at solving problems and at applying ideas. The exact opposite of the converger is the diverger. The diverger's greatest strength is in the use of imagination. The diverger has the ability to view concrete situations from many different perspectives. As a result, the diverger is good at generating ideas and at recognizing problems.

The assimilator is best at inductive reasoning and in assimilating disparate observations into an integrated explanation. The assimilator's greatest strength is in the ability to construct theoretical models. The exact opposite of the assimilator is the accommodator. The accommodator is best in those situations where one must adapt to specific immediate circumstances. The accommodator is good at implementing plans, engaging in new experience, and at risk-taking. The accommodator is more of a risk-taker, than are individuals with the other three learning styles.

Techniques of education

A person's learning style preference affects the degree to which various pedagogical techniques facilitate learning (Kolb 1978). An 'abstract conceptualization' person learns best from theoretical readings, case studies, and solitary thinking, while finding exercises, simulations, and talks by experts to be not helpful. A 'concrete experience' person finds student feedback helpful, but theoretical readings not helpful. 'Reflective observation' individuals find that lectures are best in facilitating learning. 'Active experimenters' do not find lectures to be helpful, but student feedback, homework, projects, and small group discussions are helpful. Thus, it is possible to relate various pedagogical techniques with different learning styles.

Randolph and Posner (1979) use Kolb's learning style model to place various pedagogical strategies and techniques into one of four categories: (I) reflective-theoretical; (II) reflective applied; (III) active-applied; and (IV) active theoretical (Figure 2). They also argue that the purpose of teaching is not simply to cover the subject matter, but to produce a change in behavior. Thus, the four pedagogical categories are defined by the desired changes to be brought about. For example, Quadrant I focuses on the acquisition of knowledge. Here the student is expected to learn certain theories and to be able to explain them. In Quadrant II, the emphasis is more applied, with the student developing an appreciation for the theories, along with the ability to apply them to real events. In Quadrants I and II, the nature of the student's participation and involvement is reflective, with the latter being more applied and the former more abstract.

In Quadrants III and IV, the student becomes an active participant. On a more concrete level, Quadrant III focuses on a change in attitudes and skill development. Here the student is expected to act on the theories by experiencing and coping with actual or simulated situations. In Quadrant IV, the student's activities become more abstract, while actively becoming involved in testing and developing theories and hypotheses. The focus in Quadrant IV is on a change in understanding.

Entrepreneurial Learning Style Preference

Colleges of business administration can significantly improve their contribution in entrepreneurial education if research regarding the psychological nature of entrepreneurs can be translated into more effective training of potential entrepreneurs and the further development of current entrepreneurs. A description of the linkage between the psychological characteristics of the entrepreneur and learning style theory begins with a review of the decision-making process which is used in becoming an entrepreneur.

The decision to become an entrepreneur can be seen as a series of five interrelated steps. The first step is for the potential entrepreneur to recognize an opportunity to innovate. Drucker (1985) claims that this is the necessary characteristic that all entrepreneurs have in common. After an opportunity is recognized, the entrepreneur needs to develop alternative courses of action to take advantage of this opportunity. Next, the various alternatives must be evaluated. Then, the best alternative is selected. Finally, the selected alternative is implemented.

Necessarily, the successful implementation of the five steps in the decision to become an entrepreneur requires some facility with each of the four learning abilities. Thus, the entrepreneur, in order to be effective, as any other learner, needs all four different abilities - concrete experience (CE), reflective observation (RO), abstract conceptualization (AC), and active experimentation (AE).

Looking first at the active experimentation/reflective observation dimension, our understanding of entrepreneurial behavior indicates a primary preference for action. After all, opportunities and innovative ideas must be acted upon to effectuate entrepreneurship. Litzinger (1965) draws a distinction between entrepreneurs, who are goal- and action-oriented, and managers, who merely carry out policies and procedures in achieving the goals. Similarly, the individual psychological characteristics of an entrepreneur, basically the needs to achieve and to dominate, the greater tolerance for novelty, and the perception of controlling one's environment, tend to infer an active posture, as opposed to a reflective one. Thus, an entrepreneur is expected to favor active experimentation, rather than reflective observation.

On the abstract conceptualization/concrete experience dimension, the preference of an entrepreneur is not as clear. In fact, it is precisely the conflict between concrete experience and abstract conceptualization that leads to what Kolb (1976) refers to as 'creative tension'. To be creative, one has to be freed from the constraints of a previous focus on abstract concepts and to experience anew. Schrage (1965) found that an accurate awareness of the environment was more important than either achievement or power motivation in distinguishing the successful entrepreneur from others. McMullan (1976) describes the creative process as a synthesis of problem-finding and problem-solving. Thus a creative person is one who is able to coordinate activities in each of the different modes of learning. Consequently, both the abilities are important to entrepreneurs with the balance between them varying with individual entrepreneurs depending on whether problem-finding or problem-solving is more important for innovation.

Research Methodology

Sample and procedures

The subjects employed in this research were senior undergraduate business students and MBA students (n=416) from AACSB accredited institutions. The findings of a number of previous research studies, including those of Borland (1975), Brockhaus (1975), Rupkey (1978), and Sexton and Bowman (1983), indicate that students who express entrepreneurial intentions, that is, future entrepreneurs, exhibit psychological traits which are characteristic of entrepreneurs. Therefore, to identify the entrepreneurial differences among the students, they were compared on several psychological characteristics that have been associated with entrepreneurs (McClelland, 1961 and 1965; McClelland and Winter, 1969; Hornaday and Bunker, 1970; Pandy and Tewary, 1968; Schere, 1982; Hornaday and Aboud, 1971). The measures used were: Rotter's Internal/External Locus of Control Scale (Rotter, 1966); Budner's Intolerance of Ambiguity Scale (Budner, 1962); and Steers' Manifest Needs Questionnaire (Steers and Braunstein, 1976). In addition, the students were administered Kolb's Learning Style Inventory (1976). The objective was to determine if the distinguishing psychological characteristics of entrepreneurs are associated with different learning style preferences.

Hypotheses

It is hypothesized that these entrepreneurial characteristics of the subjects will exhibit greater association with active experimentation and lesser association with reflective observation. More specifically, the individual hypotheses are:

> *Hypothesis 1*: Entrepreneurial characteristic need for achievement will be positively correlated with active experimentation (AE) and negatively correlated with reflective observation (RO).

Hypothesis 2: Entrepreneurial characteristic need for affiliation will be negatively correlated with active experimentation (AE) and positively correlated with reflective observation (RO).

Hypothesis 3: Entrepreneurial characteristic need for autonomy will be positively correlated with active experimentation (AE) and negatively correlated with reflective observation (RO).

Hypothesis 4: Entrepreneurial characteristic need for dominance will be positively correlated with active experimentation (AE) and negatively correlated with reflective observation (RO).

Hypothesis 5: Entrepreneurial characteristic exhibited by Budner's AT Scale will be negatively correlated with active experimentation (AE) and positively correlated with reflective observation (RO).[1]

Hypothesis 6: Entrepreneurial characteristic exhibited by Budner's Insolubility Dimension will be negatively correlated with active experimentation (AE) and positively correlated with reflective observation (RO).

Hypothesis 7: Entrepreneurial characteristic exhibited by Budner's Complexity Dimension will be negatively correlated with active experimentation (AE) and positively correlated with reflective observation (RO).

Hypothesis 8: Entrepreneurial characteristic exhibited by Budner's Novelty Dimension will be negatively correlated with active experimentation (AE) and positively correlated with reflective observation (RO).

Hypothesis 9: Entrepreneurial characteristic exhibited by Rotter's Internal-External Locus of Control Scale will be negatively correlated with active experimentation and positively correlated with reflective observation.[2]

On the abstract conceptualization/concrete experience dimension, the preference of the entrepreneur is not as distinct as both abilities are important to entrepreneurs, with the balance between them varying in

156

accordance with whether problem-finding or problem-solving is more important for innovation. Hence, no hypotheses regarding the entrepreneurial characteristics of the subjects will be made with respect to the differing degree of association between concrete experience and abstract conceptualization.

Results

The results of the statistical analysis are presented in Table 1. The correlation overall support the general hypothesis that entrepreneurs have a 'preferred' learning style that is active as opposed to being passive and reflective. More specifically, Hypothesis 1 is supported completely by the data as need for achievement is positively correlated with active experimentation and negatively correlated with reflective observation. Hypotheses 2 and 4 are supported in that the need for affiliation is positively correlated with reflective observation and need for dominance is negatively correlated with reflective observation. Neither of these latter two needs were significantly correlated with active experimentation. Hypothesis 3 is supported by the significant negative correlation of need for autonomy with reflective observation. However, need for autonomy rather than being positively correlated with active experimentation was correlated negatively at a significant level. Hence, the support for the 'preferred' active learning style appears to come more from the influence of the reflective observation pole than the active experimentation pole along the active experimentation/reflective observation dimension.

The same can be said for the impact of the remaining psychological variables. The influence along the active experimentation/reflective observation dimension appears to come from the reflective observation pole. For Hypotheses 5 through 9, no significant correlation between the entrepreneurial characteristic and the active experimentation scale score was found. However, support for each of these hypotheses, except Hypothesis 7, was observed by the hypothesized significant correlation with the reflective observation scale score.

Implications

Given that the entrepreneur tends to prefer one of the active learning styles, either that of the accommodator or that of the converger, it would be best to utilize the pedagogical techniques which are best suited to such learning styles. Figure 2, in Quadrants III and IV, presents pedagogical techniques which address active learning styles.

Unfortunately, the potential entrepreneur is more likely to experience the reflective-theoretical teaching style of Quadrant I as most business school academics are assimilators with particularly strong skills in abstraction and reflection (Kolb 1976). An alternative to this traditional approach where the student is passive rather than active is the one in which the instructor becomes a learning process facilitator. In such an approach, the instructor utilizes learning exercises such as: role playing; management simulations; structured exercises; and focused learning-feedback situations. Importantly, the student is given an active role. Students are required to reflect on what they experienced in an exercise, and to develop generalizations through small discussion groups. Hypotheses formulated by the discussion groups are tested with additional learning exercises. Consequently, all four learning abilities are used and developed.

Just as Kolb's model does not favor one learning style over the others, neither is there one best pedagogical approach for all courses. From Figure 2, however, it may be noted that the entrepreneurial student would best benefit from an active involvement in the learning process. The instructor serves as a facilitator in the learning process, interactively involving the potential entrepreneur as an integral part of the learning process. Entrepreneurial ability is not taught, it is recognized, evaluated, and developed.

Table 1: Correlations Between Learning Style Inventory Scores and Entrepreneurial Psychological Characteristics

Characteristic	Concrete Experience Conceptualiza-tion (CE)	Reflective Observation Experimentation (RO)	Abstract (AC)	Active (AE)
Need for Achievement	-.14**	-.30***	.13**	.10*
Need for Affiliation	.12**	.16***	-.20***	.02
Need for Autonomy	-.08	-.09*	.09*	-.12**
Need for Dominance	-.20***	-.21***	.10*	.04
Budner's AT Scale	-.02	.15*	-.03	-.04
Budner's Complexity Dimension	.03	.16***	-.05	-.06
Budner's Insolubility Dimension	-.07	.02	-.03	-.02
Budner's Novelty	.01	.10*	-.03	.03
Rotter's I-E Locus of Control	.08*	.16***	-.18***	.03

* $p \leq .05$, one-tailed test
** $p \leq .01$, one-tailed test
*** $p \leq .001$, one-tailed test

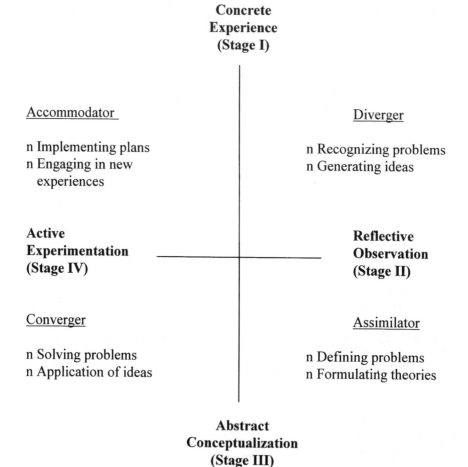

**Concrete
Experience
(Stage I)**

Accommodator

n Implementing plans
n Engaging in new
  experiences

Diverger

n Recognizing problems
n Generating ideas

**Active
Experimentation
(Stage IV)**

**Reflective
Observation
(Stage II)**

Converger

n Solving problems
n Application of ideas

Assimilator

n Defining problems
n Formulating theories

**Abstract
Conceptualization
(Stage III)**

Figure 1: Kolb's Learning Model

**Concrete
Experience
(Stage I)**

III. Active-Applied | II.Reflective-Applied
Changes in skills and attitudes | *Changes in appreciation*
n Role Plays | n Movies
n Management simulation | n Applied lecture
n Structured exercises | n Dialogue
n Processing discussion | n Limited discussion
n T-Groups | n Cases
n Diaries | n Problem exam
n Field projects | n Programmed instruction
 | (skills)

Active   **Reflective**
Experimentation   **Observation**
(Stage IV)   **(Stage II)**

IV. Active-Theoretical | I. Reflective-Theoretical
Changes in understanding | *Changes in knowledge*
n Focused learning groups | n Theory lecture
n Argumentative discussion | n Required readings
n Experiments/ research | n Handouts
n Suggested readings | n Programmed instruction
n Analysis papers | (concepts)
 | n Theory papers
 | n Content exam

**Abstract
Conceptualization
(Stage III)**

**Figure 2: Conceptual Grid of Learning Styles and Pedagogical
Techniques**

Notes

[1] The lower the score on Budner's Intolerance of Ambiguity Scale the greater the tolerance for ambiguity.

[2] The lower the score on the Rotter Internal-External Locus of Control Scale the more internal the subject's locus of control.

References

Atkinson, J. W. (1957) 'Motivational Determinants of Risk Taking Behavior,' *Psychology Review*, Vol. 64, pp. 359-72.

Borland, C. (1975), 'Locus of Control, Need for Achievement, and Entrepreneurship,' unpublished doctoral dissertation, University of Texas.

Brockhaus, R.H. (1975) 'IE Locus of Control Scores as Predictors of Entrepreneurial Intentions,' *Proceedings of the Academy of Management* (Academy of Management), pp. 443-445.

Brockhaus, R. H. (1980) 'Risk Taking Propensity of Entrepreneurs,' *Academy of Management Journal*, Vol. 23, No. 3, pp. 509-20.

Budner, S. (1962) 'Intolerance of Ambiguity as a Personality Variable,' *Journal of Personality*, Vol. 30, pp. 29-50.

Cole, Arthur H. (1959) *Business Enterprise in Its Social Setting* (Cambridge, MA: Harvard University Press).

Collins, O. F., D. G. Moore, and D. B. Unwalla (1964) *The Enterprising Man* (East Lansing, MI: MSU Business Studies).

Cooper, Arnold (1975) 'Technical Entrepreneurship: What Do We Know?' in Clifford Baumbeck and Joseph Mancuso (eds), *Entrepreneurship and Venture Management* (Englewood Cliffs, NJ: Prentice-Hall).

DeCarlo, James F., and Lyons, Paul R. (1979) 'A Comparison of Selected Personality Characteristics of Minority and Nonminority Female Entrepreneurs,' *Proceedings of the Academy of Management*).

DeCarlo, James F. and Lyons, Paul R. (1981) 'Curriculum Determinants for Entrepreneurship Training,' in Donald L. Sexton and Philip M. Van Auken (eds), *Entrepreneurship Education* (Waco, TX: Baylor University), p. 96.

Douglas, Merrill E. (December 1976) 'Relating Education to Entrepreneurial Success,' *Business Horizons*, pp. 40-44.

Drucker, P. E. (1985) 'The Discipline of Innovation,' *Harvard Business Review*, Vol. 63, No. 3: pp. 67-72.

Flavell, J. (1963) *The Development Psychology of Jean Piaget* (New York: Van Nostrand Reinhold Co.).

Harvey, O. J., Hunt, D. and Schroeder, H. (1961) *Conceptual Systems and Personality Organization* (New York: John Wiley,).

Hornaday, John and Bunker, C. S. (Spring 1970) 'The Nature of the Entrepreneur,' *Personnel Psychology*, pp.47-54.

Hornaday, John and Aboud, John (Summer 1971) 'Characteristics of Successful Entrepreneurs,' *Personnel Psychology*, pp. 141-153.

Kogan, N. and Wallach, M. A. (1964) *Risk Taking* (New York: Holt, Reinhart and

Winston).

Kolb, David A. (Spring 1976) 'Management and the Learning Process.' *California Management Review*, pp. 21-31.

Kolb, David A., (1978) *Learning Style Inventory: Technical Manual*, rev. ed., (Boston, MA: McBer & Co.).

Komives, J. L. (1972) 'A Preliminary Study of the Personal Values of High Technology Entrepreneurs, ' in *Technical Entrepreneurship: A Symposium* (Milwaukee: Center for Venture Management).

Lachman, R. (1980) 'Toward Measurement of Entrepreneurial Tendencies,' *Management International Review*, Vol. 20, pp. 108-116.

Litzinger, W. D. (December 1965) 'The Motel Entrepreneur and the Motel Manager,' *Academy of Management Journal*, pp. 268-281.

Mancuso, Joseph (1975) 'The Entrepreneur's Quiz,' in Clifford Baumbeck and Joseph Mancuso (eds), *Entrepreneurship and Venture Management* (Englewood Cliffs, NJ: Prentice-Hall).

McClelland, David C. (1961) *The Achieving Society* (New York: Van Nostrand).

McClelland, David C. (November-December 1965) 'Achievement Motivation Can Be Developed,' *Harvard Business Review*, pp. 6ff.

McClelland, David C. and Winter, D. G. (1969) *Motivating Economic Achievement* (New York: Free Press).

McMullen, W. E. (Fourth Quarter 1976) 'Creative Individuals: Paradoxical Personages,' *The Journal of Creative Behavior*, pp. 265-275.

Mescon, T. S., and Montanari, J. R. (1981) 'The Personalities of Independent and Franchise Entrepreneurs,' in *Proceedings of the Academy of Management*, pp. 413-17.

Meyer, H. H., Walker, W. B., and Litwin, G. H. (1961) 'Motive Patterns and Risk Preferences Associated with Entrepreneurs,' *Journal of Abnormal and Social Psychology*, Vol. 63, No. 3, pp. 570-74.

Mill, J. S., 'Principles of Political Economy with Some Applications to Social Philosophy', (1848) in J. A. Schumpeter (ed.), *History of Economic Analysis* (New York: Oxford University Press, 1954).

Palmer, M. (1971) 'The Application of Psychological Testing to Entrepreneurial Potential,' *California Management Review*, Vol. 13, No. 3, pp. 32-38.

Pandy, J. and Tewary, N. B. (December 1968) 'Locus of Control and Achievement Values of Entrepreneurs,' *Journal of Occupational Psychology*, pp. 649-662.

Randolph, W. Alan and Posner, Barry Z. (July 1979) 'Designing Meaningful Learning Situations In Management: A Contingency, Decision-Tree Approach,' *Academy of Management Review*, pp. 459-467.

Roberts, E. B. (1968) 'A Basic Study of Innovators: How to Keep and Capitalize on Their Talents,' *Research Management*.

Rotter, Julian B. (1966) 'Generalized Expectancies for Internal Versus External Control of Reinforcement,' *Psychological Monographs: General and Applied*, Vol. 80, No. 1: whole no. 609.

Rotter, J. B., and Mulry, R. C. (1965) 'Internal Versus External Control of Reinforcement and Decision Time,' *Journal of Personality and Social Psychology*, Vol. 2, pp. 598-604.

Rupkey, R. H. (1978) 'Entrepreneurial Potential and Assessments,' unpublished doctoral dissertation, Pepperdine University.

Schere, J. (1982) 'Tolerance of Ambiguity as a Discriminating Variable Between

Entrepreneurs and Mangers,' *Proceedings of the Academy of Management* (Academy of Management), pp. 404-408.

Schrage, H. (November-December, 1965) 'The R & D Entrepreneur: Profile of Success,' *Harvard Business Review*, pp. 56-69.

Schumpeter, J. A. (1954) *History of Economic Analysis* (New York: Oxford University Press).

Sexton, Donald L. and Bowman, Nancy (1984a) 'The Effects of Pre-existing Psychological Characteristics on New Venture Initiations,' Presented at the Academy of Management, Boston, MA.

Sexton, Donald L. and Bowman, Nancy (1984b) 'Personality Inventory for Potential Entrepreneurs: Evaluation of a Modified JPI/PRF-E Test Instrument,' Presented at the Babson Entrepreneurship Research Conference, Georgia Tech University, Atlanta, GA.

Sexton, Donald L. and Bowman, Nancy (1983) 'Determining Entrepreneurial Potential of Students: Comparative Psychological Characteristics Analysis,' *Proceedings of the Academy of Management* (Academy of Management), pp. 408-412.

Sexton, Donald L. and Bowman-Upton, Nancy (January 1987) 'Evaluation of an Innovative Approach to Teaching Entrepreneurship,' *Journal of Small Business Management*, pp.35-43.

Sexton, Donald L. and Bowman-Upton, Nancy (Winter 1988) 'Validation of an Innovative Teaching Approach for Entrepreneurship Courses,' *American Journal of Small Business*, pp.11-21.

Steers, Richard M., and Braunstein, Daniel N. (1976) 'A Behaviorally-Based Measure of Manifest Needs in Work Settings,' *Journal of Vocational Behavior*, Vol. 9, pp. 251-266.

Vesper, Karl H. (1980) *New Venture Strategies* (Englewood Cliffs, NJ: Prentice Hall, Inc.).

Warner, H. A., and Rubin, I. M. (1969) 'Motivation of Research and Development Entrepreneurs,' *Journal of Applied Psychology*, Vol. 53, No. 3, Part 1, pp. 178-84.

Zeithmal, Carl P. and Rice, George H., Jr., 'Entrepreneurship/Small Business Education in American Universities,' *Journal of Small Business Management* (January 1987), pp. 44-50.

PART C

TARGET GROUPS OF ENTREPRENEURSHIP EDUCATION

9 Training for Successful Entrepreneurship Careers in the Creative Arts

Harold P. Welsch
Jill R. Kickul

Introduction

Over the last several decades, there has been an unprecedented proliferation of the number of entrepreneurs who start their own arts organizations. Since 1965, the number of non-profit theatres in the United States has increased from 56 to more than 400; dance companies from 37 to more than 250; opera companies from 27 to more than 100; and major orchestras from 58 to a total of 230 orchestras today. In addition, there are more than 3,000 arts agencies that assist these organizations in helping them prepare and present their performances to targeted audiences.

This level of growth coincides with the market demand and opportunities seen in the arts/entertainment industry. Americans spent nearly $400 billion, or about 8 per cent of total consumption, on entertainment in 1995. About 2.5 million people earn their living in the entertainment industry. In California, job creation in the entertainment economy has helped make up for devastating losses in the aerospace industry.

In foreign markets, entertainment has become a leading U.S. export. According to investment bankers, Varennes, Suhler and Associates, by the end of the decade, the media portion of the industry will grow 6.8 per cent per year, trailing only computers, travel and telecommunications. Not only is domestic demand booming, but exports will spark an even greater growth. The U.S. makers of films, CDs, videos, and the like, are already earning 40 per cent of their revenues ($9 billion) overseas. This should increase especially in Asia and Latin America where 'the need for more and more product is just going to grow' according to Gene Jankowski, a managing director at Varennes. The U.S. is able to reassert its leadership in global trade since no society in history has attempted to produce entertainment and information on the scale the U.S. does in the 1990s.

The creative arts offer numerous outlets, books, magazines, films, theatre, theme parks, CDs, VCRs, personal computers, and televisions. The three fundamental forces that will continue to drive the growth are globalization, technology, and demographics. Never before has the demand been so explosive or the potential for growth so great. The industry is limited only by its own creativity.

Oprah Winfrey's Harpo Entertainment Group produces her daily talk show and churns out feature films, TV movies, and Internet content. She is approaching 'billionairedom.' Forbes (1999) estimates that Jerry Seinfeld and co-creator Larry David will split some $600 million from the show's $2 billion in syndication revenues.

Puff Daddy: Entrepreneuring beyond Entertainment

Rap music has reached far beyond its ghetto origins into suburbia, mainstream, and international. It is now outselling country music. Since 1999, Puffy, a unique blend of businessman, producer, and performer wants to venture beyond sound and put his star name from everything from food to fashion. 'He loves business,' says Benny Medina, his manager of three years. He also understands brand extension and is forming a partnership with celebrity lawyer Johnnie Cochran to expand his management business beyond recording artists and professional basketball players. He also publishes Notorious, a 150,000-circulation magazine for upscale urbanites.

To crack the food business, Puffy hired Denise Bonds, a well-known soul food chef and consultant. The third of his upscale Caribbean-cuisine restaurants will open in Chicago. He also plans a line of frozen food, condiments, and juices. He recently launched a clothing line, and hired a former, Ralph Lauren marketing executive to run it. Jeans, jackets, collared shirts, and T-shirts will be sold in Macy's, Bloomingdales, and specialty stores like Fred Segal. Puffy is promoting the line in his videos, concerts, and personal appearances. He is also courting film roles, establishing a TV and film production arm, and exploring new media delivery systems, such as the Internet.

Three Entrepreneurs Create Dreamworks

Dreamworks is a multimedia entertainment company created by three entrepreneurs, director Steven Spielberg, music producer David Geffen, and former Disney executive Jeffrey Katzenberg. Dreamworks plan to make 12 movies a year by the end of the decade, as well as television shows, records, toys, and computer software. While the trio only contributed $100 million, they will control 66 per cent of the company. On top of their $1 million salaries, the three principals will receive 66 per cent of the profits in exchange for 1/10 of the equity investment. Six months after they created their far-flung entertainment empire, they rounded up more than $2 billion in commitments to bankroll Dreamworks SKG. More cynical market watchers compare the elite list of wealthy individuals and corporate investors to star-struck teenagers, but a surprisingly large contingent of analysts believe the investors, while in for an admittedly bumpy ride, could experience a very profitable one too.

Dreamworks plans to implement some new ideas in policy, including splitting equity with all employees (even secretaries), and giving shares of gross movie revenue to artists, writers, and animators. In addition to a new studio, plans for a theme park are also being considered. With all these elements in place, Dreamworks intends to create a new complete entertainment industry segment, fully operational by the year 2000.

Developing Strategies for Change: Steppenwolf Theatre Company

In 1974, under the leadership direction of Terry Kinney, Gary Sinise, and Jeff Perry, the Steppenwolf Theatre Company began performing plays in a church basement in Highland Park, Illinois. Steppenwolf was founded on a commitment to the principles of ensemble collaboration and artistic risk. The theatre's mission was to advance the vitality and diversity of American theatre, while trying to delicately maintain the original impulses of the founding group. For many years throughout the 1980s, Steppenwolf was playing to nearly sold out houses, with a 92 per cent subscription rate.

However, in the early 1990s, the theatre industry was facing an erosion in the size of its audiences. Steppenwolf s quality and style of many of the productions disappointed critics and audience members. Many of the long-standing loyal patrons of the 1980s did not renew their subscriptions. It was evident the Steppenwolf needed to change its strategy and focus on two areas: artistic development and changing people's attitudes and perceptions about the theatre.

For this changing strategy and focus, the founding members began to plan new seasons farther in advance in order to allow time for critical selection. Funding was set aside in order for the company to hire a resident dramaturge to assist in play development. Readings for a play would be held for emerging playrights, directors, and designers. Subscribers would be invited to attend these works as well as a lecture series about each play offered by Steppenwolf at no additional charge. A smaller Studio Theatre was set aside to help nurture smaller, local theatre companies, and provide them with marketing and promotional support. Steppenwolf also announced its 'Next Step Campaign,' a long-range program of theatre expansion, endowment, and artistic initiatives to support and define the company's artistic development into the next decade and century.

Maintaining Flexibility Through Collaboration: Cinnabar

Cinnabar is a Hollywood props maker that operates its business on a project-by-project basis. On one particular day, it could be working on a commercial, the next day on a film, and on the following day on a television special. Cinnabar's co-founder, Jonathan Katz, must be able to oversee and manage each product for a different client within the entertainment field. As an entrepreneur, Katz must find a highly temporary alliance comprised of industry experts and professionals to complete a project. Building relationships and alliances must be done in a timely and efficient manner with not only creative specialists but also with legal, financial, and business managers. These type of alliances has helped Cinnabar record a profitable $8 billion in revenues, up from 7.1 billion the year before.

The Powerful Match of Entertainment and Retail

Among retailers, hot new entertainment properties and their accompanying licensed merchandise have become one of the stores' most important means of attracting customers and converting them to repeat purchasers. This has become especially true as new entertainment technologies have come to the forefront. Limited to the LP record as the sole retail product, there was limited opportunity for retailers to attract movie and other entertainment fans. The introduction of computer software, music CD, video game, and videotape has shifted the market from the $8 billion record industry of the early 80's to an entertainment entity worth at least $50 billion today. This figure could easily double as a newer technologies such as digital videodisc and virtual reality come to market (Hisey, 1995).

Licensed properties are one of the hottest factors in cross merchandising, since licensing products sell more quickly than the average branded product that retailers carry. It is also much more of an impulse buy because consumers want to collect the whole set and not just one piece of the product program. Cross merchandising is considered to be one of the most efficient tools for exposing a product to a large number of consumers. By forging partnerships, both retailers and vendors can increase sales and add to their consumer base. It provides a better exposure to the display of products, encourages sales, and shows consumers that there is commitment to the product.

Arts and Entertainment Entrepreneurship

Developing the arts-artists, organizations, constituencies, and arts environments - has become an increasing challenging and demanding possibility for entrepreneurship educators. Economic, social, political, and aesthetic pressures are forcing creative artists and their support services to face tough decisions. These decisions must balance conflicting interests in a context of tightening resources, more intense competition, and greater demands for accountability without losing the creative thrust. There are approximately 2 million self-employed artists in the U.S., with an expected growth rate of 15 per cent over the next ten years (Bureau of Labor Statistics, 1994). Underlying this growth lies the opportunity for entrepreneurship educators to assist and facilitate this new market and its support system. Perceptive educators and administrators can aid these

171

individuals by making them aware of the interdisciplinary nature of entrepreneurship permeating their selected professions.

By exposing the creative arts student to entrepreneurial practices and skills, these potential artists will be better able to recognize and pursue new opportunities and keep abreast with the dynamic field of the arts. Entrepreneurship, as recommended by Porter and McKibbin (1988), Ray (1990), and Bagby and Stetz (1994) has the potential to be an integrative base in an artist's education by facilitating communication across disciplinary boundaries. One method to enhance the liberal/creative/performing arts education is to include courses in entrepreneurship that can ultimately assist students in becoming more competitive in marketing their artistic talent or service to the community.

The Market Potential in Entrepreneurship Education

As the number of self-employed artists continues to grow, the market potential in educating these individuals in the skills and competencies of entrepreneurship will increase. Specifically, there are two markets (as depicted in Figure 1) that serve as growth potential for entrepreneurship educators: the primary and secondary markets. The primary market consists of *writers, visual artists, performing artists, graphic designers, musicians, photographers, screenwriters, and film/video producers.* For the secondary market, this group consists of *agents, fundraising and development, promoters, distributors, lobbyists, and operations and management personnel.* This latter market includes the complex infrastructure, invisible to the general public, that functions beyond and behind what is seen on stage, on the film, or on the canvas. It is an industrious network of management leaders and employees who are facilitating the production and distribution of artistic products and services.

Both of the primary and secondary markets are interrelated in the functions and operations that they can provide each other in making a creative enterprise successful and profitable. In order for one market to be successful, the other market must contribute in supporting its efforts and endeavors. For instance, a theater may rely upon their actors, dancers, and musicians in conducting their performance, but other support systems are necessary including administrators, promoters, and production and operation managers. It is both the primary and secondary markets that can become new areas for development in education in fostering this interrelationship between entrepreneurship and the arts.

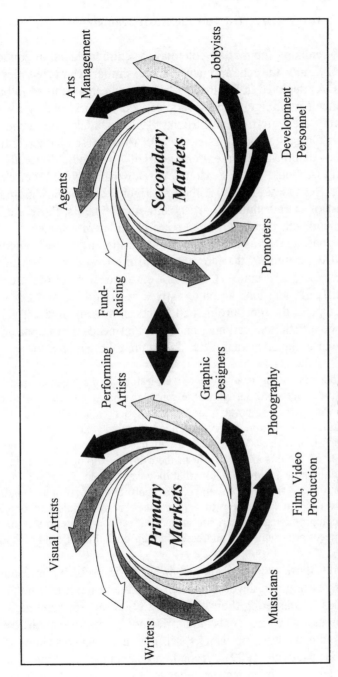

Figure 1: The Primary and Secondary Markets

Similarities between the Artist and the Entrepreneur

In addition to realizing the market potential for entrepreneurship education, both the artist and the entrepreneur share similar characteristics and opportunities. As depicted in Figure 2, artists have been attributed to having a high tolerance for ambiguity, perseverance, self-reliance, ability to adapt, autonomy, and creativity (Pufal-Struzik, 1992; Dudek, Berneche, and Berube, 1991; Guastello and Shissier, 1994). All of these characteristics or traits have been demonstrated in entrepreneurially-oriented individuals (e.g., Hornaday and Aboud, 1971; Sexton and Bowman, 1984; Welsch and White, 1981; Hornaday, 1982). Although Figure 2 does not include an exhaustive list of the attributes of artists and entrepreneurs, these are some of the fundamental characteristics often research and demonstrated.

Besides sharing these similar personality traits, artists also encounter problems and opportunities that are critical to the overall success of their creative enterprise (see Figure 3). As with entrepreneurs, artists are faced with many difficult decisions and alternatives in promoting and advancing their careers. One of the most problematic aspects of being an artist is being able to balance artistic, educational, and financial needs and opportunities. An entrepreneur in the arts exemplifies this in the following anecdote:

> I remember graduating from college, well-trained in the technical aspects of my creative profession, but with little sense of what it was really like out in the real world. It is important to include in our education more skills to survive in this competitive, unpredictable profession, which is also a business. For the artist, their needs are threefold: they need to understand what possible strategies and options are available to them in developing their professions; they need to know how to seek for what they want whether its marketing their talents or finding financing to support their profession or venture; and, they ultimately need to know how to achieve their career goals and objectives without compromising their artistic mission. It is unfortunate to say but most of these needs are usually not addressed in their discipline or field of study.

Underlying these requirements are the specific problems encountered by an artist in starting and developing their creative profession. First, artists face difficulties in marketing their expertise to their appropriate audiences. This stage includes setting goals and priorities, assessing qualifications, networking, and consulting job listings, services, and agencies (Longley and Abruzzo, 1991; Hoover, 1989). Second, artists must also find financial support in order for their project or endeavor to survive and succeed. This effort consists of often seeking innovative financing methods for their creative enterprise including support from both private and public foundations. As artists, they have many opportunities available (i.e., grants, fellowships, and awards) that can assist them in financing their career. Most of this support can come from foundations, corporations, government agencies, private individuals, and service organizations (American Council for the Arts, 1990, 1991; Grant, 1991; Reiss, 1986). Given these options, artists need to understand how to prepare grants and proposals that could produce the type of assistance they are seeking. Finally, both entrepreneurs and artists encounter various legal and technical issues surrounding their creative enterprises. This includes the requirements for starting a business and the selection of a legal structure that would be most beneficial to an entrepreneur's or artist's growth. In addition, artists and entrepreneurs often have other concerns that include negotiation, the writing of contracts, copyrights, trademarks, and patents that are associated with the survival of a small business (Grant, 1994; Hoover, 1989).

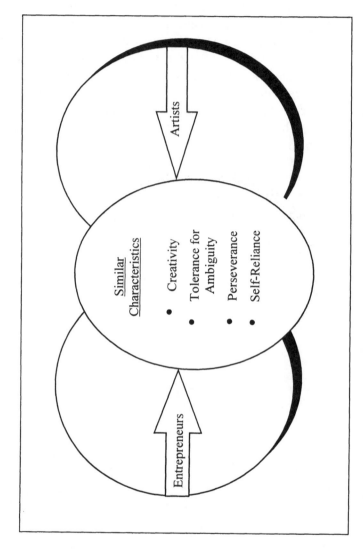

Figure 2. Characteristics of Entrepreneurs and Artists

Similar
Characteristics
- Creativity
- Tolerance for Ambiguity
- Perseverance
- Self-Reliance

Artists

Entrepreneurs

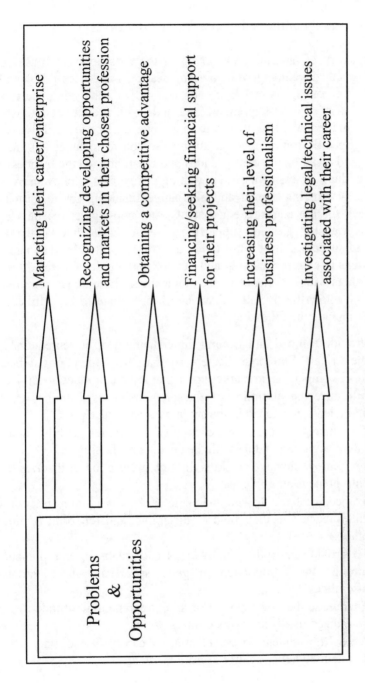

Figure 3: Problems and Opportunities for Artist

177

Entrepreneurship in the Arts Themes and Objectives

The framework of an Entrepreneurship in the Arts course is based upon identifying and developing strategies for dealing with these problems and obstacles. The overall course approach begins with analyzing the process and characteristics of entrepreneurs and ends with presentations based on how each individual plans to create their own enterprise in the arts (see Table 1). Specific topics covered during the course include: (1) enacting venturers and creators: the business idea and creativity; (2) the business plan and individual assessments; (3) writing of grants, fellowships, and proposals; (4) finding capital and alternative financing for the artist; (5) legal issues for the entrepreneur, patents, and copyrights; (6) developing entrepreneurial strategies and supporting strategies in the arts; (7) managing growth and success. All of these topics are supplemented by readings from various areas in entrepreneurship and the arts and are demonstrated through guest speakers with experience in each topic area. These topics comprise the content and allow the overall objectives of the course to be fulfilled. The objectives include the following:

- Provide a broad and general understanding of entrepreneurship in the Private Enterprise System so that the student might become more competitive in marketing his/her artistic product or service.
- Introduce the discipline of entrepreneurship as it applies to skills and talents developed in the students' area of discipline.
- To increase the awareness of entrepreneurship and its interdisciplinary nature with the creative professions.
- To improve managerial skills through application of theories to real entrepreneurial problems.
- To become familiar with analyzing cases, observation (interviewing entrepreneurs in their field of discipline, and reporting findings to others).
- To provide up-to-date innovations and trends in entrepreneurship through the introduction of guest speakers from a variety of disciplines.
- Encourage the development of an entrepreneurial attitude that may be utilized in all endeavors of one's career.
- Assist the student in establishing a career in the fine arts and maintaining better control of his/her career.

Table 1: Course Calendar

DATE	TOPIC	READINGS/ASSIGNMENT GUEST SPEAKERS
September 16	Introduction to Class The Entrepreneurial Perspective: Process and Characteristics	
September 23	Enacting Venturers and Creators: The Business Idea and Creativity	Jones and Christy: Chapters 1-5 Personal Assessment Exercise #1 Readings: 'A Whack on the Side of the Head' by Roger von Oech 'Killer Phrases: The Enemies of Ideas' by Charles 'Chic' Thompson
September 30	The Business Plan Individual Assessment	Jones and Christy: Chapters 10-14 Personal Assessment Exercise #3 Readings: 'How to Write a Winning Business Plan' by Keith Schilit CASE DUE: The George Lucas Case
October 7	Business Plan and Individual Assessment Cont. Writing of Proposals and Grants	Jones and Christy: Chapters 10-14 (if you read it before, you are all set!) Readings: 'Seeking Support for Your Project' by Deborah Hoover
October 14	Finding Capital Alternative Financing for the Artist	Jones and Christy: Chapters 15-17 Personal Assessment Exercise #4 and #5 Readings: 'Net Profit' in Film maker

DATE	TOPIC	READINGS/ASSIGNMENT GUEST SPEAKERS
October 21	Legal Issues for the Entrepreneur Patents and Copyrights	Jones and Christy: Chapter 7 CASE DUE: Boston Ballet
October 28	Developing Entrepreneurial Strategies Developing Supporting Strategies in the Arts	Jones and Christy: None Readings: 'Why Every Business will be like Show Business' by Joel Kotlin and David Friedman 'The Entrepreneurial Mind' by Jeffry Timmons
November 4	Managing Growth and Success	Jones and Christy: Chapters 18-19 CASE DUE: DePasse Entertainment and Creative Partners (MoTown Productions, A and B)
November 11	Presentations of Personal Plan Assessment	If you are presenting on this date, please provide an outline and any other supplemental material worth noting to the class on your personal plan assessment
November 18	Presentations of Personal Plan Assessment	If you are presenting on this date, please provide an outline and any other supplemental material worth noting to the class on your personal plan assessment • ENTREPRENEURIAL INTERVIEW DUE • PERSONAL ASSESSMENT DUE

Student Testimonials of Entrepreneurship in the Arts

Through these objectives, students are afforded the opportunity to analyze problems and concerns related to entrepreneurship and their careers. The following are student testimonials based on their perspective of the themes and how their translation of the topics discussed in the course in relation to the success of their own creative enterprise.

Upon graduating in June of this year, I will be yet another designer in the huge sea in the industry of theater. However, I will have several advantages over many graduates in the lighting field. One of these advantages is that I have trained at one of the top five theater conservatories in the nation with some of the nation's leading designers. It will enable me to build a network of connections with other designers in the field and become a consultant to various theaters in my region of the country. In addition to this advantage, I will also have the business knowledge to complement my technical skills in my industry. The course, Entrepreneurship in the Arts has taught me about the intricacies involved in starting my business including realizing new entrepreneurial opportunities, and sources of financing available to artists.

I plan to market myself in the entertainment business with a strong focus on opening up new ideas and concepts about women in the industry. My focus will be on the film, modeling, and recording industry. I know that this is a broad spectrum of avenues to take, but in this business you have to be well-rounded if you are a performance artist because the competition is so vast and wide that your chances are very slim. Besides modeling for United Colors of Benneton, I have been a dancer/performance artist for different shows and productions. The opportunities that are in the market/industry I am going into are the use of my creative individuality and using all of my different creative venues to pursue success. Entrepreneurship in the Arts has allowed me to foresee some of the problem areas that I need to concentrate on in order to become a success in my industry. Furthermore, it has given me the opportunity to be able to clarify my own goals and objectives before I begin my own venture.

I have been dancing more or less my entire life; seriously, for the past eight years. Ever since I could appreciate what I was doing as an art form, I knew I wanted dancing, and performing to be a permanent part of my life. Two years ago, I was appointed dance director of a summer performing arts camp. It was this experience that inspired the idea of running my own dance company. By having to develop a personal plan in the Entrepreneurship in the Arts class, I am better able to comprehend the rationale of developing a course of action that includes a vision statement and an industry analysis.

Moreover, I am better able to understand what is involved in the daily operations, organization, and management of a dance company.

Conclusion: Entrepreneurship Courses are Not Limited to Business Schools

By integrating a course in entrepreneurship tailored towards the growing demands and needs of liberal/creative/performing artist, as well as its related spin-off activity, educators in business schools and their collaborators will be assisting and facilitating this new market and its support system. With concentrated efforts toward assisting the arts profession, entrepreneurship instructors follow the recommendation of many other educators (e.g., Ray, 1990; Bagby and Stetz, 1994). This recommendation asserts that an expanded curriculum needs to be proposed that encompasses a larger number of disciplines including the liberal/creative arts. In addition, the teaching of entrepreneurship should be integrated into other courses and specialties. This challenge may seem like an overarching task, but one that needs to be integrated into a student's growth and development of their chosen concentration.

Finally, by incorporating an entrepreneurship course specifically for art students, there are additional opportunities for small business programs. These opportunities include supplementary funding from patrons of the arts that value programs that can assist individuals to develop their entrepreneurial skills as they begin their independent enterprises. These patrons can provide funding from both public and private institutions that support the notion that relevant learning for career success may not necessarily be found in a single discipline. This type of philosophy is exemplified in the quote by E.A. Prieve (1980) which asserts, 'The arts must survive as a business to thrive as art.'

References

American Council for the Arts. (1992). *Money for Visual Artists*. Washington, D.C.: Author.

American Council for the Arts. (1990). *Jobs in Arts and Media Management*. Washington, D.C.: Author.

Anonymous. (1999). How today's hottest celebrities build value in a name. *Forbes, March 22*, 180-186.

Bagby, D. R., and Stetz, P. (1994). Can entrepreneurs be taught? *The Art and Science of Entrepreneurship Education Vol., 1*, 23 - 3 1.

Bureau of Labor Statistics. (1994). *Occupational Projections and Training Data*. Washington, D.C.: Author.

Dubek, S.Z., Beneche, R., Berube, H., and Royer, S. (1991). Personality determinants of the commitment to the profession of art. *Creativity Research Journal, 4(4)*, 367 - 389.

Grant, D. (1994). *The Artist's Resource Handbook*. New York: Allworth Press.

Grant, D. (1991). *The Business of Being an Artist*. New York: Allworth Press.

Guastello, S.J., and Shissler, J.E. (1994). A two - factor taxonomy of creative behavior. *Journal of Creative Behavior, 28(3)*, 211 - 221.

Hisey, P. (1995). Retail, entertainment merge for 90's success. *Discount Store News*, June 19, p. 45.

Hornaday, J. (1982). Research about living entrepreneurs. In C. Kent, D. Sexton, and K. Vesper (Eds.), *Encyclopedia of Entrepreneurship* (pp. 26 - 27). Englewood Cliffs, N.J.: Prentice Hall.

Hornaday, J., and Aboud, J. (1971, Summer). Characteristics of successful entrepreneurs. *Business Quarterly*, 76 - 79.

Hoover, D.A. (1989). *Supporting Yourself as an Artist: A Practical Guide*. New York: Oxford University Press.

Langley, S. and Abruzzo, J. (1991). *Jobs in Arts and Media Management*. New York, N.Y.: Doubleday.

Porter, L.W., and McKibbin, L.E. (1988). *Future of management education and developments Drift or thrust into the 21st century*. New York: McGraw Hill.

Prieve, E.A. (1980). *Marketing the Arts*. New York: Praeger.

Pufal - Struz, K.I. (1992). Differences in personality and self - knowledge of creative persons at different ages. *Gerontology and Geriatrics Education, 13(1 - 2)* , 71 - 90.

Ray, D. (1990). Liberal arts for entrepreneurs. *Entrepreneurship Theory and Practice Winter*, 79 - 90.

Reiss, A.H. (1986). *Cash In: Funding, and Promoting the Arts*, New York: Theatre Communications Group, Inc.

Roberts, J. (1995). A piece of the action. *Newsweek, December 18*, pp. 48 - 54.

Sexton, D.L., and Bowman, N. (1985). The entrepreneur: A capable executive and more. *Journal of Business Venturing, Winter*, 129 - 140.

Welsch, J.A., and White, J.F. (1982). Converging on characteristics of entrepreneurs. *Frontiers of Entrepreneurship Research, Spring*, 504 - 515.

10 The Perceived Needs, Benefits and Potential Target Markets for Entrepreneurship Education

Sumaria Mohan-Neill

Abstract

Entrepreneurship education (EE) programs appear to be in the growth phase of the product life cycle. Marketing theory provides us with a framework within which to analyze the growth and development of this particular educational service category. Undoubtedly, growth in any product/service category is fuelled by a need and demand by target markets, who perceive significant benefits of the product/service offering. A combination of primary and secondary data sources are used to address the research questions.

The more significant contribution of this paper is its exploration of the needs and demand for EE programs from the customer's perspective. Using primary data collected during focus group discussions and in-depth interviews, rich, qualitative insight and understanding about the views of potential target markets were revealed. Many important issues were discussed in the focus group, but the primary research questions addressed in this paper are as follows: 1) Who would be interested in EE programs (what are the potential target markets)? 2) What are the perceived needs which could be satisfied by EE programs (what are the benefits)? and 3) What type (content and process) of EE programs would satisfy the needs of the potential target markets?

Introduction

A few years ago, an arrogant, first-year doctoral student suggested that we did not know enough about entrepreneurship to be teaching courses in it. She suggested that we needed to focus more on research, so that we could learn more about the area before we attempted to teach it. Almost a decade later, entrepreneurship education programs seem to be flourishing. They appear to be in the growth phase of the product life cycle. Sulski (1997) reported 'Around the country, MBA students are flocking to entrepreneurship programs, which are growing at unprecedented rates'. What are some of the reasons for this growth? Do we know significantly more today about the field, so that there is some theoretical framework within which we can teach the subject?

To some extent, marketing theory provides a framework for analyzing the growth of and interest in entrepreneurship education programs. Is the growth phase need and market-driven? Undoubtedly, growth in any product category is fuelled by a need and demand by target markets, who perceive significant benefits of the product/service offerings.

This paper utilizes two types of data in its quest to address issues concerning EE. First, it employs secondary data from the literature, and then it uses primary data to probe deeper into issues concerning the need and demand for EE programs from the customer's perspective. Primary data from potential target markets is viewed as critical because as Plaschka and Welsch (1990) reported 'One criticism is that business schools follow a 'product' approach rather than a 'customer' approach to education. All too often, schools like to pump out whatever they have rather than what is needed.' Primary data collection utilized focus group discussions and in-depth interviews to obtain qualitative insight and understanding into the views of potential target markets for EE programs. What are the perceived benefits provided by EE programs, and which potential target markets would be interested in such benefits?

Research Objectives

The following are the principal research questions addressed in this paper:

1. Who would be interested in EE programs (what are the potential target markets)?

2. What are the perceived needs which could be satisfied by EE programs (what are the benefits)?
3. What type (content and process) of EE programs would satisfy the needs of the potential target markets?

Methodology

Two types of methodology were utilized. The first methodology involved a computerized search of secondary data sources. An online search engine called FIRSTSEARCH was used. The key search phrase used was 'entrepreneurship education'. Journal articles retrieved were evaluated based on the relevance to the research issues in this paper.

The second research methodology involved collecting primary data from a focus group and in-depth interviews. There were sixteen subjects in the focus group. The session lasted two and a half hours and was videotaped for later analysis. Subjects were very forthcoming and articulate in their views and opinions. Focus groups reflect both the advantages and disadvantages of qualitative research. The most significant disadvantage relate to small sample size, which is often correlated to samples that are not representative of the population of interest. However, in this case there was a great deal of diversity in the sample (Figure 1).

The age of sample ranged from 20 to 46 years old, with a mean of about 31 years and median of 30 years; about 69 per cent per cent were female. The over-sampling of women fits with the over-representation of women in entrepreneurship. Mohan-Neill (1991) reports 'Seventy-five per cent women-owned enterprises in existence in 1991 were still in existence three years later compared to 66 per cent of all companies'. The focus group participants all had some college and some work experience. They were either full or part-time students at a private university with less than 10,000 students. Only three participants were full-time students with no current work responsibilities. What was particularly remarkable about the sample was the ethnic and global diversity represented. There were 56.3 per cent US born and 43.8 per cent foreign born (Figure 1; Argentina, Cyprus, Mexico, Malaysia, Bahamas). There were 56.3 per cent whites, 12.5 per cent blacks, 6.3 per cent Hispanics and 25 per cent other categories of race. Some had first hand experience with their own or family-owned businesses. What they all had in common was the fact they were all enrolled in an experimental entrepreneurship course, (Figure 2).

186

Results and Discussion

The first part of the results focuses on the existing literature and data related to the research issues in this paper. The second part or the analysis digs a bit deeper using the focus group results to help understand the issues addressed.

Overview of Literature (Secondary Data)

What are the potential Target Markets for EE?

Essentially, this question relates to the first research question which asks 'Who would be interested in EE programs?'. Hills and Welsch (1986) surveyed nearly 2000 students, and found 80 per cent expressed an interest in taking one or more Entrepreneurship/new venture courses. Solomon and Fernald (1991) reported on the findings of 3 of most extensive studies on entrepreneurship and small business education in US based on SBA surveys conducted in 1979, 1982 and 1986. They reported that 'according to the National Federation of Independent Business, forty per cent of today's entrepreneurs have no formal education beyond high school; eight per cent are high school dropouts.' They suggested that there are 2 markets for EE. The first market involve lifelong learning employing non-credit programs. The second market involves conventional business education programs.

The trends suggest that EE is in the growth phase of the PLC and the market is expanding. According to Solomon and Fernald (1991), 'small business and Entrepreneurship showed considerable growth from 1979 to 1986'. They also report that 'The field of small business management and Entrepreneurship education is growing and continues to show signs if significant growth in the next decade, not only in the US but worldwide'. Robinson and Haynes (1991) used a sample of 232 US universities with 10,000 students of more. They reported that entrepreneurship education has 'unprecedented growth in past fifteen years'. Boberg and Kiecker (1988) predicted that demand for Entrepreneurship education will outstrip resources. According to Katz and Green (1996) 'Entrepreneurship today represents a growth industry in policy making and education worldwide'.

Criticisms of Business Education and Opportunities for EE

Criticisms of business education relate to the second research question of 'What are the perceived needs which could be satisfied by EE programs?'. Often in marketing, opportunities are derived from solving problems or fulfilling unmet needs. In the case of EE, opportunities can be derived from addressing some of the criticisms leveled at business schools. In their discussion of the status of management education, Plaschka and Welsch (1990) report that 'One criticism is that business schools follow a 'product' approach rather than a 'customer' approach to education. All too often, schools like to pump out whatever they have rather than what is needed.'

Neck (1981) suggests that top-down approach to education and training does not seem to cater adequately to the needs of small businesses and entrepreneurs. He charges that the small business sector has been effectively removed from the planning, development, implementation, and evaluation of programs. 'Much of criticism focuses on lack of creativity and individual thinking required at both undergraduate and graduate levels.' Solomon and Fernald (1991).

Designing EE Programs

There is sufficient criticisms of business education which should help to determine the type of design(s) of EE programs which may satisfy customers' needs (i.e. students needing EE). Plaschka and Welsch (1990) published a very interesting paper on 'Emerging structures in entrepreneurship education: Curricular designs and strategies.' They provided a history of entrepreneurship education and they proposed two models of evolving entrepreneurship education. Framework A has two dimensions; dimension 1 is related to the number of entrepreneurship courses, while dimension 2 is based on the degree of integration of entrepreneurship courses. Framework B also has two dimensions; dimension 1 is related the stages of transition in a firm, while dimension 2 is based on a functional approach, which adds entrepreneurship courses according to the disciplines that may be required in an entrepreneurial undertaking (Plaschka and Welsch, 1990).

Plaschka and Welsch (1990) suggested that if Stevenson (1981) is correct in describing Entrepreneurship as an integrative activity based upon the capacity to understand very complex dilemmas regarding purpose, possibilities, and tools, then Plaschka and Welsch (1990) argue that 'we must follow non-traditional processes in designing entrepreneurship programs'. They suggested that a 'holistic and multidisciplinary perspective is needed'.

Solomon and Fernald (1991) proposal of two distinct markets suggest two very different types of programs for the target markets. The first market concern lifelong learning which involves non-credit programs, while the second market involves conventional business education programs.

Katz and Green (1996) report that many types of resources for entrepreneurship education are currently available. The may make it easier to design appropriate programs.

Results from Focus Group (Primary Data)

The methodology allowed for many probing questions, for clarification and follow-up. What are the perceived needs and what are some characteristics of the target market (i.e., profile of people who need and want Entrepreneurship programs)? What are the perceived benefits of Entrepreneurship programs? What are some of the features of such need-satisfying Entrepreneurship programs? These questions are very connected for obvious reasons.

Attitudes towards small versus large Companies and Entrepreneurship

Before addressing the research questions directly, the focus group was used to gain some insight into the attitudes and opinions of participants. During the first part of the focus group, participants were asked to discuss the advantages and disadvantages of working for a large versus a small company. An interesting interactive exchange ensued (a more detailed analysis of the results of this segment of the focus group will be presented in another forum). It is important to note that when asked if they wanted to have their own business at some point in the future, the majority strongly agreed, irrespective of their small or large business employment stance.

Only two women said they absolutely did not want their own businesses. Both came from families that had their own small business. One woman (AP) responded, 'I would never want to own a business. My father did. He worked too many hours'. However AP also said that she is currently working for a very small entrepreneurial market research firm and she loves the independence, flexibility and the ability to wear many hats. She is treated as a partner in all respects, except for financial responsibility, which is exactly what she wants. The second woman (LC) said her family owned a business in her native Argentina, but the employee-related problems were very bad, and she did not want to deal with such problems. She is a Ph.D. chemist and had worked for large chemical companies in the past. She is currently on the job market, and prefers large companies because of the resources available.

One participant (RL) who had strongly defended his employer (a large telecommunications company) said that in spite of his perceived advantages of working for a large company versus a small company, 'Self-actualization only happens when you work for yourself'. Another man (DH) who worked for small insurance agencies and is currently employed by a large bank, suggested that it does not matter whether you work for a large or small company, 'in one you make a big corporation rich, in the other you make the owner rich'. DH also wanted to have his own business, but he said that after taking the entrepreneurship class he realized 'there is a lot more to owning a business. I need to put away enough money to start a business. I want to do it the right way, rather than doing it blindly.'

A woman in the group (BR) thought she was giving her energy and effort to someone else (the companies she worked for). She wanted to give herself a chance to channel her energy and effort into her own business, so when she gets older she would have something to show for it.

Another woman (DM) wanted a home-based business when she starts having children for life cycle reasons. One woman (SR) suggested that small or large, 'there is no such thing as job security anymore'. She also wanted a business which would fit her life and temperament. SR continues to work for a very large company, but is looking forward to starting her own business.

Even though there were differences of opinion concerning some issues, **the consensus was that small company or large company, there is no company like your own company.** The following summarizes reasons why people were interested in their own company or an entrepreneurial venture.

There was a generally positive feeling about seeing the end result of one's work, especially with the customer.

> 'There is nothing more satisfying than doing a job well and seeing the results of your job and seeing a satisfied customer.'

People want to get back what they've given to a company:

> 'Over the years, working for other companies, I don't really have much to show in the last ten to fifteen years.'

Others indicated they wanted to be their own boss, to achieve a sense of fulfillment:

> 'Working for yourself is the only way to achieve self-actualization - *efforts* come back to you, whether they are good or bad.'
> 'The desire to see 'my product' on the shelf - to create something and for the monetary reasons.'

There were also a few people that *felt strongly* about not wanting to have their own business. Some negative opinions were expressed and included, primarily, too many hours and too much responsibility. It is also interesting to note that the people who expressed the desire not to own their business came from environments with family-owned businesses. 'It's too much responsibility and you have to work a lot more. It's too much pressure.'

EE: Is there a Need? What are the Benefits?

The participants are all currently enrolled in an experimental entrepreneurship course 399/499 (Figure 2). The focus group was conducted during the 12th week of a fifteen-week semester. By this time, they were already familiar with the demands of the course. Many found it very different and very demanding compared to the 'regular courses' in the MBA program. Many were surprised by how much was involved in planning a new venture, but they all agreed that this was valuable whether someone was going to start their own business or stay with a larger employer.

AP who had previously said that she absolutely did not want to own a business said, 'You can be entrepreneurial in your own department. Everyone taking the class could apply something they learned to their own work environments'. RL said 'This is the type of course that pulls it all together and integrates it all.' SR said she took the traditional capstone course, which is case-based, and this made more sense for a capstone course. LC, the Ph.D. chemist who wanted to continue working for a large company said, 'This course should be required for every MBA student. They should learn how to write a business plan, and how to pull it together.' SR and many others agreed that the most valuable feature of the course was what AP expressed 'This course brings it all together...marketing, management, finance...'.

Is there a Need for an MBA Concentration?

When asked, the majority of people in the group agreed that there was a need for some type of MBA concentration. However, some interesting qualitative insight was obtained as the discussion proceeded. Many used the 399/499 as a basis for their belief that a concentration would be of value. However, LC who agreed that an MBA concentration was a good thing, asked 'Why would an entrepreneur get an MBA?' DM who currently has his own construction company responded that 'People in the start-up phase of a business cannot afford $1500 a course.' A this point many people agreed but suggested that 'an entrepreneurial concentration' was valuable to anyone irrespective of where they were employed. JH who had worked with a major pharmaceutical company and who is currently in the start-up phase of her own speciality clothing company quoted her brother who had his own direct marketing business for a number of years. She said she asked him what was very important for someone interested in starting their own business. He said jokingly, 'After they have their head examined, education, education, education.'

Who needs it?

Many people working full-time with large companies are reimbursed for an MBA. There was consensus that an MBA program has immediate value for people in their current jobs, since any company can benefit from an entrepreneurial employee. However, there are also long-term benefits, since many participants expressed an interest in eventually starting their own business in the future. This is particularly important because when people get to the start-up phase, they generally do not have extra time of money to get a formal education. Therefore, it is more reasonable and economical to get an education now.

What additional Courses would be of Value? How should they be structured?

It appeared that people used the 399/499 as a starting point for their views. Figure 2 is a summary of the 399/499 course. Many agreed that more time would be helpful for coverage of the material in the course. MHM suggested 'use the 399/499 as a starting point and divided it up into sections.' She also suggested making the existing MBA courses 'more entrepreneurial'. ES, who is with a small family-owned management company suggested 'Study start-up companies or small companies, successes and failures; have entrepreneurs come in; come in and talk about successes and failures.' AP recommended 'cover negotiation skills, presentation skills, pricing topics'. BR wanted 'more communications/pr and computer related courses'. Many were also interested in courses related to growth/management strategies for small businesses. JH suggested including 'goal setting'. LC suggested that more time was needed to incubate the idea before actually writing the business plan. A 'Creativity/Innovation New Production Development course as a precursor to the Business Plan course.'

Some suggested a certificate program, but even though it seemed to be a reasonable option for some, others argued that for them it would not be practical because their employers would pay for an MBA program but not for a certificate in Entrepreneurship. So, it appeared that there were two potential target markets. People who pay for their own education may be more interested in shorter, more non-traditional types of programs such as certificates and seminars or workshops. People who are employed by large companies who are funding their education need the MBA degree, but the concentration could be in entrepreneurship.

Implications/Future Research

It appears that the growth of EE programs are need and market-driven. People differ in their opinions concerning the advantages and disadvantages of working for a small or large company, but there is consensus that companies can no longer offer job security. Our sample seem to believe that if you plan to work very hard, you may as well do it for yourself, or in an environment where you have more control and a better quality of life. EE was perceived to be a very valuable component of business education, independent of one's current employment status. People valued the hands-on learning.

The strongest conclusion of this study is that undoubtedly there is a need for EE programs. It is also clear that there are two different markets for EE, and consequently two types of programs are needed. One is the MBA-type program, which satisfies employers, and people with long-term entrepreneurial goals or intrapreneurial tendencies. The second is non-degree programs which satisfy entrepreneurs with more immediate needs. The students in this sample are older and more experienced. They also represent the growing number of part-time business students at lesser known schools. They tend to be more demanding concerning the relevance of their education. This study is important because it fills a gap concerning the opinions of that growing 'non-traditional student market', who are tougher and more savvy customers compared to 'traditional students' who are represented in the previous studies.

This initial research employed qualitative methodology because the intent was to gain a rich and deeper understanding of the issues. No apologies are made for the methodology. It succeeded in its hypothesis and idea generation objective. The next phase is to develop a measurement instrument which can be administered to a larger sample in ordered to test the hypotheses generated in this study. We can now present a large sample specific choice options in a survey format. The results of such a study can help in the design and implementation of EE programs. Other interesting findings of this project will be presented in other papers.

The 1st year doctoral student of ten years ago is older and hopefully a little wiser. She realizes that while we cannot teach people how to become passionate about their business idea or venture, we could provide them with tools that give their inherent passion for a new business venture a better chance of success. We can also employ marketing research methodologies to learn how to design EE programs which better serve the appropriate target markets.

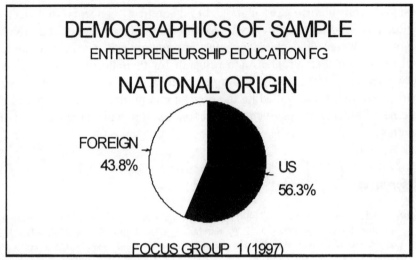

Figure 1. Sample Diversity

Course Objectives:

To develop a thorough understanding of the business plan and its role in strategic planning and decision-making in a new or existing venture.

Course Requirements and Format:

1. Critique of two existing business plans (published plans) with respect to their strengths and weaknesses.
2. Written business plan for student's venture of choice, with special emphasis on marketing strategy.
3. Weekly oral presentations on research related to essential components of business plan.
4. Written drafts of segments of business plan.
5. Written weekly activity log describing use of time related to research and other activities related to development of business plan.

The course is team taught by a full-time marketing professor (B.S. Biology; M.S. Chemistry; MBA Marketing and Finance; Ph.D. Marketing; two years experience as an R&D chemist with an entrepreneurial firm; seven years in academia-teaching and research) and a marketing consultant

195

with her own firm (M.S. in History; over ten years experience as a small business consultant). Presentation of theoretical concepts and lecture material varies with the topic area. Usually about 50 per cent of class time is devoted to lecture and questions and the remaining 50 per cent to student oral reports on their progress and research for their business plans. It is a very interactive class. Early in the semester, a class was devoted to basic market research tools, including the used of computerized databases and the Internet. Students were given a hands-on session with databases and the Internet.

References

Boberg, A.L. and Kiecker, P. (1988). Changing patterns of demand: Entrepreneurship education for entrepreneurs. In B.A. Kirchhoff, W.A. Long, W. Ed McMullan, K.H. Vesper, and W.E. Wetzel (Eds), *Frontiers of entrepreneurship research*, pp. 600 - 661, Wellesley, MA: Babson College

Hills, G.E. and Welsch, H.P. (1986). Entrepreneurship behavioral intentions and student independence characteristics and experiences. In R. Ronstadt, J.A. Hornaday, R. Peterson, and K.H. Vesper (Eds), *Frontiers of entrepreneurship research*, pp. 173 - 186, Wellesley, MA: Babson College.

Katz, J. and Green II, R. (1966). Academic resources for entrepreneurship education, *Simulation and Gaming*, 27(3) 365 - 375.

Mohan - Neill, S.I. (1996). interactions between Gender, Opportunity Structure, the desire for career change and entrepreneurial aspirations. Presented 1996 UIC/AMA Research Symposium on the Marketing/Entrepreneurship interface, San Diego, CA.

Neck, P.H. (1981). Education and training for small business. *Proceedings of the International Symposium on Small Business*, Berlin, October.

Plaschka, G.R. and Welsch, H.P. (1990). Emerging structures in entrepreneurship education: Curricular designs and strategies. *Entrepreneurship: Theory and Practice*, Spring 1990, 55 - 71.

Porter, L. (1994). The relation of entrepreneurship education to business education. *Simulation and Gaming*, 25(3), 416 - 420.

Robinson, P. and Haynes, M. (1991). Entrepreneurship education in America's major universities. *Entrepreneurship: Theory and Practice*, Spring 1991, 41 - 51.

Solomon, G. and Fernald Jr., L. (1991). Trends in small business management and entrepreneurship education in the United States. *Entrepreneurship: Theory and Practice,* Spring 1991, 25 - 40.

Stevenson, H.H. (1986). Harvard's experience with a new entrepreneurship program. In D.L. Sexton and R.W. Smilor (Eds) *The art and science of entrepreneurship*, pp. 389 - 402. Cambridge, A M: Ballinger.

Sulski, J. (1997). Entrepreneurial hopefuls flock to earn MBAs. *Chicago Tribune*, April 20, 1997, Section 1B, pp 3, 10 - 11.

11 Developing a Corporate Entrepreneurship Training Program

Donald F. Kuratko
Kelli M. Hurley
Jeffrey S. Hornsby

Corporate Entrepreneurship: an Introduction

The contemporary thrust in entrepreneurship as the major force in American business has led to a desire for this type of activity *inside* enterprises. While some researchers have concluded that entrepreneurship and bureaucracies are mutually exclusive and cannot coexist (e.g., Morse, 1986; Duncan et al., 1988), others described entrepreneurial ventures within the enterprise framework (Kanter, 1985; Kuratko and Montagno, 1989). Successful corporate ventures have been used in many companies, including 3M, Bell Atlantic, AT&T, Acordia, and Polaroid (McWilliams, 1993). Today there is a wealth of popular business literature describing a new 'corporate revolution' taking place thanks to the infusion of entrepreneurial thinking into larger bureaucratic structures. This infusion is referred to as corporate entrepreneurship (Kuratko *et al.*, 1993) or intrapreneurship (Pinchott, 1985). Why has this concept become so popular? One reason is that it allows corporations to tap the innovative talents of its own workers and managers. Steven Brandt (1986, p. 54) puts it this way:

> Ideas come from people. Innovations is a capability of the many. Hat capability is utilized when people give commitment to the mission and life of the enterprise and have the power to do something with their capabilities. Non commitment is the price of obsolete managing practices, not the lack of talent or desire.

Gifford Pinchott (1985) defined 'intrapreneurship' as entrepreneurship inside of the corporation where individuals will 'champion' new ideas from development to complete profitable reality. Other authors have expanded this definition by including the need to recognize that entrepreneurial activities revolve around organizational sanctions and resource commitments for the purpose of innovative results (Miller and Friesen, 1983; Burgelman, 1984; Kanter, 1985; Alterowitz, 1988). While on the surface this concept may appear straightforward, a number of authors have concluded that corporate entrepreneurship which he labeled administrative, opportunistic, initiative, acquisitive, and incubative. Incubative entrepreneurship refers to the creation of semi-autonomous units within the existing organization for the purpose of sensing external and internal innovative developments; screening and assessing new venture opportunities, and initiating and nurturing new venture developments.

Karl Vesper (1984) developed three major definitions of corporate entrepreneurship, which he identifies as (1) new strategic direction; (2) initiative from below; and (3) autonomous business creation. Vesper's study illustrates that corporate entrepreneurship could be any one of these individual types, as well as any or all possible combinations. Similar to schollhammer's incubative form, the 'initiative from below' approach, where an employee undertakes something new (i.e., an innovation), best represents the type of corporate entrepreneuring activity that has empowered people in a leadership sense. Stevenson and Jarillo (1990) proposed a definition of entrepreneurship that would strengthen the understanding of corporate entrepreneurship. They stated, 'entrepreneurship is a process by which individuals - either on their own or inside organizations - pursue opportunities without regard to the resources they currently control' (p.23). In this vein Guth and Ginsberg (1990) stressed that corporate entrepreneurship encompasses two major types of phenomena: new venture creation with existing organizations and the transformation of organizations through strategic renewal.

All of these concepts appear to be summarized by Zahra (1991) when he stated:

> Corporate entrepreneurship refers to formal and informal activities aimed at creating new business in established companies through product and process innovations and market developments. These activities may take place at the corporate, division (business), functional, or project levels, with the unifying objective of improving a company's competitive position and financial

performance. Corporate entrepreneurship also entails the strategic renewal of an existing business (p. 262).

Specific Elements for Corporate Entrepreneurship

What conditions or stops must be followed in order to succeed with corporate entrepreneurial strategy? These steps are described below.

Step 1: Developing the Vision

The first step in planning an entrepreneurial strategy for the enterprise is sharing the vision of innovation that executives wish to achieve. Since it is suggested that corporate entrepreneuring results from the creative talents of people in the organization, then employees need to know and understand this vision. Brandt (1986) stressed the importance of shared vision within a strategy that seeks high achievement. This shared vision requires identification of specific objectives for corporate entrepreneuring strategies and the programs needed to achieve those objectives. Kanter (1985) described three major objectives and their respective programs designed for innovations. These are:

Objective #1	Making sure that current system, structures, and practices do not present insurmountable roadblocks to the flexibility and fast action needed for innovation.
Objective #2	Providing the incentives and tools for entrepreneurial projects.
Objective #3	Seeking synergies across business areas, so that new opportunities are discovered in new combinations at the same time that business units retail operating autonomy.

Step 2: Developing Innovation

The next step for corporations is to develop innovation as the key element in their strategy. Schroeder (1990) examined the importance of innovation within the corporate environment as a key to competitive strategy. Innovation is described as chaotic and unplanned by some authors (Peters, 1987) while other researchers insist it is a systematic discipline (Drucker, 1985). Both of these positions can be true depending upon the nature of the innovation. One way to understand this concept is to focus on two different types of innovation—radical and incremental (Dent, 1990).

Radical innovation represents the inaugural breakthroughs that have been launched (personal computers, Post-it Notes, disposable diapers, overnight mail delivery). These innovations take experimentation to determined vision which are not necessarily managed but must be recognized and nurtured.

Incremental innovation refers to the systematic evolution of a product or service into newer or larger markets. Examples include microwave popcorn, popcorn used for packaging (to replace Styrofoam), frozen yogurt, etc. Many times the incremental innovation will take over after a radical innovation introduces a breakthrough. The structure, marketing, financing, and formal systems of a corporation can help implement incremental innovation.

Both types of innovation require vision and support. This support takes different steps for effective development. For example, Howell and Higgins, (1990) emphasize the need for a **champion** - the person with a vision and the ability to share it. And finally, both types of innovation require an effort by the top management of the corporation to develop and educate employees concerning innovation and entrepreneurship-referred to as **top management support**.

Step 3: Development of Venture Teams

The third step is to focus upon venture teams. Venture teams and the potential they hold for producing innovative results are being recognized as the productivity breakthrough of nineties. There's certainly little doubt that their popularity is on the rise. Companies that have committed to a venture team approach often label the change they have undergone a 'transformation' or a 'revolution.' This new breed of work team is a new strategy for many firms. They are referred to as self-directed, self-managing, or high-performance, but a venture team includes all of those descriptions (Lee, 1990 and Wolff, 1989).

In examining the entrepreneurial development for corporations, Reich (1987) found that entrepreneurship is not the sole province of the company's founder or its top managers. Rather, it is diffused throughout the company where experimentation and development go on al the time as the company searches for new ways to build on the knowledge already accumulated by its workers. Reich's definition of collective **entrepreneurship** follows.

> In collective entrepreneurship, individual skills are integrated into a group: this collective capacity to innovate becomes something greater than the sum of its parts. Over time, as group members work various problems and approaches, they learn about many such small-scale adaptations, effected throughout the organization, is to propel the enterprise forward (p. 81).

In keeping with Reich's focus on collective entrepreneurship, venture teams offer corporations the opportunity to utilize the talents of individuals but with a sense of teamwork.

The net result of many such small-scale adaptations, affected throughout the organization, is to propel the enterprise forward. In keeping with this focus on collective entrepreneurship, venture teams offer corporations the opportunity to use the talents of individuals but with a sense of teamwork. An excellent example is Signode, a $750-million-a-year manufacturer of plastic and steel strapping for packaging and materials handling, located in Glenview, Illinois. The company's leaders wanted to chart new directions to become a $1 billion-plus firm. In pursuit of this goal, Signode devised an aggressive strategy for growth by developing 'new legs' for the company. It formed a corporate development group to pursue markets outside the company's core businesses but within the framework of its corporate strengths. It also formed venture teams, but before launching the first of these tope management identified the firm's global business strengths and broad areas with potential for new product lines: warehousing/shipping; packaging; plastics for non-packaging, fastening, and joining systems; and product identification and control systems. Each new business opportunity suggested by a venture team was to have the potential to general $50 million in business within five years. In addition, each opportunity had to build on one of Signode's strengths: industrial customer base and marketing expertise, systems sales and service capabilities, containment and reinforcement technology, steel and plastic process technology, machine and design capabilities, and productivity and distribution know-how.

This criteria was based on 'business-to-business' selling only because Signode did not want to market directly to retailers or consumers. The basic technology to be employed in the new business had to already exist and there had to be a strong likelihood of attaining a major market share within a niche. Finally, the initial investment in the new opportunity had to be $30 million or less. Based on these criteria, Signode began to build its 'V-Team' (venture team) approach to intrapreneurship. It took three months to select the first team members and initial teams had three common traits: high risk-taking ability, creativity, and the ability to deal with ambiguity. All six participants were multidisciplinary volunteers who would work full-time on developing new consumer product packaging businesses. The team members came from diverse backgrounds: design engineering, marketing, sales, and product development. They set up shop in rented office space five miles from the firm's headquarters. The six teams were not able to develop remarkable new ventures. However, the efforts did payoff for Signode as one venture team developed a business plan to manufacture plastic trays for frozen entrees that could be used in either regular or microwave ovens. The business potential for this product was estimated to be in excess of $50 million a year within five years. Thus, the V-Team experience rekindled enthusiasm and affected morale throughout the organization. Most importantly, the V-Team approach became Signode's strategy to invent their future rather than waiting for things to happen (Kuratko and Hodgetts, 1995).

Step 4: Structuring for an Intrapreneurial Climate

In re-establishing the drive to innovate in today's corporations the final, and possibly most critical step, is to invest heavily in entrepreneurial activities that allow new ideas to flourish in an innovative environment (Goddard, 1987). This concept, when coupled with the other specific elements of a strategy for entrepreneurship leadership, enhances the potential for employees to become idea developers. In fact, in developing employees as a source of innovations for corporations, researchers have found that companies need to provide more nurturing and information sharing activities (Hisrich, 1985/1986). In addition to supporting entrepreneurial projects, there is a need to develop a climate that will help innovative-minded people reach their full potential (Quinn, 1990). The perception of an innovative climate is critical for stressing the importance of management's commitment to not only the organization's people but also to the innovative projects (Schuler, 1986; Sathe, 1988; Brown and Meresman, 1990). (See Table 1 for Critical Elements)

Table 1: Critical Elements in Intrapreneurial Environments

The presence of explicit goals:	These goals need to be mutually agreed upon by the worker and management so specific steps are achieved.
A system of feedback and positive reinforcement:	This feedback is necessary in order for potential inventors, creators, or intrapreneurs to realize there is acceptance and reward.
An emphasis on individual responsibility:	Confidence, trust, and accountability are key features to the success of any innovative program.
Rewards based upon results:	A reward system that enhances and encourages others to risk and to achieve must be established.

Kuratko, D.F., Hornsby, J.S., Naffziger, D.W., and Montagno, R.V., 'Implementing Entrepreneurial Thinking in Established Organizations,' *Advanced Management Journal*, (1993), (Winter), 30.

Studies conducted by Kuratko, Montagno and Hornsby (1990, 1992) investigated the types of factors which foster an intrapreneurial climate. The Intrapreneurship Assessment Instrument (IAI) was developed to provide for a psychometrically sound instrument that represented key entrepreneurial climate factors in the existing corporate entrepreneurship literature. The responses to the IAI were statistically analyzed and resulted in five identified factors: Management Support for Intrapreneurship, Work Discretion, Reward Reinforcement, Time Availability, and Organizational Boundaries.

Corporate Entrepreneurship Training Program

As a way for organizations to develop key environmental factors for entrepreneurial activity, a Corporate Entrepreneurship Training Program can serve as a manipulation to induce the change needed in the work atmosphere. A summary of an actual program based on the factors identified by Kuratko, et al. is presented to provide a general understanding of a training program designed to introduce an entrepreneurial environment in the company. This award-winning training program (recipient of two awards from the American Society for Training and Development, ASTD) was intended to create an awareness of entrepreneurial opportunities in the organization. The program consisted of six four-hour modules, each designed to move participants to the point of being able to support intrapreneurship in their own work area. The modules and a brief summary of their contents are as follows:

1. **Introduction to Entrepreneurial Management**. An enthusiastic overview of entrepreneurial thinking is provided. Participants are challenged to think innovatively and the need for 'breaking out of the box' in today's organizations is emphasized. Participants learn about the entrepreneurial activities at such well known companies as Hewlett Packard and 3M. A review of current management practices demonstrates how innovation and cultural change are necessary if organizations are to survive in today's competitive marketplace. Participants apply their learning by analyzing and contrasting two video cases that describe entrepreneuring at Du Pont and Polaroid. For each company, participants identify what distinguishes the activity as entrepreneurial.

2. **Thinking Creatively**. The process of thinking creatively is foreign to most bureaucratic organizations. The misconceptions about thinking creatively are to be reviewed and a discussion of the most common creativity inhibitors is presented. Participants complete several exercises which will facilitate their won creative thinking. Participants first consider several thinking patterns and, using video vignettes, identify them in people. For example, one character exhibits 'black and white' thinking; another has a high degree of functional perception. Other theories, such as left-brain/right-brain thinking, are also discussed. Participants then assess their own creativity and create a

long-term structured program to enhance the ability, often by focusing on resolving personal issues or problems.

3. **Idea Development Process**. Participants at this point are given the opportunity to generate a set of specific ideas on which they would like to work. The process includes examining a number of aspects of the corporation including structural barriers and facilitators. Additionally, participants determine needed resources to accomplish their projects. Participants are instructed to meet in groups and utilize evening time to flush out intrapreneurial ideas that they will present the next day.

4. **Assessing Entrepreneurial Culture**. The Intrapreneurial Assessment Instrument is provided and described which assesses the level of entrepreneurial culture within the organization. Participants complete the survey and results will be fed back to all participants. Areas for improvement are addressed during the remaining seminar topics.

5. **Barriers and Facilitators to Entrepreneurial Thinking**. The most common barriers to innovative behavior are reviewed. Participants complete several exercises which help them deal with barriers in the work place. In addition, video case histories are shown which depict actual corporate entrepreneurs that have been successful dealing with corporate barriers. An interesting result is that since the participants are usually mid-level managers, they realize they are often both the source and the victims of the barriers they identify.

6. **Action Planning**. Up to this point, participants have examined several aspects of facilitators and barriers to behaving innovatively in their organization. During this time each participant is asked to complete a personal action plan that sets a goal, establishes a work team, assesses current conditions, determines necessary resources, develops a step by step timetable for project completion, and a method of project evaluation. Participants can also be assigned to groups for this activity. Top management is encouraged to provide support for the projects, evaluate their completion and reward entrepreneurial activity.

In order to assess whether the training program impacted the organization's culture a study was conducted on 111 low to mid-level managers in a large Midwestern company known as The Associated Group (Kuratko, Montagno and Hornsby (1990). The research study included three steps. First, the IAI was administered to all participants to obtain a baseline concerning their perceptions of the firm's culture. Second, the participants participated in all phases of the training program (except the assessment component) described earlier. Finally, the IAI was readministered four months following the training. A control group who completed the IAI at both times but did not participate in the training was utilized to provide an unbiased comparison for training program results. The results of the research study showed a significant increase in all factors following completion of the Corporation Entrepreneurship Training Program. While these findings suggest that there is some validity to the training program it is important that each firm who utilizes this or any type of training evaluates its effectiveness.

After reviewing these elements, it becomes apparent that change is inevitable in the corporate structure if entrepreneurial activity is going to prosper. The change process consists of a series of emerging constructions of the people, the corporate goals and the existing needs.

Process and Support

We developed our corporate entrepreneurship training program over twelve years. It evolved into its present form as we presented it numerous times and made changes based on participant feedback and further research.

Corporate Entrepreneurship training that is viewed as a one time activity cannot succeed. The more widespread the understanding of incorporate entrepreneurship, the more likely it is that real cultural changes will occur in the organization. The organizations for whom we have worked understand that. They all have attempted to repeat the program for as broad an audience as possible.

One fact continues to surprise participants: the amount of work they can accomplish is such a short time. Invariably, when told they must create comprehensive business plans in a condensed time frame, participants claim it cannot be done. But they do create plans - in most cases, quite good ones. In one organization, we were told the plans presented were better than most planning documents currently accepted within the firm.

Despite the program's success, we have noted several issues that may limit its value and the effectiveness of corporate entrepreneurship as a strategy. 'Slack time,' or free time to develop ideas, is critical for corporate entrepreneuring's success. So are reward systems for corporate entrepreneurs. But participants have consistently said that top management will not provide those prerequisites. Top management in many organizations, while supporting the entrepreneurial concept, has sometimes failed to support the culture visibly. Without that support, a corporate entrepreneurship program cannot work. Whether real or imagined, such blocks will prevent intrapreneuring from reaching its full potential.

To bring about the fundamental cultural change needed to promote corporate entrepreneurship in an organization, top management must create an integrated strategy for the change effort. Corporate entrepreneurship, as it is taught in our training program and others, can be used to implement strategic objectives. But top management first must articulate the strategy clearly and reflect it in specific organizational goals.

Results from Corporate Entrepreneurship Training

Corporate Entrepreneurship Training is best illustrated with an example of The Associated Group (mentioned above). Under the vision and direction of L. Ben Lytle, Chairman and CEO of The Associated Group, a startling restructuring plan was put into effect during 1986 in order to facilitate the entrepreneurial process. In 1983 the company was operating as Blue Cross/Blue Shield of Indiana and was literally bogged down in its own bureaucracy. As a result the Associated Group (the new name taken by the company rather than Blue Cross/Blue Shield of Indiana) was losing ground in a fast-paced, changing insurance industry. However, in 1986 after initiating a corporate entrepreneurship training program, Lytle divided the company legally, emotionally, physically, geographically, and culturally into operating companies named Acordia Companies, ranging in size from 42 to 200 employees.

The opportunities for entrepreneurial individuals within the organization began to expand with the development of these 'mini corporations,' which were designed to capture market niches and innovatively develop new ones. Each separate Acordia company has an individual CEO, Vice President, and outside board of directors which delegated full authority to run the business. In 1986 The Associated Group was one large corporation with 2,800 employees serving only the state of Indiana with all revenue generated from health insurance. By the end of 1991, 1800 days had gone by and culminated a five-year strategic plan to restructure and infuse entrepreneurial thinking into the organization. The results had the company employing 7,000 people in 50 different companies, serving 49 states and generating over 25 per cent of its $2 billion in revenue in lines of business outside health insurance. It provides an example of effectiveness that corporate training can have in capturing the imagination of the entire company. It uncovers 'builder-types' in the company seeking challenge and accountability of their ideas and innovative abilities.

There are currently 32 Acordia Companies where corporate clients can obtain all types of insurance-related services including commercial property and casualty coverage, group life and health insurance, third party claims administration for self-insured benefit plans, and employee benefits consulting. In order to institute self-perpetuating change in the Acordia network, the mini corporation CEOs are encouraged (and rewarded through stock options) to expand business and then spin off certain parts of the business either geographically or by specialty when there are 200 employees or there are too many management layers. In addition, the CEOs are evaluated on their ability to identify and nurture additional potential CEOs within their own organization. One concise example of the Acordia concept is Acordia Corporate Benefits, Inc., which was incorporated as a Third Party Administrator and Insurance Agency in the state of Indiana effective December 1, 1990. Its approved mission was to market and administer insurance and insurance-related products to employers with 50 or more employees, excluding customers that fall within the missions of any other Acordia companies. (There were 23 original Acordia companies formed out of The Associated Group, formerly Blue Cross and Blue Shield of Indiana and today there are 32 companies.) Generally speaking, employers in the manufacturing and service industries with fewer than 1,000 employees are targeted, while geographically there is a restriction to employers located in the northern half of the United States.

Michael D. Houk, the company's new CEO, described the company's

209

entrepreneurial birth out of a major Blue Cross and Blue Shield organization. On December 1, 1990, 97 employees staffed the new company and prepared to move to a new facility February 1, 1991. During that 60-day period, we began to build our new culture, the culture of a company whose future was totally dependent upon the results it produced. From the first day, we eliminated the multiple levels of management that employees had been accustomed to. Each employee was hired by a vice president in our company who reported directly to the president. No more supervisors, managers, or directors to stagnate the communication channels. We also converted from a 37.5 hour work week to a 40-hour work week, added an employee profit-sharing plan, a dress code, raised expectations, and set up our new facility with our new work flows in mind. All these changes combined, allowed us to eliminate over 30 positions from the operation that had been handing the business prior to December 1, 1990. Attitudes began to change ever so slowly at first, but each day we saw some improvement. When we moved out of the old 15-story building to our new, one-level facility on February 1, 1991, we realized a significant increase in the morale and excitement of our employees. Our employees began to take greater pride in where they worked and how they worked. As a result, service to our customers improved. Our clients were no longer unknown employers, and employees who generated work now were our clients upon whom our future would be built.

'...During that first year, we went on to add an Employee Advisory Committee that meets monthly with the president to continually refine our corporate policies and practices, our culture. We've implemented a weight-loss program for our employees, a totally no smoking facility, quarterly all-employee meetings, dress-down day every payday, an annual family picnic, a Christmas lunch, etc., all organized and run by employees elected by their peers. But have we been successful financially? In a word...yes!...'

During 1991, revenues exceeded $10 million and net income before taxes exceeded $1.8 million, a pre-tax return on revenue of over 18 per cent. The second full year was even better, and pre-tax net exceeded $2.2 million, a 22 per cent increase over 1991. During 1992, over 40 per cent of net income came from outside Indiana and over 20 per cent of the net income was from non-health sources. Acordia Corporate Benefits was now licensed as a third-party administrator and life and health insurance agency in over 20 states, concentrating in the Midwest. Acordia Corporate Benefits began to consider diversification either geographically, by product, or into non-health products. In 1993, the company added a new product line, Flexible Benefits Administration, which increased revenues by over $1 million in the

210

first year. Also, Acordia Corporate Benefits acquired a large Indianapolis-based property and casualty insurance agency during the first quarter of 1993 increasing revenue an additional $3.5 million.

By the end of 1993, annual revenue increased to over $16 million, with pre-tax net income approaching $3 million, and an employment base of approximately 160 employees, all in a span of three years. More importantly, this particular Acordia made the transition from a business totally dependent upon the health insurance business and employers in Indiana alone to a business operating in over 20 states, with over one-third of revenue from non-health products (Kuratko and Hodgetts, 1995, pp. 484 - 485). Thus, the Acordia strategy is to 'concentrate and divide,' which leads to continuous innovation, growth, and entrepreneurial development. Acordia now ranks 7th in Business Insurance's worldwide broker rankings. Corporate entrepreneurship is a risk and it has to start somewhere - sometimes small and corporate controlled. But if it starts, there is the likelihood of greater success. People become more comfortable with the idea, confidence builds, results occur, and soon the first corporate assigned projects evolve into more autonomous ventures that reach farther out before being required to report into administrative structure. The key steps of vision, innovation, venture teams, and innovative climate need to be developed for corporate entrepreneurship to become a reality.

The major thrust behind corporate entrepreneurship is a revitalization of innovation, creativity, and leadership in our corporations. It appears that corporate entrepreneurship may possess the critical components needed for the future productivity of our organizations. If so, the recognizing the objectives, requisites, and range of potential training activities are most important in establishing entrepreneurial strategies in contemporary organizations.

References

Alterowitz, Ralph (1988) *New Corporate Ventures*, John Wiley & Sons, New York.

Brandt, Steven C. (1986) *Entrepreneuring in Established Companies*, Homewood, Illinois, Dow Jones/Irwin Company.

Brown, Rick and Meresman, Joseph L. (September 1990) 'Balancing Stability and Innovation to Stay Competitive,' *Personnel*, pp. 49 - 52.

Burgelman, R. (1984) 'Designs for Corporate Entrepreneurship,' *California Management Review*, pp. 26, 154 - 166.

Dent, Harry S., Jr. (June 1990) 'Reinventing Corporate Innovation.' *Small Business Report*, pp. 31 - 42.

Duncan, W. Jack. et al. (May - June 1988) 'Intrapreneurship and the Reinvention of the Corporation,' *Business Horizons, pp.*16 - 21.

Goddard, Robert W. (March 1987) 'Recharge the Power Shortage in Corporate America,' *Personnel Journal*, pp. 39 - 42.

Guth, W.D. and Ginsberg A. (1990) 'Corporate Entrepreneurship,' *Strategic Management Journal*, (Special Issue #11), pp. 5 - 15.

Hisrich, Robert D. and Peters, Michael P. (1986) 'Establishing a New Business Venture Unit Within a Firm,' *Journal of Business Venturing*, pp. 307 - 322.

Howell Jane M. and Higgins, Christopher A. (Summer 1990) 'Champions of Change; Identifying, Understanding, and Supporting Champions of Technology Innovations,' *Organizational Dynamics*, pp. 40 - 55.

Kanter, Rosabeth M. (Winter 1985) 'Supporting Innovation and Venture Developing Established Companies,' *Journal of Business Venturing*, 1;1, pp. 47 - 60.

Kuratko, Donald F. and Hodgetts, Richard M. (1995) *Entrepreneurship: A Contemporary Approach*, (3rd ed.), (Ft. Worth, TX: HBJ/ Dryden Press).

Kuratko, Donald F., and Hornsby, Jeffrey S. (1997) 'Developing Entrepreneurial Leadership in Contemporary Organizations,' *Journal of Management Systems*, Vol. 8 #1, pp. 17 - 24.

Kuratko, Donald F., Hornsby, Jeffrey S., and Montagno, Ray V. (August 1992) 'Critical Organizational Elements in Corporate Entrepreneurship,' Presentation to the Academy of Management, *Proceedings Abstract*, p. 424.

Kuratko, Donald F., and Montagno, Ray V. (October, 1989) 'The Intrapreneurial Spirit,' *Training and Development Journal*, pp. 83 - 87.

Kuratko, Donald F., Montagno, Ray V., and Hornsby, Jeffrey S. (1990) 'Developing and Intrapreneurial Assessment Instrument for an Effective Corporate Entrepreneurial Environment,' *Strategic Management Journal*, 11, pp. 49 - 58.

Kuratko, D.F., Hornsby, J.S., Naffziger, D.W., and Montagno, R.V. (1993) 'Implementing Entrepreneurial Thinking in Established Organizations,' *Advanced Management Journal*, pp. 28 - 33.

Lee, Chris (June 1990) 'Beyond Teamwork,' *Training*, pp. 25 - 32.

Miller, D. and Friesen, P.H. (1982) 'Innovation in Conservation and Entrepreneurial Firms: Two Models of Strategic Management,' *Strategic Management Journal*, 3, pp. 1 - 25.

Morse, C. Wesle (December 1986) 'The Delusion of Intrapreneurship,' *Long Range Planning*, 19; pp. 92 - 95.

Peters, Thomas J. (1987) *Thriving on Chaos*, New York, NY: Harper & Row.

Pinchott, Gifford (1985) *Intrapreneuring*, New York NY: Harper & Row.

Quinn, Susan R. (February 1990) 'Supporting Innovation in the Workplace,' *Supervision*, pp. 3 - 5.

Reich, Robert B. (May - June 1987) 'The Team As Hero,' *Harvard Business Review*, p. 81.

Sathe, Vijay (Winter 1988) 'From Surface to Deep Corporate Entrepreneurship,' *Human Resource Management*, pp. 389 - 411.

Schollhammer, Hans (1982) 'Internal Corporate Entrepreneurship' In C. Kent, D. Sexton and K. Vesper (editors), *Encyclopedia of Entrepreneurship*, (Prentice Hall: Englewood Cliffs, NJ).

Schroeder, Dean M. (1990) 'A Dynamic Perspective on the Impact of Process Innovation Upon Competitive Strategies,' *Strategic Management Journal*, 2, pp. 25 - 41.

Schuler, Randall S. (1986) 'Fostering and Facilitating Entrepreneurship in Organizations: Implications for Organization Structure and Human Resource Management Practices,' *Human Resource Management*, 25, pp. 607 - 629.

Stevenson, H.H. and Jarillo, J.C. (1990) 'A Paradigm of Entrepreneurship: Entrepreneurial Management.,' *Strategic Management Journal*, (Special Issue 11), pp. 17 - 27.

Vesper, K.H. (1984) 'Three Faces of Corporate Entrepreneurship: A Pilot Study,' *Frontiers of Entrepreneurship Research*, (Wellesley, MA; Babson College), pp. 294 - 320.

Wolff, Michael F. (November - December 1989) 'Building Teams - What Works,' *Research Technology Management*, pp. 9 - 10.

Zahra, S.A. (1991) 'Predictors and Financial Outcomes of Corporate Entrepreneurship: AN Exploratory Study,' *Journal of Business Venturing*, 6, pp. 259 - 286.

12 Becoming a Successful Corporate Entrepreneur

Peter A. Koen

Abstract

This paper discusses a course in corporate entrepreneuring taught to students from large companies. The success of the course was amazing with start - up funding approved for seven of the thirteen business ventures developed. The course is divided into four sections. The 1st part reviews the key factors for corporate venture success, the 2nd part evaluates the organizational and cultural factors, the 3rd part provides guidance in how to develop a business case, and the final portion is the development of an actual business venture in student's company. Key criteria, determined from the executive champions working with the venture teams, for obtaining start-up funds were corporate strategic fit, the teams understanding of the business, the market and the product and their ability to develop a comprehensive business plan.

Introduction

Intrapreneuring[1] is inherently frustrating and difficult [2 - 5]. But why should it be? Perhaps the typical technical professional is inadequately trained. To this end a unique intrapreneurial course was introduced into the Masters of Technology Management (MTM) course taught at Stevens Institute of Technology. The success of the course was amazing, with corporate funding obtained for seven of the 13 business ventures that the students developed. This paper reviews the structure of the course and the key criteria used by the executive champions in determining their funding decision.

Pedagogical Overview

Five criteria were determined to be necessary for the student to succeed with an intrapreneurial project. First they needed to understand the key success factors associated with successful ventures. This was done by reviewing the literature and giving lectures on the key criteria which previous investigators had learned. The second criteria was to develop an awareness of the corporate and political environment which affected corporate venturing in their company. This was accomplished by requiring the students to evaluate the venturing process in their company, along with an evaluation of both successful and unsuccessful ventures. The third criteria was to obtain the support of an executive champion within their company. The authors own experience along with the results of previous studies [6 - 8] have indicated the importance of having an executive champion. The fourth criteria was to provide the students with experience in preparing a business case. The majority of students taking the course needed to gain experience in preparing a business case since students develop an actual business case for a real venture in their respective company as the final project. Only seven per cent of the 42 students taking this course had ever done a business case. This criteria was met by allowing the students to develop a business case for a software based business simulation [23]. The fifth criteria was to provide the students with support in preparing the final project business case. This was done by meeting with the student teams during the course as well as requiring the students to prepare a preliminary presentation on their venture mid way through the program.

The Course

The course is divided into four parts and is taught weekly for two half hours over a fourteen-week period. The course syllabus is shown in Exhibit 1. The foundation portion, or first part, deals with a reviews of the literature and a discussion of the key success factors which separate successful from unsuccessful corporate ventures. The company portion, or second part, review the organizational and cultural factors effecting the success of new projects. The remaining two parts deal with the development of a business case. The simulation portion, or third part, allow the student to develop a business case for a simulation. In the final portion, the students develop an actual business venture for their company in teams of from three to four persons. The majority of teams consist of members from their own company - although two of the 13 teams consisted of members from more than one company.

Part I - The Foundation (Weeks 2 through 4)

The principal purpose of this portion of the course is to allow the students to learn the key success factors which separate successful from unsuccessful corporate ventures. The students evaluate the key finding from 10 studies done in corporate venturing [5, 9 - 16]. The key findings from these studies are to:

- Choose ventures based on market needs rather than technological capability [9, 10, 16, 17].
- Expect corporate venturing to be difficult and expect negative financial returns for at least 4 years [9, 10].
- Maximize success by choosing ventures where the market conditions are favorable (i.e. low number of competitors, high industry growth rate and lack of a dominant competitor) [13].
- Choose products that are proprietary [9, 10].
- Enter the market aggressively both in investment intensity and marketing strategy in order to obtain rapid market share [9, 10, 13].
- Choose ventures where there is good strategic fit [5, 11, 16].

Based upon this foundation the students understand the key issues associated with successful corporate ventures. In order to reinforce these concepts the students are required in their first case to evaluate both a successful and unsuccessful venture in their company. Invariably, they found that the factors discussed above played a pivotal role in their own companies.

Exhibit 1 - Course Syllabus

Lecture	Topic	Lecture	Case Presentation or Simulation
1	Introduction and Course Overview	•	
	Part I - Foundation		
2 and 3	Corporate Venture Lessons	•	
4	Case I - Students evaluate a successful and unsuccessful venture in their company		•
	Part II - Organizational and Cultural Factors		
5	Venture Organizations in Established Companies	•	
6	Organizational and cultural factors which effect ventures	•	
7	Case II - Students evaluate the venture process and organizational structure in their own company		•
8	Comparison of Intrapreneuring (Starting projects in large companies) to High Technology Entrepreneuring (Starting your own high technology business)	•	
	Part III - The Simulation		
9	The Business Plan	•	
10	Orientation to the Simulation	•	
11	Case III - Students prepare a Business Plan for Simulation and run simulation		•
	Part IV - The Business Venture		
12	Case IV - Students prepare a preliminary presentation of their venture		•
13 and 14	Final Presentation of Business Venture		•

The actual course sequence is slightly different and was modified for this exhibit so that all of the lectures for each part could be sequenced together. In actuality, lectures 9 and 12 are given earlier in the sequence.

Exhibit 2 - The Business Plan

Section	Topic	Pages
1	*Executive Summary* Summarizes the highlights of the project including the identification of unmet customer needs, strategic fit, strategic and financial reward, risks and major assumptions and the initial recommendations and milestones.	1
2	*Scope* Describes what the project encompasses, unmet customer needs, strategic fit and a product generation map [26].	1
3	*Market and Customer Definition* Describes how the market is segmented, practice, usage and trends in the market place and a customer need competitor comparison.	2
4	*Competitor Analysis* In this section the competitors to the venture are evaluated including market share, level of commitment, strengths, weakness, trends, patent/licensing issues as well as potential threats.	1
5	*Why this venture will win?* In this section the students describe the key project targets and explain how achieving these targets will allow the venture to 'win' and achieve competitive advantage. Further the strategic and financial value to the business are restated here.	1
6	*Market Entry Strategy* In this section the student describes how the product will be introduced, including a channel, pricing and promotion and advertising strategy.	1/2

Part II - Organizational and cultural Factors (Weeks 5 through 8)

Organizational and cultural factors along with management behaviors play a significant role in determining venture success [5, 18]. Both successful and unsuccessful organizations are reviewed [19 - 22]. In case II, the students evaluate the processes and organizational structure in their own company for doing a venture so that they can better understand the obstacles and hurdles which they are likely to encounter.

Exhibit 2 - The Business Plan (Continued)

Section	Topic	Pages
7	**Technology Strategy** In this section the student formulates a technology strategy for the project including a discussion of core competencies [27], a Technology Limit analysis [28, 29], a proprietary position statement along with an analysis of where (internal, strategic alliances, etc.) all the technologies will be obtained from.	2
8	**Operational Strategy** In this section the operational strategy and supply chain describing the linkage between the product through delivery to the customer is described. In addition the fit with existing capabilities and capacities are also indicated.	1/2
9	**Project Plan** A PERT or Gantt chart showing an overview of the entire project are indicated here. The initial workplan showing major milestones, timing and responsibility are also included.	1
10	**Project Organization** The initial project team along with the required time requirements are indicated here.	1/2
11	**Financials** Detailed financials over a five - year period including RONA, and IRR are included in this section.	1
12	**Risk Assessment** The major risks and assumptions associated with this project along with their potential impact are discussed in this portion of the business plan.	1
	Total Pages	12 1/2

Part III - The Simulation (Weeks 9 through 11)

Only seven per cent of the students participating in this course had ever developed a business case. In order to gain experience in doing this the students developed one for a business simulation [23]. The business case that was developed, which followed the same format (see Exhibit 2) as that required for the final business venture, emphasized the risk and assumptions [24, 25] associated with the start-up rather than focusing on elaborate financials. The students indicated that this step represented an important learning step prior to Part IV.

Part IV - The Business Venture (Weeks 12 through 14)

All ventures require an executive champion within the company who is typically a senior management executive, is a supporter of the project and is capable of directly or indirectly influencing resources to the start-up. The participants are required to complete and present the business case to the executive champion and a multi-company executive review panel at the conclusion of the course.

As an incentive, all teams obtaining funding were given an 'A' for the course. The rationale for doing this was that any team that could obtain funding for a venture in a fourteen-week period from a large corporation had an excellent understanding of the intrapreneurial process and was entitled to an 'A.'

The actual idea for the venture was left to the students taking the course. However, the chosen venture must meet two criteria. First, the project cannot already be in the company's product pipeline nor cannot it be an incremental improvement to an existing project. A description of four of the seven ventures which received funding are shown in Exhibit 3. For confidentiality purposes the remaining could not be discussed.

Exhibit 3 - Examples of Intrapreneurial Projects

World Wide Web Browser (Large - Telecommunications Company - greater than $10 billion in sales)

This project involved the development of a Internet web browser to allow small businesses to make non-complex changes to there phone service. The user would access the companies web site through the Internet and revise their phone service accordingly. Changes would then be sent to the appropriate service department. Previously, such changes were handled by a large telephone support staff.

Cleaning Methodologies (Large Flavoring Company - greater than $1 billion in sales)

This project involved process methodologies that are used to clean and deodorize processing equipment in order to reduce down time. The current process required the complete disassembly of their manufacturing equipment in order to assure that no residuals from a previous flavoring run were left. Even a low residual concentration from the previous run, in the parts per million, could potentially contaminate the new run. Typical down time for the cleaning was 1 - 2 days. The new process would allow in-situ cleaning to be done in 2 hours.

3D Animation Art (Small Consumer Products Company - approximately $30 million in sales)

This was for the development of a new consumer product for the company where animation art could be printed on a thermoplastic. This project made use of the companies core competency in printing on a 3D thermoplastic surface and developing alliances with movie studios for the animation art.

Interactive PC Technology (Large Chemical Company - greater than $10 billion)

This project involved the development of an interactive computer technology so that technical education can be available at both international and domestic sites. Considerable technical training is required at this international company with concomitant large travel costs and time away from the job. This project was directed at developing sophisticated multimedia software, along with appropriate hardware purchases, to allow the technical professional at any company site to be trained without having to travel to the education center.

Student Population

The MTM program consists of mainly (94 per cent) students from large companies in the NJ area - such as AT&T, Lucent, Exxon, Allied Signal and Merck. The average age of the student is 36, 76 per cent had one or more direct reports and 38 per cent had advanced degrees. The 42 students were taught in two separate classes, and were divided into 13 teams.

Research Methodology

The questionnaire designed by MacMillian et. al. [30] and Siegel [31] to determine the key decision criteria used by venture capitalists was modified to fit with a corporate venture (see Table 1). Each executive champion was asked to evaluate on a 5 point scale (i.e. 5 being essential and 1 being irrelevant) the key factors which were crucial to the funding decision. In a similar manner, the key obstacles associated with corporate venturing were evaluated by MacMillian, et. al. [24] in a previous study were similarly modified (see Table 2). The questions were similarly evaluated on a 5 point scale ranging from significant to irrelevant obstacles.

Results

Completed questionnaires were obtained from all 7 of the executives from the start-ups which received funding. However, only 1 executive survey was obtained from the projects which were not funded, despite repeated conversations and requests. Therefore, no comparison could be made between the executive champions who were on the funded start-ups and those were start-up funding was not obtained.

The results are shown in Tables 1 and 2 respectively. No obstacles, as indicated in Table 2, achieved a high rating. This was probably due to the fact that Table 2 consists of only projects which were funded and the executive champions judged the obstacles to be small. The executive champion from the project, which did not receive funding, also did not rate any area as being a significant obstacle (i.e. rating of 5).

The criteria used by the executive champions to evaluate the projects provide a better picture. The figure below indicates the percentage of executive champions who rated a criteria as a '5' or essential.

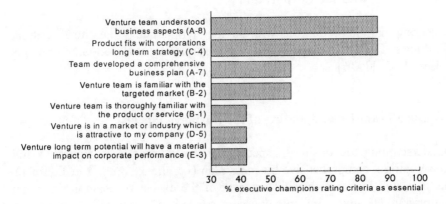

Figure 1: Percentage of Executives who Rated Criteria as Essential (i.e. '5')
The nomenclature in the parenthesis for each horizontal bar denotes the criteria designation from Table 1.

The two most important criteria indicated by the executive champions are understanding the business aspects of the venture along with strategic fit. All, but 1 of the executives, indicated that these two areas were essential. This latter executive rated each of these areas as a '4'.

The next two areas rated as 'essential' by over 50 per cent of the executive champions was the development of a comprehensive business plan and that the team be familiar with the targeted market. The remaining three areas, rated by more than 40 per cent of the executive champions, were familiarity with the product or service, developing a product for an attractive industry and a venture which will have material impact on corporate performance.

Discussion

Obtaining executive champion support remains a key criteria for obtaining start-up funding in large corporations [4, 5, 8]. However, the key criteria that they utilize has not been previously evaluated.

223

Strategic Fit with the Corporation

Ensuring that the product fits with the long term strategy (i.e. the 2nd criteria in figure 1) of the corporation is not surprising and supports previous research [5, 11, 16].

Venture Team Understanding of the Business Aspects

Understanding the business aspects (i.e. the 1st criteria in figure 1) and developing a comprehensive business plan (i.e. the 3rd criteria in figure 1), as indicated by more than 50 per cent of the executive champions, is not surprising. However, few employees have ever had the experience in putting together a business case. Only seven per cent of the 42 students taking this course had ever done a business case. However, being able to do a business case belies the real question. The majority of these technically trained students do not understand the key processes, organizational issues and key hurdles which lead to a successful business case. Roberts [32] evaluated business cases submitted to venture capitalists by similarly trained individuals and found deficiencies in 70 per cent of the cases, with the most significant ones occurring in the marketing, management and financial portions. Therefore, one of the key learning experiences this course provides is the understanding of how to prepare a business case, hopefully with few deficiencies.

Venture Team Understanding of the Market

Understanding the market is another criteria found to be important by the executive champion. This finding stresses the importance of being market and customer driven. Supporting ventures in new markets even with known technology has been shown to be less successful than developing products for known markets. [9, 10, 16, 17].

Venture Team Understanding of the Product or Service

Having familiarity with the product or service is also another criteria. This may almost seems obvious. This result indicates that the venture team should work in areas that it thoroughly understands rather than to jump to a totally new area, that appears exciting, but where the team has no in-depth experience.

Market Attractiveness to the Company

Choosing a venture in a market which is attractive to your company also seems obvious. This probably remains an essential criteria for projects in a course such as this since start-up funding is usually difficult or impossible to obtain in most large companies out of the normally yearly funding cycle. Projects which do get funded, out of this normal sequence, need to be especially attractive to the corporation and the executive champion.

Material Impact on Corporate Performance

The last essential criteria, having a project that will have material impact on corporate performance, goes along with previous findings of choosing product that fit with the corporations long term strategy [5, 11, 16].

Comparison with the Venture Capitalists most frequently cited Criteria

The seven most frequently cited criteria by venture capitalists [33] were capability of sustained effort $(A - 1)^2$, familiarity with the market (B - 1), ten times financial return in 5 - 10 years (E - 1), demonstrated team leadership in the past (B - 3), team evaluates and reacts to risk well (A - 2), investment can be made liquid (not included in the survey in this paper) and significant market growth (D - 1). Only one of these criteria, familiarity with the market (B - 1), was also in the most frequently cited criteria of the corporate executive champions.

The differences can be attributed to two factors. The importance of the venture team represents a key criteria in determining the attractiveness of a proposal to venture capitalists. Their capability for sustained effort, leadership ability and ability to react to risk all are critical to the venture capitalists funding decision. However, the importance of the team to the eventual success of the project was less important in obtaining start-up funding since many of the projects were continued by new teams. These new teams would often have only a few or only one member from the class team which developed the original business case. The 2nd factor is that the venture capitalists are looking for a significant financial return and a venture in a significant market growth rate. The corporate executive champion, while desirous of a project with large financial return, probably does not expect such a project to be developed during a 14 week course sequence. Choosing a product in an attractive market continues to represent a key criteria by venture capitalists. However, this study and others [5, 11, 16] indicate that strategic fit and attractiveness to the company are more important to the corporation.

Conclusions

The results of this study confirm the frequently cited positions that strategic fit and the quality and knowledge of the team preparing the business case are key determinates for obtaining start-up funding in large corporations. Of the seven criteria in figure 1, four had to do with the experience of the team. Two of the remaining three were concerned with strategic fit and the last one was concerned with the material impact on corporate performance.

Understanding the business aspects of the venture and the need to develop a comprehensive business plan represent key skills required by the venture team to be successful. Perhaps, this is the most critical deficiency with probably few employees in large companies having these skills. Courses, such as this allow the students to develop and practice these critical skills.

Table 1: Champion Funding Criteria used to evaluate the Venture

Criteria	Mean[a]	Standard Error of Mean
A. Venture Team		
1. Capable of sustained effort	3.00	.62
2. Able to evaluate and react to risk	3.43	.49
3. Articulate in discussing venture	4.14	.26
4. Attends to detail	4.14	.14
5. Able to accept criticism	3.71	.42
6. Is compatible with champion	2.88	.46
7. Developed a comprehensive business plan	4.29	.29
8. Understood the business aspects.	4.85	.14
9. Developed a good working relationship with champion.	3.57	.37
B. Venture Team Experience		
1. Thoroughly familiar with product/service	4.14	.34
2. Thoroughly familiar with the market targeted by venture.	4.57	.20
3. Demonstrated leadership ability in the past.	3.29	.57
4. Has track record relevant to venture	2.86	.51
5. Venture team comes highly recommended	2.71	.47
6. Already familiar with venture team	3.00	.54
C. Characteristics of Product or Service		
1. The product/service is proprietary or can otherwise be protected	2.57	.57
2. The product/service is expected to enjoy easy market acceptance	3.57	.20
3. The product/service has been developed to the point of initial demonstration	3.71	.36
4. Product fits with corporations long term strategy	4.86	.14
D. Characteristics of the Market		
1. The target market enjoys a significant growth rate	3.57	.53
2. The venture will stimulate an existing market	2.86	.51
3. The venture will create a new market	2.71	.42
4. Competition in the market will be minimal for the first three years.	2.14	.46
5. The venture is in a market or industry which is attractive to my company	3.86	.55

E. Financial Considerations

1. Venture generates a return equal to at least 10X the investment within 5 - 10 years	3.00	.66
2. Champion controls the initial funding	2.71	61
3. Venture long term potential will have a material impact on corporate performance	4.00	.44
4. Venture IRR will be greater than 25 per cent	2.85	.40
5. Initial investment required is low	3.14	.34

[a] Evaluated on a 5 point scale. 5 = an essential factor which is crucial to the funding decision; 1 = an irrelevant factor to the decision making process.

Table 2: Obstacles to obtaining Start-up Funds

Criteria	Mean[a]	Standard Error of Mean
A. Misreading the Market		
1. Imperfect market analysis	2.00	.45
2. Underestimate of competition	1.83	.48
3. Underestimate of initial selling effort required	1.83	.31
4. Underestimate of barriers to entry	1.67	.49
B. Inadequate Corporate Support		
1. Lack of real commitment to venture	2.83	.48
2. Competition for resources within company	3.83	.31
3. Lack of fit with corporate strategy	2.00	.63
C. Inadequate Planning		
1. Poor cost estimation	2.16	.60
2. Underestimation of funds needed	2.17	.60
3. Lack of contingency plans	2.50	.56
4. No clear definition of failure	2.16	.54
5. Lack of adequate time to evaluate venture	2.00	.37
6. Lack of adequate time to prepare venture	2.00	.45
7. Lack of comprehensive business plan	2.00	.68

D. Venture Team		
1. Inability to attract a team to do the venture	1.40	.25
E. Champion		
1. Lack of time to evaluate venture	2.00	.37
2. Lack of authority to approve venture	2.83	.60
3. Lack of time to obtain support from champion	1.60	.40
F. Corporation		
1. Lack of clear mission regarding venture activity	2.20	.58
2. Lack of process regarding venture activity	3.00	.52
3. Lack of patience regarding new entrepreneurial activities	2.33	.33
4. Inadequate venture funds available	2.83	.65
5. Difficulty in dealing with venture activity	2.50	.43
6. Lack of time to support	2.67	.42

[a] Evaluated on a 5 point scale. 5 = significant obstacle; 1 = irrelevant or not relevant to the venture.

Notes

[1] Intrapreneuring is a word coined by Pinchott [1] and refers to the process of creating innovation within a corporate organization.

[2] The nomenclature in the parenthesis denotes the criteria designation from Table 1.

References

Biggadike, E.R. (1976) Corporate Diversification: Entry Strategy and Performance *Harvard University Press*, Boston, MA.

Biggadike, E.R. (1979) The Risky Business of Diversification *Harvard Business Review*.

Burgelman, Robert A. (Winter 1984) Managing the Internal Corporate Venturing *Process Sloan Management Review*, pp. 33-48.

DeSarbo, W. MacMillian, I.C. and Day, D.L. (1987) Criteria for Corporate Venturing Importance Assigned by Managers *Journal of Business Venturing*, 2: pp. 329-350.

Dunn, D.T. (October 1977) The Rise and Fall of Venture Groups *Business Horizons*, pp. 32-41.

Hlavacek, J.D. and Thompson, V.A. (April 1978) Bureaucracy and Venture Failures. *Academy of Management Review*, pp. 242 - 247.

Kantor, R.M. (June-July 1982) The Middle Manager as Innovator. *Harvard Business Review*, p. 61.

Kantor, R.M., and Richardson, L. (1991) Engines of Progress: Designing and Running Entrepreneurial Vehicles in Established Companies - The Enter-Prize Program at Ohio Bell, 1985-1990 *Journal of Business Venturing*, 6: pp. 209-229.

Kantor, R.M., North J., Bernstein, A.P., and Williamson, A. (1990) Engines of Progress: Designing and Running Entrepreneurial Vehicles in Established *Companies Journal of Business Venturing*, 5: pp. 415-430.

Kantor, R.M., North J., Richardson, L. Ingols, C. and Zolner, J., A. (1991) Engines of Progress: Designing and Running Entrepreneurial Vehicles in Established Companies: Raytheon's New Product Center *Journal of Business Venturing*, 6: pp. 145-163.

Kantor, R.M., Richardson, L., North J., and Morgan, E. (1991) Engines of Progress: Designing and Running Entrepreneurial Vehicles in Established Companies; The New Venture Process at Eastman Kodak, 1983 -1989 *Journal of Business Venturing*, 6: pp. 63-82.

Knight, Russel M. (1987) Corporate Innovation and Entrepreneurship: A Canadian Study *Journal of Product Innovation Management* 4: pp. 284-297.

MacMillan, Ian C. And George, R. (1985) Corporate Venturing: Challenges for Senior Managers, *Journal of Business Strategy*, pp. 34-43.

MacMillan, Ian C., Block, Zenas and Narashimha, P.N. (1986) Subba Corporate Venturing: Alternatives, Obstacles Encountered, and Experience Effects, *Journal of Business Venturing*, 1: pp. 177-191.

MacMillan, Ian C., Siegel, Robin and Narasimha, P.N. (1985) Subba Criteria used by Venture Capitalists to evaluate new venture proposals. *Journal of Business Venturing* 1: pp. 119-128.

MacMillan, Ian C., Zemann, Lauriann and. Narasimha, P.N. (1987) Criteria Distinguishing Successful from Unsuccessful Ventures in the Venture Screening Process. *Journal of Business Venturing* 2: pp. 123-137.

MacMillian, I.C. and Day, D.L. (1987) Corporate Venturing into Industrial Markets: Dynamics of Aggressive Entry *Journal of Business Venturing*, 2: pp. 29-39.

McGrath, Rita Gunther and MacMillan, Ian C. (July-August 1995) Discovery Driven Planning *Harvard Business Review* pp. 4-12.

Merino, D.N. (1990) Development of a Technological S-curve for Tire Cord Textiles *Journal of Technological Forecasting and Change*, 37: pp. 275 - 291.

Merino, D.N. (1989) Managing Advances in Polymer Technology *Journal of Polymer Processing Institute*, .9: pp. 1-9 1.

Miller, A. and Camp, B. (1985) Exploring Determinants of Success in Corporate Ventures *Journal of Business Venturing*, 1: pp. 87-105.

Ohe, T., Honjo, S., and Merrifield, D.B. (1992) Japanese Corporate Ventures: Success Curve *Journal of Business Venturing*, 7: pp. 171-180.

Pinchot, Gifford (1985) Intrapreneuring, *Harper & Row*, New York, NY.

Prahalad, C.K. and Hamel, G. (May - June 1990) The Core Competence of the Corporation. *Harvard Business Review*, 68: pp. 79-91.

Quinn, J.B. (Spring 1979) Technological innovation, entrepreneurship, and strategy. *Sloan Management Review* 20: pp. 19-30.

Roberts, Edward B. (1991) Entrepreneurs in High Technology, *Oxford University Press*, New York, NY.

Siegel, Robin, Siegel, E., and MacMillan, I.C. (1988) Corporate Venture Capitalists: Autonomy, Obstacles and Performance *Journal of Business Venturing*, 3: pp. 233-247.

Smith, Jerald R. and Golden, Peggy A. (1987) Entrepreneur: A Simulation *Houghton Mifflin Company*, Princeton, NJ.

230

Sorrentino, M. and William, M.L. (1995) Relatedness and Corporate Venturing: Does it Really Matter *Journal of Business Venturing*, 10: pp. 59-73.

Souder, William E. (May 1981) Encouraging Entrepreneurship in the Large Corporation, *Research Management, pp.* 18-22.

Sykes, H.B. (June 1986) Lessons from a New Ventures Program *Harvard Business Review*, pp. 69-74.

von Hippel, E. (1977) Successful and Failing Internal Corporate Ventures: An Empirical Analysis, *Industrial Marketing Management* 6: pp. 163-174.

Wheelwright, S.C. and Sasser, W.E. Jr. (May - June 1989) The New Product Development Map. *Harvard Business Review*, pp. 112 -120.

13 Curriculum Development for Australian Family Business Education and Training

George Tanewski
Claudio Romano
Xueli Huang
Kosmas Smyrnios

Abstract

It is well acknowledged that education and training are important to all business sectors. Research has shown that training greatly increases productivity and improves business performance, especially in small- and medium-size enterprises. In spite of its importance, literature on the education and training needs of family businesses is lacking. Given the importance of educational programs, the objectives of this study were to review, analyze, and synthesize family business programs offered internationally, to identify the education and training needs of Australian family businesses, and to recommend a set of educational and training courses for family business based on the issues identified in this investigation. To enhance the validity and reliability of the results, a multi-method approach was adopted. A profile of family business programs offered internationally was developed through a widespread literature search and review of CD-ROM databases and the Internet. In addition, a national cross-sectional survey of 5,000 enterprises was undertaken to identify the education and training needs of Australian family businesses. Textual data were analyzed using content analysis procedures in NUD-IST. Data from questionnaires were analyzed using quantitative techniques.

Several key educational and training areas for family businesses were identified. These are in the areas of strategic management and operations such as finance and quality management. The present study also outlines a number of themes and topics that could be used in family business educational and training programs. These findings as well as the theoretical rationale for developing educational and training programs for family businesses are discussed.

Introduction

Family businesses are significant contributors to the wealth of the Australian economy. Recent national survey findings show that family businesses account for 83 per cent of all businesses and employ about 50 per cent of the private-sector workforce in Australia (Smyrnios, Romano, and Tanewski, 1997; Smyrnios and Romano, 1994). Similar findings have been reported in the US (Francis, 1993; Upton, 1991; Ward and Aronoff, 1990) and other west European countries (Lank, 1995; Dyer, 1986; Stoy Hayward and The London Business School, 1990).

Education and training are important to all sectors of the business community. Research has shown that training greatly increases productivity and improves business performance, especially in small- and medium-size businesses (Marshall, Alderman, Wong, and Thwaites, 1995; Steinburg, 1993). Training needs in family business are expected to be high since the majority of family businesses are classified as small business, and these enterprises are less likely to employ trained and/or skilled managers. As reported by Stanworth and Gray (1992) in their study of small business in the UK, the quality of management in small firms suffered not only from a limited number of managers available, but also from lack of management training to upgrade the managerial knowledge and skills.

Family businesses also have specific learning needs. They are different from other firms, since they mix business with their day-to-day family life, adding the complexity of family life to the business challenge. Thus, they face a range of issues surrounding three key aspects in running their family business: the firm; the owner; and the owner's family. To be successful in a family business, owners have to strike a balance between the best interests of business and the well-being of the family. To do so, owners continuously learn how to formulate and to adopt appropriate policies, they assimilate and recognize the dynamics surrounding these three key aspects, and they acquire knowledge and develop skills which can be used to identify and to solve difficulties brought about by the interplay of these dynamics.

Given current fierce competition in the market place and the growing demand for additional knowledge and skills in the management of family businesses, the need to have an edge against competitors through education and training in the area of family business is increasing. Recognizing this increasing need, education and training programs have been established in many countries and have become a major business. A number of universities are devoting considerable time and better facilities in educating family business owners (Vinturella, Elstrott, and Galiano, 1993).

Unfortunately, education and training programs for Australian family businesses are relatively scarce. Only two universities, Bond University in Queensland and Southern Cross University in New South Wales, are actively involved in family business. In addition, family business educational programs that were initiated recently in Australia are still in their early stages of development. Therefore, it is very important to bridge the gap between the need and provision of family business education and training in Australia.

It is acknowledged that education and training programs should be based on the practical needs of family businesses, and ideally a thorough needs assessment should be conducted. Hence a worldwide literature review and information search of family business education and training was conducted to identify these needs and provide an assessment of education and training programs. This process has resulted in an extensive list of family business programs offered worldwide. In addition, the Australian Family and Private Businesses Survey (Smyrnios, Romano, and Tanewski, 1997) identified a number of potential educational and training needs and problems. The findings of the present survey and literature review have laid a solid foundation for the development of comprehensive educational and training programs that meet the specific needs of Australian family businesses.

Family businesses exist in two social systems: business and socio-familial systems. Thus, owners of family businesses face challenges not only from operational business areas such as competitive markets, planning, financing, marketing, but also from areas associated with ownership and family. Given these systems, family businesses demand a unique knowledge base, skills, and experience to maintain an appropriate balance between business interests and the well-being of the family.

Traditional business programs are primarily concerned with the economically rational and impersonal behavior of business organizations. Participants in these programs are taught the benefits of achieving economic goals, particularly profits, whereas family related issues and emotional behaviors in business are rarely mentioned.

Entrepreneurship Exceptions are courses run in 'Entrepreneurship' and 'Small Business Management', programs that handle issues relating to family business. By definition, an entrepreneur is 'one who can recognize an opportunity in the marketplace and is willing to marshal the resources necessary to exploit that opportunity for long-term personal gain' (Sexton and Nowman-Upton, 1991, p.19). Hence, entrepreneurship is the basis for most family businesses. Families have been found to play a crucial role in fostering so called entrepreneurial qualities in their siblings, and by providing necessary financial and human resources support in setting up a business.

Notwithstanding these findings, the association between entrepreneurship and family business have been largely overlooked. As Dyer and Handler (1994) pointed out, entrepreneurship typically deals with two major issues: the characteristics of an entrepreneur and the conditions for initiating a successful business. In other words, entrepreneurship primarily focuses on issues in the early stages of business development, and largely ignores issues an entrepreneur may face during subsequent stages of business development.

Small Business Small business management has been developed in recognition of the unique needs and challenges confronting small businesses. There are a number of definitions of small business categorized according to either employee numbers, or levels of control, or scale of operation. The Australian Bureau of Statistics (ABS) defines a small business as either a non-manufacturing organization that employs less than 20 full-time employees or a manufacturing business which employs less than 100 full-time employees (ABS, 1995). Consequently small businesses are more likely to face difficulties in obtaining human and financial resources because of the size of their capital and employment. Thus, educational and training courses for small business have focused on how to establish, manage, market, and finance a business rather than family related issues (e.g., Dixon, Hodgetts, Kelmar, and Kuratko, 1991).

In other words, it appears that current Australian educational programs do not address specific areas relating to family business, such as succession, family business dynamics, estate planning, communication, and conflict resolution. Clearly, it is important to develop education and training courses that focus on the special needs of Australian family business.

Underdevelopment of family business theory

Over the last decade, research output into family business has increased in North America and Europe. Most of this research has concentrated on the special needs of family businesses including succession (e.g., Handler and Kram, 1988; Lansberg, 1988); culture (e.g., Astrachan, 1988; Dyer, 1986); cross-cultural comparisons (Donckels and Fröhlich, 1991); strategic planning (e.g., Daily and Dollinger, 1992; Lyman, 1991; Ward, 1987); conflict (e.g., Dyer, 1989; Lansberg, 1988); organizational structure (e.g., Kahn and Henderson, 1992); and gender issues (e.g., Lyman, 1988).

Despite this quantity of research, theorizing in the field of family business is at its formative stage. A number of factors have contributed to the slow development of theory. First, several problems are inherent in studies of family business (Brockhaus, 1994). Such problems include: a shortage of robust secondary data; difficulties in eliciting cooperation from family business members; and the large variety of family businesses. Second, most early research was primarily prescriptive (Swartz, 1989), which has less utility for theory building. Finally, most recent research has employed a range of theoretical frameworks or used different measurement instruments, which has made it difficult to compare and generalize findings.

Lack of theory in family business has become an issue of growing concern. Wortman (1994) noted in his comprehensive review of theory and research in family businesses that there is no unified paradigm. In line with this view, Wortman (1994) recommended the adoption of a typology of theory and research in order to lay some common foundation for future research in family business.

Problems relating to theory development in family business has left many aspects regarding the behavior of family businesses unexplained, or at best, only partially explained. This problem could impose substantial costs on the development of education and training programs for family business in Australia. Lack of understanding of phenomena in this field has made it very difficult to generalize findings of research. Coupled with the wide spectrum of family businesses and a dearth of robust secondary data, the relevancy of course materials developed overseas to Australian family business is questionable. As a result, it will be difficult to make full use of the course materials developed overseas, and expensive field research is indispensable in the process of course development for Australian family business.

Need to develop programs devoted to Australian family business

There are many educational programs for family businesses available overseas (e.g., Northeastern University's Center for Family Business; Oregon State University's Austin Family Business Program; Manchester University's MBA Family Business Management Program). Comparable programs are not available in Australia. Clearly there is a need to develop national or regional programs that address the needs of family businesses. These special needs relate to Australia's unique legal and taxation system, multiculturalism, and geographic and demographic considerations.

Carsrud (1994) stressed the need to create unique programs based on the specific needs of family businesses. Carsrud (1994) also noted that 'each market is different' and emphasized that 'each program will have a unique mission' (p. 44).

Given that Australian family businesses are operating under a unique set of macro- and micro-environmental factors, coupled with an underdevelopment of theory, a unique program should be developed to meet these special needs.

Aims and purposes of this study

The objectives of this study were threefold:

1. to review, analyze, and synthesize family business courses offered internationally;
2. to identify the education and training needs of Australian family businesses; and
3. to recommend a set of educational and training courses for Australian family business based on the issues identified and from the results of the review.

Method

Scope of investigation

In order to enhance the validity and reliability of findings, this study employed a multi-method approach. Family business programs offered internationally were searched and reviewed on CD-ROM databases and the Internet. A national cross-sectional survey identified educational and training needs of family businesses.

Qualitative data. A literature review and information search was conducted worldwide on several databases. These databases included ABI/Global (January 1992 to December 1996); Sociofile (January 1971 to December 1996); Psyclit (January 1990 to December 1996); ABIX (The Australia Business Intelligence, Volume 3, 1996); DAO (Dissertations Abstracts on Disc, January 1993 to September 1996) and the World Wide Web (Internet).

Quantitative data. A cross-sectional quantitative survey was conducted using a stratified sample of 5,000 businesses obtained from Dun and Bradstreet (1996) based on state, location, industry, and sales (Smyrnios, Romano, and Tanewski, 1997). The Australian Family and Private Business Questionnaire (AFPBQ) comprises 10 sections: Background of the Business, Current Ownership, Management of the Business, Succession and Retirement Plans, Family Business Issues, Banking and Insurance, Planning the Growth of the Business, Management Development and Training, Alternate Investment, and Background of the Owner. This study reports findings primarily concerned with education and training issues. Data were electronically scanned by computer and responses were analysed using SPSS for Windows (Norusis, 1993).

Qualitative data search parameters

The literature review and information search on family business educational programs was conducted with key words seeking approach. Key words were: family business, closely held business, small business, small enterprise, training, education, university, management program, course, forum, seminar. A number of string word combinations also were used to produce relevant literature results. For instance, 'family business' was combined with 'training' to cover literature that encompassed 'family business' and 'training'.

Results from CD-ROM database searches, on the whole, were found to be too broad. This is understandable, given the nature and contents of the educational and training courses and programs. A worldwide Internet search complemented CD-ROM search results. There are 19 search and directory services currently available on the Internet and three widely used services. *Infoseek, Alta Vista,* and *Yahoo* were chosen to perform search requests. It was expected that some of the matches would overlap, and the overlapping matches once viewed in one service were highlighted throughout all the searches. Thus, those highlighted matches were ignored from subsequent searches on the topic. Emphasis also was placed on the various family business centers in North America and Europe, since they are major institutions conducting family business education and training.

Internet search results were richer, specific, and relevant in content compared with the findings from the CD-ROM databases investigation. The Internet probe covered information on university course syllabi, programs, workshops, forums, topics, issues, articles, newsletters, and events.

Qualitative data analysis procedures

A content analysis approach was considered appropriate for the purposes of this evaluation. According to Manning and Cullum-Swan (1994, p. 464) content analysis is 'a qualitatively oriented technique by which standardized measurements are applied to metrically defined units and these are used to characterize and compare documents'.

The content of each family business program, either located on the Internet or in various university libraries, was first perused in hard-copy form. Those documents (n=32) deemed appropriate for analysis were either transcribed or scanned as word processing (text) files and then converted into textual database files. The initial analysis began by content analyzing all textual database files and frequencies were generated for all words. All prepositions, the indefinite and definite articles, and proper nouns were excluded from the word count.

The word list and their respective concordances were analyzed more closely in context (Strauss and Corbin, 1991). About 50 key words (e.g., succession, communication, taxation) and short phrases (e.g., strategic management, board of directors, management planning) gathered from these textual database files were used in further analysis.

These 50 key words or short phrases were then content analyzed with the aid of Non-Numerical Unstructured Data Indexing, Searching and Theorizing (NUD-IST 3.0) software program (Richards, Richards, McGalliard, and Sharroch, 1994). NUD-IST was used because of its comprehensive text searching and indexing facilities. The program also assisted in developing themes from qualitative data. Word lists, phrases, and their respective concordances were verified in context. This process focused on de-contextualising data segments and re-contextualising them in locations with segments containing similar properties. Themes and their respective categories were then compiled with examples until they were 'saturated' (Turner, 1981, p. 231) and the frequency of each instance was noted.

A number of international universities (e.g., The University of Manchester; Duke University; Baylor University; Oregon State University) and private professional entities (e.g., Montreal Institute for Family Enterprise; Family Business Roundtable Inc.; Arthur Andersen) provide programs for family business (Vinturella et al., 1993). Some universities do this through several departments. To be consistent in the content analysis, each organization was considered a unit of analysis. Thus, if two or more departments in a university offered family business programs, these were merged to represent the same institution.

Results

Program providers and participants

Family businesses require both technical and management training. Technical training refers to those technical functions which are specific to a particular industry, such as information technology, CAD, and flexible manufacturing. Although family relationships may increase complexities involved in managing a family firm, the technical expertise needed for production is probably the same for family and non-family businesses. Thus, technical training programs may not necessarily differ between these two types of enterprises.

Since 70 per cent to 80 per cent of family businesses fall into the category of small business, technical training is usually provided, sometimes funded, through various government-aided programs, by various industry associations, specialized technical consulting firms, community technical colleges, and universities. Moreover, these professional institutions also provide either *general or industry-specific management* education and training for small business.

Management education and training are provided predominantly by universities, specifically by various university-based Family Business Centers or Centers for Entrepreneurship. In the US, over 60 universities offer family business programs, while a further group of non-university entities provide programs for family businesses (Vinturella et al., 1993).

Various programs or topics can be offered targeting specific segments. Several criteria are available for this purpose and they include: business interests (family business members vs. professionals), family membership (member vs. non-family members), generation (senior vs. junior), participation (participating vs. non-participating family members), and position (shareholders vs. managers). As a starting point, it is meaningful to use family business membership as a criterion to categorise the participants. A detailed segmentation of these participants is shown in Figure 1.

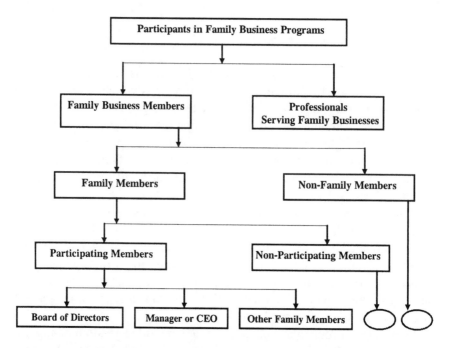

Figure 1: Segmentation of Participants in Family Business Programs

Types of Programs

In segmenting family business programs it is important to recognize the special features in managing a family business. To successfully operate a family business, mangers require both family and business knowledge, and skills to deal with these issues. Thus, programs can be divided into two broad groups: family - and business - related areas. We also acknowledge that these two areas are closely interrelated, as shown in Figure 2.

242

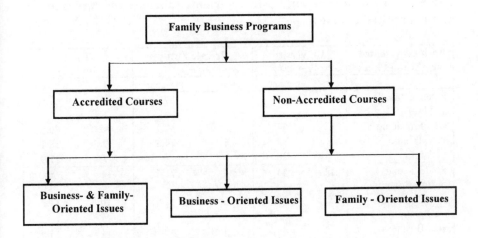

Figure 2: Types of Family Business Programs

Family business programs can be broadly classified into two categories: non-accredited and accredited. Non-accredited programs involve various levels of training, which does not lead to any formal academic awards. These programs tend to be short-term and include forums, seminars, and roundtable meetings. Programs are predominantly concerned with practical skills and knowledge related to successfully running a family business.

In contrast, accredited programs tend to be long-term educational courses in which participants attain an academic qualification. Accredited courses are usually concerned with both practical and theoretical issues in family business.

Non-accredited courses

Business-oriented themes and topics A contextual analysis of training programs provided in information from 32 organizations was undertaken using NUD-IST. Themes to emerge from this analysis are summarized in Table 1, and include strategic and business planning, management of growth, financing, leadership development, human resources management, and marketing.

Table 1: The most frequent business-oriented themes and topics in non-accredited courses

Business-oriented themes and topics	University ($n = 25$)		Private Entity ($n = 7$)		Total ($n = 32$)	
	f	per cent	f	per cent	f	per cent
Finance, taxation, and law	17	68	4	57.1	21	65.6
• Financing	11	44	4	57.1	15	46.9
• Taxation	8	32	1	14.3	9	28.1
• Law	7	28	0	0	7	21.9
Strategic and business planning	11	44	5	71.4	16	50
• Strategic planning	7	28	3	42.9	10	31.3
• Business planning and strategy	7	28	4	57.1	11	34.4
Human resource management	13	52	3	42.9	16	50
• Human resource management	5	20	2	28.6	7	21.9
• Compensation	6	24	1	14.3	7	21.9
• Team building	6	24	2	28.6	8	25
• Recruitment	1	4	3	42.9	4	12.5
Governance	10	40	4	57.1	14	43.7
• Board of advisors	3	12	1	14.3	4	12.5
• Board of directors	7	28	2	28.6	9	28.1
• Council, constitution, and governance	2	8	2	28.6	4	12.5
Leadership development	8	32	1	14.3	9	28.1
Management of growth	4	16	1	14.3	5	15.6
Marketing	3	12	2	28.6	5	15.6
Family business dynamics	4	16	0	0	4	12.5

Table 2: The most frequent family-oriented themes and topics in non-accredited courses

Family-oriented themes and topics	University (*n* = 25)		Private Entity (*n* = 7)		Total (*n* = 32)	
	f	per cent	f	per cent	f	per cent
Succession	19	76	6	85.6	25	78.1
• Succession in general	5	20	2	28.6	7	21.9
• Succession planning	9	36	3	42.3	12	37.5
• Leadership succession	4	16	1	14.3	5	15.6
• Ownership succession	4	16	1	14.3	5	15.6
• Successor	5	20	1	14.3	6	18.8
• Succession management and process	3	12	0	0	3	9.4
Conflict resolution	16	64	7	100	23	71.9
• Family member	10	40	3	42.9	13	40.6
• Family and business	9	36	5	71.4	14	43.8
Estate planning	10	40	3	42.9	13	40.6
• Planning process	8	32	2	28.6	10	31.3
• Planning options and techniques	2	8	1	14.3	3	9.4
Communication	8	32	5	71.4	13	40.6
• Family and business	6	24	3	42.9	9	28.1
• Family member	2	8	2	28.6	4	12.5
Family dynamics and relationship	10	40	3	42.9	13	40.6
• Family dynamics	6	24	1	14.3	7	21.9
• Family relationships	7	28	2	28.6	9	28.1
Retirement	6	24	3	42.8	9	28.1
• Planning	4	16	1	14.3	5	15.6
• In general	2	8	2	28.6	4	12.5

Family-oriented themes and topics Educational and training themes can also be developed for family-oriented issues and can be geared towards family and non-family members. Topics on issues relating to family members seem to be the main areas focused on in these training programs. As can be seen from Table 1, training themes for family members include succession, estate planning, retirement planning, communication, conflict resolution, family dynamics, and relationships.

Topics related to non-family members In contrast, topics related to non-family member issues are limited and are usually oriented towards human resources management issues. Topics involve attracting and retaining non-family management; when/whether to add non-family members to the board; working with, and sometimes for, non-family managers; equitable compensation among family and non-family members; and rewarding and retaining non-family employees.

Accredited courses

As knowledge of family business management accumulates, university-based education and training providers appear to be turning towards offering more accredited courses for both MBA and undergraduates. Since 1987, the American University has offered Entrepreneurship courses at the MBA level and currently offers five subjects in: Entrepreneurship and New Venture Management; Managing Small and Growing Ventures; Managing Family Business; Entrepreneurial Leadership and Organisational Productivity; and Management and Entrepreneurship in Service Organizations

At undergraduate level, several universities in the US offer family business courses. The American University provides four subjects for undergraduates majoring in Management of the Enterprise: Entrepreneurship; Managing Human Resources; Management and Leadership Development; and Managing Information for Business Decision Making

In 1993, the University of San Diego developed an undergraduate course entitled 'Management in the Small and Family Business'. This course also has adopted an innovative delivery approach called 'Consultant Learning' which is project-oriented. Students are required to pick a consulting project, either from a list of topics suggested by the lecturer or

246

an interesting relevant topic of their own. The quality of the consulting project is then evaluated and results contribute to the students overall grade in this subject.

A content analysis of course outlines offering accredited courses in family business management was undertaken from eight universities (six from the US, one from Canada, and one from the UK). Table 3 shows themes and topics offered by these tertiary institutions. It is noteworthy that although the emphasis of these accredited courses appear to be different to non-accredited programs, they are similar in their structure and content.

Table 3: The most frequent themes and topics offered by universities in accredited family business programs

Themes and topics	f	per cent
Introduction and overview • An historical perspective • A current perspective • Demographics • Macro- vs. micro-issues, e.g., structure	8	100.0

Family business dynamics and systems
• A systems approach
   • Family system
   • Business system
• A life cycle approach
   • An organizational life cycle approach
   • A family life cycle approach
• Interactions, interrelationship, and exchange in family business
• Growth models of family business
• Competitive strengths and weaknesses
	7	87.5

Intra-personal issues • Characteristics of Entrepreneur, founder, and owner • Leadership development	4	50.0

Table 3 (cont.): The most frequent themes and topics offered by universities in accredited family business programs

Themes and topics	f	per cent
Human resources management, communication, and conflict resolution	8	100.0
• Human resources management		
• Communication		
• Team building		
• Compensation		
• Conflict resolution		
• Sibling rivalry		
• Non-family employees		
• Gender issues		
Succession management	8	100.0
• Succession planning		
• Estate planning		
• Retirement planning		
• Selection, motivation, and training of successors		
• Managing succession processes		
Strategic and business planning	6	75.0
• Strategic planning		
• Business planning		
• Source of information for business analysis		
Financial and taxation issues	7	87.5
• Financing family business		
• Evaluating family business		
• Taxation issues		
Organization and governance	6	75.0
• Board of directors		
• Family council		
• Ownership structure		
• Professionalization of family business		
• Setting up governance systems		
• Board of advisors		

Table 3 (cont.): The most frequent themes and topics offered by universities in accredited family business programs

Cultural issues, international perspective, and issues in the future	7	87.5
• Family business culture		
• Change of culture		
• Culture evolution: ethnicity, race, multinationalism		
• Implications of formalisation for the culture of the family firm		
• An international perspective		
• Future of family business		

Delivery approaches

Gibb (1995) suggested a number of pedagogical approaches that can be used to develop management capacity in small and medium size enterprises (see Table 4).

Table 4: Pedagogical approaches used for education and training small and medium sized enterprises

• Lecture: Delivery, Aids, Handouts, Video	• Seminars
• Critical Reviews	• Workshops-Issues Related/Group Discussion
• Peer 'Teaching'	• Presentations
• Problem Solving-Real	• Peer Counselling (One to One and Group)
• Debates	• Problem Solving - Simulated
• Critical Incidents Identification	• Cases
• Project Based Learning	• Role Image and Self
• Experiential Learning (Real Simulated)	• Consultant/Counseling Approaches
• Brainstorming Learning	• Personal or Partner/Group Scoring
• Interactive Video/IT Based	• Investigative (Discovery) Learning

Since a wide spectrum of pedagogical approaches are used in educational and training courses for small- and medium-sized enterprises, it can be expected that most approaches also would be used in family business programs. Gibb stressed the importance of transactional and networking approaches in management learning and education processes.

Non-accredited course delivery approach Non-accredited programs are usually short-term and flexible. They can be delivered through many approaches, including business roundtable meetings, executive breakfasts, forums, workshops, family business retreats, short - term seminars (usually half-a-day to three days), and self-paced learning via audio/video/CD materials.

In their study of learning needs of family business, Upton, Moore, Wacholtz and Sexton (8.4.97) found that the most preferred approaches used in delivering non-accredited programs in the US were business roundtable meetings and half-day seminars. Moreover, they found that financial topics and management succession were the most preferred topics covered in these forums.

Accredited course delivery approach The most widely used delivery approaches for accredited courses are lectures and case studies. Guest speakers are also used and class discussions are encouraged.

Learning needs of Australian family businesses

Although the Australian Family and Private Business Survey (Smyrnios, Romano, and Tanewski, 1997) found that family businesses were profitable and a significant number reported profits greater than 6 per cent, several potential problems were identified in our survey. A substantial proportion of family businesses indicated that they did not have a business plan in writing (36.9 per cent) nor did they have a documented succession plan (69.3 per cent) for the future ownership of their business. Overall, only 50.7 per cent of family businesses indicated that they had a formal long-term strategic plan.

Other potential problem areas included conflict resolution and management. A large number of these family businesses have not developed a formal management structure (30.9 per cent), and most of them do not have a family constitution (92.2 per cent) nor processes to resolve either family and/or business conflict (71.7 per cent).

In spite of these problems and difficulties, our survey found that management training was not highly regarded. Only 16 per cent of family business owners indicated that they have a clearly defined and documented strategy for training and development of family members, while 34 per cent reflected the same for non-family employees.

With regard to attending formal training courses, 44 per cent of owners attended formal training courses focused on family directors, while 43 per cent of non-family senior managers working in family businesses had participated in some form of senior management training. A large number of family business owners indicated that their learning objectives were to improve management skills (46.9 per cent), to obtain technical information (36.6 per cent), and to improve their industry knowledge (33.8 per cent).

Regarding future interest in training and owners' preference to the type of delivery approaches, Australian family businesses prefer non-accredited compared with accredited courses. This result is in line with Upton *et al.* (8.4.97). Preferred topics of Australian family business owners involved strategic management issues such as growing the family business (33.4 per cent), followed by operational issues such as finance (26 per cent) and quality control (16 per cent). However, the least regarded topics were setting up a family constitution (5.4 per cent) and establishing a family council (2.4 per cent).

Discussion, Implications and Recommendations

Obviously, education and training should, in principle, address the needs of the target audience and help solve their problems. While few published studies have been found on the needs of family business members, two approaches have been used to study and categories the organizational problems of family businesses. They are function-based and life cycle based approaches. The former approach groups the problems identified by organizational functions, such as marketing, accounting, human relations, internal management, and external management (Walsh, 1988). The latter approach classifies problems based on organizational life cycles and stages of development, such as conception and development, commercialization, growth, and stability (Kazanjian and Drazin, 1990). These authors also suggested that management at each stage of development confronts a unique set of problems. For example, Kazanjian (1988) found that organizations during their initial growth stages had more problems in sales and marketing. Although these researchers have focused on business-related areas, they have shed some light on problems that might confront family business, since family firms require similar skills to address business related issues (Upton et al., 8.4.97). However, there is little description in the literature of the characteristics of each stage and how to define the various stages.

Family businesses operate not only under a business system, but also under a socio-familial system. Thus, family related problems need to be addressed in educational and training programs. On the whole, both family business and entrepreneurship researchers seem to adopt an entrepreneur life-cycle approach. Hence, entrepreneurship researchers devote most effort to investigating family influence on the entrepreneur's personalities; and the role that families play during the start-up stages of a new venture. Family business researchers tended to focus their efforts on issues that entrepreneurs might confront near the latter stages of their career paths, such as succession (Wortman, 1994).

Dyer and Handler (1994) recently proposed a conceptual framework to study interactions of family and entrepreneurship dynamics from the perspective of an entrepreneur's career path. He suggested that intersection of family and entrepreneurial dynamics can be considered at four 'career nexuses': early experience and family influence of the entrepreneur; family's role in venture initiation; hiring family members in the business; and involvement of family members in succession. This conceptual framework is instrumental to understanding the complex linkages between family businesses and entrepreneurship, particularly at the early and late stages of the business. However, investigating the complex relationships among entrepreneur, family, and business during stages of growth and stability appear to be relatively unexplained.

Since owners of family businesses are confronting issues of both business and family, these two conceptual frameworks are instrumental to the development of education and training courses for family businesses. Thus, it is recommended that a set of educational and training courses for family businesses be organized according to their business functions and to their life cycle. Moreover, given the wide spectrum of potential participants in family business educational programs, both non-accredited and accredited courses are proposed.

Each type of course has its unique advantages and disadvantages, and more importantly, they should be set up in such a way as to complement each other. For example, non-accredited courses might provide up-to-date topics to participants, and act as an important channel for collecting learning needs of the participants. These learning needs could be used as key inputs into the accredited courses in order to keep the content and subject matter relevant and attractive to family businesses. Accredited courses enable participants to delve into theoretical issues, which, in turn, can be utilized as crucial inputs into non-accredited courses. As a result, participants in non-accredited courses might also receive more theoretical grounding, which would provide a better basis for explaining behavior of family businesses.

References

Astrachan, J.H. (1988). Family firm and community culture. *Family Business Review, 1*(2), 165-189.

Australian Bureau of Statistics (ABS). (1995). *Small Business in Australia* (Government Publications 1321.0). Canberra: Australian Bureau of Statistics.

Brockhaus, R. H. S. (1994). Entrepreneurship and family business research: Comparisons, critique, and lessons. *Entrepreneurship: Theory and Practice, 19*(1), 25-38.

Carsrud, A. L. (1994). Meanderings of a resurrected psychologist or, lessons learned in creating a family business program. *Entrepreneurship Theory and Practice, 19*(1), 39-48.

Daily, C.M., and Dollinger, M.J. (1992). An empirical examination of ownership structure in family and professionally managed firms. *Family Business Review, 5*(2), *117-136.*

Dixon, B., Hodgetts, R., Kelmar, J., and Kuratko, D. (1991). *Effective small business management.* (Australasian ed.). Sydney: Harcourt Brace Jovanovich.

Donckels, R. and Fröhlich, E. (1991). Are family businesses really different? European experiences from STRATOS. *Family Business Review, 4*(2), 149-160.

Dun and Bradstreet. (1996). DFB database obtained from author. 479 St. Kilda Road, Melbourne, Victoria 3004, Australia.

Dyer, W.G., Jr. (1986). *Cultural change in family firms.* San Francisco: Jossey-Bass.

Dyer, W.G., Jr. (1989). Integrating professional management into a family owned business. *Family Business Review, 2*(3), 221-235.

Dyer, W. G. J., and Handler, W. (1994). Entrepreneurship and family business: Exploring the connections. *Entrepreneurship Theory and Practice, 19*(1), 71-83.

Francis, B.C. (1993). Family business succession planning. *Journal of Accountancy, August,* 49-51.

Gibb, A. A. (1995, June 18-21). *Learning skills for all: The key to success in small business development?* Paper presented at the The 40th World Conference of International Council for Small Business, Sydney.

Handler, W.C. and Kram, K.E. (1988). Succession in family firms: The problem of resistance. *Family Business Review, 1*(4), 361-382.

Kahn, J.A. and Henderson, D.A. (1992). Location preferences of family firms: Strategic decision making or 'Home Sweet Home'? *Family Business Review, 5*(3), 271-282.

Kazanjian, R. K. (1988). Relation of dominant problems to stages of growth in technology-based new ventures. *Academy of Management Journal, 31*(2), 257-279.

Kazanjian, R. K., and Drazin, R. (1990). A state-contingent model of design and growth for technology based new ventures. *Journal of Business Venturing, 5*(3), 137-150.

Lansberg, I. (1988). The succession conspiracy. *Family Business Review, 1*(2), 119-143.

Lyman, A.R. (1988). Life in the family circle. *Family Business Review, 1*(4), 383-398.

Lyman, A.R. (1991). Customer service: Does family ownership make a difference? *Family Business Review, 4*(3), 303-324.

Manning, P. K., and Cullum-Swan, B. (1994). *Narrative, content, and semiotic analysis.* Thousand Oaks: SAGE Publications, Inc.

Marshall, J. N., Alderman, N., Wong, C., and Thwaites, A. (1995). The impact of management training and development on small and medium-sized enterprises. *International Small Business Journal, 13*(4), 73-90.

Norusis, M. J. (1993). *SPSS for Windows: Base System User's Guide (Release 6.0).* Chicago: SPSS Inc.

Richards, J., Richards, L., McGalliard, J., and Sharroch, B. (1994). Q.S.R. NUD-IST 3.0 for Microsoft Windows (Version 3.0). Melbourne: Qualitative Solution and Research, LaTrobe University.

Sexton, D., and Nowman-Upton, N. (1991). *Entrepreneurship: Creative and growth.* New Tork: MacMillian Publishing.

Smyrnios, K., and Romano, C. (1994). *The Price Waterhouse/Commonwealth Bank Family Business Survey 1994.* Melbourne: Syme Department of Accounting, Monash University.

Smyrnios, K., Romano, C., and Tanewski, G. (1997). *The Australian Private and Family Business Survey 1997.* Melbourne: The Monash University Private and Family Business Research Unit, Monash University.

Stanworth, J., and Gray, C. (1992). Entrepreneurship and education: Action-based research with training policy implications in Britain. *International Small Business Journal, 10*(2), 11-23.

Steinburg, C. (1993). Taking training for granite. *Training and Development, 47*(2), 7-8.

Stoy Hayward and The London Business School. (1990). *Managing the family business in the UK.* London: Author.

Strauss, A.L. and Corbin, J. (1990). *Basics of Qualitative Research: Grounded Theory Procedures and Techniques.* Newbury Park, CA.: Sage.

Swartz, S. (1989). The challenges of multidisplinary consulting to family-owned business. *Family Business Review, 2*(4), 329-340.

Turner, B. (1981). Some practical aspects of qualitative data analysis: One way of organising the cognitive processes associated with the generation of grounded theory. *Quality and Quantity, 15*, 225-247.

254

Upton, N.B. (1991). The Institute for Family Business at Baylor University. *Review of Business, 13*, 6-9.

Upton, N., Moore, C., Wacholtz, L., and Sexton, D. (8.4.97). *A comparative analysis of learning needs of family-owned and entrepreneurial firms* [Internet]. Available: http://199.103.128.199/fambiznc/cntprovs/orgs/baylor/papers/95ifbpa.htm.

Vinturella, J., Elstrott, J. B., and Galiano, A. (1993). *University programs for family businesses: Survey and projections* : In Director's Manual, International Family Business Program Association.

Walsh, J. P. (1988). Selectivity and selective perception: An investigation of managers' belief structures and Information processing. *Academy of Management Journal, 31*(4), 873-896.

Ward, J.L. (1987). *Keeping the family business healthy: How to plan for continued growth, profitability, and family leadership*. San Francisco: Jossey-Bass.

Ward, J.J., and Aronoff, C.E. (1990). To sell or not to sell. *Nation's Business, 78*, 63-64.

Wortman, M. S. J. (1994). Theoretical foundations for family-owned business: A conceptual and research paradigm. *Family Business Review, 7*, 3-27.

14 Entrepreneurship Education for Professionally Qualified People

Cecile Nieuwenhuizen
Albert van Niekerk

Introduction

Entrepreneurship education for professional people is versatile. It can satisfy various needs. Small business knowledge is necessary for the professional person who wants to start and manage a practice. Apart from this general need of professional people, the same knowledge can be applied to other business opportunities which are so often presented to professional people for evaluation and utilization. Knowledge of at least some crucial business principles and practices is essential to ensure informed evaluation of opportunities and successful start-up and management of the practice or enterprise.

The success factors of entrepreneurs, as identified by research and the type, role and importance of entrepreneurship education for professionally qualified people are highlighted.

Abstract

Although professionally qualified people often have to establish and manage a practice or enterprise, they are usually not regarded as typical candidates for entrepreneurship education. Their exposure to business management and related subjects and experience in the field is generally limited. They are often aware of this, but do not have a very positive attitude towards studies in this field. They have neither the time nor the desire to study again and even if they are so inclined, they might not know which course to study at which institution.

Insufficient attention is given to the advantages of entrepreneurship education for professionally qualified people. The advantages of this kind of education include a strong multiplier effect, due to the professional person's well developed-skills and knowledge which can combine perfectly with business knowledge. Entrepreneurship education for professional people creates awareness and develops business and management skills which can lead to improved opportunities, a higher income and job creation.

Entrepreneurship education for professional people is versatile. It can satisfy various needs. Small business knowledge is necessary for the professional person who wants to start and manage a practice, for example a lawyer, dentist, psychologist or medical doctor. Apart from this general need of professional people, the same knowledge can be applied to other business opportunities which are so often presented to professional people for evaluation and utilization. Examples of these are the psychologist who develops a method to identify entrepreneurs or managers; the doctor who discovers a new medicine or remedy; the lawyer who identifies a property development project or the teacher who wants to start a mathematics or computer training center. Knowledge of at least some crucial business principles and practices is essential to ensure informed evaluation of opportunities and successful start-up and management of the practice or enterprise.

A real-life and recent example of a dentist who realized the possible value of specific entrepreneurship education will be used to illustrate the advantages and importance of entrepreneurship education for professional people.

A case study of Dr Albert Van Niekerk is presented in this paper

Dr Van Niekerk is an example of a professional person who developed his entrepreneurship potential by enrolling for a course in small business management. As a dentist, he developed a dental product, but he realized that he did not have sufficient knowledge to market the product. He enrolled for a small business management course in 1996 and passed with a distinction. During his time of study he started applying the knowledge he had gained. He submitted the marketing plan, as part of the course, for a presentation of the product he had developed to interested parties. In November 1996 he closed a $40 million contract with an American pharmaceutical firm. He attributes a significant part of his success to the small business management knowledge he had gained. Albert lives in Germany, from where he operates his business. He received distance education from Technikon Southern Africa and since the finalization of his contract with America; he has been regarded as an international entrepreneur.

The success factors of entrepreneurs, as identified by research, and the extent to which Albert complied with them will be discussed. We will compare his behavior and knowledge to the success factors. We will also look at his strengths, his weaknesses, and how he learned and developed his entrepreneurial abilities.

The type, role and importance of entrepreneurship education for professionally qualified people will be highlighted.

Dr Albert van Niekerk attended the conference and delivered a part of the paper to relay his experiences and achievements personally.

Introduction

'Unless you try to do something beyond what you have already mastered, you will never grow.'

Ronald E. Osborn

Professionally qualified people are often satisfied with their qualifications which are usually passports to successful professional careers. However, they soon realize that there are options within their situations and they have choices to make, such as becoming and remaining employees for large, state or other institutions, operating their own mediocre or successful practices or applying their professional knowledge to become successful business people. In some instances they are in the position to combine two or more of the options.

According to McClelland, the person's need for Achievement will determine his/her option. The response of Calvin Coolidge, thirteenth President of the United States, to the question 'Exactly why don't you want to be President again?' is a good example of the frustrations often experienced by professionally qualified people. His answer 'Because there's no room for advancement' (Van Ekeren, 1994:12) is certainly shared by many professional people. The achievement motivated successful accountant, lawyer, doctor, will have a desire for advancement, and being a successful accountant, lawyer, doctor there will be, like in the case of the President, no room for advancement, unless they can combine it with their entrepreneurial talent.

The concern of entrepreneurship and small business management educators is the person with a high need for achievement, more specifically the entrepreneurial, professionally qualified person. This is the person who is interested in the additional dimension of development, the development of his/her entrepreneurial skills. The professor in psychology who is simultaneously involved in his own practice and eventually establishes and is involved in a center for assistance of AIDS patients differs remarkably from the state psychologist who is satisfied with this single career. The entrepreneurship educator is concerned with the professional portrayed in the first example. Our duty, as educators, is to assist the professionally qualified person in becoming professional in an additional field of expertise to ensure the development of his potential as a businessperson.

The Type of Entrepreneurship Education Required for Professionally Qualified People

From interviews and experience it was identified that entrepreneurship education for professional people has to be:

- practical
- applicable
- analytical
- relevant
- How to...
- short
- basic
- goal-directed
- specific and
- on a need-to-know basis.

The reason for these requirements is that they usually do not study to obtain a qualification, but to acquire information for a specific, business-related purpose.

The role of entrepreneurship education for professionally qualified people

Three important roles of entrepreneurship education for professionally qualified people were identified by observation and interviews:

To teach professionally qualified people how to start and manage a practice

Small business knowledge is needed by the professional person who wants to start and manage a practice, for example a lawyer, dentist, psychologist or medical doctor;
Generally professionally qualified people have two main problems:

- They do not know how to establish their practices. For example they do not know how to analyze their market; what market research needs to be done and how; how to do feasibility and viability studies and as well as forecasts and budgets.
- They have insufficient or no knowledge about the basic business functions. Examples are that they often do not know the basics of marketing and frequently confuse it with advertising; they do not know how to develop an efficient and effective administrative system; or they do not understand financial principles to ensure optimum financial performance.

To teach professionally qualified people how to evaluate a business opportunity

Business opportunities are often presented to professional people for evaluation, utilization and investment. They need the knowledge and must develop the analytical, business-related skills to enable them to evaluate a business opportunity effectively. This knowledge and skills will enable them to invest their money in profitable enterprises which will assist small business growth and in addition they will be able to provide valuable input.

To teach professionally qualified people how to develop their own innovative ideas and innovations into profitable enterprises

Professionally qualified people often have unique business opportunities. Examples are that they:

- do research related to their professions and in the process discover innovative products - the engineer who discovers a new way of designing and manufacturing reinforced concrete slabs for multi-store buildings
- identify business opportunities related to their fields of expertise - the mathematics teacher who starts a computer training center
- identify business opportunities diverse from their fields of expertise but due to their exposure, other interests and availability of capital are in the position to pursue it - the lawyer who becomes involved in property development.

Often they do not know how to evaluate the viability of the product or how to develop it into a profitable enterprise.

The importance of entrepreneurship education for professionally qualified people

Under normal circumstances professionally qualified people have easier access to finance, as they are regarded as low risk clients by financial institutions. It is therefore relatively easy for them to start a practice, a new enterprise or make an investment in an enterprise.

The high income potential of professional people creates the availability of finance. An example is the successful plastic surgeon who earns a high income which makes it possible to develop and market a range of advanced skin care products. He is a keen entrepreneur and markets his product as well as his services uniquely through beauticians. In addition to this, he has excellent public relations skills participating in actuality programs on television and granting interviews to fashion magazines. His practice as well as his skin care products is immense successes, while other plastic surgeons battle to survive.

Professional people often have a hobby or an interest from which they would like to earn an additional income, for example, the general practitioner who owns an airplane knows he can charter his plane out, but lacks the necessary business skills such as marketing and planning to do so - consequently his investment remains nothing more than a hobby.

Professional people often become bored with their professions and need diversification, an anesthetist may buy a farm and eventually farm full-time when he retires.

The above illustrates that it is easier for professional people to start their own enterprises which are often more profitable and sustainable than the efforts of, for example, unemployed, basically educated people. The combination of the availability of funds and entrepreneurship education will result in an increase in the establishment of these types of enterprises. This will cause improved job opportunities; more successful practices; more innovative products and services and more available funds invested correctly and less loss of capital invested wrongly by uninformed professional people.

The Success Factors of Entrepreneurs as the Foundation of Entrepreneurship Education

If we know what makes entrepreneurs successful, we can develop focused entrepreneurship training and educational programs. When the success factors of entrepreneurs have been identified, they can be used as guidelines for the content of entrepreneurship education and training programs.

Thorough research was done to identify the success factors of entrepreneurs. As this is not the focus of this study, the research methodology will not be relayed in detail.

Research to identify success factors of entrepreneurs

Through interviews with twenty managers from a specific financial institution, successful entrepreneurs and a literature study, 49 potential success factors of entrepreneurs were identified. Subsequently, 86 questionnaires were completed by managers, advisors and entrepreneurs and through a statistical process of prioritization and elimination, 18 success factors of entrepreneurs were identified. Success factors are those factors contributing to the successful establishment and management of a small business. This does not mean that a successful entrepreneur has all the success factors.

With regard to the eighteen success factors, a clear distinction could be made between

- personal characteristics
- management skills

The success factors were divided into these two categories and each factor was defined.

Important Personal Characteristics of Entrepreneurs

Considerable research has been done to describe a typical entrepreneur. Findings have shown that there is no such thing as a typical entrepreneur!

> Peter Drucker (1966:22), well-known management consultant and writer, said the following about the profile of an entrepreneur: 'Some are eccentrics others painfully correct conformists; some are fat, and some are lean; some are worriers; some relaxed; some drink quite heavily, others are total abstainers, some are persons of great charm and warmth; some have no more personality than a frozen mackerel.'

Personal characteristics identified as key success factors are not personality traits. Rather, they are personal characteristics relating to the way entrepreneurs manage their enterprises. The personal characteristics of entrepreneurs that relate directly to their enterprises were the focal point of the research interviews. This means that people have specific personal characteristics in respect of the enterprise they run. However, the same characteristics are not necessarily evident in other facets of their lives.

The key success factors regarding personal characteristics are defined as follows:

a. Perseverance: Entrepreneurs are confident in themselves and their enterprises and persevere despite setbacks, obstacles and difficult situations. They can make immediate decisions, but have enough patience to complete a task and achieve a goal. They do not lose heart when they make mistakes or fail.

b. Commitment to enterprise: Entrepreneurs give everything to establish and build the enterprise. They prove their commitment by using personal funds in the enterprise; taking a bond on a house, working long hours to achieve success in the business; initially being satisfied with a lower standard of living and possibly little or no income from the enterprise.

c. Involvement in enterprise: Entrepreneurs are personally involved in their enterprises and know what is happening at all levels and in all divisions of the enterprise. They perform tasks themselves and communicate directly with staff and others involved in the enterprise, such as suppliers and clients.

d. Willingness to take risks: Entrepreneurs usually try to avoid unnecessary risks by using opportunities to spread risk. For instance, they find investors to provide financing, make special arrangements with suppliers to obtain stock on consignment and conclude special payment agreements with suppliers and service providers. A business opportunity should be exploited in a well-planned manner. It is clear that, rather than taking risks, they evaluate risk and try to eliminate it which is in line with the findings of Brockhaus,

e. Good human relations: Entrepreneurs are strongly involved with people. They realize that they cannot be successful in isolation. They motivate their employees and know how to build up contacts to benefit the enterprise. It is important for them to establish long-term relationships and build up good relations with suppliers, clients and others involved in the enterprise.

f. Creative and innovative: Creativity distinguishes an entrepreneur from competitors. Often entrepreneurs do not have a radically new method, but they do have a method that meets a client's needs in a better way.

> To raise new questions, new possibilities, to regard old problems from a new angle, requires creative imagination.
>
> Albert Einstein

g. Positive attitude and approach:

> Entrepreneurs use failure as a learning experience. The iterative, trial-and-error nature of becoming a successful entrepreneur makes serious setbacks and disappointments an integral part of the learning process. The most effective entrepreneurs are realistic enough to expect such difficulties. Furthermore, they do not become disappointed, discouraged, or depressed by a setback or failure. In adverse and difficult times, they look for opportunity. Many of them believe that they learn more from their early failures than from their early successes. They believe in their own ability. (Kuratko and Hodgetts, 1992:54).

This quotation indicates that entrepreneurs remain positive despite setbacks, failures and disappointments. This does not mean that they do not become discouraged when things do not go smoothly, but they usually deal with these situations positively. We often read of successful entrepreneurs who have lost all they owned sometimes more than once, only to start again from the beginning. Success is achieved by using negative experiences positively and learning from mistakes.

Important Functional Management Skills of Entrepreneurs

The management skills of an entrepreneur indicate how well the entrepreneur can perform important activities in an enterprise.

The following is a definition of management skills identified as success factors:

a. Plan the enterprise before establishing it: A well-thought-out business plan ensures that the entrepreneur can establish the enterprise confidently, because the necessary research and planning has been done.

Entrepreneurs often plan very informally, because they do not have time to draft a formal business plan or simply because they do not know how. Despite the lack of formal training, entrepreneurs are often successful. Formally or informally planning an enterprise is essential before an enterprise can be established. It is desirable to formally plan and draft a business plan, since it has the following advantages:

- Fewer mistakes will be made because problems can be identified in the planning stage - the entrepreneur will therefore be wiser as a result of the planning.
- Entrepreneurs are obliged to address all the important factors of the planned enterprise and will therefore depend less on purely instinctive and crisis decisions. This prevents stress.
- Future-oriented action.
- The planning stage is an ideal opportunity for testing ideas.

b. Have management skills and use advisors and/or experts when necessary: Entrepreneurs usually know, or find out very soon, what their strengths and weaknesses are (in respect of the enterprise they are operating or wish to operate). It is then logical for entrepreneurs to start an enterprise in which they can use their personal characteristics and management skills effectively. Entrepreneurs usually deliberately and instinctively choose enterprises in which they feel comfortable. This ensures a good relationship between them, the enterprise and the environment.

An important element of entrepreneurship is that entrepreneurs must be aware of the management skills they do not have. Entrepreneurs compensate for these lacking skills by:

1. using other people such as employees, consultants, contractors or professional experts; and/or
2. developing themselves and making conscious efforts to fill these shortcomings by learning from others, attending courses, reading or studying.

c. Client service: Client service, combined with good human relations, ensures that an entrepreneur is sensitive to the client's needs. Personal service is important. Administrative and technical factors are also important for good client service.

d. Knowledge of competitors: Successful entrepreneurs know who their competitors are, how many there are and how influential they are, what each one's market share of the target market is and what the quality of their products is like. They know how to distinguish themselves from competitors to ensure and expand market share. They investigate their competitors' strengths and weaknesses and use a competitor's weakness as an opportunity in the enterprise.

e. Market-oriented: Successful entrepreneurs are market-oriented. They know who their target market is, what the target market's requirements and needs are and how to meet these needs profitably.

Many aspiring entrepreneurs are so in love with their product-service idea that they ignore the market; they assume it will sell... The market road is strewn with product-service ideas that were heavily - and many times cleverly - advertised and went bust. (Burch, 1986:79).

f. Realise the importance of quality products/services: A quality product does not necessarily imply an expensive one. However, customers expect the quality of the product to be in relation to the price demanded. Value for money is important. Successful entrepreneurs aim to provide quality products to customers and still turn a profit. To do this, costs must be kept under control without affecting the quality of the products. Quality products and services contribute to the marketing of the enterprise, because they ensure new clients through the personal recommendations of existing, satisfied clients.

g. Bookkeeping for personal purposes: Successful entrepreneurs realize they need to understand their bookkeeping systems. Simplicity and usability are the most important characteristics of the system.

The usefulness of the information made available through the bookkeeping system is vital. The information must be understood so that decisions can be made to better manage the enterprise. Insight into the application of the information is the main purpose of bookkeeping for the entrepreneur.

h. Insight into costs, income, profit, loss and so on: Entrepreneurs know how to calculate profit and what it means to make a loss. They know which costs are essential for survival and understand the implications of increased expenditure. This management skill is closely related to the ability to use income judiciously.

i. Ability to use income judiciously: Successful entrepreneurs exercise financial discipline and understand how money should be spent and what it should be spent on to ensure success. Entrepreneurs must constantly make decisions on expenses to be incurred. They have and develop the ability to make the right decisions for ensuring growth.

It is important to remember that although each management skill is important, few or no successful entrepreneurs have all these skills.

Management Courses for the Development of Entrepreneurial Abilities

The success factors of entrepreneurs give a clear indication of the training and educational needs of entrepreneurs. A thorough literature study (Timmons, 1991; Burch, 1986; Marsh, 1992) proved that most of these success factors can be improved by training and education. To ensure the development of the wide variety of success factors, the expertise of various disciplines and fields of specialty is required.

As a lecturer in management, the focus of the courses developed addresses the management-related success factors. The same can be done by other subject experts, for example the development of programs for increased creativity by psychologists or for better human relations by human resources or communication experts.

The success factor, **have management skills and use advisors and/or experts when necessary,** indicates that successful entrepreneurs are aware of the management skills they do not have. As mentioned, the means by which they compensate for these lacking skills is by **developing themselves and making conscious efforts to fill these shortcomings by learning from others, attending courses, reading or studying.** In addition to this, the other functional success factors indicate the important managerial areas crucial to the effective development of entrepreneurs. This is were entrepreneurship educators in the field of management can and should perform a major role.

In the Business Management Department of Technikon Southern Africa small business management courses were developed in line with the needs of entrepreneurs that could be addressed by experts in the various business functions. The range of six-month short courses developed, and in the process of development are:

How to establish your own small business
Marketing for a small business
Financial management of a small business

Management of a small business
Important information for starting a small business
How to franchise your own business
Alternative methods of obtaining a small business
Growth and the different phases of a business
Entrepreneurial skills
Computers in Small Business.

Dr Van Niekerk enrolled for and completed the Marketing for a small business course. This course would probably be regarded as very elementary and too basic by important professors, researchers and theorists in management. However, intellectual snobbery has no place in entrepreneurship education, as the proof of the pudding is in the eating. Results are what matter. Let us look at the positive results of a basic small business management course.

The Result of Entrepreneurship Education

The success of Dr Albert Van Niekerk - A combination of professional expertise and entrepreneurship education

Professional Background

Dr. Albert van Niekerk studied dentistry and the science of dental materials. His ability to combine science and technology resulted in the viability of the world's first low- fusing fully synthetic dental glass-ceramic system. This combination of art, science and technology led to synthetic dental products which meet the highest demands placed on the dental team today.

He lectures internationally on fulfilling the high esthetic demands placed on the dental team through the combination of art and science.

Dr. Van Niekerk has published several publications and heads the research and development program for two German dental ceramic manufacturing companies.

Currently he is working on a new synthetic bio-active glass for which a European community grant was granted. The products from this research will revolutionize dental and medical implant technology.

Development of the Product

1980 The Minister of Health of the German Democratic Republic, (DDR) ordered the Karl-Marx University in Leipzig, Germany, to develop a ceramic without relying on natural, raw materials from the West. In the same year Prof. Dr Gerhard Gehre, in close co-operation with the company Keradenta, started to work on a concept of producing synthetic dental ceramics, eliminating impure natural minerals. The science of synthetic materials was already known to the industry but not in the field of dental ceramics.

1984 Gehre discovered that the stability of a synthetic ceramic can be controlled with synthetic oxides. This was one of the most important discoveries in the history of dental ceramics and opened many alternatives and new possibilities in dental technology.

1987 Dr Van Niekerk discovered the stability of synthetic glasses through multiple firing processes at temperatures between 900° C and 1000° C.

1989 The first synthetic dental metal ceramic bridge was constructed.

1991 Drs Leonhard Meyer and Albert van Niekerk developed a synthetic dental metal ceramic system for the company Keradenta-Wilde.

1992 The first synthetic dental metal ceramic system was introduced by Keradenta-Wilde at the International Dental Show in Koeln, Germany. Dr Van Niekerk found that through the controlled crystallisation of the mineral phases synthetic dental ceramics have a flexible and stable thermal expansion coefficient as well as unlimited properties and behavior which could be changed objectively. Prof Dr Klimm, University of Dresden, and Dr Van Niekerk started pioneer work in the field of full ceramic inlays and laminated veneers utilizing synthetic ceramics. This was the start of the low-fusing, full synthetic dental ceramic systems. Drs Meyer and Van Niekerk developed the first synthetic titanium ceramic.

1993 Dr Van Niekerk started to work on 'the one-in-all' ceramic system that can be used in all the different application fields of dental ceramics. Dr

Meyer initiated a low-fusing bonding system and, together with Dr Van Niekerk, they developed the first low-fusing (680° C) synthetic ceramic bonding system for resin/composite veneering. In the same year Drs Meyer and Van Niekerk developed a low fusing-synthetic ceramic staining system.

1995 The introduction of full synthetic dental metal ceramics. To date Feldspar had been replaced by synthetic oxides. With the introduction of other high purity oxides, inconsistencies and undesirable, impure, raw materials are eliminated. Van Niekerk and Dr Kaplan Diedrich developed low-fusing synthetic ceramics which function on the principle of capillary forces and diffusion, and the first low-fusing dental synthetic ceramic aid products were introduced to the market by **SPRINGBOK Dental GmbH** and **Optimal Dental GmbH**, Germany.

Identification of Weaknesses

Although these synthetic products revolutionized the dental world, sales were extremely low and the products hardly accepted in the market place.

Dr Van Niekerk analyzed the situation and concluded that the most important part of success was the marketing management of the product about which nobody in the company knew anything or possessed the knowledge or experience of marketing management.

Possible Solutions

He decided to solve this problem by identifying several possibilities which included the following:

- Reading literature on marketing management
- Employing consulting professionals
- Enrolling for a marketing management seminar
- Enrolling for an official education program at an educational institute.

Studies in Small Business Management

He decided to enroll at an educational institution which offered:

- a six-month marketing management for small business course
- which course had to combine a practical application with a theoretical background.

He drew up his practical marketing plan and marketing strategy assignment on the synthetic products and asked that his assignment should be evaluated critically. He passed with distinction.

In addition Dr Van Niekerk read extensively to broaden his knowledge base on marketing.

Application of Studies

After his practical assignment had been marked, he took the assignment and changed the 'Questions' headings to normal headings indicating the headings of a marketing strategy and marketing plan.

He then presented the marketing plan to the company's staff and they started to work exactly according to the marketing plan.

Results

The results were phenomenal. The company negotiated a 40 million US$ contract and an international distribution channel (worth millions if you want to build up such a distribution channel) which represents 52 different countries.

The synthetic dental products are selling extremely well, are well accepted in the market place. Star products changed into cash cows resulting in a positive cash-flow.

Today, synthetic dental ceramic products are becoming market leaders and the science together with the associated products has launched the dental industry into a new future benefiting both dental team and patient.

The Extent to which Albert complied with the Success Factors

Although rather unusual, Dr Van Niekerk possessed all the **personal characteristics** of a successful entrepreneur:

- He **created** a product by
- **committing** extensive time and energy in the development and refinement of the product.
- He **persevered** by gaining additional information to make an
- **innovative** product available to the industry and the client.
- **Personal involvement** in the research and development process as well as in the establishment of the enterprise
- ensured an **innovative product**, an awareness of the needs of the company and the determination to ensure a general application of the product.
- He was prepared to take **moderate risk** by applying his time, energy and capital to the development of the product instead of earning more money in his dental practice.
- In spite of setbacks in different phases of the product development and when the finished product was available and nobody interested in it he **persevered and remained positive**.
- His **personal relations** with staff, colleagues and people in general is experienced as very positive.

   With regard to the **functional management skills** SPRINGBOK Dental, Dr Van Niekerk's existing company was:

- well planned and
- well managed and therefore financially successful,
- he has a good knowledge of his competitors,
- provides excellent client service and quality products.
- The bookkeeping system of the company is managed by a
- professional financial specialist but Dr Van Niekerk is responsible for the financial management of his company as
- he understands the information required and provided by the accountant.
- In spite of financial success he uses his profit and income judiciously by exercising financial discipline and instead of becoming complacent

and satisfied with his financial situation he is always on the lookout for new opportunities.

It is clear that Dr Van Niekerk adheres to most of the functional management skills. However, with regard to the new product he realized that he was product-oriented and that he had to become market-oriented in order to make a success of his new product. He embarked on the marketing management for a small business course and for the first time learned about important issues such as segmenting the market and target markets. He applied his new knowledge and afterwards realized that specific functional management skill was a critical success factor for his business. Without developing the particular skill his chances for success was limited.

When asked about his entrepreneurial success as founder of Atari, Nolan Bushell responded,

> The critical ingredient is getting off your butt and doing something. It's as simple as that. A lot of people have ideas, but there are few who decide to do something about them now. Not tomorrow. Not next week, but today. The true entrepreneur is a doer, not a dreamer.(Van Ekeren, 1994:17)

This quotation is relevant to people like Dr Van Niekerk.

Conclusion

The importance of entrepreneurship education for professional people cannot be overstated, as the benefits for the communities and the improvement of professional practices and businesses at various levels are clear, as illustrated by Dr Van Niekerk. By combining the process of identification of entrepreneurial success factors with the development of appropriate courses, the needs of entrepreneurs can be addressed by specialists in various fields of expertise. Together we, entrepreneurship educators, can help to transform professionals into professional business people and in the process add value to the most valuable asset: intellectual capacity.

The aim of Britain's Graduate Enterprise Program (GEP) was to improve the interest in self-employment of first-time graduates in the United Kingdom from 0.3 per cent to two per cent as in the USA. The 1985 outcome of the GEP proved that more new enterprises were established by graduates and it created additional employment. In addition it proved that 90 per cent of the participants would have deferred their entrepreneurial activities by a few years or would never have started their own enterprises if they had not taken part in the program. The target of two per cent of graduates initiating their own enterprises was reached in many colleges. This experience is an illustration of the value of entrepreneurship education and proves the benefit of timeous entrepreneurship education in ensuring business start-up.

> It takes vision to realize the potential of an international market for an enterprise. However, this vision can only be broadened through education, which in the end will ensure your survival.
>
> Albert Van Niekerk

References

Brockhaus, R.H. (1980b). Risk taking propensity of entrepreneurs. *Academy of Management Journal*, 23:509-520.

Brown, R. (1990). Encouraging enterprise: Britain's graduate enterprise program. *Journal of Small Business Management*, October, 71-77.

Burch, J.G. (1986). *Entrepreneurship*. New York. John Wiley.

Kroon, J. and Moolman, P.L. (eds) (1992). *Entrepreneurskap*. Potchefstroom. Sentrale Publikasies.

Kuratko, D.F. and Hodgetts, R.M. (1992). 2nd ed. *Entrepreneurship, A Contemporary Approach*. Fort Worth: USA. Dryden.

Malan, D.J. (1990). *Entrepreneurs- en Bestuurspotensiaal vir Kleinnywerhede*. Magister Commercii, UNISA.

Marsh, R. (1992). *Business Success in South Africa*. Cape Town. Struik.

Merz, G.R., Weber, P.B. and Laetz V.B. (1994). Linking Small Business Management with entrepreneurial growth. *Journal of Small Business Management*. 32(4) Oct.: 48-60.

McClelland, D.C. (1986). Characteristics of Successful Entrepreneurs. *Journal of Creative Behavior*, 21(3):218-232.

Pickle, H.B. and Abrahamson, R.L. (1990). 5th ed. *Small Business Management*. New York: USA. John Wiley.

Tate, C.E., Cox, J.F., Hoy, F., Scarpello, V. and Stewart, W.W. (1992). *Small Business Management and Entrepreneurship*. Boston: USA. PWS-Kent.

Timmons, J.A., Smollen, L.E. and Dingee, A.L.M. (1994). 3rd ed. *New Venture Creation: Entrepreneurship for the 21st century* (4th edition). Boston: Irwin.

Van Ekeren, G. (1994). *Speaker's Sourcebook II*. Prentice Hall: USA

PART D

NETWORKS IN ENTREPRENEURSHIP EDUCATION

15 Youthful Enthusiasm and Market Realities: Matching Students with Businesses in a Global Economy

Dusty Bodie
Kevin Learned
Nancy K. Napier

Abstract

This paper describes a unique tripartite partnership linking education, government and business in an effort to teach international business and entrepreneurship students to manage in a global economy. Boise State University, the Idaho Department of Commerce and the Idaho business community and Chambers of Commerce have joined forces in developing and growing an internship program that is gaining increasing regional and national recognition. This paper describes how the program developed, how it works, and the benefits and challenges to each of the parties involved.

Introduction

Global forces are driving entrepreneurs to look beyond their borders for opportunities and to meet competition from abroad. Individual states in the US are encouraging their firms to move into the international arena as a way to grow and build employment with the states. To pursue such opportunities, these firms need employees who understand and can thrive in the global economy. In response, over the past three years three entities

279

in the State of Idaho - business, government and education - have learned to work together closely to facilitate the education of a new generation of global entrepreneurs.

In this paper we describe briefly the forces driving business, government and education, the building of a relationship among the three groups and some of the ways we have collaborated including a student internship program. The paper next describes the internship program. Finally, we briefly mention some of the activities that have grown out of this unique venture.

Business, Government and Education

Forces driving business

Today small firms can operate globally because of access to communications systems and to data and information made widely available through low-cost technology. This access clearly makes doing business globally more affordable for all sizes of firms, but it is critical for resource-constrained small and medium-sized firms. Fax, telephone, e-mail, computers and the internet all facilitate communications and make data sources like the National Trade Data Bank in the US and various internet data bases accessible to the smallest of businesses.

Small firms traditionally participating only in the domestic economy now face competition and find opportunity outside their national boundaries. For example, in Idaho a firm that rebuilds used telephones taps the developing economy market. Thus it was forced to think and operate globally from its founding. Another small Idaho company makes high end decorative pillows and screens from raw materials procured through European antique dealers. 100-year-old brocades and fringes simply are not available in North America.

Forces driving state governments

State governments are aggressively promoting and supporting their own businesses as a means of increasing employment for their citizens. However, they are under pressure to reduce costs and operate more efficiently. Thus, many are creative at establishing alliances and finding other co-operative means to conduct their affairs. Within the State of

Idaho, the Departments of Commerce and Agriculture share the costs associated with a trade office in Guadalajara, Mexico. The Department of Commerce has an informal arrangement with is counterpart in Alberta, Canada to exchange staff, thus allowing each state/province to inexpensively market its products in the other.

Forces driving universities

Universities are being asked to offer both international business and entrepreneurship courses, preferably in an integrated format. Global business is exciting to students and the demand for international business education is skyrocketing at our university. But international business students realize their opportunities may well be within the small and medium enterprises, perhaps one they found themselves, and are asking for entrepreneurship education. Our entrepreneurship students are finding some of the businesses they want to start require knowledge of global supply and market issues. They are asking for more education in global business. From an economic perspective, rapidly increasing numbers of small and medium enterprises are entering into cross-border transactions (e.g. Idaho, a predominantly small business economy, has seen the number of firms exporting products grow from several hundred to nearly a thousand over the past five years). From a disciplinary perspective, the literature (e.g. Giamartino, McDoughall, and Bird, 1993) has suggested more interplay between entrepreneurship and international business. Conferences such as this one and the recently concluded International Conference for Small Business further support the idea of blending issues facing SME's with what is occurring globally.

Blending the forces

These forces converged in Idaho three years ago when Boise State University pursued a grant from the US Department of Education that would enhance international business education. We collaborated in the proposal with the State Department of Commerce and our local Chamber of Commerce to develop a joint proposal. The proposal, subsequently funded, was titled 'The Idaho Connection' and developed on the theme of building links and co-operative activity among government, private business and higher education to further international business education and development within our state.

281

To support the project, the Department of Commerce and the Chamber of Commerce each agreed to donate a portion of key staff time over a two-year period to implementation. Over the life of the grant we carried out a number of collaborative activities:

Team teaching - two new courses were team taught by a faculty member and a staff member of either the Department of Commerce or the Chamber of Commerce.

Joint project management - the three groups met monthly to review the project, work on upcoming activities, and stay informed about the activities of each.

Joint purchases and use of equipment - the university began a course on business interpreting and translation and needed equipment to support the course. The Department of Commerce purchased the equipment, which allowed the language department faculty and students to support businesses in the state, one of the Department of Commerce's goals.

Joint conferences - the three entities jointly produced three workshops: 'Doing Business in North American', 'Emerging Nations Workshop', and 'Case Study Writing using Businesses in the Region'.

Joint internship program - together the three developed a unique internship program designed to identify high potential students, train them and place them in businesses attempting to participate in the global market. Following we discuss the internship program.

Developing the Internship Program

Our university has long had an internship program whereby we offer credit for work experience under the guidance of an instructor. However, the program is unstructured and somewhat random. Businesses potentially interested in interns contact the university who posts the internships on a bulletin board. We decided to develop a new internship program specifically focused on international business, targeted toward high potential students. In this section we describe the specific needs of each of the three groups, their strengths, and how the internship program spoke to each.

Needs of each

SME's, speaking through the Department of Commerce and the Chamber of Commerce, were frustrated. They frequently had international trade leads, but neither the time nor the experience to follow them up. In several cases, such firms had participated in trade missions led by the Department of Commerce. These frequently generated so many leads that the companies felt overwhelmed and rarely followed up systematically. Further, few firms had access to or knowledge of how to use the various international trade and related databases available through CD-ROM and the internet.

The Department of Commerce wanted to help businesses in the state build their sales and employment but lacked resources to assist individual firms. Statistics generated by the department showed not only that the payoff for businesses successfully entering into international trade was great but also that jobs in the export-import fields tended to pay more than other jobs. But it was often hard to convince our Idaho firms to attempt international business when they knew so little about it.

The university needed to prepare its students to be active players in the global economy. We sought means of giving students practical experience to enhance their studies in international business and entrepreneurship. But we did not know how to recruit those businesses which could offer a quality international business experiences to our students.

Strengths of each

The Department of Commerce provided infrastructure. It had access to data bases which at the time were not available through the university. It provided access to overseas markets through its offices and co-operative ventures in Mexico, Taiwan, Canada and Japan. Most importantly, it provided leadership through the Director of the International Business Division of the Department. He became the champion to spearhead the program within the government reaching out to the Department of Agriculture and others interested in international trade. His efforts to merge the interest of the Department, the business community and the university were crucial to the initial and subsequent success.

The business community provided the qualified businesses ready and able to direct students in international projects. The International Business

283

Committee of the Chamber of Commerce not only helped to identify businesses, but provided critical support for the program as well.

The university had access to energetic, qualified students. Through its International Business office, and the close co-operation of professors in Modern Languages, Public Affairs/International Relations and Business, the university could identify and recruit a range of capable students for consideration. Due to the success of the grant application with the US Department of Education (which had been the impetus for the three groups to talk initially), funding was available for a faculty co-coordinator to supervise the academic aspects of the program.

Internship Program Mechanics - how it works

Student recruitment

The most crucial component is having a supply of capable, willing, strong students who are able to work with little supervision and to take the initiative with firms who sometimes know little about international trade. In addition, because the program has high visibility, placing only outstanding students is vital to the reputation of the university.

Students are invited to apply through notices posted on College bulletin boards, by making classroom announcements and by asking faculty and students to nominate candidates. Once the program had some 'graduates' those student became the most important recruitment tool. At a minimum, students must have a 3.0 g.p.a., upper division standing and some language proficiency. In addition, we seek evidence of work ethic, ability to adapt and ability to take initiative.

Once students apply, we use a multi-stage screening process. First students are selected by the faculty advisor for further consideration based upon their resumes and recommendations. Next the faculty advisor interviews each likely candidate. Those remaining in the pool are interviewed by the Department of Commerce co-coordinator. He and the faculty advisor then discuss each student and make matches with candidate companies. Finally, the student and the faculty advisor call on the company to introduce the student. The company may veto the student if it does not believe the recommended match is satisfactory.

Company recruitment

The Department of Commerce assembles the list of candidate companies. They normally begin with firms that have made inquiry for assistance in trade lead follow up. We make announcements at various meetings of potential candidates such as the Chamber of Commerce International Business Committee and the Department of Commerce's quarterly state-wide meeting and ask the Department and the Chamber to publicize the program in their newsletters. Chamber and department executives and faculty also recruit firms from their personal experience. Like the students, the best recruiting came after the program had initial success. We have had several repeat customers and they spread the word to other firms who then approach the Department of Commerce.

The criteria for firm selection focuses on the firm's need for assistance, whether there is a manager willing to spend time with the students to clarify expectations and monitor progress, and the nature of the project itself.

Training and placement of students

Students are placed for a semester and work approximately 20 hours per week without pay. Once firms and students are chosen and matched, each student attends a three-day training program designed specifically for interns. The training program is co-ordinate by the Department of Commerce and conducted jointly by the Department, directors of international banking in several of our local banks, and freight forwarders. The goal of the training is to provide the students an overview of the types of practical problems they might face, some of the resources (both people and data bases) available to them, and to impress upon the students the importance of being flexible and taking initiative. Both trainers and trainees report a high level of satisfaction with the training. Each semester the training program is revised to take into account trainer/trainee comments and new information.

Informal training also takes place through conversations with the faculty advisors and through the student network of prior interns. We try to impress upon the students the importance of professional behavior and performance. Because of the quality of the students we have recruited to the program, to date, this has not been a problem.

On-going monitoring of internships

During the first several weeks of the internship, the faculty advisor maintains close contact with each student and business. Throughout the semester, students prepare a weekly report, which is submitted to the faculty advisor, the firm and the Department of Commerce. If there appear to be any problems developing, the faculty advisory talks with the student and the firm.

All students submit a final written report at the end of the semester. The faculty advisor, the Department of Commerce and the firm each receive a copy of the report. The faculty advisory assigns a grade of pass or fail based upon the report. To date, all students have passed. In addition, the Department of Commerce has conducted post-semester debriefings between the students, the faculty advisors, the companies and the department. The Department has also maintained an on-going briefing report updated for each cohort of students.

Program Lessons

We have now completed three years in this program. The following are some of the lessons we have learned:

1. Number of students. We have learned that the maximum number of students we can successfully supervise is six. The program is very time intensive for both the faculty advisor and the Department of Commerce. This means the program must remain a small one, but this size allows close monitoring and the ability to solve problems before they become serious. The small size also allows us to assure quality by keeping the program prestigious among students.
2. Quality of students. Student quality is of utmost importance. We have been careful to select only top quality students. For example, one summer the pool of available students was deemed too weak. We suspended the program for the summer and concentrated on recruiting stronger students for the following fall. By placing only high quality students, we have insured a continuing stream of quality internship projects.
3. Business selection. The firms who have been most pleased and successful in the program have managers who have a good sense of

286

their needs and who are willing to accept suggestions from students. In addition, they must be willing to make the commitment to give the students some of their time each week. Projects do not seem to have similar characteristics. They have ranged from a 'long-distance' internship conducted by email and telephone between the student and the business, to identifying possible target countries for a type of internet hardware, to locating sources of supply for high end antique fabrics, to developing a marketing plan for exporting agricultural products to Mexico.

4. Faculty advisor. A key to the success of the program is a committed faculty advisor who is interested in the program, the students and our relationship with our partners. We ask advisors to serve at least an academic year on the program. To date, they have worked without additional compensation, although occasionally we have been able to provide a course release.

5. Ongoing monitoring and continuous improvement. The close monitoring by the faculty advisor and Department of Commerce has allowed us to solve small problems before they became large ones. The requirement of weekly reports keeps the students on task throughout the semester, helping to avoid the end of semester crunch typical of semester long projects. The debriefing process has allowed for continuous improvement each semester.

6. Importance of tripartite relationship. The relationship between the university, the business community and the Department of Commerce has allowed us to provide a quality internship experience for our students while assisting our local businesses to penetrate the global market place. The relationship between the three entities brings credibility to the program and a ready source of students and internship opportunities. By drawing upon our individual strengths, we have been able to develop a program far superior to any we might have done alone.

Program Results and Benefits

In addition to the educational benefits all professors hope to gain for their students, this program has had a number of other results:

1. Of the nearly thirty students who have participated in the program to date, approximately half have received job offers from their host companies.
2. The prestige of the program has recruited additional students to our international business major and raised the awareness overall of our students in international business.
3. Much of our international business curriculum deals with the large, multi-national business environment. The internship program has exposed our international business students to the inner workings of small and medium enterprises.
4. Because the internships are typically with SME's, our entrepreneurship students have become more aware of the possibilities of international business. As a side note, our entrepreneurship and international business clubs are considering merging since the students see a high level of overlap between the two areas.
5. Our local firms have gained exposure to international business systems and processes that they might never have been aware existed. For example, many SME's are unaware of the possible uses of the internet.
6. The internship program has helped build a strong relationship between the university and the business community. It is helping break down the old notion that all we do is teach theory without practicality.
7. We believe business in our state is improved due to this program. Nearly 30 businesses have gained exposure to international business through our student interns.

A Reflection on the Tripartite Relationship

Perhaps the most important benefit to come from this program is the relationship between the university, the Department of Commerce and the business community. We have not only served the needs of each entity, but in the process have become colleagues outside of our traditional boundaries to our mutual benefit and the benefit of our constituencies. The trust that has been built as a result of the joint development and implementation of the internship program now allows us to work together in many ways: we recommend students for jobs, we serve on committees, we write grant applications, we sponsor joint workshops and teach together and we do research. We look forward to developing other programs with our colleagues for the betterment of our students and our economy.

Reference

Giamartino, G.A., McDougall, P.P., and Bird, B.J., (1993), International Entrepreneurship: The State of the Field, *Entrepreneurship Theory & Practice*, 18(1), pp. 37-42.

16 Entrepreneurship - an Introduction: they said 'don't do it'

Alison Morrison

Abstract

This paper presents an example of collaboration between an entrepreneur and educator in the development of entrepreneurship teaching material. This takes the form of a learning package which serves as a comprehensive introduction to entrepreneurship. With the generous sponsorship of the entrepreneur, David Levin, this was developed over a year period, 1995 to 1996, and consists of a video, supporting student workbook, case study, and tutors' guide. The key stages of the development of the material, piloting procedure, teaching strategy, and case study and teaching notes are now presented.

Introduction

In 1994 David Levin, a leading UK entrepreneur, was appointed as Visiting Professor at the University of Strathclyde, Glasgow, Scotland. When he met Dr. Alison Morrison he enquired as to her area of teaching specialism, to which she replied 'entrepreneurship'. David exclaimed, 'You won't believe how long I've waited to hear that entrepreneurship is being taught within a university What can I do to help?' Consequently, it was agreed that they would collaborate in the development of a learning package which would serve as an introduction to entrepreneurship. With the generous sponsorship of Professor Levin, this was developed over a year period, 1995 to 1996, and consists of a video, supporting student workbook, case study, and tutors' guide. The key stages of the development of the material, piloting procedure, teaching strategy, and case study and teaching notes (Appendix 1) are now presented.

Learning Package Development

Dr. Morrison commenced the process through the development of a case study and teaching notes titled 'They Said "Don't Do It"' (Appendix 1). In addition, a supporting text, which consolidated the range of associated literature, was written in the form of a student work book. The combination of these documents enabled a set of learning objectives to be identified, and verified with Professor Levin.

These were to:

- identify and understand the range of entrepreneurial characteristics, traits, and behaviors which contribute to achieving a successful venture;
- gain an insight into key social influences on entrepreneurial behavior;
- develop an appreciation of entrepreneurial qualities which contribute to successful/growth ventures; and
- be able to identify key challenges facing entrepreneurs, and the means of addressing them.

The case study, text and learning objectives provided the framework for the production of the video which follows the career development of David Levin. Furthermore, it enabled effective structuring of the content in support of the learning objectives. It was recognized that the material would require additional tutor guidance information in order that the learning experience was effective. Therefore, a Tutors' Guide was compiled outlining: learning objectives; intended user groups; teaching strategy; and case study summary, questions and answers.

291

Piloting Procedure

On completion the material was piloted with four disparate groups of students. Their profiles varied considerably with respect to age group, core curricula of study, post- and under-graduate levels, international grouping, and educational institutes. Feedback from each of the pilot sessions was requested and communicated relative to the following three questions.

First, the students were asked what key messages, relative to entrepreneurship, remained with them on completion of the session. These are summarized as follows:

- You have to have a dream and the determination to see it through.
- Don't let anyone stop you - believe in yourself.
- Anything is possible, even if the opportunity does not seem obvious to others.
- Positive thinking and self-confidence are major factors in achieving success.
- Do not be afraid to stand out from the crowd.
- It leaves you with a positive sense - a will to achieve everything that you want to achieve.
- You need to have a passion for what you do and desire to excel.
- Never see situations as 'bad', but as opportunities which may not seem obvious to others.
- Be willing to accept personal responsibility for every aspect of your business.

Second, the students were asked what features they most liked about the video. There responses were:

- The honesty and frankness of Professor Levin in his account of his career development.
- The material was presented in an unpretentious, unassuming manner, which was informative and interesting.
- It was personally inspirational in the presentation of a specific role model with whom the students could identify.
- It provided an insight into the development of a family business.
- The style of presentation was relaxed, easy and enjoyable to watch.
- The opportunity to see the three business operations, which were the focus of the video, in action.

Finally, students were asked as to any additional information which they would like not covered in the video. They said that they would welcome a greater insight into any problematic phases which David Levin may have experienced during his career.

Teaching Strategy

As previously stated, there are four, inter-linked components to the learning package. The first is the accompanying text titled 'Entrepreneurship: an Introduction'. The second is the case study 'They Said Don't Do It' included in Appendix 1 of this paper. The third component is the video 'They Said Don't Do It', and finally, the Tutors' Guide represents a support mechanism. Drawing on the information presented in the Tutors' Guide the sequencing of the teaching strategy is recommended as follows:

- students should have access to the case study and prepare the end questions prior to coming to class;
- tutor and student discussion should take place in class relative to the case study and end questions;
- the video is then presented and is followed by discussion structured around expansion, and deepening, of the answers to the questions at the end of the case study, and addressing the stated learning objectives of the package;
- at the end of the class students should be directed to copies of the text 'Entrepreneurship: an Introduction' for private study to reinforce the concepts and approaches identified through the mediums of case study, class discussion, and video.

Conclusion

This paper provides a model of how learning materials have been developed in collaboration with industry, satisfying clearly identified learning objectives. The value of the contribution of Professor Levin cannot be understated, nor can the level of commitment which he brought to the project. It is considered that the consistently positive response from the pilot student groups serves as a testimonial to the quality of the resource, and the effectiveness to the learning experience.

Appendix 1: Case Study they said 'don't do it'

This case study is based on David Levin a well-known and respected entrepreneur in the United Kingdom. Born in Glasgow, Scotland his businesses are now based in UK's capital, London. He developed his business interests from 1964 starting modestly at the Royal Oak in Yattendon, Berkshire, moving to the prestigious property of the Capital Hotel, Knightsbridge, London. This case documents Levin's entrepreneurial route, which he describes as 'walking a lonely road' along which he met plenty of people who advised him 'don't do it'. The case considers the personality, characteristics and social circumstances which led to his successful arrival at the destination - or has he still to arrive?

For nearly 30 years Levin had been an entrepreneur at the forefront of British hotel keeping at the Capital Hotel in the heart of London's Knightsbridge area. Most people in the hotel industry who knew Levin - and most people did - saw him as an enigma. His quiet, Glaswegian accent and careful speech masked, you suspect, strong passions and great determination. He managed at the same time to be a maverick and an establishment figure, part elder statesman, part enfant terrible.

Despite his assertion that he had always been earnestly committed to maintaining a low profile, he is a former Justice of the Peace, once deputy chairman of the London Tourist Board, was chairman of the British Hospitality Association in 1992, is a Fellow of the Hospitality and Catering International Management Association, and was a Founding Member of the Restaurateur Association. Furthermore, in 1995 he was appointed Visiting Professor at the Scottish Hotel School, University of Strathclyde. As though all these accolades were not enough, Levin was also named Restaurateur of the Year 1992, and Hotelier of the Year in 1994. The judges of these awards praised him for his leadership, inspiration, development and handling of staff - particularly chefs, Richard Shepherd, Brian Turner, Philip Britten and Gary Rhodes - and his ability always to stay ahead of the business.

Levin grew up in the close Jewish community of Pollokshields in Glasgow, the son of an electrical wholesaler. It was a comfortable existence, but he longed to escape its confines. 'I had an enormous fascination for other foods and other countries, which was unheard of in those days', he smiled. His entrepreneurial ambition exhibited itself early in life. 'At the age of 15 or 16, I decided I wanted to get into the hotel business but, I must tell you, I wanted to own my own hotel and a luxury one, too' he recalled, appearing slightly amazed at his own daring and determination. Levin's father went 'mad' when he heard of his son's plans, which were so contrary to his aspirations for his son to enter the 'professions' such as law or medicine.

After his first job at Glasgow's Central Hotel Malmaison Restaurant, under chef Etienne Vacher, who then ordered him to the newly-established Scottish Hotel School, he had a meteoric rise through the ranks of British Transport Hotels, becoming a general manager at the age of 27. Though he has had many triumphs since then, his complete turn around of the worst performing, and the worst food of all the BTH hotels, the humble Lochalsh Hotel in the North of Scotland, is something he is still immensely proud of. This success promoted him to take the entrepreneurial option and go it alone.

In 1964 Levin bought a rundown hostelry, the Royal Oak, in Yattendon, Berkshire for £14,000. Within a year, the Royal Oak had found its way into the Good Food Guide and Levin had made a £14,000 profit. He was content enough, but in the late 1960s he seized the opportunity to achieve his ambition in the shape of the 60 bedroom Capital Hotel on Basil Street, London, a discreet stone's throw from Harrods. He built it with the help of the £1,000 a room grant handed out by the Development of Tourism Act of 1969 and his one time partner, Ian Copeland, a director of Capital and Countries, the property company which developed the Knightsbridge site. From that moment in 1969 when Levin came across the site in Basil Street he has been a man prepared to take risks. 'People said I was crazy to develop a new hotel there,' Levin said. How wrong they were was testified by the hotel's unremitting popularity from the start. With hindsight, Levin was amazed that he had the confidence in his early thirties to do what he did, and that a bank was prepared to support him.

After five years Levin bought out Copeland's shares and since then he has been a lone entrepreneur. It is a loneliness which means a lot to him. 'I thought at first I'd like someone to share my troubles with. But I felt uncomfortable. Otherwise I don't have a reason. It's the way I am,' Levin said. Not even his wife, Margaret, whose gift for interior design is increasingly apparent in the Capital, has a share in the company.

The lonely road led him next door to the Capital where he soon established the less formal L'Hotel, with its chic wine bar-cum-restaurant, Le Metro. Then he 'invented' the now renowned Chef Gary Rhodes and installed him in the Greenhouse Restaurant. Like the hotel ventures, the trade thought a restaurant down a quiet mews in Mayfair, a dead duck. Levin didn't point out that Hay's Mews contained an all-night taxi drivers' garage. The public flocked. He was given the same thumbs down about his latest enterprise, the 180-seater Peoples Palace restaurant in the concrete monstrosity of the South Bank complex in London. It reopened in January 1995 and is run by the next generation Levin - his son Joseph. The Capital now turns over more than £4m per year, and the other ventures contribute a further £4m to annual turnover, and this figure is still rising.

Levin's management style is unusual. 'I take the shape of the board of directors - chairman, managing director, marketing director, and personnel director,' Levin said. 'At weekends I am in the habit of washing my cars, an occupation which surprises my family, but it helps me to think, and actually I'm having a board meeting. It means a lot of conflicting aspects within me. I suppose the nearest thing I have to a partner is Barclays Bank'. Not surprisingly Levin leans heavily on his lawyers, accountants and other professional advisers with whom he has regular meetings, but they have no share in the business and, unlike members of a board, can stand aside from it. However, Levin believes that his total involvement in the management of his business is one thing. Becoming a slave to it is another. 'A large part of my life is my family,' he said 'It worries me that people whom I look around at aren't able to sustain a happy family.'

Longevity of employment is something which Levin values, and it hurts him personally when a protégé leaves. As did the Capital's chef Richard Shepherd in 1977, who was lured away by the promise of the partnership with Peter Langan, at Langan's Brasserie in London, which was to prove so fruitful. The same feelings were experienced in 1996 when chef Gary Rhodes made his move from the Greenhouse Restaurant to work for the large Gardner Merchant catering company.

'I've been fortunate in maintaining a certain continuity in the people who work for me,' Levin said; 'one could say that they should enjoy the success of the company. But that conflicts with my aim to hold 100 per cent of the company to myself.'. In order to address this conflict Levin set up a non-contributory discretionary pension fund in which the lease of the Capital was vested. The trustee of the pension fund is the company, and 'I'm the company,' he said. 'The pension fund is worth millions. It's a gift from me to certain individuals. It's my way of saying: 'it has solid foundations.' When asked what it was worth in real terms to fund members? 'It has not quite reached the equivalent of two-thirds of final salary. And I believe in big salaries,' he replied. 'Not partnerships but provides a powerful incentive to stay put!' Is this the personnel director speaking? Or the chairman? It is difficult to tell.

When he speaks of the future it is obvious that neither his enthusiasm for the hotel industry nor his entrepreneurial spirit have been dimmed by time. Forever the maverick, Levin has told his pension company that he will be retiring at 64. At 62, there is still much to motivate him for the next two years. However, even though retirement may be looming, Levin is still thinking of new projects - 'there is a real need for new restaurants in the middle market'. It is hard to believe he will do more than move on to the pavement of the lonely road and direct the traffic. This man believes that everyone has it in them to climb their own mountain as he has climbed his. 'The road may be lonely, but the view from the top is superb - I have no regrets', he concluded.

Teaching Notes: They said 'don't do it'

Case summary

This case presents a profile of a man with a complex persona, often seemingly at conflict within himself. Levin is unorthodox but seeks the trappings of the traditional establishment. He is dedicated to his businesses, but wants to be known as a family man. His stated commitment to maintaining a low profile is at odds with the wide range of accolades which he has sought and/or been awarded. He wants to share the business with his loyal staff, but retention of 100 per cent equity is of prime importance.

In terms of entrepreneurial behavior and characteristics Levin exhibits the classic of: an early and driving ambition; a vision recognizing opportunities where others see none; creativity, attention to detail, and continuous innovation; and a need for independence and an inner locus of control despite presiding over a multi-million pound empire. These characteristics are underpinned by strong management capabilities, and supported by a team of professional advisers.

One of the major social influences on Levin's entrepreneurial behavior appears to have been his up-bringing within the Glasgow Jewish community which he found claustrophobic. Thus, family background, social up-bringing, and perhaps to a certain degree, social marginality were motivating factors towards his chosen career path. His attitude towards providing a pensions fund for loyal staff could be taken as having derived from his formative social setting. A further social influence which Levin himself highlights is that of the effect of his achievements during his time within British Transport Hotels. The confidence gained from this success represented a deciding influence towards taking the entrepreneurial route.

Case Study Questions and Answers

(i)   *Entrepreneurial motivation*

Q. What triggered Levin's entrepreneurial behavior?

A. Students should be guided to draw from the case study key motivational influences in the development of Levin's entrepreneurial behavior. These may include his family background and social setting, experience within the industry sector, and in-born characteristics and personality traits such as creativity, drive and desire to achieve, and self-confidence.

(ii)   *Rewards*

Q. For Levin, what rewards of an economic and social psychological nature can be identified as a result of his entrepreneurial behavior?

A. It is clear that the rewards for Levin are far more than monetary. Students should consider the reward driven motivations which urged him forward at different stages in his career development. In doing so the distinction and links between economic and social psychological rewards should be identified and discussed, focusing on the relationship of these to question (i).

(iii) *Challenges*

Q. What key challenges did Levin encounter during his career and how did he overcome them?

A. At each of the four key stages in Levin's career he met different types of challenges. These included access to financial resources, lack support from advisers, fear of loss of reputation, etc.. Students should identify what action Levin took at each stage in addressing these challenges and what features from questions (i) and (ii) contributed in the taking forward of his initiatives.

(iv) *Organizational structure*

Q. Did Levin's road need to be lonely?

A. Levin chose to develop his career as a solo entrepreneur. There were other options open to him, such as recognition of family input and involvement of members in the control of his businesses. Alternatively, a partnership or team approach involving appropriate persons outwith the family could have been adopted. Students should be guided to discussion relatively to the merits of different organizational structures in the achievement of entrepreneurial goals.

(v) *Future*

Q. Is there such a thing as a life-cycle for entrepreneurs? Will Levin ever retire?

A. Students should be guided to consider the perspective of entrepreneurial behavior over a person's life-cycle and whether it can be turned on and off as required. Given the profile of

Levin the students will be in a position to assess how this relates to him. They should consider what the future may hold for Levin. Alternatives may be: sell the businesses and become a full-time family man; abdicate to his son Joseph; bring in partners; and/or other alternatives.

(vi)   *Entrepreneurs*

Q. Could you emulate the entrepreneurial career development of Levin?

A. Final discussion should center on what it takes to be an entrepreneur, and ask students to assess their potential. This closing session should aim to inspire students that if they have the passion and the will they have the potential to develop a successful entrepreneurial career.

17 Establishing a Cross-faculty Entrepreneurship Program for Undergraduates

Mike Yendell

Abstract

The University of Strathclyde in Scotland, highly regarded by employers in industry and commerce, had, until recently, offered the majority of students little opportunity to develop entrepreneurial capabilities. The Strathclyde Entrepreneurship Initiative, established in February 1996, now offers elective classes to students throughout the University, complementing their cores studies.

The program is described, as well as the learning approaches used.

Innovations include a full credit interactive computer-based class 'An Introduction to Entrepreneurship', which will be demonstrated, and also a creativity class. Some results from student evaluations are discussed, as are wider issues including alumni and entrepreneur involvement, and interactions with academic colleagues university-wide.

Introduction

Background: The University of Strathclyde, Glasgow, Scotland

The University of Strathclyde was founded by a benefactor, John Anderson, who left a bequest in 1796 for the creation of a University which would become 'A Place of Useful Learning'. Every student and every member of the University's staff know these few words. They set the

301

core values of the University and were as appropriate in 1997 as they were 200 years ago. While Strathclyde has a long tradition, that tradition is not a classical tradition, rather, it is linked to the historical excellence of Scottish expertise in science, engineering, and business, as well as to the world-wide entrepreneurial activities of Scots in times past.

The University is structured in five Faculties: Arts and Social Sciences, Business, Education, Science and Engineering. Total student numbers registered for diplomas and degrees are approximately 17,000, of whom approximately 11,000 are on four year undergraduate programs: the 1996 undergraduate intake was 3,146 students. The university's undergraduate students are predominantly from the local, West of Scotland, population, but there are also significant numbers of overseas students. A recent trend has been an increase in the numbers of mature students.

The University's activities impact all levels of education, from the training of primary school and secondary school teachers, through undergraduate and postgraduate study and research, to a Learning in Later Life program. At postgraduate level, Strathclyde has a significant number of distance learning students based in countries throughout the world. The following table shows the University's graduation profile for 1995.

Table 1

Strathclyde Graduates 1995						
Degree	Arts.	Busin.	Educ.	Engin.	Science	Total
Undergraduate	423	567	348	661	533	**2532**
Postgraduate Diploma	32	223	588	35	9	**887**
Higher Degree	50	808	14	229	236	**1337**
TOTAL	**505**	**1598**	**950**	**925**	**778**	**4756**

The University of Strathclyde has a reputation for quality in both teaching and research, and for the relevance of these to the needs of industry. The University's Teaching Quality Assessment ratings place it in the top ten universities in the UK. Strathclyde graduates have the knowledge needed for an industrial or commercial career, and because the style of education equips them to work effectively within the organizational structure of their future employer, they are in high demand: the proportion of Strathclyde graduates whose first employment was in industry and commerce in 1993 (the latest available data) was 32 per cent greater than the UK average.

Scientific and engineering research at Strathclyde is world class in many areas. Academic staff are encouraged to work closely with industry. Intellectual property earnings are the largest in the UK. These earnings have generated $37M in the last 13 years, and approach those of Massachusetts Institute of Technology, who generated $39M over the last 10 years.

Strathclyde has an international outlook. Significant numbers of students come from overseas, and academic staff are encouraged to network with the best in their field of study internationally. The Strathclyde MBA is delivered through a number of overseas centers and as a result the University has been awarded the prestigious Queens Award for Export, normally only awarded to industry. Strathclyde has also been particularly successful at securing European funds for research, for projects which support the EU West of Scotland Regional Strategy, and for student and staff interchange programmes.

As a result of these and other innovative developments which generate income to support the growth of the University, Strathclyde is recognized within the UK and elsewhere for its entrepreneurial approach to developing its own activities. However, prior to the formation of the Strathclyde Entrepreneurship Initiative in February 1996, only students from a limited number of departments within the University, and mostly those in the final year of study, had access to entrepreneurship education. Through the Strathclyde Entrepreneurship Initiative, students in any year or Department can now take Entrepreneurship classes, earning credits towards their degree.

The Local Economic Background

The Scottish economy and its development needs

Scotland, a country of five million people, is an integral part of the United Kingdom, but has a distinct culture, and a very close-knit business community. Historically a hub of international trading, heavy engineering and shipbuilding, Glasgow and the West of Scotland have tremendously entrepreneurial origins. Edinburgh, Scotland's capital city which is just 40 miles away in the East of Scotland, also has a substantial industrial history, but here, the emphasis is on financial activities. Scotland is proud of its educational heritage and its schools and universities are respected world-wide. It is the quality of this educational system, together with Scotland's position within, but on the rim of the European Community, which has been responsible for the substantial development of science and technology-based businesses in recent years. However, the major technology players have been branch factories of multinational companies.

By comparison with Asia and North America and, indeed, the South East of England, Scotland has a low business birthrate. A broad range of cultural and historical issues lie behind this situation, but in Scotland, in the last few years, a major change in attitudes and perceptions is leading to a significant change to this situation for the long term benefit of the economy.

The need for knowledge-based entrepreneurs

In the 21st century, substantial new wealth will be created through the commercialization of knowledge, with emphasis on the creation of new science and technology based business activity. New opportunities will be created by new technology, and the speed of reaction of the entrepreneurial company, or the entrepreneurial division within a large company, will be vital if the opportunities are to be effectively exploited in increasingly competitive global markets. And as large companies shrink their workforce and increasingly subcontract to smaller specialist companies, new companies must continually be created to satisfy these needs. Because mass employment can no longer be guaranteed by labor-intensive industries, large numbers of new businesses are essential. But it is not sufficient for new businesses to be formed, they must survive and grow if the economy is to thrive. They must be created by intelligent, competent entrepreneurs who have specialist knowledge within their field of business. The Scottish economy needs an increasing number of such individuals.

According to the 1996 OECD report, 'The Knowledge-Based Economy', more than half of total GDP in the rich economies is already knowledge-based, and high tech industries have almost doubled their share of manufacturing output in the last two decades, to around 25 per cent, with knowledge-intensive services growing faster. Further, according to the Economist's World Economic Survey (Sept. 1996), by one reckoning, 'knowledge workers' now account for eight out of every ten new jobs.

Development of such new knowledge-based businesses, and linkages between them and universities, is a key new element in the European Union requirements laid down for Regional Development programs for the period commencing 1997, a major plank of the Scottish Enterprise strategy, and is addressed in the October 1996 Bank of England Technology Report.

But without highly educated, creative individuals with an entrepreneurial mindset and access to enterprise skills, no government strategy for business creation will succeed. Such 'people' issues, unfortunately, have often been ignored by management theorists and economists, who themselves are 'facing a huge challenge learning how to measure the performance of the knowledge-based economy' (OECD, 1996). Within the University of Strathclyde, the Fraser of Allander Institute, an economic research Institute which maintains a model of the Scottish Economy has recently taken particular interest in this issue through collaborative research on innovation across the EU and a major research project on entrepreneurship within the UK Economy.

The Scottish enterprise business birth-rate strategy

As a result of substantive studies of this issue, Scottish Enterprise, the economic development agency for Scotland, established a strategy (Improving the Business Birth-rate - A Strategy for Scotland, Scottish Enterprise, 1993) to increase the business birth-rate throughout the country. This program addressed a broad range of issues, in each case aiming to use limited amounts of public sector money to stimulate lasting change. Issues covered include sources of finance - stimulating the development of the UK Alternative Investment Market (AIM), supporting organisations of business angels, supporting regional programs to deliver courses to potential entrepreneurs, and, of particular relevance to this conference, supporting enthusiastic teams within the educational system, to embed enterprise and entrepreneurial elements within education at all levels, through a program entitled 'From Primary to plc.'

In the four years since the publication of this Strategy, dramatic changes have taken place throughout the country. Enterprise programs are operating at all levels of society. Within the education sector, these operate at school level, both primary and secondary, in the community through programs such as 'NFTE', imported from New York City, in Further Education and in the Universities. Scots are responding well: the impact of the programs is becoming evident in the business birth-rate statistics.

At the school level, both Primary and Secondary, Strathclyde University's Center for Enterprise Education provides a range of services in support of school wishing to embed enterprise elements within their curriculum. A learning resource center develops and publishes materials for use in schools (these materials are now in use in schools in many countries world-wide) and conferences and teacher education programs provide opportunities for schoolteachers to develop their skills, with a target of training one teacher in every school in Scotland. As a result of this program, 80 per cent of Scotland's primary schools now have a teacher trained in enterprise education, and secondary programs are developing well. Other programs, such as Young Enterprise (for which Strathclyde provides the annual examinations), and the new International Achievers program, give secondary school students an opportunity to experience realistic business situations.

Structuring the Strathclyde Entrepreneurship Initiative

Focus

The University made a decision during 1995 to develop an entrepreneurship program, not only in support of the needs of the Scottish economy, but also because students were increasingly conscious of the need to take control over their own careers, and to develop a portfolio of skills and abilities which would equip them for their futures in a rapidly changing environment.

Unlike many University entrepreneurship programs which offer undergraduate or postgraduate programs in Business Schools specifically for those who have already decided to develop an entrepreneurial career path, it was decided that Strathclyde's initial program should be at undergraduate level, and have, as its prime objective, the support of students with core disciplines throughout the University. The program should be seen as an adjunct, not an alternative, to in-depth study of core disciplines in any of the Universities five Faculties of Engineering, Science, Education, Arts and Social Studies, or, indeed, of Business.

Because of the increasing level of interest and related activity in schools in Scotland, and a desire to maintain that interest while students are at University, and also because of a view that conventional 'linear track' university education may have the potential to have a negative effect on the development of an individual's entrepreneurial characteristics, it was considered important that the entrepreneurship program be accessible by students in their early years of study.

Elective classes would be available to students from all departments of the University, in any year of study. The University's credit-based degree structure, in which every first and second year student has the option of taking two classes (out of twelve) each year from departments outwith his/her department of study, lends itself to providing an internal market. In this way, students taking, as core subjects, the University's industrial oriented programs of business education, applied science and engineering, might become equipped to become the 'knowledge entrepreneurs' of the 21st century.

Emphasis is placed on the commercialization of knowledge gained in study of core subjects, on internationalization, and on issues associated with high-growth businesses.

Academic reporting

The Director of the Initiative reports directly to Professor John Spence, Pro-Vice Principal of the University.

The Initiative is administered, for financial and operational purposes, within the Strathclyde Business School, the University's Business faculty. However, it has a cross-faculty remit. For this reason, its academic reporting line has been structured in such a way to allow all five Faculties an involvement in the decision making in relation to class content, teaching approach, assessment etcetera.

The **Entrepreneurship Academic Advisory Group** was created to provide the first stage in the University's academic approval quality procedures for the Initiative and facilitates the process for new class or course proposals developed by the Strathclyde Entrepreneurship Initiative. Documentation on new classes/courses which are recommended for approval by the Advisory Group are then passed to the Strathclyde Business School Academic Committee for formal approval via the normal Faculty reporting mechanism.

Because the Initiative's activities are cross-faculty, this is a cross-faculty Group. It has five Faculty Representatives, at senior level, delegated by the Vice-Dean (Academic) of each Faculty, and provides the mechanism to ensure that the academic requirements of all five Faculties are taken into account as the Entrepreneurship Initiative develops. All members are appointed on the basis of their academic position within their Faculty, and their interest in and knowledge of entrepreneurship issues. Its Chairman is Professor Norman Clark, who has interests in the contribution of entrepreneurship to economic development internationally, and whose early research related to entrepreneurship in India.

Design of the Program of Undergraduate Elective Classes

Learning approaches

> 'In my work, I meet with many entrepreneurs. A common trait is that they read widely, but rarely does this include standard management texts. Instead, they prefer to read about how other people have grown their businesses'

John Anderson, Head of Entrepreneurial Services, Price Waterhouse, Glasgow. The Herald, 26 Nov. 1996. *John Anderson's MBA Thesis, entitled 'Local Heroes' provided the insights which led to a series of publication about recent Scottish Entrepreneurs entitled 'Local Heroes'.*

Entrepreneurs have historically learned how to develop their businesses not through formal study, but through their own experience, through asking for help from experts and also through talking to, and reading about, others who have experienced similar situations. They go

308

through an incremental learning process, continually developing their knowledge and skills. Perhaps the main challenge for entrepreneurship educators is to create appropriate classroom and project situations in which learning of this nature takes place.

Entrepreneurs identify opportunities, create ideas and decide on their actions on the basis of a mixture of creativity, rational analysis and intuition. Creativity is a key issue, and for this reason a full elective class in creativity has been developed. Rational analysis is crucial also: many of the standard business techniques are appropriate here. The intuitive element, the ability to take decisions on the basis of the brain's powerful ability to sift information and relate situations to the individual's full knowledge base, is essential also - entrepreneurs know that it is frequently more important to take a decision quickly than to await a full analysis. Yet without experience, it can be dangerous to trust intuition. Effective entrepreneurs need to know when to invest time and money in structured analysis and when to trust their intuition.

In developing the learning approaches for the Strathclyde Entrepreneurship Initiative therefore, emphasis was put on experiential learning, in which the students actively participate, by analyzing case study situations when they know they will have to contribute to discussions, working on projects in teams, making presentations, and learning interactively through computers. Maximum exposure was given to real-life situations: they are exposed to professionals whose work supports growth companies, and of course to the experiences of actual entrepreneurs, both through case studies and, 'live', in the classroom. It was decided that class tutors who work within the Initiative should ideally have first hand experience of entrepreneurial activities within a growth company environment.

The classes were designed to maximize the benefits students gain from such participation, and approaches vary depending on the topic or issue being taught. While classes are developed with clearly defined learning objectives for each session, they are not structured rigidly within the individual disciplines of a vertically structured business school, rather, they address the issues in a more holistic, multidisciplinary manner. Approaches used include:

- Open-ended Case Studies
- Entrepreneurs in Class
- Guest Presenters
- Group Projects

- Video Case studies
- Multimedia
- Computer Aided Learning
- Workshops

The Strathclyde Entrepreneurship Initiative team work with specialists to develop their classes, and associated learning materials, for example with members of Strathclyde's Center for Academic Practice and with the Scottish representative of the European Case Clearing House.

Resources - teaching staff needs

The Strathclyde Entrepreneurship Initiative team initially comprised, in addition to the Director and secretary, a lecturer, seconded on a temporary basis (now complete) from within the Business School and a part time teaching assistant. A new lecturing post is now in the process of approval and this will shortly be advertised.

Because the team is small, an inherent difficulty exists, however, in supporting the above learning approaches which are very labour intensive, requiring substantial academic staff time. Preparation time is substantially greater than the normal lecturing approach, and class sizes need to be small, with an absolute maximum of 50 students per class. Yet the Entrepreneurship Initiative receives its resources on the same basis as all other departments at the University who, typically, teach by more conventional lecture-based approaches with large class sizes.

This led to an examination of the potential for the use of IT, and the decision to develop, with financial support from Scottish Enterprise, an interactive computer-based module as an introduction to key knowledge issues within entrepreneurship. There is a need for students to develop a sound knowledge of key business matters, and an understanding of the full range of issues which impact the creation of an entrepreneurial business activity. By using computer-based teaching, with interactive exercises, for the knowledge elements of the program in an introductory class, large numbers of students could be introduced to Entrepreneurship issues. This, then, enables later classes taught in a 'live' participative manner to be much more effective because the students will already have the necessary knowledge base. The computer-based approach is particularly well suited to this need, and allows large numbers of students to study with minimal tutor involvement freeing up staff time for smaller numbers to take the remaining classes.

This approach addresses a key problem with the chosen cross-faculty approach: timetabling. There are very few timetable 'slots' available to students in departments across the University. So a self-study, self-timed approach provides a good solution to this issue also.

This approach was adopted, the new computer-based class (Z1.104) proving very effective, students particularly liking this method of learning, and requiring much lower levels of tutor support than traditional methods.

1996/7 Program

Classes offered

Four classes were offered, each with no required pre-requisites. Classes focused on the development of entrepreneurial knowledge, skills and behavior. Learning approaches were designed to enhance those personal qualities and capabilities, which will enable students to seize entrepreneurial opportunities as their careers develop.

Students are assessed throughout the semester, rather than by formal examinations.

Z1.104 Entrepreneurship: Business Start-up Toolkit (Multimedia)
1 Credit

An Introduction to Entrepreneurship

A highly innovative multi-media based class in which students learn through interactive computer-based study, at times to suit themselves. Developed in conjunction with a company providing hands on assistance to new start businesses in Scotland, the Euroventure Group, and using authoring software developed by the University's MENTOR unit within the Management Science Department, this class takes advantage of substantial experience of multimedia teaching of undergraduates. Students are guided through the processes involved in developing business ideas, building

311

teams, assessing markets and shown how to successfully transform a business idea through to start-up stage.

Z1.105 Entrepreneurship: Personal Creativity   1 Credit

This innovative class assists students to develop their personal creativity and problem solving capabilities. In this way, the potential available in their knowledge, experience and assets in general can be released. In addition, through considerable group interaction, the value of the creative team is emphasized.

Z1.102 Entrepreneurship: New Venture Creation   1 Credit

A broad and realistic introduction to the process of new venture creation, this class examines the ways in which entrepreneurs approach the creation and development of their own businesses. It then takes students through the sources of new venture business ideas, business planning, commercialization of products/services, assessment of market and financial viability, sourcing of start-up funds and issues associated with the successful management of the venture.

Z1.103 Entrepreneurship: Knowledge, Science and Technology-Based Businesses   1 Credit

The process of entrepreneurship is examined, with emphasis on the commercialization of knowledge, science and technology. Through the use of case studies based on start-up and growth of actual knowledge-based businesses, students will develop an understanding of the issues associated with innovation, commercialization and management. This class is particularly appropriate to science and engineering students, together with those business students considering careers in this sector.

Student evaluations

Overall, student evaluations of the pilot runs of the four initial classes were very encouraging. Comments such as 'The hardest work of my classes this Semester, but the best' or 'Case studies and guest speakers showing the application of the knowledge, were very effective' and 'At last, some useful knowledge' are obviously very encouraging to the class tutors. However, for the student to enjoy their studies is only part of the task: did they learn what we wanted them to learn? Again, in general our assessments show that they did: not only were we very pleased with their assignments, but the external panels who reviewed the student project presentations, composed of financiers and professionals who support businesses, were very complementary of our students' work.

Exit questionnaires

In their exit questionnaires for semester 2 classes, the following percentage of students responded 'agree' or 'strongly agree' when asked if the class met their expectations in relation to:

Table 2

	Z1:103	Z1:104	Z1:105
Enhancement of career opportunities	79%	69%	50%
Development of entrepreneurial potential	87%	86%	63%
Exposure to the practicalities of the business environment	83%	79%	61%
Development of personal skills	67%	48%	71%
Improvement in business management skills	58%	69%	50%

They were then asked a range of questions relating to their evaluation of the class, and again, the following percentages of students agreed or strongly agreed with the following statements:

Table 3

	Z1:103	**Z1:104**	**Z1:105**
The content was appropriate	75%	90%	88%
Teaching methods were well chosen	83%	72%	85%
The tutor knew the specialism	96%	69%	89%
I was stimulated to find out more information	46%	55%	50%
The assignments were well chosen	68%	79%	57%
My interest in the class increased as the class progressed	62%	65%	61%
The class was valuable in developing skills & techniques in entrepreneurship	83%	76%	82%
I would recommend the class to other students	75%	93%	75%
I understand how to build a team	83%	76%	78%
I developed team participation skills	67%	56%	82%

In examining these evaluations, perhaps the weakest points relate to the level of stimulation to find out more information. This needs to put in perspective, however in relation to the fact that each class is an elective, just one twelfth of a year's work for the student, and the level of work expected of students in these classes is higher than most anticipate when they sign up - so that the pressures on the students from other classes militate against spending more time on related study.

In relation to Z1:104, the computer-based class, it is interesting to note that this class carries the highest proportion (93 per cent) who would recommend it to other students, but as one would expect bearing in mind the mode of study, the lowest proportion (48 per cent) considered that they had developed personal and team participation skills.

Students were asked a range of 'free text' questions as part of the evaluations. Among regular responses were the benefit of the teamwork, the feeling of increased confidence, and an understanding that creation and building a new enterprise is 'an actual process - it isn't just luck'. Perhaps one of the nicest responses was from a student in my colleague Dr Alison Morrison's class: 'It's nice to find someone who cares - I mean, about us entrepreneurs - those of us who want to be employers, not just employees'.

Wider Issues

Alumni

The benefit to an entrepreneurship program of Alumni involvement is immeasurable. The advantages of bringing entrepreneurs and professionals into the classroom have been well borne out by the responses of students in the evaluations. The messages Alumni give are real, the commitment to their businesses and their employees is tangible, and the students can relate to them because they studied at the same university. The younger they are, the greater the empathy with students.

Strathclyde University is fortunate at having some very successful young alumni entrepreneurs, including the Scottish Entrepreneur of the year for 1996, who was more recently, in May 1997, awarded the accolade of joint Worldcom World Young Business Achiever in Canada.

To stimulate continued interest among the University's Alumni, the Initiative organised, in January 1997, a series of seminars for Alumni with funding from a local enterprise support agency, Lanarkshire Development Agency. This was very successful, and as a result will be run again in 1998.

The seminars were delivered by experienced professional trainers, actively involved in supporting entrepreneurs who are creating successful growth businesses. Active entrepreneurs contributed by offering accounts of the attractions and pitfalls of entrepreneurship, drawn from recent personal experience. Over 70 Strathclyde Alumni, all scientists or engineers, attended these seminars, gaining practical insights into the real world of the entrepreneur. 50 of these expressed strong interest in establishing businesses at the end of the series.

Strathclyde Alumni can move forward from this seminar series for selection for the Lanarkshire Development Agency's very successful Entrepreneurship Program, which has created 46 companies employing 1,500 people with sales in excess of £21 million, and is an important element of the Scottish Enterprise Business Birth-rate Strategy.

Related departmental programs within Strathclyde

Complementary programs relating to entrepreneurship have been developing in a number of departments across the University for some

315

years. These have already provided diverse external impacts - from culture change within primary and secondary schools, through the economic benefits of new business creation, to government policy-making. These programs provide the strong foundations from which the Strathclyde Entrepreneurship Initiative is now building, and are outlined in Appendix 1.

This range of programs within Strathclyde University greatly enriches the Strathclyde Entrepreneurship Initiative's educational programs by providing a continuum of understanding relating to innovation and entrepreneurship.

Strathclyde Entrepreneurship Education Forum

Since the inception of the Strathclyde Entrepreneurship Initiative in February 1996, it has had as a prime commitment the enhancement of an entrepreneurial culture throughout the academic staff within the University. This is essential in the achievement of a cascade effect which will, in time, be reflected in the teaching environment. In turn, this will impact on the cultural values and attitudes of our students, hopefully, to the betterment of their career opportunities and the economy of Scotland as a whole.

In support of this, with funding from the Glasgow Development Agency, the Initiative established an **Entrepreneurship Education Forum** with regular monthly meetings for those directly involved in entrepreneurship education, and other interested parties within, and external to the University of Strathclyde. This interchange of best practice and experience is stimulated by meetings, presentations, structured discussion and workshop sessions. The Forum aims to act as a support group, nurturing awareness and attitudes towards entrepreneurship and associated educational issues.

The program for 1996/7 is attached as Appendix 2.

Relationships and partnerships with external entities - Academic, Business, and Public Sector

A highly practical educational program of this nature could not possibly be delivered in academic isolation. Academic networking is normal within

316

universities, and this is addressed through the conference circuit and through actively seeking out relevant specialists internationally. However, interaction with practitioners is even more important.

All Initiative team members therefore network regularly with all sectors of the business and support community, locally, nationally and internationally, identifying key individuals and developing personal contacts through appropriate organizations.

Individuals and organizations with whom the team currently work are listed in Appendix 3.

The Future

The Strathclyde Entrepreneurship Initiative has had a successful first year. Its strength lies in the fact that it supports, rather than replaces, core studies.

Students are increasingly aware that their period at University provides the best opportunity they will ever have to equip themselves for their future. Interest in the Elective Classes operated by the Strathclyde Entrepreneurship Initiative is high, and growing. The University's Principal, himself a member of the Economic Committee of the Dearing Commission which is examining the future of Higher Education in the UK, with a long term perspective, is committed to the program.

The Initiative's future is secure. Its students will ensure that it maintains and grows its activities.

18 Stimulating and Fostering Entrepreneurship Through University Training - Learning Within an Organizing Context

Bengt Johannisson
Dan Halvarsson
Eva Lövstål

Abstract

Entrepreneurship, when perceived as an organizing endeavor, opens the field for more context-oriented and less person-oriented strategies for developing new ventures and employment. More room is given to different teaching methods, including cases. It also invites to partnerships between universities and other educational institutions and different stakeholders in the surrounding community. In this paper we propose that an 'open' university provides a platform for effective training in entrepreneurship. Inversely, the new objectives of Swedish university - to disseminate is knowledge - e.g. to the business community can e.g. be accomplished by turning emerging firms into live cases in courses in entrepreneurship. The paper reports such an undergraduate course involving 90 students and 30 emerging and new firms in a project where the students operated as junior consultants and mentors. The findings suggest that the course literally had made sense, e.g. of the difference between an established company and an emerging firm. The interaction with the entrepreneurs has also given the students an increased self-confidence and made them revalue their own competencies - also as entrepreneurs.

Entrepreneurship and the new Role of the University

During the recent decades the practicing and theorizing of entrepreneurship has been more intensive than ever. New and small firms are the major contributors to new jobs, a fact originally pointed out by Birch (1979) and since then proven to be valid in most Western industrialized countries. In e.g. Sweden, 70 per cent of new jobs originate in new and small firms (Davidsson 1995). The academic community is today providing a number of images of entrepreneurship which try to explain this phenomenon. For a long time these were mainly structured according to who the entrepreneur is and what s/he does. The trait approach, identifying different personal attributes of the entrepreneur has been thoroughly researched by behavioral scientists, with McClelland (1961) and Rotter (1966) as prominent early contributors. What entrepreneurs do has mainly been a concern for economists, cf. Binks and Vale 1990 for an overview.

Here we choose to join a third road leading to the understanding of entrepreneurship, that of *how* venturing is pursued, i.e. by deploying resources creatively according to opportunity, cf. Stevenson and Jarillo 1990. There are three major reasons for this focus. First, entrepreneurship is very much an organizing endeavor, involving not just the entrepreneur but also a number of other stakeholders (Gartner et al. 1992). Second, several images of entrepreneurship have been identified and researched including political entrepreneurs (Casson 1982), corporate entrepreneurs (Burgelman 1983), community entrepreneurs (Johannisson and Nilsson 1989), cultural entrepreneurs (Spilling 1991), bureaucratic entrepreneurs (Teske and Schneider 1994), and university entrepreneurs (Chia 1996). Obviously different kinds of entrepreneurs have different personal backgrounds and have widely different missions; the way they carry out their work may however unite them. Third, if we are going to bridge academic research and education in entrepreneurship and the practice thereof we need an image of entrepreneurship which invites to different kinds of exchange between the two 'worlds'. The image of entrepreneurship as an organizing endeavor invites rather to educational challenges than to attempts to change the personality of individuals.

319

The awareness among universities in Sweden of the need for education and training in entrepreneurship and small business management has increased dramatically in the 1990s. Recently the first comprehensive survey of all such was published within the context of a general review of training for entrepreneurship in the Swedish education system (Johannisson and Madsén 1997). The study includes both shorter courses and long programs (lasting for at least one semester). Out of 70 academic courses/programs identified at business and technical universities, all but 18 were established in the 1990s. This Swedish boom in academic education in entrepreneurship and small business management does however not mean that they all aimed at practicing entrepreneurship. In 68 cases the researchers were provided with course/program objectives. These revealed that while in 25 cases the aim was to teach *about* entrepreneurship and small business management alone, 20 courses/programs did provide the students with a tool kit for innovative projecting and/or business venturing. Most of the programs did include comparatively intensive exchange with the business community, i.a. implying everything from practitioners teaching to qualified internships. These activities were by far the most appreciated by the students. The educational staff found very much stimulation in student exchange in the comparatively small student groups.

Our understanding of the situation in Sweden is that due to weak entrepreneurial traditions, any training for entrepreneurship must include the context of the educational institution. 'Context' here refers to the environment which is jointly enacted by the focused (educational) institution and different stakeholders. At least in a Scandinavian setting the primary, here referred to as the 'organizing', context, is spatially demarcated. The 'organizing context' supports the organization, here the educational system, in realizing its objectives by infusing self-confidence and providing recourses. The municipalities in Sweden are quite independent and financially strong. If educational efforts become decontextualized there is an obvious risk that efforts promoting entrepreneurship, in high school or at the university, will become only superficial and never take root in the Swedish culture. In the above mentioned research, commissioned by the Swedish Ministry of Education and Industry, we thus suggest that young pupils at junior high school should mainly be encouraged to pursue their natural entrepreneurial behavior (cf. Hjorth and Johannisson 1997) while those at senior high should be encouraged to practice organizing in different projects. Only on the university level should the instrumentality of launching concrete ventures be taught. This means that the lifeworlds of the students and the school training feed into each other.

The need for a contextual approach to teaching entrepreneurship and training also have a more pragmatic source. Recently the obligation of all Swedish universities to actively make their knowledge available to stakeholders in the regional setting has been stated. Besides doing research and teaching, Swedish universities are in the years ahead expected to through dialogue disseminate research findings, make students' reports available, arrange seminars for practitioners, and volunteer as speakers at different occasions. Obviously this demand for knowledge diffusion offers an entrepreneurial challenge for all Swedish universities. The objective of this paper is to report how one university, Växjö, has responded to this challenge in an undergraduate course in entrepreneurship and business development.

The outline of the paper is as follows. In the next section we briefly present our image of appropriate education and training for entrepreneurship. Then we introduce the design of an undergraduate course with its objective of giving the students insights into entrepreneurship and small business. Section 4 reports an evaluation study carried out among both students and involved new businesses. In the last section lessons for teaching/training and for further research are summarized.

Challenges in Entrepreneurship Training and Education

Our objective is not to provide a comprehensive framework for training and education in entrepreneurship at the university level but rather to raise some critical issues and choices to be considered when designing courses and programs. However, our general perspective is that only if students are actively taking part in the process will learning take place. That is, any qualified education program should include dialogue, or rather polylogue (Hjorth and Johannisson 1997) involving all students in the knowledge creation.

As already indicated, a basic choice is whether the objective is to provide knowledge *about* or *in* entrepreneurship and small business. If the ambition is only to provide some understanding of the prospects and obstacles for business venturing and development, traditional lectures will suffice, possibly trimmed with guest lectures by entrepreneurs and site visits. If however knowledge in entrepreneurship is aimed for, there is not only a general need for action/experiential learning (Revans 1982, Schön 1983). Learning processes then also have to include the context of the university (Johannisson and Madsén 1997). This contextual approach means intimate collaboration with the business community and its different organizations.

The reasons while the boundaries between the university and the surrounding community have to be perforated if entrepreneurial capabilities are to be trained are two. First, if venturing is going to be practiced, the arena, the market, is outside the academic setting. Second, since important knowledge relevant for venturing success is tacit knowledge, entrepreneurial capabilities can only be acquired by exchange with other experienced persons. As pointed out by Nonaka and Takeouchi (1995) transfer and elaboration of tacit knowledge take place in socialization processes, by personal networking.

There is however a third option between a general acquaintance with entrepreneurship and the small business sector on one hand, and capabilities for own venturing on the other. One research into successful family business in Sweden suggests that genuine entrepreneurs combine vision and action, shunning planning. However, in a highly institutionalized society, all firms need management competencies such as planning. Thus, by training the students to become managers in the small and/or growing firm, a strategic dilemma will be coped with. Such a graduate business program has for many years been offered by Växjö University; detailed features thereof are reported elsewhere (Johannisson 1991).

Teaching and Education for entrepreneurship is both an easy and a difficult task. Easy because as children we were all entrepreneurial in our behavior. Children, especially at the ages of 5-12, are self-confident, imaginative, and social, spontaneously experimenting with their perceived reality. This behavior, usually addressed as 'play', has in principle very much in common with prospective venturing. Both entrepreneurs and children enact their environments, cf. Weick 1995. The challenge thus is to preserve, or even enforce children's natural entrepreneurial talents during their upbringing. In this endeavor the education system, as one of society's major institutions, obviously has a considerable responsibility, at least in trying to avoid an 'unlearning' of entrepreneurial capabilities.

Our understanding of entrepreneurship as an organizing endeavor performed by mutually inspiring and mutual supportive individuals in combination with images of child development suggests a stepwise strategy for promoting entrepreneurship in the education system. The effective general curriculum for the Swedish education system, as a proclaimed theory very much supports the promotion of an entrepreneurial learning mode. In junior high this would mean providing an extended 'playground' where inherent entrepreneurial capabilities are tamed to incorporate a further substantive input into the children's emerging knowledge base. In senior high school practicing organizing in terms of projects - across disciplinary and school boundaries - should be encouraged. Such a focus would advance the student's ability to exploit opportunities and ward of problems (or even turning them into opportunities) jointly with other student and additional persons. Again, these projects may cover any theme, not just a business oriented. Our report on different kinds of entrepreneurs provides one argument, the importance of having the young students making their own choices. Taking initiative and responsibility accordingly is another.

We thus propose a broad approach to the training for entrepreneurship at the compulsory school. This does not only fit into the sociobiological development of the young individual; it seems also compatible with existing attitudes to entrepreneurship in Sweden. Also Australian experiences suggest that training activities directly focusing business venturing have little impact if not embedded in the general promotion of entrepreneurial behavior (Morris and Wingham 1996). Children must learn to control their own knowledge creation through self-reflection before applying knowledge instrumentally to the field of business venturing. Nevertheless, Sweden's compulsory school offers a number of projects aiming at promoting entrepreneurship. These projects include for example venture-idea competitions in junior high and Young enterprise in senior high school.

We believe that, if students are properly prepared in the high school through entrepreneurial training, concrete venturing may become a natural ingredient on the university level. In mature entrepreneurial cultures, such as in the USA, student-venturing activities are also frequent, e.g. Vesper 1990. In other cultural settings, such as the Swedish one, where entrepreneurship has to be explicitly encouraged at the university level, a bridging strategy may be needed. Below we will elaborate on such an approach.

In developed economies with a less favorable business climate direct interface between the business community and the education system is rare. The role of a bridging function may be played by public and private organizations and associations (including the businesses' own), which promotes entrepreneurship and small business. Such agencies are frequent in these economies. However, the above mentioned report by Johannisson and Madsén (1997) reveals that in Sweden these organizations are not deeply involved in the implementation of courses and programs in entrepreneurship and small business management. Possible explanations include lacking (pedagogic) competencies, protection of their own preserve or simply that they have not been properly invited.

In Sweden universities are now expected to not just conduct research and education: they should also actively disseminate their accumulated knowledge to the regional society in general and the business community in particular. The ultimate challenge in our mind is to merge these different missions in concrete projects. This ambition should appeal to an entrepreneurial mind. An undergraduate course recently offered at Växjö University is introduced next as an illustration.

Junior Mentoring and Consulting in Live Cases - A Road to Entrepreneurial Insights

Background

The course 'Entrepreneurship and Small Business Development' deals with issues related to small-business management, entrepreneurship and new business creation. It is a compulsory five-week component within a two-year program in business administration and management. Offering the course at the end of the program means that the participating students have a general experience in academic work as well as broad knowledge in the field of business administration and management. They have among other things studied marketing, financial accounting, management control, and logistics. During these five weeks the students work on a full-time basis, focusing exclusively on this particular course.

This course on entrepreneurship and small-business management was originally developed in 1994 and was offered at Växjö University the following two years. This experience lead to the decision to completely redesign the course before it was offered in 1997. It became apparent that the course contents and pedagogics did not meet our ambition to teach for entrepreneurship. The course, as currently designed, was held for the first time in February and March of 1997, 90 students participated.

Linking students with entrepreneurs

The course has a number of stakeholders other than the students (and university staff). The other main role was played by local (nascent) entrepreneurs. A couple of weeks before the start-up of the course the students, in groups of three, were linked with entrepreneurs who either were planning to start a business or had recently started one. Thus 30 entrepreneurs (90/3) were enrolled. The students were encouraged to immediately contact 'their' entrepreneur(s), get acquainted, and to discuss the intended collaboration before the course actually started. In the course evaluation, elaborated in the next section, several students stressed the importance of having such an opportunity. Their experience was that coming to a mutual agreement with regard to the terms for collaboration required a lot of time and effort. The students stressed the importance of building trust before the concrete work.

The reasons for linking students with entrepreneurs are threefold. *Firstly*, by being involved in emerging, or recently started, businesses the students have the opportunity to work in a setting characterized by *both* entrepreneurship and small-business management. A small firm's starting-process provides, in our view, a common ground for discussing and reflecting upon both phenomena. By being a part of a business's starting-phase the students get a better understanding of entrepreneurship as a process of emergence. They also gain an increased a more relevant knowledge about small businesses' specific characteristics and conditions and what management technologies may be applicable to them.

Secondly, by co-operating with living entrepreneurs each group of student is not just provided with unique cases to work with but with an ever-changing segment of the business reality. Our experience from previous years, when all student groups used the same designed and formal case, is that such a case, even if based on existing companies and real events, does not provide variety enough to stimulate the students' creativity, responsibility, and enterprising capacity. Written cases instead stimulate an imitating behavior: students do copy each others case reports! Real cases, in contrast, require committed students who take charge and are able to fulfill their obligations. What is especially interesting in a learning context is that living cases also call for sensitivity on the part of the students for the entrepreneurs' experiences and ideas. The students learn to become good listeners, an entrepreneurial capability. Our approach further encourages the students to have a critical and reflective attitude toward the theories being provided by textbooks and lectures. Since, as indicated above, the academic image of entrepreneurship is still shifting, their criticism is very valuable.

A third reason for involving entrepreneurs is that they themselves can gain from such a collaborative effort. In the starting phase of the venturing career, entrepreneurs can be short of self-confidence, time, resources, and legitimacy. It is well known that starting an own business is a very lonely task, hence a need for a confidant. Usually nascent and new entrepreneurs know very little about how to administer a business. During the course, the students represented additional management capacity, could, by using their own networks, provide further resources. By formalizing some of the ideas of the entrepreneur, even into a business or market plan, the students may help the entrepreneur to acquire needed legitimacy with other stakeholders such as the bank, and suppliers and customers.

The course as an organizational endeavor-involving local advisory agencies

In order to get access to new entrepreneurs, and acquire general support the course organization was set up as a joint venture involving several local advisory agencies, cf. Figure 1 one the next page.

The agencies primarily appeared as recruiters of entrepreneurs. Through their daily contacts with nascent and new entrepreneurs who where looking for different kinds of support, they were able to select, and convince entrepreneurs to take part in the student project. In order to qualify, the entrepreneurs however had to meet two criteria. First, they either had to be in the process of preparing a business start-up or have been running their business for no more than two years. Secondly, they had to be susceptible to such a collaboration and positively interested in and willing to share and discuss their experiences and business ideas with external parties, e.g. students. If these criteria were met, there were no further restrictions. Consequently, the entrepreneurs who participated in the course were, with respect to age, sex, education and experience etc., quite diverse. They also represented a wide range of businesses, from art gallery to snack production.

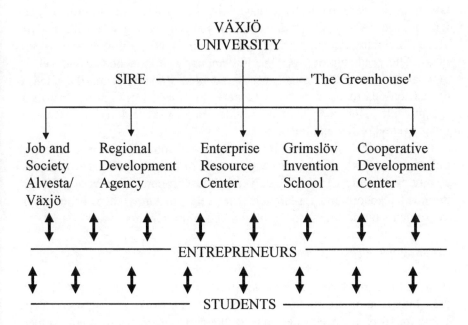

Figure 1: The Organizational Setup of the New-Venture Education Project

The new-business agencies also participated in the process, in the actual performance of the course. Firstly, they provided the entrepreneurs, as well as the students, with general support throughout the whole course. Equally important was their special input of practical experience. Several representatives of the agencies gave lectures to the students, based on their experiences from new-business creation and small-business management.

Due to its business idea and its location, representatives of 'The Greenhouse' were naturally engaged in the project, cf. Figure 1. 'The Greenhouse', is an organization that aims at stimulating venturing activity at the university and supporting those students who want to enact business ideas. The organization, located on campus, was launched and is run by graduates. During the course these graduated students primarily acted as discussion partners for the students as they worked on fulfilling assignments. They also helped provided more practical services, such as the provision of fax and telephones.

The project was designed to cover all objectives of a Swedish university-education, research, and transfer of knowledge to the (business) community. Thus SIRE, the university's entrepreneurship research unit, provided teachers and researchers with relevant knowledge, primarily to the students but indirectly also to involved entrepreneurs.

Creating networks

Besides the formal vertical network illustrated in Figure 1, we also invited the students to create spontaneous horizontal networks among themselves. The aim was to encourage the students to learn from their student colleagues by exchanging experiences. Before the course started we asked the students to write down their names, telephone numbers, and three words that reflected their main personal competencies. These competencies could originate in previous studies or venturing activity, in temporary employment, talents, or hobbies. A comprehensive list of this information was compiled and distributed to each student, who then had a systematized source of peer experience, knowledge and further network resources. This group of almost one hundred students represents an enormous collective source of competencies.

The aim of the 'directory' of students' competencies was to encourage the students to embark on more active networking. Our experience from previous courses was that students verbally advocate networking but had difficulties in practicing it. For example, when we, at the first lecture, asked the students if they would contact a student colleague if they knew that s/he had knowledge within an area that they were dealing with, almost all responded affirmatively. When we a week later asked how many actually had been in contact with a peer student friend for consultation, only a few hands were raised.

The assignments

The assignments within the course were of two kinds, practical and theoretical. The practical assignment was an issue discussed only between the students and their entrepreneur. Without interference from teachers, the students and the entrepreneurs had to agree on suitable tasks, depending on the entrepreneur's needs and the students' capabilities and specific competences. As a consequence the tasks varied substantially between the groups. Some student groups did not focus on a particular issue, but acted rather as a supportive discussion partner in a more general sense. Others worked on more clearly defined projects, such as designing a home page for World Wide Web or preparing an advertising leaflet. Despite this great variety, most work actually related to marketing. It seems as though many entrepreneurs have difficulties in dealing with marketing issues, due to either lack of time or limited knowledge. At the same time, they seem to realize the importance of marketing for the success of the business. For many entrepreneurs, then, the students represented at least a temporary solution for this marketing dilemma.

Our role as teachers was to encourage the students to use their 'student network' when solving these practical assignments. Furthermore, 'The Greenhouse' and other agencies played, as already mentioned, a supportive role in this work. The main idea for not intruding was to force the students to take own initiatives and personally take responsibility for their actions. In other words, we created a supportive context wherein the students had to take own initiatives. Consequently, we did not evaluate their substantive practical work; instead we stressed that they, together with the entrepreneurs, had to decide when they had fulfilled their obligations. We also stressed that missing concrete outputs would not be rated as a course failure. Most important was that the students actively reflected upon the collaboration and revealed an ability to learn from both mistakes and successful actions.

329

The academic assignments dealt with four different topics. These are presented in Table 1.

Table 1: Academic Assignments

Topic	Focus	Presentation
'To Be an Entrepreneur'	The entrepreneur	Written report Informal discussions
'To Start a Business'	The venturing process	Written report Informal discussions
'To Do Business in Small and New Firms'	Running a business	Written report Formal presentation and discussion
'To Learn through Collaboration and Practice'	Student's own learning process	Written report Formal presentation and discussion

The four topics were dealt with in three written reports, two shorter ones and one more elaborated. The students were told to reflect upon and discuss both empirical experience, gained in their co-operation with entrepreneurs, and theoretical issues, covered by the course literature. Each topic was followed by an oral presentation in seminar groups of about fifteen students guided by a teacher. During the discussions the students could compare and learn from other students' experiences and reflections. The same topic was discussed in several reports and on several group meetings. By forcing the students to treat the same subject more than once, we hoped to evoke a reflective learning process, similar to the hermeneutical spiral.

Summary: Positioning against conventional case approach

In this subsection we briefly position the 'live-case' approach presented above against our own previous approach. In many respects the earlier version of the course design probably resembles those adopted in other university contexts.

Table 2: Juxtaposing Conventional and Live Case Approach

CASE FEATURES	Conventional Analytical Case Approach (adopted 1995 - 6)	Experiential Live Case Approach (introduced 1997)
Objective	Managing change in the small firm	Coping with the ambiguities of entrepreneuring
Case design	Sequential and analytical by original design	Emergence by dialogue between students and entrepreneurs
Basic pedagogic	Group work, role play	Self-reflection
Student participation	Traditional, passive	Sounding board for new entrepreneurs
Role of teacher	Providing ambiguity in a structured simulated setting	Providing order in an ambiguous real world
Textbook contents	Organization theory, small business, networking	Entrepreneurship theory, start-up manuals, networking
Outcome	Confusion-avoidance of graduate program	Insight and curiosity - increased self-confidence

Over the three years the course 'Entrepreneurship and Small Business Development' has been offered at Växjö University it has covered five weeks in total, whereof approximately the equivalent of two weeks of full-time work had to be used for case work. With respect to the course objective it has changed from providing an understanding of management challenges in small (family) business to that of coping with emergence and liabilities of newness in organizations. While the written case was presented in sequences (1995 three, 1996 two), the situations in the live cases obviously developed as a spontaneous, organic process which reflected self-organizing features.

Basic pedagogic adopted in the conventional-case approach was small-group analytical assignments were the students where assigned different fictitious roles. In the live-case reflection upon own learning processes in the dynamic setting of an emergent firm was the methodology adopted. This means that the students' role remained rather passive in the formal case setting while in the live situation the students with the function as a sounding board for new entrepreneurs worked both as junior mentors and junior consultants. The role of the teacher in the conventional-case design was to add some ambiguity to the present documentation of the case: various events which may be critical to the company where successively communicated to the students. In the live-case situation, where the original setting automatically produced uncertainty, the role of the teacher was rather to provide some stability, e.g. if the expectations of the entrepreneur concerning the student contribution became unrealistically high. Textbooks used in the conventional case included organization theory ('virtual organizations'), information about the small-business sector in general, and on networking in particular. When the live cases were launched organization literature was replaced with literature on entrepreneurship and learning, a popular monograph on the pros and cons of running a small firm and a start-up guide.

Below we will present a thorough evaluation of the live-case course. Positioning against the conventional-case version however suggests however that the live-case approach, by inspiring more commitment as well as time for self-reflection, provided some insight into entrepreneurship and also appetite for continued studies in the field. When the conventional-case approach was applied during the two previous years the course mainly lead to confusion: questioning that which before had been taken for granted in the students management courses without providing a distinct alternative. The students had problems with the written examination (supplementing the case): a few minor essays some major course messages were to be put in context to demonstrate that the message of the course had been understood. The 1997 student groups did not have the same such problems when recontextualizing the knowledge they acquired both at the university and in the field.

Evaluating the Course and the Collaboration with Living Entrepreneurs

The evaluation format

Both the students and the collaborating entrepreneurs were asked to answer a questionnaire concerning their the live-case projected reported in the previous section. The students were surveyed in connection with a compulsory seminar hence all delivered completed forms. Of the 30 entrepreneurs 19 responded no follow-up of non-respondent).

The students were approached with the following requests/questions:

QS 1: Use three keywords to characterize the collaboration with your entrepreneur(s).

QS 2: Use three keywords to characterize your image of how your entrepreneur(s) experienced the collaboration.

QS 3: How many times have you or any member of the group been in touch with your entrepreneur(s) (a) by phone, (b) visiting the firm, and (c) personally outside the firm?

QS 4: How many peer students outside your own group have you contacted ideas or advice to use in you collaboration with the entrepreneur(s)?

QS 5: What unique things did you learn during this course?

QS 6: What did you learn about entrepreneurship and small business during the theoretical sections of the course?

The entrepreneurs where asked to answer the questions below:

QE 1: Use three keywords to summarize the collaboration with the students

QE 2: How many times have you been in touch with (any of) the students (a) by phone, (b) visiting the firm, and (c) personally outside the firm?

QE 3: Do you have any plans to stay in touch with the students?

QE 4: State what in your mind is the most positive experience of the collaboration.

QE 5: State what in your mind is the most negative experience of the collaboration.

Adopting a strategy inspired by 'grounded theory approach' (Glaser and Strauss 1967) we have analyzed the open-ended responses sequentially. Similar answers have been categorized into first-level conceptual groups and these are then, if well-grounded, been collapsed into second-order categories for which distribution of responses are reported (percentages).

Exploring keywords - tracking the outcome of student/entrepreneur exchange

In order to tap the project participants' ability to intuitively communicate their impressions of the course, they were each asked to summarize these in three keywords.

As Table 3 below reports the same three second-order categories of keywords emerged with respect to both the student's own experiences and their perceptions of the entrepreneurs outcome of the collaboration.

The entrepreneurs' own image of the collaboration (QE1) reveals a similar profile where 46 per cent of the respondents indicated an inspiring exchange of ideas. Another 30 per cent found the collaboration interesting and 18 per cent enjoyed themselves. Only six per cent are negative, mainly because they were not prepared for what it meant to host a group of students.

Table 3: Students' Perceived Outcome of the Collaboration (QS1, QS2)

Second order characteristics	First-order characteristics	per cent	First-order characteristics	per cent
	Students' Own experiences		**Entrepreneurial experiences according to the Students**	
The practical work (50/71)	Qualified learning due to live cases	28	Stimulating collaboration	32
	Increased self-awareness	8	Useful collaborative	22
	Lack of time	6	Labor supplement	9
	Close to reality	4	Unclear rules of collaboration	5
	Difficulty committing the entrepreneur	4	Committing the entrepreneurs	3
The subject (25/11)	Insight into the small business sector	19	Import of new perspectives	4
	Encouragement for a venturing career	3	Access to a previously unknown world	4
	New perspectives on business activity	3	Confirmation of own ideas and strategies	3
The relationship itself (25/18)	Enjoyable encounters	11	Junior mentorship	7
	Creative dialogue	9	Lack of time	7
	Favorable atmosphere	5	Building trust	4
		100		100

Elsewhere we argued that personal networking is instrumental in the venturing process. The framework outlined here suggests that learning generally benefits from human intercourse. In order to capture the extent of networking within the course context we inquired about both student/entrepreneur peer-student exchange. There are few differences between the students and the entrepreneurs with respect to images of frequency and location of their exchange. Since several of the students may have called the entrepreneur or visited her/his firm on different occasions the slightly higher values for the entrepreneur are expected. Considering their less developed personal network it is not surprising that the students more often remember (casual) encounters on arenas outside the firm/the subcontractor.

Table 4: Encounters Between the Students and the Entrepreneurs (average frequencies) (QS3, QE2)

Encounter mode	According to the students	According to the entrepreneurs
By phone	4.6	5.4
Site visits by students	3.7	4.1
Personal contacts on neutral arenas	1.3	1.0

While the level of exchange between students and entrepreneurs met expectations we were surprised by the insignificant exchange between students within the course but outside the task group. On the average less than two (1.9) peers where contacted for advice on issues related to the role as junior mentor/consultant. Students are obviously not used to communicate with peers for instrumental purposes in the educational setting. In this case we even asked the students to take advantage of competencies which the schoolmates may have as private persons, a request which obviously was perceived as especially unfamiliar.

Critical overall experiences

In Table 5 the extraordinary experiences of the course according to the students are summarized.

Table 5: Unique Lessons by the Students (QS 5)

Main lessons derived from the open answers

* A comprehensive understanding of the differences between entrepreneurship and management	26 %
* A deep insight into the everyday life of a (prospective) owner-manager in a small firm	22 %
* Enhanced ability to apply theory to practice	19 %
* Motivation to take own initiative and responsibility	19 %
* A more general understanding of business as a field of study	11 %
	100 %

Asking the students about the benefits of the theoretical, academic parts of the course almost half of the responses concerned increased knowledge about the persons and operations within small-business sector and its role in the Swedish society. Another third of the answers pointed out the enhanced understanding of entrepreneurship and what it takes to adopt entrepreneurial behavior. One out of ten students reported increased awareness of personal networking in entrepreneurial processes as a major lesson. Remaining answers mainly concerned acquaintance with the proper terminology in the field.

The entrepreneurs were asked as well about the costs and benefits of the student exchange. Negative lessons were lack of time, more relevant not being properly prepared to participate in the collaboration which appeared as a quite complex project to inexperienced entrepreneurs. One third of the respondents had no negative experiences at all to report. The encounter with enthusiastic students was the major benefit to almost half of the entrepreneurs and further advantages divided equally between increased supply of new ideas and an extended resource base.

Two out of three entrepreneurs, when asked, declared that they intended to keep in touch with the students. Those entrepreneurs who were not interested argued that the project was concluded and/or that they wanted to take the opportunity to host new students (which in some cases has been implemented). The entrepreneurs' own suggestions for improving collaboration with the university were mainly two: to extend the time period of the collaboration and to broaden the interface with the university. That, 18 out of 19 responding entrepreneurs wanted collaboration with another student group implies that the bridging between the university and the business community achieved by the course has created healthy further expectations.

Conclusions - Implications for the Education of and Research into Entrepreneurship

Obviously the reorientation of education of entrepreneurship from a traditional-case design to a live case approach has improved the quality of the course. Students have managed the formal examinations approximately as successfully as before but in addition become considerably more interested in the subject and have made significant contributions to the promotion of entrepreneurial activity in the vicinity of the university. An intriguing finding is that, when tested for their 'entrepreneurial capability' (Johannisson et al. 1997), these students had lower test values than their peers from 1995 (6.6 and 7.2 respectively (maximum 12)). One possible explanation is that the new design of the course, by bridging the laboratory milieu of the university and the complex outside world, initiated a different kind of learning experiences. On one hand the students' self-confidence was enhanced, on the other they became aware of the complexity and unpredictability of the venturing process. That was reflected in the test procedure where extreme - and by the test procedure highly valued items - were avoided by the tested. These items simply appeared as ideal or naive.

The project clearly states that the interaction with the new entrepreneurs, and the role of mentor and consultant, has increased the students' self-confidence. Before the 'confrontation' arranged within the course the students were uncertain about their ability to contribute to business development. We believe that by providing a new perspective, entrepreneurship as emergence, we have provided a healthy criticism of the management rationale. The course creation itself, which was presented as a pioneering endeavor to the students, turned out to an entrepreneurial experience of enactment. This experiential learning illustrates how education, research, and transfer of knowledge to society should not be considered as three conflicting demands on universities but as a potential for university entrepreneurship.

The course project has also provided a number of research challenges. There is a need to further investigate how to bridge the academic world and the world of practice. One way to do this would be further inquiries into 'knowledge of acquaintance', as opposed to the knowledge by description, produced by pure desk research as a road to scientific knowledge, not the least in the field of entrepreneurship. Yet another challenge is to further investigate the contextual approach to business development, whether in the teaching or in the practicing of entrepreneurship.

References

Birch, D. (1979) *The Job Generation Process.* Cambridge, Mass.: MIT.

Binks, M. and Vale, P. (1990) *Entrepreneurship and Economic Change.* London: McGraw - Hill.

Burgelman, R. A. (1983) 'Corporate Entrepreneurship and Strategic Management: Insights from a Process Study.' *Management Science.* Vol. 29, pp. 1349 - 1364.

Casson, M. (1982) *The Entrepreneur.* Oxford: Robertson.

Chia, R. (1996) 'Teaching Paradigm Shifting in Management Education: University Business Schools and the Entrepreneurial Imagination.' *Journal of Management Studies.* Vol. 33, No. 4.

Davidsson, P. (1995) 'Culture, structure and regional levels of entrepreneurship.' *Entrepreneurship and Regional Development.* Vol. 7, No. 1, pp. 41 - 62.

Gartner, W. B., Bird, B. J. and Starr, J. A. (1992) 'Acting As If: Differentiating Entrepreneurial from Organizational Behavior.' *Entrepreneurship Theory & Practice.* Spring 1992, Vol. 16, No. 3, pp. 13 - 31.

Glaser, B. G. and Strauss, A. L. (1967) *The Discovery of Grounded Theory: Strategies for Qualitative Research.* New York: Aldine De Gruyter.

Hjorth, D. and Johannisson, B. (1997) 'Training for Entrepreneurship: Play and Language Games - an Inquiry into the Swedish Education System.' Paper presented at *IntEnt 97.* Monterey, Cal., USA., Jun 25 - 27.

Johannisson, B. (1991) 'University Training for Entrepreneurship: Swedish Approaches.' *Entrepreneurship and Regional Development.* Vol. 3, No.1, pp. 67 - 82.

Johannisson, B., Landström, H. and Rosenberg, J. (1997) *University Training for Entrepreneurship - An Action Frame of Reference.* SIRE WP 1997:1. Växjö: Växjö University.

Johannisson, B. and Madsén, T. (1997) *I entreprenörskapets tecken - en studie av skolning i förnyelse.* Närings- och handelsdepartementet, Ds. (1997):3. Stockholm: Fritzes.

Johannisson, B. and Nilsson, A. (1989) 'Community Entrepreneurs: Networking for Local Development.' *Entrepreneurship and Regional Development.* Vol. 1, No. 1, pp. 3 - 20.

Morris, R. and Wingham, D. (1996) 'Educating for our Future: Creating Enterprising Youth.' Paper presented at *Internationalizing Entrepreneurship Education and Training.* Arnhem/Nijmegen, June 1996.

McClelland, D. (1961) *The Achieving Society.* Princeton: D. Van Nostrand.

Nonaka, I. and Takeuchi, H. (1995) *The Knowledge - Creating Company.* New York: Oxford University Press.

Rotter, J. R. (1966) 'Generalized Expectancies for Internal Versus External Control of Reinforcement.' *Psychological Monographs.*

Revans, R. W. (1982) *The Origins and Growth of Action Learning.* Lund: Studentlitteratur.

Schön, D. (1983) *The Reflective Practitioner. How Professionals Think in Action.* New York, N.Y.: Basic Books.

Spilling, O. R. (1991) 'Entrepreneurship in a Cultural Perspective.' *Entrepreneurship and Regional Development.* Vol. 3, No. 1, pp. 33 - 48.

Stevenson, H. H. and Jarillo, C. (1990) 'A Paradigm of Entrepreneurship: Entrepreneurial Management.' *Strategic Management Journal.* Vol. 11, Special Issue on Corporate Entrepreneurship, pp. 17 - 27.

Teske, Paul and Schneider, Mark (1994) 'The Bureaucratic Entrepreneur: The Case of City Managers.' *Public Administration Review.* Vol. 54, No. 4, pp. 331 - 340.

Vesper, K. H. (1990) *New Venture Strategies.* Revised edition. Englewood Cliffs: Prentice Hall.

Weick, K. (1995) *Sensemaking in Organizations.* Sage: Thousand Oaks.

19 University-based Entrepreneurial Outreach: a Case Study of the Midwest Entrepreneurial Education Center

Kelli M. Hurley
Donald F. Kuratko

Abstract

The purpose of this paper is to illustrate the viable integration of The Midwest Entrepreneurial Education Center into The Institute for Entrepreneurship at Ball State University. The integration took place in December of 1996 and the existing programs were maintained and eventually expanded with a seamless transition. The paper's sections delineate the critical components involved in this unique transition.

Background

The Midwest Entrepreneurial Education Center (formerly a stand-alone corporation) moved from a collaborative position to one of seeking a permanent partner for absorption of key programs. Ball State University's Institute for Entrepreneurship was in an unique position to provide a seamless transition of the Center's programs to the Institute. B.S.U.'s program director had served on The Midwest Entrepreneurial Education Center's board and had worked closely with the Center's president for over a decade. This relationship of trust and confidence was the foundation for a productive plan to carry on key programs such as FastTrac I_{TM} and FastTrac II_{TM}. In addition, the Institute for Entrepreneurship at Ball State University was beginning to emerge as a leader in entrepreneurial training and development for the State of Indiana. With the proper funding, the Institute could maintain and expand current programs of The Midwest Entrepreneurial Education Center as well as develop new initiatives for entrepreneurial companies throughout the State of Indiana.

Integration

The Midwest Entrepreneurial Education Center is now located in the College of Business at Ball State University. Its mission is to help Midwest entrepreneurs build growing, profitable businesses by offering practical, high quality educational programs and activities, while serving as the focal point for encouraging the further development of an entrepreneurial economy in the Midwest. It's specific objectives include:

- development of programs to enhance the business-building capabilities of aspiring and practicing entrepreneurs.
- development of a program to assist executives in transition who are interested in entrepreneurial growth opportunities.
- facilitation of entrepreneurial education activities for a larger geographic area, utilizing the latest communication technologies.
- participation in activities that encourage an early interest in entrepreneurship among youth.
- development of programs for successful companies that want to expand the growth of entrepreneurship within their own organizations.

Purpose

The purpose of this paper is to outline, in a case study format, the stages of integration for this Center to develop inside of a university, as well as the financing alternatives needed to expand the Center's capabilities. This approach may serve as an international model for university-based centers.

Our Entrepreneurial Economy - The Environment for Entrepreneurship

Entrepreneurship is the symbol of business tenacity and achievement. Entrepreneurs have been the pioneers of today's business successes. Their sense of opportunity, their drive to innovate, and their capacity for accomplishment have become the standard by which free enterprise is now measured. This standard has taken hold throughout the entire world.

We are experiencing an 'Entrepreneurial Revolution' in the United States. This revolution will be as powerful to the twenty-first century as the Industrial Revolution was to the twentieth century (if not more!) Entrepreneurs will continue to be critical contributors to economic growth through their leadership, management, innovation, research and development effectiveness, job creation, competitiveness, productivity, and formation of new industry.

To understand the nature of entrepreneurship, it is important to consider two perspectives of the environment in which entrepreneurial firms operate. The first perspective is statistical, providing actual aggregate numbers to emphasize the importance of small firms in our economy. The second perspective examines some of the trends in entrepreneurial research and education in order to reflect the emerging importance of entrepreneurship in academic developments.

Predominance of New Ventures in the Economy

The past decade has demonstrated the powerful emergence of entrepreneurial activity in the United States. Many statistics illustrate this fact. For example, during the past ten years, new business incorporations averaged 600,000 per year. Although many of these incorporations may have been sole proprietorships or partnerships previously, it still demonstrates venture activity, whether it was through start-ups, expansion, or development. More specifically, 807,000 new small firms were established in 1995, an all-time record.

Small enterprises are the most common form of enterprise-established relationships regardless of industry, and most small businesses consist of a single establishment. More than half of all businesses employ fewer than 5 people. More significantly, almost 90 per cent of firms employ fewer than

343

20 people.

This employment number is important, since the small entrepreneurial firms have created the most net new jobs in the U.S. economy from 1977 to 1990. In addition, the smallest of our enterprises have created a steady supply of net new jobs over the business cycle from 1977 to 1990.

The Age of the Gazelles

New and smaller firms create the most jobs in the U.S. economy. The facts speak for themselves. The vast majority of these job-creating companies are fast-growing businesses. David Birch of Cognetics, Inc., has named these firms 'gazelles.' A gazelle, by Birch's definition, is a business establishment with at least 20 per cent sales growth every year from 1990 to 1994 (the last year for which Cognetics has complete numbers), starting with a base of at least $100,000. Despite the continual downsizing in major corporations, the gazelles produced 5 million jobs and brought the net employment growth to 4.2 million jobs.

Innovation

Gazelles are leaders in innovation, as shown by the following:

- New and smaller firms have been responsible for 55 per cent of the innovations in 362 different industries and 95 per cent of all radical innovations.
- Gazelles produce twice as many product innovations per employee as do larger firms.
- New and smaller firms obtain more patents per sales dollar than do larger firms.

Growth

Note how these growth data indicate the current 'Age of the Gazelles':

I. During the past ten years, business incorporations have averaged more than 600,000 per year, with 1995 experiencing an all-time high of 807,000.

II. Of approximately 21.5 million businesses in the United States (based

344

on IRS tax returns), only 14,000 qualify as 'large' businesses.

III. The compound growth rate in the number of businesses over a 12-year span is 3.9 per cent.

IV. Each year about 14 per cent of firms with employees drop from the unemployment insurance rolls while about 16 per cent new and successor firms - firms with management changes - are added each year. This represents the disappearance or reorganization of half of all listed firms every five years!

V. By the year 2010, demographic estimate, 30 million firms will exist in the United States, up significantly from the 21.5 million firms existing in the mid-1990s.[1]

Entrepreneurial Support

In the early 1980s, the economy in Indiana experienced a significant downturn due to the disruptive changes affecting many of the state's traditional industries. In response to the loss of jobs and changing industry conditions, the state government launched an effort to create and build an entrepreneurial base. Three organizations were created to provide a boost to the new business creation mandate: The Corporation for Innovation Development (CID); the Corporation for Science and Technology (CST); and the Indiana Institute for New Business Ventures (INBV). Each of these organizations received state support.

CID became the state's first venture capital fund with an initial capitalization of $10,000,000. State support consisted of $3,000,000 in tax credits provided to the investors in CID's initial fund.

CST focused its efforts on creating an environment supportive of technological development, and designed a financing program to develop promising technologies. CST initially received funding of approximately $10,000,000 annually, primarily to support the development of new technologies and technology based businesses.

INBV developed conferences, seminars and programs for those interested in improving their entrepreneurial capabilities, and provided direct one-on-one counseling to start-ups and emerging company owners. INBV operated on an initial budget of approximately $425,000.

These three organizations provided a foundation for entrepreneurial development in the state, and helped focus considerable attention on the importance of entrepreneurs to the future of the state's economy. As a result of the formation of CID, CST, and INBV, many other initiatives and programs supportive of entrepreneurial businesses were developed throughout the state. Today, there are a considerable number of organizations providing services to small, emerging businesses. While many of these programs are providing value, others are not. Additionally, the sheer number of service providers, often duplicating each other's efforts, has created a confusing landscape for those in need of the services provided.

The Midwest Entrepreneurial Education Center has a major interest in providing management improvement assistance to those companies capable of having a positive economic impact on their communities. In addition, it has a major interest in serving as the catalyst and 'lighting rod' to create and foster an environment of entrepreneurship in the state. The Midwest Center intends to become universally recognized as the leading organization supporting and advocating entrepreneurs. This is a void that is widely acknowledged in the marketplace.[2]

The Midwest Entrepreneurial Education Center

Ball State University's Entrepreneurship program has received numerous national awards including 'Top 25' best Schools by *Success Magazine*, 'Top Ten Entrepreneurship Programs in North America' by *Entrepreneur Magazine*, and 'Top Twenty' U.S. MBA programs in Entrepreneurship by *Business Week Magazine*. The program's director, Dr. Donald F. Kuratko has published over 100 articles on Entrepreneurship and has written several books including: *Entrepreneurship: A Contemporary Approach, Entrepreneurial Strategy*, and *Effective Small Business Management*.

In 1996, Ball State University's Institute for Entrepreneurship absorbed the Midwest Entrepreneurial Education Center, which will enhance its community outreach tremendously. The Midwest Entrepreneurial Education Center reaches six states: Michigan, Illinois, Indiana, Ohio, West Virginia, and Kentucky. The Center's initiatives are currently focused on developing its FastTrac I_{TM} and II_{TM} programs which train and educate potential entrepreneurs, experienced entrepreneurs, high growth companies, and youth.

346

Mission

The Midwest Entrepreneurial Education Center is located at the College of Business at Ball State University. Its mission is to help Midwest entrepreneurs build growing, profitable businesses by offering practical, high-quality educational programs and activities, while serving as the focal point for encouraging the further development of an entrepreneurial economy throughout the Midwest.

Objectives

The Midwest Entrepreneurial Education Center's key objectives include:

- development of programs to enhance the business capabilities of aspiring and practical entrepreneurs.
- development of a program to assist executives in transition who are interested in entrepreneurial growth opportunities.
- facilitation of entrepreneurial education activities for a larger geographic area, utilizing the latest communication technologies.
- participation in activities that encourage an early interest in entrepreneurship among youth.
- development of programs for successful companies that want to expand the growth of entrepreneurship within their own organization.

Initiatives

Potential entrepreneurs

Premier FastTrac I$_{TM}$ Premier FastTrac I$_{TM}$ emphasizes entry strategies for start-up ventures through 32 hours of course work. Entrepreneurs identify business opportunities, research the market, expand business concepts, obtain solid information about launching new ventures, and develop feasibility plans.

347

Experienced entrepreneurs

Premier FastTrac II$_{TM}$ Premier FastTrac II$_{TM}$ provides training for existing business owners on planning, researching, and evaluating the strategic growth and operational aspects of their businesses. This 45-hour program culminates in the development of a viable business plan for the entrepreneur's venture.

High growth companies

Corporate Entrepreneurship and Innovation Corporate Entrepreneurship Training is an intensive training seminar involving the development of managers' entrepreneurial abilities within existing corporations. The major thrust of this program is to enhance the creative and innovative potential of managers and their environments for fast growing companies throughout the Midwest. Emphasis throughout the program is placed on energizing and reinventing the organization through enhanced customer service, new product development, and diversification projects.

Youth programs

Yess! Mini-Society The YESS! (Youth Empowerment and Self-Sufficiency)/Mini-Society curriculum uses an experience-based, self-organizing, interdisciplinary approach to teach youth, ages 7 to 12, about entrepreneurship, decision making and critical thinking - while enhancing learning in mathematics, reading, and other core subject areas, and encouraging the exploration of personal values.

EntrePrep EntrePrep is a program for talented, motivated high school juniors. It is designed to provide the fundamental concepts and skills for becoming an entrepreneur and starting up a business. In addition to laying a solid foundation in entrepreneurship, EntrePrep offers internship experiences with start-up businesses and helps students explore the process of evaluating and making recommendations to new ventures.

Community Programs

Successful Entrepreneurs Seminar Series Another initiative of the Midwest Entrepreneurial Education Center will be to create a quarterly series of 1/2 day seminars featuring 'Entrepreneur of the Year' recipients from the state of Indiana.

Women Entrepreneurs Program This specialized program, delivered by successful women, will concentrate on the planning, organizing, evaluating, and creation of a viable business venture. Through a special guidebook entitled, *The Entrepreneurial Decision,* idea creation, business plan development, and action plan steps will be developed.

MEEC Competitive Analysis

Currently there are four other centers that operate within the Midwest Entrepreneurial Education Center's reach. They include: DePaul University's Entrepreneurship Program, Institute for Entrepreneurial Studies at the University of Illinois at Chicago, University of Louisville, and Xavier Entrepreneurial Center at Xavier University.

The following tables are broken down into three segments and analyze the top Entrepreneurial Centers across the United States. The first table is focused on analyzing the specific programs or centers that are within the Midwest Entrepreneurial Education Center's market. The second set of tables detail thirty-five centers from across the country. Seven components from each of these centers will be illustrated in this section. This will include Faculty, Curriculum, Research, Student Activities, Community Outreach, Awards, and Recognition and Resources. The final tables identify some of the unique student and outreach activities that other centers offer.[3]

The Midwest Entrepreneurial Education Center has a great opportunity to enter new markets in Indiana, Michigan, and Ohio. Currently there are no other centers operating in these markets which gives the Midwest Entrepreneurial Center a significant lead in deciding which areas that they should expand the FastTrac I_{TM} and II_{TM} programs.

The University of Louisville (Kentucky), Xavier (Ohio), DePaul (Illinois), and the Institute for Entrepreneurial Studies at the University of Illinois at Chicago concentrate their outreach in the areas surrounding the centers in which they operate.

The University of Louisville does not currently have an Entrepreneurship Center, but it is in the process of establishing one. Graduates can earn a concentration in the MBA program or the joint Masters of Engineering/MBA program. Like Ball State, Entrepreneurship classes are offered via interactive video-conferencing. Louisville offers training and seminars through its Family Business Center. The Faculty of the University of Louisville participate in FastTrac I_{TM} and II_{TM} programs. In 1996, *Success Magazine* rated the University of Louisville as one of the up and coming programs in the country.

Xavier already has a presence in the Cincinnati area. Their involvement in the community has extended to numerous partnerships with local and regional organizations and various community economic development projects. They also sponsor three half-day programs with the Chamber of Commerce. However, Xavier has also hosted some big name speakers in the past year which would include Tom Peters, Stephen Covey, and Ken Blanchard. In addition, Xavier does not offer the FastTrac$_{TM}$ programs which would allow Midwest Entrepreneurial Education Center possible access to Cincinnati's market.

Xavier does not consider publications or research as part of their mission. The Midwest Entrepreneurial Education Center may take advantage of this deficiency. Considering Dr. Kuratko has been a consulting editor for Dryden Press series in Entrepreneurship, he has the opportunity to keep up with the latest trends in Entrepreneurship. In addition, the research and publications he has completed lend a great deal of credibility to his name and the program.

The biggest challenge the Midwest Entrepreneurial Education Center faces would be in Illinois, and more specifically the Chicago area, because of the current competition. Both DePaul University and the University of Illinois at Chicago share the Chicago market in Illinois. Both are well-

350

respected programs and have gained national recognition. Together, they have formed the Collegiate Entrepreneurs of the Midwest and are developing into a national organization. DePaul initiated a Small Business Institute in 1972 and has aided over 800 Chicago area businesses. Community outreach is extended locally to businesses including start-up and minority owned businesses. The University of Illinois runs a family business council for CEO's of a significant number of family firms. These practices pose a strong barrier to the Midwest Entrepreneurial Education Center's entry of the Chicago area market.

Overall, within the Midwest Entrepreneurial Center's six state market there is substantial opportunity for entry and growth.

Leadership

Executive Directors

The Midwest Entrepreneurial Education Center's leadership begins with two Executive Directors who are responsible for planning, development, and management of the specialized training and consulting services designed to enhance the effectiveness of emerging entrepreneurial firms throughout Indiana and the Midwest.

Associate Director

The Associate Director's responsibilities include implementing and creating marketing objectives, developing the Center's newsletters and promotional materials, and directing the administrative and marketing efforts of the Premier FastTrac$_{TM}$ programs.

Director of Youth Programs

The Director of Youth Programs is responsible for the marketing, recruitment of teachers, follow-up, and coordination of activities and programs for YESS! Mini-Society. In addition, he/she is responsible for the planning and developing of the EntrePrep program, which includes the recruitment of mentors and high-school juniors.

351

Student/Graduate Assistance

Due to the high overhead associated with an administrative assistant, the Center has decided to engage the resources available from the university. Currently, the Midwest Entrepreneurial Education Center's assistance includes one student assistance, who works 20 hours per week, and one graduate assistance, who works 10 hours per week. Their combined responsibilities include: answering the phone, copying and collating binder materials, typing letters, developing PowerPoint presentations, database entry and maintenance, and other miscellaneous administrative work as assigned.

MEEC Board of Directors

The Midwest Entrepreneurial Education Center is overseen by a 20 member Board of Directors. This 20 member Board consists of top professionals and executives throughout Indiana. The MEEC Board meets quarterly to review strategic plans, MEEC growth, and any developments that may have occurred since the last meeting.

A new Model for Universities

The Midwest Entrepreneurial Education Center (MEEC) at Ball State University has worked to create a niche of quality education for entrepreneurs. This unique niche is very different than previous small business seminars that have been offered to entrepreneurs at a much lower cost and quality content from non-entrepreneurial educators. MEEC differs from these organizations not only by the quality of the program and the entrepreneurial educator that instructs the sessions, but also by the level of 'class' that is associated with the lecture, speakers, dinners, presentations, and corporate environment that is exhibited.

Because MEEC is supported by independent revenue (corporate sponsorships) and seminar fees, the Center has become a unique model for universities to emulate. The Center is currently sponsored by ten private organizations. Due to university ties, corporate sponsors, and outreach capabilities, the Center truly has become a public and private partnership.

Support for potential and experienced entrepreneurs is of the essence as the world is moving toward a more entrepreneurial economy. In order to produce quality entrepreneurial education programs to encourage the development of entrepreneurs, universities with successful Entrepreneurship Programs and Centers must take the lead in non-credit areas. For an entrepreneurial economy to continue and flourish, outreach centers, like MEEC will have to take the responsibility in establishing these programs across the United States and the world.

In conclusion, the Midwest Entrepreneurial Education Center believes strongly that universities across the country can begin to offer similar outreach programs to help continue the growth of the entrepreneurial perspective. Because of this belief, MEEC's vision is transpired through the following famous quote by Peter F. Drucker, 'The entrepreneurial mystique? It's not magic, it's not mysterious, and it has nothing to do with the genes. It's a discipline. And, like any discipline, it can be learned.' The Midwest Entrepreneurial Education Center stands by this quote and is proud to offer this level of program.

Notes

[1] Adapted from Donald F. Kuratko and Richard M. Hodgetts, *Entrepreneurship: A Contemporary Approach* 4th ed. (Dryden Press: Harcourt Brace & Co., 1998)
[2] Information obtained from a report by David C. Clegg, Consultant, Indianapolis, IN.
[3] Competitive Analysis provided by Catherine Basso, Ball State University.

PART E

VARIOUS ASPECTS OF ENTREPRENEURSHIP EDUCATION

20 The Use of Enterprise Training Programs as a Mechanism for Assessing Entrepreneurial Suitability

Colette Henry
Albert Titterington

Abstract

When it comes to new venture creation, few would disagree that there is no obvious 'formula' for success. However, it helps if the new product or service being proposed is innovative, competitive and market driven. In addition, the promoter should normally possess at least some of the key traits and abilities deemed to be so critical to successful entrepreneurship, such as drive, determination and risk-taking ability.

This paper begins by considering the various theories concerning the ideal personality profile for a successful entrepreneur and tests these theories against the profiles of a real group of aspiring Irish entrepreneurs at the pre-feasibility stage. The paper also looks at how an appropriately designed enterprise support program can not only provide critical business training to optimize the chance of successful set-up, but can also act as a mechanism for testing entrepreneurial suitability. The authors suggest that using enterprise programs to identify successful entrepreneurs can not only help to reduce the risk of failure but can also assist in rationalizing State and/or private investment.

By presenting the evaluation results of the pilot run of the Coca-Cola National Enterprise Award scheme, the authors attempt to address the issues of determining entrepreneurial suitability, developing entrepreneurial talent through training and predicting entrepreneurial success.

Introduction and Background

Over the years, various authors have attempted to develop a typical personality profile for the successful entrepreneur. Menger (1950), and even as far back as von Wiesner (1927), underlined the importance of management and leadership in successful entrepreneurship, while Drucker (1985) emphasized the ability to innovate systematically. Meredith et al (1982) listed five core traits of the typical entrepreneur: self-confidence, risk taking activity, flexibility, need for achievement, and a strong desire to be independent. Garavan and O'Cinneide (1994), suggested that, to be a successful entrepreneur, it was desirable to come from 'two learned, successful, entrepreneurial parents, to have work experience and an adequate education'.

Some researchers have taken a different approach to the study of entrepreneurship and tackled the problem of investigating what stimulates an individual to leave secure employment and take on the social, psychological and financial risks associated with starting a new business. Others have chosen to address the issue of whether entrepreneurs can be taught and, if so, what is the role of entrepreneurship education and training.

The life cycle approach to conceptualizing entrepreneurial careers, for example, gave nine major factors which can influence an individual: educational environment, personality, family environment, employment history, adult development history, adult non-work history, current work situation, current perspective and current family situation (Brodzinski et al 1989). Caird (1992) developed a measure of enterprising traits called General Enterprise Tendency (GET). This comprehensive system of measurement included a range of questions within various categories: the need for achievement (12 questions); internal locus of control (12); creative tendency (12); calculated risk tendency (12) and six questions on the measured need for autonomy.

However, the success or failure of small business start-ups involves more than the personality characteristics of the entrepreneur. The proposed product or service of the new business venture must be innovative, market oriented and, to some degree, relative to the entrepreneur's own area of expertise.

Naturally, difficulties can arise for the potential entrepreneur within any of these phases, even if the individual appears suited to an entrepreneurial career (on the basis of personality or psychometric tests). It is important, therefore, that the aspiring entrepreneur receives sufficient support and guidance when planning the new business venture.

There is no doubt that adequate grant aid and financial investment at the early stages of business set-up can significantly accelerate commercialization, however, the benefits of non-financial support mechanisms such as business training, mentoring and advice are often considerably underestimated. In fact, it is the authors' opinion that such support is often critical in not only ensuring a match between the entrepreneur and the proposed product or service idea but also in facilitating the individual through the four stages of enterprise development identified by Hirisch.

Garavan and O'Cinneide (1994) reviewed six entrepreneurial education and training programs in Europe - Ireland (1), Italy (1), Spain (1), England (1) and France (2). They identified five objectives which were common to all of the programs:

1. identify and prepare potential entrepreneurs for the start-up or advancement of their own high technology/knowledge based business venture
2. enable participants to prepare business plans for the new ventures which were based on identified market segments
3. focus on issues that were critical to implementing an entrepreneurial project such as market research and analysis of competitors, financing the business, legal and taxation issues, etc.
4. enable the development of autonomous behavior, the taking of risks and acceptance of responsibilities
5. enable participants to be in a position to launch high technology/knowledge based business ventures at the end of the program.

Objectives

It is clear that enterprise-training programs can yield a number of benefits for both participants and providers alike. There is a need for such benefits to be properly measured and evaluated. Wickham and Wedley concluded in their 1990 study of the NEP (New Enterprise Program) that entrepreneurship programs can, in fact, yield very positive results, as did Webb et al in 1982 and Henry and Titterington in 1996. Fleming, in her 1993 paper, emphasized the need to assess the performance of entrepreneurship education and chose the former IDA Student Enterprise Award (now the Forbairt Student Enterprise Award) as the basis of her research. Garavan and O'Cinneide's (1994) detailed analysis of the end results of the six training programs they reviewed gave powerful support to the proposition that such training programs are effective in aiding entrepreneurs to launch successful businesses.

This paper begins by looking at the various theories concerning what is the best personality profile for a potential entrepreneur and then tests these theories against the profiles of a group of real entrepreneurs at the pre-feasibility stage. In addition, an evaluation of the training that these entrepreneurs received to help them develop their new business ventures is presented. Based on the specific experiences of The Coca-Cola National Enterprise Award scheme, the authors of this paper attempt to address the issues of determining entrepreneurial suitability, developing entrepreneurial talent through structured training and predicting entrepreneurial success.

The Study

Explanation and rationale

The Coca-Cola National Enterprise Award (CCNEA), a joint initiative of Coca-Cola Atlantic (Drogheda) and Dundalk Regional Technical College, was designed to promote graduate entrepreneurship throughout the island of Ireland. The pilot program, funded by The Coca-Cola Foundation in Atlanta (USA), was launched in January 1996 and targeted graduates of third level educational establishments with the aim of encouraging and developing entrepreneurial talent through training. In order to qualify for entry, applicants had to hold a diploma, degree or higher qualification, and have a business idea at feasibility or pre-feasibility stage.

Program structure and content

This pilot project contained many unique features in terms of focus, content and targeted results. It combined structured training with financial reward and an academic qualification, all within a competitive framework. Managed by Dundalk RTC's Regional Development Centre, the scheme comprised a series of six intensive business training modules, individual assessment sessions and meetings with experienced mentors. The program was delivered over a six-month period with participants offered the opportunity to work towards a recognized qualification and compete for a prize fund of £18,000.

Training

The formal training, delivered by Dundalk RTC's Business School, concentrates on what have previously been identified as the critical aspects of business planning, i.e.:

1. Generating the business proposal
2. Determining legal and financial requirements
3. Planning the business operation
4. Planning the market strategy
5. Monitoring/controlling business operations and quality
6. Planning the human resource development

The topics are modeled on the 'Owner-Management Business Planning' program, a set of standards designed by the UK small firms lead body for those preparing to set-up and be responsible for the management of their own business. These standards are linked to the UK's NVQ (National Vocational Qualification) system and allow participants to work towards the achievement of a level 3 qualification. Due to the wide geographical spread of participants, (applications were invited from all 32 counties in Ireland), the number of formal training sessions was minimized and a comprehensive training manual was designed as both a reference and distance learning support tool.

361

The emphasis on training in a wide number of areas is important in order to provide the entrepreneurs with the necessary skills to run their businesses. Drucker (1985) in particular believes that successful entrepreneurship is a behavioral rather than a personality trait and something that people can be taught so that they can in fact learn to behave 'entrepreneurially'. Duggan (1996), further supports this view when he stresses the need for 'high quality innovation project management' as a requirement for successfully bringing new ideas to the market place.

A particularly interesting part of the training element is the mentoring input. Garavan and O'Cinneide (1994) stress the importance of mentoring or facilitating in the enterprise training programs they reviewed. In the CCNEA scheme this was organized through Forbairt (the Irish government agency responsible for the development of new and indigenous businesses) using a group of experienced mentors with strong management and marketing backgrounds.

Thirty-five graduates were chosen to participate in the pilot scheme and these were selected solely on the basis of their business ideas. These graduate entrepreneurs joined the scheme in April 1996 and completed their business plans in September 1996. The additional work required for the NVQ qualification had to be submitted by the end of November and the candidates were informed of the results during the weeks which followed.

Research Methodology

The research study set up to run in parallel with the CCNEA project involved the questioning of participants pre, during and post their participation in the program. The objective of the first part of the study was to acquire further personal information on the participating entrepreneurs and to investigate their reasons for joining the program. To this end, paper based questionnaires were designed to determine the participants' age, gender and family situation. Participants were also asked about their educational background and work experience and whether they had been involved in any previous business venture. In addition, the group was asked to rate themselves against a list of key entrepreneurial characteristics and business skills and to explain what they hoped to gain by participating in the scheme.

The second part of the study, carried out half way through the project, sought to evaluate the effectiveness of the program itself in terms of how the participants perceived the overall quality of the training, the benefits they derived, and whether or not their original expectations had been met. Having completed the formal training element of the program, participants were again asked to rate their knowledge of key business skills so that a comparison could be made with the responses they gave prior to commencing the program. The issue of work experience was further investigated to determine its relevance to the proposed business venture. Participants were also asked to state whether they had any management or sales experience, which was going to deal with sales in the new business, and what their own role would be.

The third part of the study sought to evaluate the mentoring, assessment, qualification (NVQ) and competitive elements of the program. In this respect, the questionnaires were administered upon completion of the entire project with the intention of gauging participants' overall opinions of the support they had received. The group were asked to comment on the amount of work and time commitment required during the program and whether this was more or less than they had expected. Participants were also asked how they felt the program impacted upon the development of their business ideas, on their entrepreneurial abilities and on their own personal development. Finally, the group was asked for their suggestions for improving the program.

Results

The results of this comprehensive three-part study are divided into two main categories. The first deals with the analysis of the individual participants, comparing them against the 'typical' entrepreneurial profile, as described in the literature. The second deals with the effectiveness of the program, presenting the participants' evaluation of the various support elements they received and how these impacted upon the development of themselves and their business ideas. In terms of responses, the first part of the study yielded a 100 per cent response rate, i.e. 35 responses out of the 35 individuals surveyed. By the time the second part of the survey was administered, two of the participants had dropped out of the scheme for work related reasons, leaving 33 to be surveyed and of these 30 useable responses were received. The third and final part of the survey yielded 25 responses out of the 33 surveyed.

Part I: Analysis of the individuals

General As mentioned above, the thirty-five individuals surveyed were all participants in a new graduate enterprise-training program - The Coca-Cola National Enterprise Award. Each of these aspiring entrepreneurs were of Irish origin (i.e. from one of Ireland's 32 counties), had a business idea at the feasibility or pre-feasibility stage, and had received a third level education to at least diploma standard. Most of the participants were single men, with women accounting for only 20 per cent of the final group selected. Seven of the participants (4 men and 3 women) had children dependant upon them and two of the women were pregnant (each with their second child) at the time of joining the scheme. The business ideas proposed by the participants covered a wide range of industry sectors with some 86 per cent (30 business ideas) in manufacturing and the balance in the service sector.

Age Whilst there was no specific age limit laid down for participants, the criteria for entry to the program required that applicants had to have graduated during or since 1990. The actual age of those selected to participate ranged from 20 to 35 years, with the bulk of participants (48 per cent) falling into the 25-29 age group and the balance split almost equally between the 20-24 and 30-35 age groups.

Educational background and work experience In accordance with the program's entry criteria, all of the participants possessed a third level qualification from a recognized College or University. Information was then gathered concerning participants' specific area of education. It was found that 40 per cent of participants' educational background was in business or marketing related subjects, 14 per cent in engineering and the balance in other areas. The analysis also revealed that 31 per cent of participants' education appeared to be directly relevant to their proposed business idea.

It was significant that almost all of the participants (97 per cent) had gained work experience, with the majority of participants (over 70 per cent) in gainful employment at the time of joining the program. Such

364

experience ranged in type and duration with over 70 per cent of participants having more than three years work experience. The survey also revealed that 44 per cent of the participants had work experience which was directly related to the industry sector of their proposed business idea.

Motivation In order to assess the various motives for setting up in business, the participants were asked to give their reasons for deciding to go into business for themselves. Only a few of the group (4 participants) had experience of their family business which may have helped develop in them an early ownership mentality, giving them a 'taste' for self employment, as well as an insight into the amount of work and commitment required. For the most part, the group's responses fell into three categories, as illustrated in table 1 below.

Table 1: Reasons for Wanting to Set-up in Business

To be successful and make money	To be own boss and be independent	For personal achievement or to realize own ambition
6 (17%)	16 (46%)	13 (37%)

About one third of the participants had been involved in, or at least attempted to set-up, previous business ventures, some of which had been modestly successful and some of which had failed either before or shortly after start-up.

Self Ratings - entrepreneurial characteristics In order to further analyze the type of individual taking part in the program, the participants were asked to rate themselves against a list of key characteristics deemed to be critical to entrepreneurial success. Using a scale of 1 to 5, where 1 is the lowest rating and 5 is the highest, the participants were asked to rate their level of enthusiasm, need for achievement, initiative taking, risk taking, innovativeness, leadership, commitment and determination, confidence, communication and judgment abilities.

A surprisingly confident group, most of the participants gave themselves very high ratings against all of the characteristics, with only a few individuals rating themselves lower than a 3. A summary of the ratings is presented in table 2 below.

Table 2: Summary of Self Ratings - Entrepreneurial Characteristics

Entrepreneurial Characteristics	Percentage of Participants scoring in each rating					Average rating
	1	2	3	4	5	
Enthusiasm	0	0	6	37	57	4.51
Need for Achievement	0	0	11	28	60	4.48
Taking Initiative	0	0	9	57	34	4.25
Calculated Risk Taking	0	9	20	43	28	3.34
Innovativeness	0	0	11	43	46	4.34
Leadership	0	6	14	54	26	4.00
Commitment / Determination	0	0	23	34	43	4.20
Confidence	0	0	23	51	26	4.02
Ability to Communicate	0	0	28	51	20	3.40
Judgment	0	3	28	57	11	3.77

Note: Percentages may not total 100 due to rounding

It is interesting to note that enthusiasm and need for achievement attracted the top ratings with 57 per cent and 60 per cent of the participants rating themselves as a 5 respectively. The lowest number of 5's was given to judgment and communication skills, as well as to leadership and confidence, characteristics, which are particularly important in individual-promoted ventures.

Self Ratings - business skills In order to assess the participants' preparedness for setting up in business, the individuals were asked to rate their knowledge in a number of key business areas. Once again, a rating scale of 1 to 5 was used and the results of this analysis are presented in table 3 below.

Table 3: Summary of Self Ratings - Business Skills

Business Skills	Percentage of Participants scoring in each rating					Average Rating
	1	2	3	4	5	
Raising Finance	9	20	48	20	3	2.90
Sales Management	9	14	43	28	6	3.09
Cashflow Management	14	14	37	26	9	3.00
Staff Development	14	11	23	40	11	3.23
Contract Law	26	28	28	6	11	2.49
Safety Legislation	28	20	23	17	11	2.63
Employment Law	28	31	23	9	9	2.37
Stock Control	17	23	31	14	14	2.86
Work Scheduling	9	9	37	40	6	3.26
Quality Control	9	28	14	28	20	3.23
Quality Standards	9	26	28	23	14	3.09
Market Information	9	14	37	37	3	3.11

Note: Percentages may not total 100 due to rounding

It was interesting to note that the participants did not rate themselves as highly on business skills as they did on entrepreneurial characteristics. In fact, the average rating registered in the business skills section was 2.94, with most of the respondents giving themselves ratings of 3 or less against almost all of the skills listed. This compares with an average rating of 4.03 in the entrepreneurial characteristics analysis where most of the participants rated themselves as 4 or more against the majority of the characteristics listed.

The lowest scores appeared in the legal areas, (i.e. contract law, safety legislation and employment law), with average ratings of between 2.37 and 2.63. Skills such as raising finance, cashflow management and sales also attracted low ratings with average scores of 2.9, 3 and 3.09 respectively.

Part II: Effectiveness of the program

Expectations Participants were asked to list their main expectations from the program prior to embarking on the training sessions proper. Expectations ranged from gaining an opportunity to test the feasibility of the business idea to gaining new skills and knowledge in the general area of enterprise preparation. A summary of participants' main expectations is provided in table 4 below.

Table 4: Participants' Expectations

Support and guidance on setting up a business	12*	Create realism for Business ideas	2
Completion of Business Plan	11	Opportunity to compete for the prize fund	1
To gain new skills and training	4	Make new contacts	1
Marketing/Business skills	3	No expectations	1
Advice on running a small company	2	One-to-One Sessions	1
To Gain Experience	2	To get access to different experts	1
Get help with Financial Planning	2	A quality program	1
To explore and develop the business idea	2		

* Figures indicate frequency of response and may not equal the total number of participants due to multiple answers.

At the end of the formal training sessions participants were asked whether or not they felt their expectations had been met. Over 90 per cent of the participants who completed the training confirmed that their expectations had been met, with the remaining percentage saying that they were unsure.

In order to get an overall opinion at the end of the program, the participants were surveyed again on this point once all of the assessment and mentoring sessions were completed. A scale of 1 - 5 was used, where 1 indicated that expectations had not been met and 5 indicated that expectations had been fully met. This analysis showed 80 per cent of those responding registering a 4 or higher.

The survey also revealed that 21 of the 35 participants had been involved in other enterprise programs prior to embarking on the CCNEA scheme. These participants were asked to state what they hoped to gain by taking part in this initiative that they had not been able to gain from previous programs. The completion of a business plan, a recognized qualification and more assistance with focusing their business ideas were seen as the main areas of gain by the respondents.

Benefits At the end of the program, participants were asked to describe the benefits they derived from the scheme. Just under one third of the participants mentioned contact with other entrepreneurs as being the main benefit gained, with about 19 per cent stating that business training was a key benefit. Gaining a better understanding of general business operations and knowledge of marketing and legal aspects were the next highest rated benefits. Table 5 below summarizes the participants' responses.

Table 5: Benefits

Contact with other Entrepreneurs	29%	Networking	6%
Business Training	19%	Practical Advice	3%
Knowledge of Marketing and Law	16%	Researching Business Ideas	3%
Better understanding of Business Operations	16%	Access to Information	3%
Personal Development	13%	Stimulation	3%
Knowledge from Trainers	13%	Meeting Experts in Different Fields	3%
Insight into Business Success Factors	13%	In depth Training and Assessment	3%
Motivation	10%	Support	3%
Working to a Schedule	6%	Various Business Techniques	3%

Note: Percentages do not total 100 due to multiple answers.

Following on from the above analysis, the participants were asked to say what they felt was the single most important benefit they had gained from the program.

Contact with other entrepreneurs and producing a business plan were the most common responses.

New contacts In order to further analyze the response that 'contact with other entrepreneurs' was perceived as a key benefit, participants were asked whether they had made any valuable new contacts as a direct result of participating in the program. About three quarters of the participants said that they had made valuable new contacts and these ranged from potential customers for their proposed products, to suppliers and contacts in foreign markets. In addition, it was interesting that the trainers and guest speakers contributing to the program were also mentioned as useful new contact points for the entrepreneurs.

*New skills/*knowledge Participants were asked about the new skills and knowledge they had gained by taking part in the scheme. Responses ranged from marketing and financial skills through to quality control. Marketing was the most common response with over half of the group listing it as an important area in which they had gained new skills/knowledge. Table 6 below summarizes the responses.

Table 6: New Skills/Knowledge Gained

Marketing	52%	Unsure	3%
Finance	23%	Awareness of Sources of Funding	3%
Business Planning	19%	Production/Operations Management	3%
Human Resource Management	10%	Ability to seek new networks	3%
Legal Aspects	10%	Entrepreneurial Skills	3%
Better Judgment	3%	Analytical Techniques	3%
Information and Training	3%	Communications	3%
Quality Control	3%	Improved Research Methods	3%
Assertiveness	3%	Better understanding of start-up business requirements	6%

Note: Percentages do not total 100 due to multiple answers

In addition, participants were asked to say what they felt was the single most important new skill or knowledge they had gained by participating in the initiative.

370

Business planning and marketing were the highest rated skills with 19 per cent and 52 per cent of the participants listing these respectively.

Mentoring and assessment sessions The participants in the CCNEA scheme received mentoring and assessment sessions on a one-to-one basis. At the end of these the group was asked to rate these elements of the program in terms of neutral, beneficial and very beneficial. The results of this analysis are presented in table 7 below.

Table 7: Ratings of Mentoring and Assessment Sessions

Rating	Mentoring Sessions	Assessment Sessions
Neutral	24%	20%
Beneficial	36%	36%
Very Beneficial	32%	40%
Didn't attend sessions	8%	0%

NVQ qualification Part of the program involved the completion of work towards an NVQ qualification at level 3. All of the participants were offered the opportunity to obtain this qualification, and of these, 23 submitted evidence for assessment. Twenty of these candidates managed to achieve NVQ certification for various units of the course.

At the end of the program, the participants were asked how beneficial they felt the NVQ was to their project. 40 per cent of the group rated it as being beneficial to their project, with 24 per cent rating it as very beneficial and the balance rating it as being of neutral benefit. In terms of the work required to achieve the qualification and the time scale allowed, all of those who responded to this part of the survey felt that the workload was more than they had expected and felt that not enough time was given for its completion. However, more than half of the participants surveyed felt that it was important for aspiring entrepreneurs to gain certification for work completed in the area of business preparation and planning (Henry, Titterington and Wiseman, 1997).

Degree of progress In order to further test the effectiveness of the program, participants were asked to describe how the initiative affected the progress and development of their business ideas. Using a progress bar, the participants were required to mark the point to which their business idea had developed since joining the program. The results of this part of the survey are presented in table 8 below.

Table 8: Progress of Business Ideas

Point of Joining CCNEA	1	2	3	4	5	6	7	8	9	10	Point of Business start-up
	1*	0	2	2	4	8	6	1	0	1	

*Figures indicate number of participants

It was also interesting to note that, by the end of the program, 3 of the entrepreneurs reported that their businesses had already reached set-up stage. 15 of the participants said that they intended to proceed to set-up stage but needed to do more work on product development and finding investors.

Since it could be argued that the individuals who had shown significant progress, including those who had reached set-up stage, might have done so anyway, participants were asked whether they felt that they would have developed their business idea to its current stage without the help of the scheme. Most of the participants (64 per cent) stated that they would possibly not have developed their business idea to its current stage without the help of the scheme.

Personal development In order to determine how the group benefited in terms of their own personal development as a result of taking part in the CCNEA scheme, the participants were asked to rate the program's impact in this respect. On a scale of 1 - 5, where 1 represented 'no real impact' and 5 represented 'significant impact', 72 per cent of the group registered a 4 or higher. In addition, the participants were asked to say whether their confidence in their own entrepreneurial abilities had improved as a direct result of the program. Again using a scale of 1 - 5, where 1 implied 'no more confident than before' and 5 implied 'significantly more confident', 52 per cent of the participants registered a 4 or higher.

Gaps and recommendations Whilst most of the participants surveyed felt that there were no significant gaps in the program, many offered their own personal recommendations improvement. Such recommendations ranged from proposals for more group work to the inclusion of more entrepreneurs in the program. One of the main recommendations, however, was that participants should be given more time to complete the work for their business plans.

Developing a predictive model In order to make an informed prediction of those candidates most likely to succeed in their business, a comparative analysis was made of the most committed/driven candidates. The measure of commitment used in this case was the completion of the business plan within the program time frame and thus, those candidates who managed to complete their plans and competed for the prize fund were deemed to the most committed of the group. Twenty participants met these criteria and key elements of their background and personality were examined. Table 9 below gives a summary of these results.

Table 9: Summary Comparative Analysis - a Predictive Model

Cand. Ref.	Education			Work Exp.				Previous Business	Calculated Risk Taking	Comm. Ability	Judg. Ability
	Relv	Bus.	Other	Relv.	Mgt.	Sales	Other				
001	✓						✓				
005			✓		✓				✓	✓	✓
006	✓			✓				✓	✓	✓	✓
007	✓			✓		✓			✓	✓	✓
009		✓			✓			✓		✓	
013		✓					✓	✓	✓	✓	✓
014	✓			✓				✓		✓	✓
015	✓			✓						✓	✓
016	✓							✓			
017			✓	✓					✓	✓	✓
018		✓		✓	✓			✓		✓	✓
020	✓			✓	✓			✓	✓	✓	✓
021	✓			✓	✓			✓	✓	✓	✓
022		✓					✓			✓	✓
024		✓					✓		✓	✓	✓
025		✓					✓	✓	✓	✓	✓
027	✓			✓						✓	
031	✓			✓						✓	✓
032			✓			✓			✓	✓	✓

374

Those candidates registering the most checks were identified as being those most likely to succeed as they best fitted the 'typical' entrepreneurial profile. Hence, those participants whose educational background and work experience were directly relevant to their proposed business venture; had been involved in a previous business venture, and scored highly on key entrepreneurial attributes such as calculated risk taking, communication and judgement abilities, were identified as potentially the most successful entrepreneurs. Candidates 016, 022 and 005 received 1st, 2nd and 3rd prizes respectively in the competition for best business proposal. Data subsequently collected revealed that candidates 007, 014, 016, 020 and 021 have since set-up their respective businesses.

Conclusions

The survey presented in this paper shows that, even at the early feasibility and planning stage, aspiring entrepreneurs have much to gain by participating in enterprise support programs. In particular, those programs which focus on the critical aspects of implementation and offer a structured framework within which relevant research can be carried out and a business plan developed are especially beneficial. (Tables 5 through to 8 serve to demonstrate this).

In addition, the CCNEA program impacted significantly upon the personal development of the individuals involved with almost three quarters of the group reporting a significant improvement in their own entrepreneurial confidence as a direct result of taking part.

The paper also demonstrates that enterprise support programs, like the Coca-Cola National Enterprise Award, if appropriately designed, can not only benefit aspiring entrepreneurs, but can also serve as a mechanism for predicting successful entrepreneurs. Section I of the paper dealing with the analysis of the individuals shows how important data can be collected at the outset of a program to determine whether the individual participants match the educational, work experience and social profile of the 'typical' entrepreneur. The self-rating tables used served to identify which individuals possess those important entrepreneurial characteristics and business skills deemed to be critical to entrepreneurial success. Furthermore, since it is anticipated that not all participants will in fact complete their research, develop a business plan and proceed to start-up stage, support programs themselves can act as an automatic filtering mechanism, retaining only the most enthusiastic and committed candidates.

Finally, in terms of predicting future success, being able to complete the business plan within the given time frame was used as a measure of drive and commitment. In addition, various key elements concerning the candidates' background and personality were added and this formed the basis of the predictive model illustrated in table 9. It is now intended to track these candidates over the next 12 months to monitor their progress. The fact that five of the individuals identified in the table have already set-up their businesses demonstrates, at least in part, the potential viability of the predictive model. It is intended to further strengthen this model by including the use of psychometric tools, which can test more objectively for entrepreneurial suitability.

If we can use enterprise programs to predict successful entrepreneurs with a view to identifying candidates for further support, grant aid or financial investment, then the risk factors associated with small business start-ups could be significantly reduced, and State or private investment could be rationalized to ensure the optimum return.

References

Brodzinski, J.D., Sherer, R.F. and Wiebe, F.A., (March 1989) Entrepreneur Career Selection and Gender; A socialization approach, *Journal of Small Business Management 27*, pp. 37-42.

Drucker, P. (1985) *Innovation and Entrepreneurship*, Pan Books Ltd., London.

Duggan, R., (1996) Promoting Innovation in Industry, Government and Higher Education, *Journal of Long Range Planning*, vol. 29, No.4, pp.503-513.

Fleming, P., (1993) The Role of Structured Interventions in Shaping Graduate Entrepreneurship, *Internationalizing Entrepreneurship Education and Training Conference, Vienna*.

Garavan, T.N. and O'Cinneide, B., Entrepreneurship Education and Training Programmes - A Review and Evaluation, *Journal of European Industrial Training*, Vol. 18, No. 11, pp. 13-21.

Henry, C. and Titterington, A., (June 1996) The Effects of Enterprise Support Programs on the Success of Small Business Start-ups: - an analysis of the Technology Enterprise Program, paper presented at *IntEnt conference*, Arnhem.

Henry, C., Titterington, A. and Wiseman, K., (June 1997) Developing Graduate Enterprise Schemes in Higher Education - a partnership approach, paper presented at *Coventry University Enterprise Conference*.

Menger, C., (1950) *Principles of Economics*, trans. J. Dingwell, B.F. Hoselitz, Free Press,

Glencoe.

Meredith, G.G., Nelson, R.E. and Neck, P.A. (1982), The Practice of Entrepreneurship, *International Labor Organization*, Geneva.

Webb, T, Quince, T. and Wathers, D., (1982) Small Business Research, *The Development of Entrepreneurs*, Gower.

Wiesner, F. von, (1927) Social Economics, trans. A. F. Hindrich's, Adelphi, New York.

Wyckham, R. and Wedley, W., (October 1990) Factors Related to Venture Feasibility Analysis and Business Plan Preparation, *Journal of Small Business Management*.

21 Survival, Planning Performance and Growth of Business Start-ups: Management Training Matters

Tom Schamp
Dirk Deschoolmeester[1]

Abstract

The outcome of this research gives the reader insight in the growth pattern of two groups of surviving small and medium enterprise start-ups: at the one hand 'Vlerick'-starters who have enjoyed management training at the Department of SMEs at The Vlerick School of Management, and at the other hand a group of 'Others' who have not.

Secondly, some of the research findings reveal clear evidence for the relationship between entrepreneurial characteristics and managerial techniques, planning skills and the business growth pattern of the enterprises of both groups. Even so, certain combinations pointing towards the likely catalyzing effect of management training on growth-related entrepreneurial and managerial attitudes and towards the influence of those attitudinal differences on planning skills and the enterprise growth pattern are identified.

Introduction and Hypotheses

Celebrating over a decade of educational training and counseling activities for start-ups and early growth stage firms the need was felt to conduct *a follow-up study* in order to gain specific information on the survival and growth tendencies of all alumni-participants, hereafter called *'Vlerick'-starters*.[2] More important though, a profound comparative study was to be done on the profile of these start-ups and a comparable group of 'non-Vlerick'-starters (hereafter called *Others*) being aware that the generally assumed impact of management programs on entrepreneurial, managerial and self-employing attitudes of the first group would clearly disclose inter-group post-start-up profile differences.

The starting-point for this research hence was the reflection on what kind of contribution the listed management training programs (see footnote 2) have on the life cycle of start-ups. In this context abundant literature and study materials demonstrate the positive effect of participating on management training and individual counseling programs on the entrepreneurial and managerial attitudes of SME-businessmen (Gibb, 1995 and 1996; Iredale and Cotton, 1995; Klandt, Muller-Boling (ed.), 1995; Atherton and Hannon, 1996; Fuller, 1993; etc.). Part of the contributors even consider post-experience management training to be an important explanatory element for a higher survival rate and chances for growth (Rosa, Scott, and Klandt, 1996; Crant, 1996; Van Clouse, 1990). Because training is a form of education, in general, over the last two decades institutions of higher learning have experienced an increased demand for courses and management modules dealing with entrepreneurship and new venture creation. Universities and centers for continuous education have come up with a variety of course offerings, ranging from traditionally structured courses consisting of lectures, venture design projects, case-study writing, and reading to innovative courses developed to address the unique personality characteristics of the trainee. Under the latter heading most of the management programs of the Department of SMEs of The Vlerick School of Management can be categorized. Businessmen who are motivated to enroll for one or more management training programs share, gain and test expertise and almost personalized management knowledge that might eventually lead to higher economical, social and individual performances. Therefore, apart from some typical follow-up questions on what economical level the 'Vlerick'-alumni attained, their life cycle and economic or fiscal diversification, causes for their internal decision-making processes and the firm's management processes, especially toward 'planning' were questioned in depth.

H1: *Partly due to pre- and post-start-up real-live experience and their motivation or need for management training courses and counseling, 'Vlerick'-starters show a different entrepreneurial and managerial profile than their non-trained SME-colleagues. Moreover, specific selection criteria on the willingness to perform formal business planning of certain management programs makes the already existing inter-group difference even more profound.*

In other words, the need for management training is due to a difference in the pre-start-up context and past (involving skills, abilities, and experiences) as well as to the eagerness to work on all such levels. In order to validate hypothesis 1 check-lists were inserted in the questionnaire for two different places in time: firstly the founder's *(pre-)start-up* age, family and household, educational level, motivations, and secondly his *post-start-up* motivations, planning and entrepreneurial and managerial characteristics. Because the relationship between being better informed, trained and experienced and business planning abilities is existent, the least of the expectations therefore is that all Vlerick-alumni would attach a higher importance to the proficiency and systematic attitude of foreseeing future opportunities, options, weaknesses and risks or threats within their day-to-day business-planning activity than their non-trained fellows.

On the other hand, because of the crucial role of *learning about business-planning* within most of these management training programs, the selection of businessmen within the framework of these programs evidently focuses on the willingness of each candidate to plan his business in a more or less formal manner. Hence, one could easily assume that because of this selection parameter all candidates withheld would show a higher business-planning attitude after following the management course.

H2: *Based on the assumption that management training cycles positively influences the particular management technique of business planning, in general, the 'Vlerick'-starters score higher on the operational and strategic planning criteria scale (= the general tempo of realization of the* *firm, annual gains, turnover, growth of personnel and staffing (HRM), personal salary, etc.) both quantitatively and qualitatively.*

As to what Crant (1996) defined as the *proactive entrepreneurial attitude*, which can be explained by certain entrepreneurial intentions (consisting of a variety of individual differing variables) or the entrepreneurial heritage (e.g. gender, education and entrepreneurial parental role modeling), SME-businessmen with a better planning proficiency are likely to have a distinctive entrepreneurial, managerial and self-employing profile from non- or bad-planners.[3] We also believe that this will be the case for both groups of 'Vlerick'-starters and 'Others'. Distinction between the well-planning, bad-planning and non-planning entrepreneurial and managerial profile of 'Vlerick'-starters and that of 'Others' could stem from the accentuation of certain operational and strategic planning attitudes during the management training sessions.

H3: *Within both the test and control group (well-)planning businessmen differ on certain entrepreneurial and management attitudinal factors. Entrepreneurial and managerial profiles therefore strongly correlate with different planning behavior which shows great similarities with the typical emphasized aspects of business planning within the framework of 'Vlerick'-management training for SME-business-owners. And, to some extent they even determine the planning ability to plan specific items of the business household.*

As well as the eagerness to work on their planning skills, experience and management expertise, the need for defining strategy in general and business goal definition in particular not only results these inter-group planning profile differences but can implicitly be linked to *growth-to-planning related ratios* (e.g. the planning profile versus the annual growth of turnover and employment). Amongst others Olson and Bokor (1995) put following rationale straightforward: (formal)[4] business planning - being one of the major categories of strategy process research - and its content are interrelated concepts when linked to performance. Therefore, because a firm's performance is influenced by the main effects of strategy process and content as well as their interaction effect, distinctive mixtures of operational and strategic planning patterns for both tested groups will be made even more apparent when the above characteristics are linked to other parameters, i.e. the growth rate of the firm, the creation of other firms, financing methods, etc.

H4: *'Vlerick'-starters show a higher business growth rate than their non-trained counterparts, due to the inter-group operational and strategic business planning mix and the original and elementary managerial and entrepreneurial attitudinal differences.*

Because all firms of the control group were selected out of a last years' start-up database all business-owners been referred to, are still in business. Hence, no comparative survival analysis could be done. The research group will therefore focus on the *growth rate* of all these firms. All of the above hypotheses are summarized in the figures 1a and b.

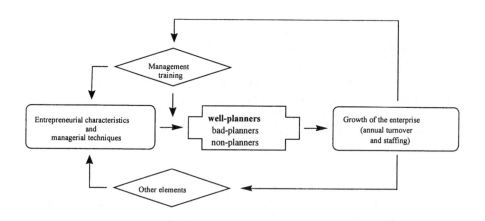

Figure 1a: Management Training as a Tool for Enhancing Operational and Strategic Business Planning

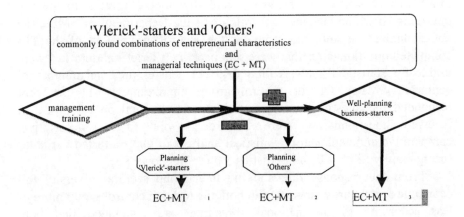

Figure 1b: Summary of Hypotheses and Research Questions: whether Management Training does or does not Positively Influence Entrepreneurial Planning Skills and Attitudes?

Explanatory value of interrelations between (a) *sets of entrepreneurial and managerial qualifications*, (b) *planning attitudes*, and (c) *business survival and growth* rate of start-ups will be sufficiently established for the group of management trained and individually counseled business start-ups.

Research Methodology

Unit of analysis

In order to assess correctly all differences in company structure, growth pattern, as well as in entrepreneurial characteristics and managerial techniques of the 'Vlerick'-starters (226 alumni in total) a control group database of 2500 SME business-owners was put together, all of them working in an independent company structure for not longer than ten years.

Through sectoral weighting 1000 SME-businessmen were selected randomly from this database (= 'Others' or the control group). Subsequently, in brief, Dillman's *Total Design Method* was followed combining data bank research, telephonic interviews, and direct mailing of questionnaires (Dillman, 1978).[5] A personalized questionnaire[6] was mailed to all 'Vlerick'-starters (= test group) and all 'Others'. Apart from specific questions about the management training at the Department of SMEs, the questionnaire was kept the same for the control group. Out of the 118 completed questionnaires that were sent back by 'Vlerick'-starters 114 were usable for statistical analysis (about 49 per cent of the total number of contacted SMEs). Of the control group approximately 11 per cent responded the questionnaire in a usable form. In total only four of all received questionnaires were discarded from further descriptive, comparative and explanatory statistical analysis of all 165 tested variables (using mainly SPSS 7.0 and Statistica 5.0 for Windows '95).

From the response rate and the inter-group sectoral diversity (all economic sectors are represented in both the test and control group more or less according to the national spreading) we concluded that both compounded groups were fairly comparable for further research and statistical difference analysis and that valid samples -one for the total population, the other by random test- were collected.

Questionnaire

Embedded in the concepts of the *guidelines* for the exploration of entrepreneurship, entrepreneurial and managerial processes, and new-firm performance by Cooper and Gascon (1992), the questionnaire was divided into three parts.

The *first part* dealt with the personal history and past and present motivational and economical situation/status of the small business-owner and the evolution in the firm's activities (employment and yearly production). The *second part* dealt with the importance that businessmen attached to the management training (positive and negative experiences, the practical use and applicability of business-planning, etc.) *Part three* checked upon the businessmen's attitude towards planning and the importance attached to another 28 entrepreneurial and managerial characteristics and techniques; encompassing personal, psychological, managerial and other entrepreneurial issues. Answers were to be formulated by crossing, (nominal and ordinal) scaling, or writing out sentences.

Descriptive Statistical Analysis:
Profiles of Flemish Business Start-ups and Early Stage Growth Firms

Within the boundaries of this article clarification of any relation, correlation and causality between business-owners' entrepreneurial, managerial and self-employing attitudes or behavior, the growth rate of their firms (including survival rates for the test group only) and the assumed influence of management training in strengthening already existing liaisons was sought. Since the touchstone for the latter two is *the ability to plan* future business properly, planning skills will be tested as the critical growth generating factor.

This part summarizes the pre-start-up profile of the starting businessmen of both groups (e.g. age, education, parental role models, pre-start-up experience, and start-up motivation).[7] Secondly, tables 1 and 2 indicate the way in which post-start-up planning skills/abilities and entrepreneurial and managerial characteristics (inclusive the motivation to continue) are affected by management training in the post-start-up stage. All variables within these tables -whether or not typically operational or strategic- were selected on grounds of their relevance to the underlying case and because they are often cited as critical success factors for small businesses (Attahir, 1995). Briefly the growth and survival rate of both groups of start-up firms will be analyzed. Where needed, T-test and/or χ^2-test results will indicate the significance of the discrepancies between samples (variables or groupings) and their average scores.

Profile of starting businessmen

'*Vlerick*'-starters are significantly younger than 'Others' (= the average Flemish SME). About 70 per cent of the test group is between 21 and 40 years old (58 per cent is in its thirties). Not even 3 per cent of the Vlerick-entrepreneurs is older than 50, which is very little compared to the 23 per cent fraction of all 'Others'. An explanation for the on average younger age of the test group population might be the *motivation and need* to follow certain management training which is clearly dropping at the age of 40 and higher. The fact that the average start-up age is only 30 years[8] can be explained by the fact that at least one important management program for starters is exclusively accessible for starting businessmen that are under 35 years old having a business-owning experience of four years at maximum.

The fact that the average 'Vlerick'-starter is younger than the starter of the control group is mainly due to its younger start-up age. As seen already, also because of the nature of some of the management programs for starting businessmen, the Department for SMEs of The Vlerick School of Management most often gathers young entrepreneurs.

The 'Vlerick'-starters population is pro rata *significantly higher educated* than the control group. Looking only to the highest degree ever took, differences get even more apparent: nearly half of the 'Vlerick'-starting businessmen has graduated university (10 per cent even with a post-graduate degree), respectively 25 per cent (6 per cent post-graduate diplomas) for 'Others'. Also one-third of the tested alumni has an equivalent degree but outside university, which is still more than 'Others' (30 per cent).

With a 15 per cent gap, the businessmen of the control group (69 per cent) are obviously more likely to originate from *entrepreneurial households* than 'Vlerick'-starters (54 per cent) (= *entrepreneurial parental role modeling*). This could also be concluded from the motivations to start up an independent business (cf. infra pre-start-up motivations). As mentioned already, this pre-start-up motivational difference does not unconditionally lead to earlier start-ups within the group of 'Others'. Some of the conditions supplementary needed will be illustrated in the following paragraphs. The peer pressure of entrepreneurial parents also link to the chosen start-up form: in total more than 39 per cent of 'Others' stated that they took over or inherited their first enterprise, which is double the 'Vlerick'-starters' score. In contrast, more than 40 per cent of all 'Vlerick'-starters started a new business on their own (28 per cent for 'Others'). Also, 'Vlerick'-starters start more often together with *one or more partners*, or institutions. In sum, this variance can be explained by the fact that 'Vlerick'-starters more frequently create *a new idea in a new configuration* using the help, knowledge and expertise of outsiders, whereas 'Others' follow the more classic family business start-up pattern.

The relation between the duration of *pre-start-up sectoral experience* and the business growth or well-doing of the firm has been a major subject in academic studies. Though, few studies came up with real evidence for a positive (causal) relationship (a.o. collected by Cooper and Gascon (1992)). Both groups are marked by a higher relative share of in-sector over outer-sector experience (> 56 per cent). In total, 10 per cent more 'Vlerick'-starters gain a frequently brief working experience (both in - and outside the actual business sectors). For the in-sector pre-start-up experience, in one on 5 cases this happens to be in a leading function, which is 6 per cent more than 'Others'. For outer-sector experience the range between 'Vlerick'-starters and 'Others' is a lot less (about 2 per cent) and varies around 12 per cent.

The much higher score on *leading or managerial pre-start-up experience* is most probably due to the longer educational curriculum of the test group and can be explained by the opportunities that highly educated post-graduate students can get in leading functions (often within their field of expertise). It also explains why for 'Vlerick'-starters the difference between the experience from not-leading functions in and outside the sector is not that big as for 'Others'. For the latter, the combination of poorer education with the entrepreneurial parental role model evidently pushes towards non-leading status inside the sector one knows the best (this apparently was the case for more then half of all 'Others'). Experiencing leadership within a real-live business situation therefore can be captured as a third possible explanation for the higher survival rate of the 'Vlerick'-starters.

(Pre-)start-up motivations will of course be linked to the already discussed age, level of education and entrepreneurial parental peer pressure, in order to complete theories of organization creation. In those the decision to behave entrepreneurial as a result of the *interaction of several factors* has been repeatedly underlined: personal characteristics, personal environment, relevant business environment, existing business idea(s) and the personal goal set. Examining why people start business and how they differ from those that do not may therefore be useful in understanding the 'motivation' that entrepreneurs exhibit during start up as a link to the sustaining behavior exhibited later (Kuratko, 1995).

In order to get an overview of the reasons why somebody begins a business activity, a range of 16 pre-start-up motivations were tested. The respondents to the questionnaire had the possibility to mark their preference three times, being the first, second and third choice pre-start-up motivation. Across all three series of answers *the challenge to become an entrepreneur* and *the challenge to become independent* are the number one and two motivations for starting up a small enterprise (> 13 per cent), both within the test and the control group. Disparity commences at the level of the third motivation: *the presence of an opportunity* for the group of 'Vlerick'-starters (about 11 per cent first choice and 14 per cent second

387

choice) and *the entrepreneurial parental role model* or the parental peer pressure for 'Others' (respectively 13 per cent and 10 per cent). The latter percentages certainly help to explain why almost 69 per cent of all 'Others' became independent entrepreneurs (cf. supra).

Other significant differences between both groups concern the respectively fourth, fifth and sixth choice: *not longer willing to work for a boss*, and *the belief in the quality of one's product*. Less chosen and therefore less determining motivations for start-up are *a logical consequence of my studies, the high participation in this firm, unemployment or joblessness, family reasons* (inheritance,...), *the wish of doing something else, liking to work hard, to earn lots of money, to become rich*, and *the personal status*.[9]

In sum, 'Vlerick'-alumni can be characterized as highly educated people (twice as many university degrees as compared to the control group), trained inside as much as outside the actual business sector in leading positions. 'Vlerick'-starters most frequently were motivated to start a business on their own. On the contrary 'Others' were highly stimulated by their parent's entrepreneurial role model, due to a greater number of 'Others' that originate from an entrepreneurial or family business environment. Also a set of differences in start-up motivations for the group of 'Vlerick'-starters was disclosed: the challenge of an opportunity, and in that way the sense for a challenge and a new product, and the ever lasting wish to be independent.

So far, the conclusion to this part of the descriptive analysis might be that 'Vlerick'-starters join our management programs to learn the techniques and ways to meet shortcomings and problem-shootings while working out an own business concept or idea, most of it the 'Others' learn while being confronted with the daily *family businesses*. Anyhow, partly due to the start-up motivations, partly due to the pre-start-up experience and expertise (age, education, entrepreneurial household,...) 'Vlerick'-starters indeed show a different pre-start-up entrepreneurial profile, which sustains hypothesis 1. In the following part elements will be searched that also underscore that participating in one or more management training programs at the 'Vlerick'-Center of SMEs deepens these inter-group post-start-up profile differences in other ways than the above, namely the *post-training survival and growth rate* of business start-ups.

Profile of the start-up firm

The absence of alarming discrepancies in the inter-sectoral division of the test and control group reassures that the samples were taken properly. Most of the firms in both groups are active in *distribution and retail*. More differentiating from the spreading of the Flemish SME business activity, 'Vlerick'-starters often do business in textile, wood and paper, transportation and communications (and a smaller part in high-tech). 'Others' matches the regional and sectoral partition in the main.

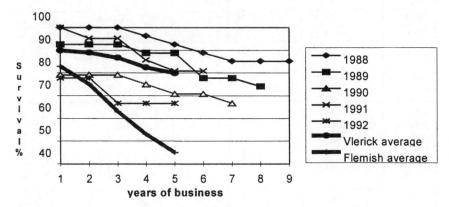

Figure 2: Survival Rate of 'Vlerick'-Start-ups Compared to the Flemish Average (in Number of Years after the Start-up) for the five Oldest Start-ups and the Average for All

Figure 2 gives an indication of the survival chances of 'Vlerick'-alumni and the average fall-out for 'Others'. Regional statistics (for Flanders) indicate that after five years more than 55 per cent of all starters stop either due to bankruptcies (negative rentability), or because of a take-over (positive rentability) of their business. This is only the case for 20 per cent only of all 'Vlerick'-alumni. Moreover, the SME-department also enrolls individuals that consider to start up a firm but after following the courses have not. These persons might be discouraged to do so by the end of the program but are nevertheless included in the above statistics. Therefore, the reader should not oversimplified consider the full 20 per cent as a stoppage of business activities in the way as it was described for 'Others'.

Table 1a: Annual Personnel and Total Production Growth Rates (in Percentages of Total Counts)

	VLERICK STARTERS	OTHERS		VLERICK STARTERS	OTHERS
Average staffing °	mean value (in absolute numbers): **4,70**	**6,95**	*Annual staffing growth*° °°	mean value (in absolute numbers): **7,69 (>)**	**5,15**
during 1987	1,10	3,95	-5 to 0**	0,87	4,50
1990	2,23	4,96	0 to 5	44,73	45,94
1993	3,15	6,73	5 to 10	14,91	17,11
1994	3,79	7,54	10 to 15	*7,01*	4,50
1995	4,64	8,15	>= 15	*8,80*	6,33
1996	6,40	8,87	missing cases	23,68	21,62
Average produc-tion°°	mean value (in absolute numbers): **24,49**	**41,20**	*Annual turnover growth*° °°°	mean value (in absolute numbers): **6,56 (>)**	**2,19**
0 to 14,99*	41,96	33,04	-5 to 0**	2,63	8,92
15 to 29,99	13,39	9,82	0 to 5	57,01	*70,53*
30 to 44,99	6,25	13,39	5 to 10	*10,52*	0,89
45 to 59,99	5,35	10,71	10 to 15	*3,50*	1,78
60 to 74,99	3,57	2,68	>= 15	*6,17*	2,71
75 to 89,99	2,67	1,79	missing cases	20,17	15,17
> 90	3,56	9,82			

*In million Belgian Francs (BEF); **In percentages; °T-test: p < .05; °°T-test: p = .005; °°°T-test: p = 0.21; °°°°T-test: p = .015.

Table 1b: Combined Box and Whisker Plots for Annual Growth in Turnover and Staffing (Growth Rate in Absolute Numbers)

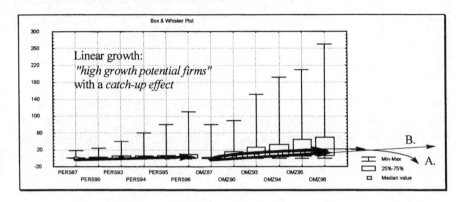

Legend:
PERS = annual level of personnel/staffing (in units); OMZ = annual level of turnover (in million BEF). A-curve = regressive versus (curve for 'Others'); B-curve = linear/progressive growth pace ('Vlerick'-alumni curve).

After one, three and five years, respectively 90, 87 and -like already said- 80 per cent of all 'Vlerick'-starters are still active. Remarkably, 'Vlerick'-starters from before 1989 are in 85 per cent of the cases *survivors in the long run.* This could be due to the originality of management training programs at the 'Vlerick'-Department of SMEs in those days, since there were no comparable alternatives at the time of starting the program and participants were admitted on the basis of criteria such as personality, motivational and activity grounds.[10] Other valid explanations for the higher survival rate include inter alia the high educational level, though more likely the function and duties fulfilled by the 'Vlerick'-starters both inside and outside the eventual business sector (cf. supra).

Table 1c: Turnover versus Staffing Growth Correlation Matrix

	GROWTH STAFFING/PERSONNEL	
	'Vlerick'-starters	'Others'
GROWTH TURNOVER	.84*	-.16

*Significant correlation (p < .05).

Furthermore, tables 1a and b show the *growth tempo of annual turnover and staffing* for both groups. Despite the resemblance of the steepness of the slopes for both graphics in table 1b the inter-group differences are obvious, the 'Vlerick'-starters survival ratio being much higher than the average survival rate for the Flemish industry and commerce. Also calculations via incremental growth ratios (= annual growth of *personnel productivity*) for both groups show that *'Vlerick'-starters grow faster*. This can be explained by the fact that they start at a smaller scale (probably due to the lesser entrepreneurial parental peer pressure (cfr. supra)) and by the *linearity* of their growth pace.

For 77 to 85 per cent of the cases of both groups (see the number of missing cases table 2a) numbers for the annual staffing and turnover display a significant difference. Start-ups of the control group have more personnel and staff members than their 'Vlerick'-trained colleagues at the moment of start-up. This difference decreases however during the post-start-up years and becomes insignificant after 1994. This is mainly due to an intense *catch-up movement* by the 'Vlerick'-starters (cf. table 1b Box and Whisker plot: the steepness of the business-growth slope). In general, 'Others' have a higher average annual production volume. But, here too 'Vlerick'-starters show a considerably higher yearly turnover growth rate (cf. table 1a). Therefore, it can be concluded that 'Vlerick'-starters grow faster both in terms of annual turnover and staffing (cf. '>').

In other words, as well as 'Vlerick'-starters distinguish themselves before the start-up, evidence for a sharpening inter-group profile difference has occurred by ways of growth and survival analysis. In globo, this underscores hypothesis 1 and the first part of hypothesis 4, sustaining a priori assumed inter-group post-start-up differences. Furthermore, the explanatory statistical analysis (see further) will give us proof that there is indeed a link between the annual growth pattern of personnel or turnover and certain entrepreneurial and managerial behavioral aspects.

Once started a business, it is very important to know what drives an entrepreneur to keep going, these reasons most of the time called *mission* or *goals*? Also interesting to know is what would be changed *if one could start all over again*? Therefore this part covers the inter-group satisfaction rate differences and present motivations. The most occurring ambition to continue the present business activities for all respondents is *to make one's firm as profitable as possible* (47 per cent of the 'Vlerick'-starters and 54 per cent of 'Others'). 'Vlerick'-starters merely want *to grow in a more controlled manner* (38 per cent), and *to build out a firm with a high marketing value* (selling price) (7 per cent). For 'Others' third in rank scores *to survive in the market* (10 per cent). *To grow as much as possible* and *to survive in employment* are not really the case for continuance for either group. Since most of the firms are still existent and growing, not surprisingly about 90 per cent of all interviewed small business-owners replied *positively towards a re-start-up scenario*.

Table 2: Planning Attitudes of 'Vlerick-'Starters and 'Others'

POST-START-UP	'VLERICK'-STARTERS		OTHERS		
Planning skills[11]	average planning attitude* and ↓ well-planners (1-2)**↓	not-planners (per cent of total)	average planning attitude* and ↓ well-planners (1-2)**↓	not-planners (per cent of total)	
- *annual* turnover° (N = 105 and 110)	2,1	65,1	5,35	2,1	62,7	10,71
- *annual gains*° (N = 106 and 109)	2,1	59,8	4,46	2,2	53,2	8,04
- *personal salary* (N = 107 and 109)	2,4	62,9	14,28	2,2	68,8	13,39
- tempo of firm realization°° (N = 103 and 106)	2,3	55,7	2,67	2,2	51,9	16,07
- *number of employees* (N = 108 for both)	2,3	70,6	9,82	2,0	66,1	8,04
- new products (N = 105 for both)	2,4	62,3	16,94	1,9	41,9	19,64
- *financial affairs* (N = 107 for both)	2,1	79,6	3,57	2,1	73,2	5,36
- risk control (N = 106 for both)	2,1	85,0	5,35	2,1	72,3	5,36
- general success rate (N = 107 for both)	2,0	72,2	1,78	2,0	68,2	3,57
- *customer attraction and image* (N = 98 and 105)	1,8	88,9	3,57	1,9	80,0	3,57

*Average planning attitude = mean value on a tree-point scale (1 = firm results were better than planned, 2 = firm results were as planned, and 3 = results were worse than planned); **well-planning percentages; °T-test: p = .000; °T-test: .05 < p < .1.

From the literature it may be concluded that there is an essential relation between the independent variable *business planning* (attitude) and the dependent variable *business growth* (performance) and that planners out-perform non-planners. Recent reviews however also have pointed to certain gaps in our knowledge of planning/performance relationships, caused by (1) the standards used to define small businesses and to assess formal planning, (2) the seldom relevant time periods during which it is measured and (3) the lack of organizational and contextual background information (Shrader, Mulford and Blackburn, 1989; Lyles, Baird, Orris and Kuratko, 1993).[12] The pre- and post-start-up examination of both groups over a period of ten years of business performance fill some of these gaps (cf. supra).

Past efforts to determine the effect of the planning process on firm performance mainly concentrated on dividing firms into those with formal planning systems and those without and related these to measures of financial, sales, turnover, etc. performance. Hence assuming that formal planners will exceed in growth of the firm that of non-formal planners.

Because of the importance of *formal business planning* - making it a persistent element of management - was stressed continuously during 'Vlerick'-*management training*, both groups of business-owners were tested here on ten operational and/or strategic planning criteria, in order to find out about the relationship between business planning behavior and the growth structure of the firm. This counts for both the quantitative aspect (no formal planning versus a (quasi) complete formal planning)[13] and the qualitative or the planning content aspect (planned badly, as expected and better than planned for) as well as for the relation to their respective business growth patterns was depicted over the last ten years. Nevertheless this time factor, planning within the framework of this research only implicitly concerns *an objective and subjective uncertainty*.[14] Business planning might therefore be more likely defined as a *proxy* for a number of organizational activities, periodic strategic management tools and characteristics such as managerial competence, managerial involvement, leadership style, and employee commitment.

For the purpose of this paper *short-term operational* (e.g. finances, employment, market...) as well as (mid-)*long-term strategic planning* (innovation/new products, general success rate of the firm, tempo of realization,...) were tested in their effect on the growth rate of the enterprise and the underlying bond with one or more entrepreneurial characteristics or management techniques. Because it is contended that strategic planning is not practiced commonly by SMEs because they do not have the time nor the funding or the personnel to engage in strategic planning,[15] and -different from operational planning- that it is difficult to identify strategic planning versus performance correlation, categorization between operational (short-term day-to-day functional area problems, -cf. table 2: *printed in italics*-) and strategic (long-range) planning will be made when examining the planning attitude versus business growth pattern relationship.

Although most of the ten items are planned, *personal salary* and *(innovation) new products* are not so intensely planned. The high importance of planning *innovation/new products* to the group of planning businessmen within both groups for their growth of annual turnover and employment/staffing will be observed in the next part. Furthermore, a clear inter-group distinction can be marked for not-planning *the tempo of the firm realization*, being another strategic planning item. More than 16 per cent of 'Others' does not plan this item (eight times the number of the test group). This does however not relate to the qualitative aspect of planning. Even though planned to a lesser ratio, 'Others' plan *the tempo of business realization* better. The relative insignificance however of this planning attitude in relation with business growth will however be demonstrated in the next part.

In conclusion to this quantitative description of inter-group planning differences, about twice as many 'Others' state that they do not plan their *annual turnover* or their *annual gains*. Other levels of planning score similarly for both groups. The next part will show however that planning *annual gains* is significantly correlated with the growth of the firm for both groups. All in all, 'Vlerick'-starters plan a lot more than 'Others', especially on *annual turnover**, *annual gains**, *tempo of realization of the firm*, *innovation/new products**, *financial affairs**, and *the general rate of success**. As the reader will find out the enterprise's growth in turnover for 'Vlerick'-starters (see table 4a) is for 97 per cent due to a combination or set of the five planning attitudes marked with asterisk. Thus far, the conclusion can be made that *'Vlerick'-starters plan more* in order to accelerate their business growth. Though, one should mitigate this amazing finding because only 22 per cent of all 'Vlerick'-starters simultaneously plan on all ten parameters (20,5 per cent for 'Others').

'Vlerick'-starters also plan qualitatively better. The second column of table 2 shows the percentages of well-planning for each item. Again there is a significant difference between values for both groups. Only *personal salary* is planned better by the small business-owners of the control group. At last, both groups are very eager to plan the *customers attraction and the firm's image* correctly. Though, as the reader will find out in the next part planning this item has however a substantial restraining influence on the enterprise growth pattern of enterprises for both groups. In sum, more 'Vlerick'-starters score higher on the quantitative (for 70 per cent of the planning items) and the qualitative element (for 90 per cent). As already observed, less planned parameters are: *innovation/new products* and the *personal salary.* The tendency no to plan *personal salary* can be related to specific Belgian fiscal regulations, and can be understood better when referring to start-up motivations, the top-seven of which does not include *to gain lots of money* or *to become rich.*

Because there is a significant difference in the planning attitude between the two groups, more evidence has been found for hypothesis 1. Outcomes of above cited studies established the general belief that management training positively influences the particular management technique of business planning (cf. hypothesis 2). In how far this relation is causal will be checked through a list of 28 planning-related entrepreneurial and managerial characteristics and techniques (table not inserted). In this way the reader will discover that planning (in its ten dimensions) in itself is strongly influenced indeed by certain (mixtures of) entrepreneurial and managerial attitudes. But, most important, results for this research question reveal that management training 'by its own' does not have that much explanatory value neither to any (positive or negative) planning attitude nor to any dimension that has been assumed. Only in combination with other entrepreneurial and managerial attitudinal factors significance was detected.

Significant discrimination between both tested groups was found for the following variables: *conceptual and rational thinking, subcontracting, human resources management,* and *stock management.* 'Vlerick'-starters and 'Others' score significantly higher on respectively the first and the latter two. Why 'Vlerick'-starters have a higher average score on *conceptual thinking* can be explained by both their higher level of education (less practical and more conceptual-theoretical) and by their willingness to start *a business from scratch,* from an own and mostly *new*

397

idea that needs to be implemented. But, more importantly for this group, through correlation and regression analysis proof has been found for the direct and predictive or causal relation between conceptual thinking and the well-planning behavior leading to business growth.

Smaller differences were noted for the items *leadership*, and *cost accounting*, scoring higher for 'Others' and for *flexibility (low salary)* and *external advise*, having a higher rate for the 'Vlerick'-starters. Once again these patterns underpin the idea that 'Vlerick'-starters try to concentrate *on how to integrate a vision into the firm's life* with outside help and through the implementation by a third party. Of these significantly differing entrepreneurial and managerial variables, in combination with *conceptual thinking*, *external advise* and *delegation of tasks* are the strongest fundaments of all kinds of planning attitudinal combinations of 'Vlerick'-starters that help to increase the firm's turnover performance and growth in staffing (= well-planning). In contrast to the exposed relation between combinations of entrepreneurial and managerial attitudes, planning attitudes and growth of the firm, in the case of 'Others' hardly any of the significantly distinguishing entrepreneurial or managerial qualifications can be tied to business growth insuring planning attitudes. This aspect will be examined in large in the following section.

Because one main effort at the end of management training programs for starting SMEs is paid for the preparation of a business-plan the act of normalization by writing one is an important touchstone of the ability and proficiency of planning *realization of the firm*. This element might partly explains why 'Vlerick'-starters try to plan their *annual turnover* and *annual gains* far more and better than 'Others'. Regression analysis cleared out that those two elements have a meaningful impact of the well-doing or growth of the business household, more exactly in both group's cases . In spite of the fact that 'Others' plan their *tempo of firm realization* better, overall 'Vlerick'-starters are superior in both the quantitative and qualitative facet of operational planning. Moreover, *'Vlerick'-starters plan far more strategically* (cf. *general rate of success, innovation/new products, tempo of realization of the firm*). If planned well and if this strategic planning attitude emanates from a conceptual way of working it will exercise a positive influence on the small enterprise growth. *Innovation/new products* -likely generating company growth for 'Others' when planned effectively or not- and *personal salary* are the least planned items for both the test and control group, though not at all negligible for this research.

The following conclusion can be made from the inter-group entrepreneurial and managerial profile differences: although no significant differences could be noted for about half of the tested entrepreneurial characteristics and managerial techniques, the remaining contrasts nevertheless match the second element of hypothesis 1, saying that there is *a remarkable inter-group profile variance been sharpened by management training*. There is however no manifest indication that one by one these differentiating entrepreneurial and managerial variables a priori determine a profitable or non-profitable business-planning attitude. Certain entrepreneurial and managerial attitude combinations however have a relative high predictive value towards planning behavior and the resulting firm growth pattern. In this they contribute to the search for hard evidence for the second part of hypothesis 3. All in all, at this stage by way of descriptive statistical analysis watertight evidence has been given for the inter-group back-ground differences before the start-up, and the perpetuation of entrepreneurial and managerial profile splitting after the start-up.

Explanatory Statistical Analysis:
Does Management Training make any Difference?

In order to learn about (causal) relationships between management training, environment, entrepreneurial and managerial (or personal) characteristics, planning attitudes and the economical profit for the enterprise the reader should keep the above figure 1b in mind.

In this part arguments in favor of, or against the fact that 'Vlerick'-starters show a higher growth rate because of their specific planning mix and elementary entrepreneurial and managerial attitudinal profile (cf. hypothesis 4) will be searched for. Therefore, firstly the *relationship between the well-planning attitude and enterprise growth* will be examined. Secondly, resulting positive correlation and regression predictive relationships will be looked upon from the perspective of the relationship with possible underlying causes, i.e. *entrepreneurial and managerial characteristics* (see hypothesis 3).

The principal issue at this stage is to determine what entrepreneurial and managerial attitudes generate what kind of operational and/or strategic planning attitudes, these -on their turn- considerably predicting business growth or loss (= EC+MT3)? As the reader goes from the right (economic growth of the enterprise) to the left end of the above figure 1a to find out about causal linkages, firstly the planning versus enterprise growth (being the sole variable that really gives objective and unbiased information) relation will be tested. One way to investigate any causal relation is by exercising correlation resulting in a selection of a pool of positively correlating entrepreneurial and managerial variables and regression analysis for all well-planning businessmen experiencing a positive average growth over the examined period.

In the case of 'Others' regression analysis in some cases (within the group of well-planners) does not have enough variance. Therefore, for 'Others' well-planning categories were fragmented. The associated table 3 learn that *strategic planning* (i.c. *innovation/new products* -being more and better planned by 'Vlerick'-starters) positively correlates with the enterprise growth structure for the two groups, whereas operational planning efforts such as *annual gains* when planned properly -this is above all expectations- catalyses economic benefits for both annual turnover and staffing. Planning the *annual turnover* predicts future business growth when correctly planned by 'Vlerick'-starters and planned no matter how efficiently by 'Others'. The immediate conclusion from these data of might be that for both groups the planning of *innovation/new products* and *annual gains* are highly determining for the growth of the firm. Notwithstanding the extremely high analogy of the planning attitude versus enterprise growth (i.e. *innovation* for all planning categories and *annual gains* for all well-planners (= master-planners)) for the control group, in the case of well-planners of 'Others' planning *annual gains* helps the enterprise grow as well as underrating the planning of *number of personnel/staffing, personal salary* and *financial affairs.*

Table 3: Business Growth Increasing Planning Components for Both Groups (+ Influence)

'VLERICK'	WELL-PLANNING OF	PLANNING OF
growth annual turnover	general rate of success annual gains	
↳ due to a set of ↱ due to a set of	risk control	annual gains innovation/new products
growth annual staffing	annual turnover	

'OTHERS'	WELL-PLANNING OF	PLANNING OF
growth annual turnover		annual turnover
↳ due to a set of ↱ due to a set of	annual gains	annual gains innovation/new products
growth annual staffing		

In the case of 'Vlerick'-starters both *innovation/new products* and *annual gains* planning attitudes (being a combination of strategic and operational planning) are an important piece fitting the planning versus growth puzzle for 'Vlerick'-starters. So, whether planned properly or not, the planning of *innovation/new products* has a positive impact on the increase of the annual turnover and number of employees of both groups. As already argued in the previous section planning more frequently and better the *general success rate, annual turnover,* and *risk control* has a high predictive value towards the increase of the annual turnover for *'Vlerick'-master-planners.* For 'Vlerick'-starters the post-training planning of *risk control* and *annual turnover* also positively relate to the yearly growth of staffing. Thus, in addition to the descriptive planning results regression analysis sheds light upon those planning attitudes that are significantly more and better planned by 'Vlerick'-starters and at the same time increase chances for business growth.

Nearly all sampled enterprises have been growing both in annual turnover and staffing during the post-start-up period (see table 1a). There is one important difference though between the average firm of both groups: the growth speed or annual growth rate of the firm. It has become clear that the growth speed of 'Vlerick'-starters is higher than that of 'Others'. In relation to the outcome of the descriptive analysis, intuitively arguments to explain any inter-group discrepancy related to the above schematized planning profiles were given. These might help to uncover the tight relationship between management training and business growth. Table 1a (see up) shows that the correlation between *the growth pattern for the annual turnover and staffing is significantly positive* for 'Vlerick'-starters (.84*), while the correlation is negative for 'Others'. Many authors argue therefore that raising employment is due to new venture creation and does not stem that much from the annual turnover growth produced by growing firms (= growth firms).[16] This information perfectly matches the information of table 3 underpinning the heavy homogeneous and resembling (well-)planning 'Vlerick'-profile for annual turnover and staffing.

Altogether, there are unmistakable indications of certain positive planning versus business growth interdependencies for both groups. In support of the first element of hypothesis 4 these interdependencies are marked by significant inter-group differences in the pools or clusters of growth-generating planning attitudes and has been summarized in the above table 3. In the following part the reader will learn about the fundamental entrepreneurial and managerial characteristics and profiles that relate the above illustrated planning profiles.

Entrepreneurial characteristics and managerial techniques versus operational and strategic planning: is management training a linking factor?

Quantitative and qualitative planning information not only provides insight in inter-group planning profiles but should implicitly be linked to *business performance-related ratios* (e.g. the planning profile versus the annual growth of turnover and employment); hence we have explained in the previous part how *operational and strategic planning* can be translated into economical performance and growth. O'Neill and Duker's (1986) findings suggest that any significant entrepreneurial or managerial parameter can be used to enhance the strategic planning and hence the performance of SMEs (Balantine, Cleveland, and Koeller, 1992). Again due to the small number of firms reporting that the performance was better than planned, the three qualitative planning categories were dichotomized into (1) performance better or equal as planned, and (2) performance worse than planned.

Through correlation and multiple regression analysis at a 5 per cent level of significance the explanatory value and causality between (sets of) entrepreneurial or managerial characteristics (independent grouping variable) and the dependent pool of (well-)planning attitudes will be examined, pre-selecting only these planning attitudes that positively influence business growth and out-selecting all restraining ones. From tripled correlation for all 28 independent entrepreneurial and managerial variables and all ten dependent operational and strategic planning variables a correlation matrix resulted containing the analysis for (1) well-planning businessmen (cf. Spearman R: R > .30) as well as for (2) the general planning attitude (*Spearman R*: .10 < R < .30).[17]

In the case of 'Vlerick'-starters, relative to this pre-selected pool of entrepreneurial and managerial characteristics which are positively correlating with all 5 business growth predicting planning attitudinal elements, regression analysis indicates in how far the growth augmenting planning attitudes are caused by what entrepreneurial and/or managerial qualifications. For both groups the entrepreneurial characteristics (EC) and managerial techniques (MT) are summarized in the figure 3 (= EC+MT3). Through regression analysis the well-planning scenarios for *annual turnover, annual gains, innovation/new products,* and *risk control* for 'Vlerick'-starters are caused for a rather indicative percentage (in-between 1,7 and 7,7 per cent) by different groups of entrepreneurial and managerial attitudes consisting out of *time management, client orientation, conceptual thinking,* and *personal ambition*. These elements are to be considered *positively influencing the growth generating planning behavior*. Apart from *external advise* and *delegation of tasks* all other significantly correlating entrepreneurial and managerial characteristics have a positive effect on the planning behavior.

Figure 3: The (Well-)Planning Entrepreneurial and Managerial Starters' Profile

'Vlerick'-starters: entrepreneurial tinted well-planning profile

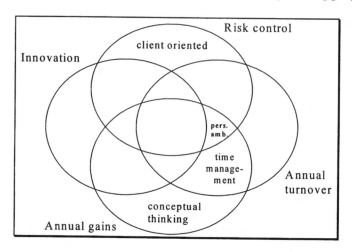

'Others': managerial tinted well-planning profile

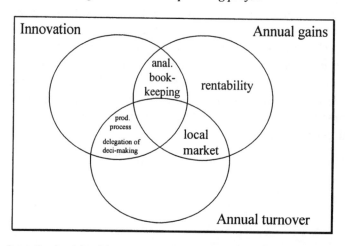

Proportional weight of the entrepreneurial and managerial characteristics on the divers growth creating planning proficiencies: for 'Vlerick'-(well-)planning starters for *annual gains* = 4 per cent; for *risk control* = variable; for *innovation/new products* = variable; and for *annual turnover* = 4 per cent; for Others' *innovation* = 17 per cent; for *annual gains* = 18 per cent; and for *annual turnover* = 10 per cent (of a total list of 28 EC+MT (cf. supra)).

Master-planning 'Vlerick'-starters plan predominantly *strategically*, the most when it comes to planning correctly the annual growth of turnover. Remarkably however two out of the four planning attitudes that correlate significantly positive with the pre-selected entrepreneurial and managerial characteristics are of *the operational kind*. Moreover, not regressing with any of entrepreneurial and managerial profile constituents for 'Vlerick'-starters is the planning of the *general rate of success*. Because of the dualistic declarative value of *personal ambition* and *conceptual thinking* for both strategic and operational planning one may conclude that only for the operational business growth yielding planning of *annual gains* and *annual turnover* of the 'Vlerick'-starters one indisputable entrepreneurial and managerial characteristic can be found (i.c. *time management*), whereas this is not the case for the respective strategic planning comportment.

For the group of 'Others' 14 overall positively correlating qualifications were selected from correlation matrix. In the case of (well-) planning 'Others' chances for growth increasing planning behavior are mainly positively linked to *analytic book-keeping, local market competition*, and *rentability*. Note that the explanatory value of these variables is much higher (4,5 to 13 per cent) than in the case of 'Vlerick'-starters. This is of course due to an *extreme low variance* between the cases included in the sample (based on the selection of all cases planning the three items simultaneously). *Production process* and *delegation of decision-making* show a dualistic relationship with planning: the latter one positively influencing planning of annual turnover and at the same time negatively influencing the planning of innovation/new products; and just the other way around for *production process*.

As argued before, SME-businessmen with a better planning proficiency would have a distinctive entrepreneurial, managerial and self-employing profile from non- or bad-planners. On that account, reference can be made to the observed inter-group planning and entrepreneurial and managerial profile discrepancies (see previous part). Also, the higher business growth rate of 'Vlerick'-starters is likely due to the inter-group managerial and entrepreneurial attitudinal differences. Because of the *economical, entrepreneurial and managerial differences* between a management trained and not by The Vlerick School of Management trained group of small business-owners remains the focus, the argumentation for the *post-start-up variance* in the evolution of the firms, can presumably to

405

some extent be assigned to this one differentiating element: *management training* (understood to be an enhancing factor for the SME business). Basic statistics, non-parametric statistics, and ANOVA/MANOVA correlation tests using 'performance/growth' as the dependent variable pointed out that management training positively influences the growth pattern of the relevant enterprises but only when stimulating those entrepreneurial and managerial business techniques that induce a better operational and/or strategic planning attitude.

On the one hand, in the case of 'Others' *education/training* does not significantly correlate at a 5 per cent level of significance with any of the determination entrepreneurial or managerial variables: neutrally with *rentability* (-.04) and *production process* (.10) and positively with *local market competition*(.15). The fact that all withheld business growth generating entrepreneurial attitudes relate neutrally or negatively to the educational item and the way in which business growth restraining entrepreneurial characteristics relate positively to '*education/training* hence mitigates the relative importance of the latter item in determining the planning profile of 'Others'. Of all positive correlating attitudinal parameters for 'Others' only *analytic book-keeping* unites around the *education/training* branch. On the other hand, the 'Vlerick'-starters (well-) planning profile correlates positively -although not significantly- with all entrepreneurial or managerial characteristics (ranging from .05 to .22 at a 5 per cent level of significance). Therefore, clustered tree structures confirm the basic relating factor to be *education/training* (cf. figure 4). Although only four entrepreneurial and managerial characteristics were found to have a considerable proportionally stimulating impact on wealth-generating planning abilities, *education/training* groups three of them at the right side of the tree structure within one Euclidean distance or range: i.e. *client orientation, conceptual thinking,* and *personal ambition*. Intuitively, the positive linkage between business growth stimulating planning profile of entrepreneurial and managerial characteristics and the element of *education/training* is more apparent for 'Vlerick'-starters, in this confirming hypothesis 3.

Figure 4: Tree Structure for all Entrepreneurial Characteristics and Managerial Techniques

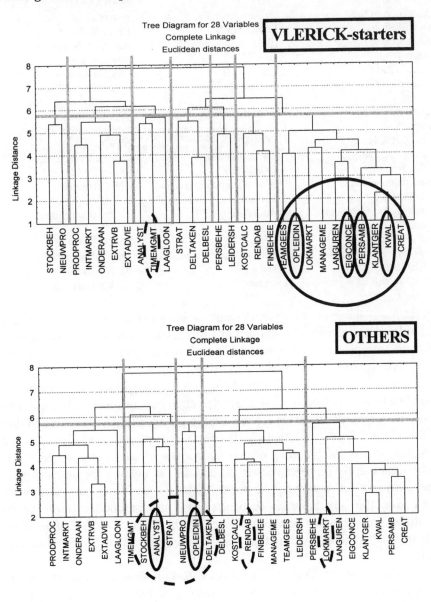

407

In sum, in the case of 'Vlerick'-starters business growth will be likely stimulated and eventually attained at a sufficient level of attention paid to certain entrepreneurial characteristics and managerial techniques, namely *personal ambition, conceptual thinking, client orientation*, and *time management*; three out of four being clear *entrepreneurial entries*. In combination these entrepreneurial elements can originate efficient and realistic planning scenarios for the *annual gains, annual turnover* and *risk control* (in 3,5 to 7 per cent of all cases). Accordingly, whether planned properly or not the planning of *innovation/new products* and *annual gains* will significantly (respectively in 20 and 29 per cent of the cases) higher the chances for enterprise growth, both in personnel and turnover!! However, the link between *innovation* and the grouped entrepreneurial attitudes was found to be inconclusive. To the 'Vlerick'-growth generating planning attitudinal combination *time management* plays a very important role.

In the case of 'Others', based on a certain degree of *analytic book-keeping* (5 to 13 per cent), *local market competition* (4 per cent) and *rentability* (all three elements being typically managerial entries) 'Others' are likely to grow both in terms of turnover (in 11 per cent of the cases) and staffing (in 51 per cent of the cases) if only the combination of *innovation/new products, annual turnover*, and *annual gains* strategy is planned. Except for paying attention to the planning of the *local market competition* (resp. .56 and .66) in the case of planning *annual turnover* and *annual gains* no significant predictive or causal links could be traced between the entrepreneurial and managerial profile and the (well-)planning of this threefold combination. Therefore, only this element makes the planning profile of 'Others' as conclusive as that of 'Vlerick'-starters. On the contrary, it has become clear that *management training by itself does not have that much explanatory value* neither to any (positive or negative) planning attitude nor to any dimension that has been assumed. Only in combination with other entrepreneurial and managerial attitudinal factors significance was detected.

Conclusion

All data and findings of this research do not entirely clarify the importance or the impact of management training on the planning of annual gains, turnover or innovation etc., neither do they explain the relationship with all other operational planning efforts for a 100 percent. Innovating however to already existing studies is the way in which the formality and content of operational and strategic planning has both been tested within one item of the questionnaire. This means that at the same time the reader gets an idea about the different planned items (qualitative element), how successful planning was experienced (quantitative element) and what kind of management was argued to lead to what positive planning result.

In support of the above correlation and implicitly hypothesis 3 some additional evidence for the critical linkage that 'Vlerick'-starters apparently make between the necessity of planning *annual gains*, the *annual turnover* and *risk control* and the management training has been found. This linkage can be explained by the set-up of most of the management training courses: normally management training courses for SME-start-ups contain different modules ranging from strategy, marketing, legal aspects, HRM, and last but not least to financial issues and related issues. Clearly the way in which general and comprehensive management concepts (involving annual growth of turnover, gains and risk control) were trained shows that this training has obviously had some influence on the management of the daily business-process. Since no relevant linkage with the educational variable was found for 'Others' any analogous linkage is however absent for the control group, again supporting the content of hypothesis 3. Except for planning risks this is hence not different from the (well-)planning attitude of 'Others'.

Confirming the content of hypothesis 4 evidence has yet been found for that *typical forms of entrepreneurial or managerial behavior* can to a certain degree of certainty contribute to the business growth (turnover and employment) but only through its energizing or multiplication effect on the operational and strategic business planning!! The assumption that 'Vlerick'-starters typically start from a personal conception or an innovative idea has been sustained both in terms of their pre-start-up profile and their post-start-up proficient planning profile. The fact that their entrepreneurial based growth related planning behavior is conditioned mainly by their *personal ambition, conceptual thinking, client orientation* and *time management* thus makes the 'full circle'. After all, the foremost important task of management training programs in general is to explicit the conceptual thinking by ways of comprehensive strategies within the socio-economical context or structure of SMEs. In the mean time only those small business-starters that signal the need for refining their conceptual thinking into *a strategy and planning proficiency* will be accepted for the management training; the search for outside help being just a symptom of this quest. Supporting hypothesis 2 outside help by a third person or a training institute -typical for 'Vlerick'-starters- is not that apparent for 'Others'.

The convergence effect of those determinants that significantly predict growth generating planning attitudes around the independent variable *education/training* for 'Vlerick'-starters (cf. figure 4) broadens possibilities for interpretation for its relative impact on *successful operational and managerial decision-making and planning skills*. In this *'Vlerick'-starters plan more and better*, they equally balance their planning attitude between operational and strategic options and consequently are able to generate a higher business growth. Thus, not surprisingly, the growth rate of both tested parameters (annual turnover and number of personnel) is significantly higher for the test group than for 'Others'. In the case of 'Vlerick'-starters this growth pattern, the pre-start-up and post-start-up entrepreneurial, managerial and planning profile (activities) could be slightly linked to the parameter *education/training*, underwriting its leverage or interaction effect on the whole process (cf. figure 1b) (hypothesis 3). This is not the case of 'Others'.

Differences in the entrepreneurial and managerial profile logically might lead to different planning abilities. But, also *other elements* (see figure 1a) could have caused any adaptation, e.g. to environmental, economical and personal uncertainties and changes. Therefore further investigation will be needed on the linkage between the pre-start-up motivation, age distribution, level of education, etc. and the actual growth pattern of the enterprise. Moreover, a very rigid selection was done only checking planning business-owners attitudinal behavior and its relation to their business growth rate. Therefore, further research ought to be done on how this relationship specifically looks like for non- and bad-planners.

Furthermore, because of the heterogeneous operational and strategically planning attitudes of the annual turnover and staffing the introduction of a typology for planning start-up SME-business-owners (more or less entrepreneurial than managerial) is very hard and rather food for thought. Another restriction to this research is that business growth has only been tested through the annual turnover and staffing. These are of course the most frequently quoted business growth parameters in academic journals and other study materials, but nevertheless the measurement of *business success* can be made more comprehensive. Amongst others critical success factors that could be included are market share, client service/satisfaction, internal decision-making processes, return on investment, strategy and governance, personnel or staffing (HRM), etc. Also, comparable examination of the partition of stopped business-owners can be done as a manner to double-check if the now selected criteria for business growth are truly typically for well-planning business-owners' profiles or not. These defined independent entrepreneurial and managerial variables and planning attitudes could of course in some cases also lead to the enterprise stoppage due to the impact of *other elements*. The latter topic has for this paper mainly been covered and compensated by the descriptive statistical analysis. At last, what could have happened to the enterprises that did not answer the questionnaire (non-response rate)? Here too more research, by ways of questionnaire or interviews, ought to be done.

Evidence has yet been found for typical forms of entrepreneurial or managerial behavior that can to a certain degree of probability (certainty?) contribute to the business growth (turnover and employment) but only through its energizing or multiplication effect on the operational and strategic business planning, among them the convergence effect of those determinants that significantly predict growth generating planning attitudes around the independent variable *education/training.*

This research will hopefully lead to further actions for experimentation with and elaboration of management training programs for start-ups and early stage growth firms by centers for continuous education. Important for local as well as federal governments throughout Europe is the fact these unique educational and vocational intertwined management programs are presumably leading to better, more equilibrated and more frequently performed ways of business planning and control. In this survival and growth sustainability ought to be further and more consistently insured for the future...

Notes

[1] The authors wish to acknowledge the financial support of the Fortis (former: General Bank (Belgium)) including the person of Katrien Leger for the data collection and the empirical research on which this study is based.

[2] The Department of Small and Medium Businesses (SMEs) of the Vlerick Leuven Gent Management School (former: De Vlerick School voor Management (University of Gent - Belgium)) has over eleven years long experience in organising management training programmes for starting SME-businessmen or business-owners. Following programmes for small business starters were organized on a pseudo-continuous base during the 1987-1998 period: '(Pre-) Starters Programme', 'SME-Challenge Programme', 'SME-Excellence Programme', 'SME-Perfection Programme', 'and Woman and Entrepreneurship'.

[3] Because it seems impossible to quantify and conglomerate the effects and entrepreneurial, managerial and self-employing characteristics of entrepreneurship inside one definite holistic structure, this research is another attempt to determine what kind of entrepreneurial-managerial-self-employing interrelations originate from what contextual business background.

[4] Most of the research concerning this category has focused on the impact of planning methods (that is, the degree of planning formality) on a firm's performance. Although there are exceptions, strong empirical support exists for the thesis that formal planning out-performs informal planning in large firms.

[5] At first the research group received 73 completed copies of the questionnaire and took the initiative to do another mailing to all remaining non-respondents backed up by a broad telephonic audit. Before the foreseen deadline another 45 questionnaires were returned. This operation totaled a very high response rate compared to other SME follow-up studies and surveys. Four questionnaires were excluded from statistical analysis for the following reasons: because of far too explosive (production or employee) growth rates which would have distorted most of the results of frequency tables or because of the stoppage of the firm's activities.

[6] The questionnaire was based upon a sixfold series of interviews with SME-businessmen in order to select and include the utmost plausible and statistical useful questions and answering possibilities.

[7] Ten years ago, the fraction of women in our management training programmes was far too little to analyze. Since then the Centre of SMEs launched the 'Women and Entrepreneurship programme'. Still, statistical analysis is insignificant compared to the total population of female entrepreneurs. No comparative study was done on this matter between the 'Vlerick'-starters and 'Others'. On the subject, see Scherer, Brodzinski and Wiebe, 1990, 'Entrepreneur Career Selection and Gender: a socialization approach', *Journal of Small Business Management*, vol. 28, no. 2, 37-44.

[8] On a national and international scale the average start-up age is 36 years old.

[9] Although 'to earn lots of money' did not count high for the first and second choice, it has got the second highest rating within the third choice category (right behind 'the challenge to become independent'), respectively 10,71 and 14,29 per cent for 'Vlerick'-starters and 'Others'.

[10] Nowadays however competition within the field of management training and counselling for start-ups is heavier then ever before and erodes our department's unique market position

413

more and more forcing us to undertake innovative steps concerning the course layout, content, selection of participants, etc.

[11] Question sets as were described by Lyles, Baird, Orris and Kurato (1993) and Bracker and Pearson (1986) formed the basis to set out *a four-dimensional ordinal planning formality and content scale* (e.g. 1 = the performance was better than planned; 2 = the performance was as planned; 3 = the performance was worse than planned; 4 = the performance was not-planned). Due to the small number of firms reporting that the performance was better than planned, the three qualitative planning categories were dichotomised into (1) *performance better or equal as planned*, and (2) *performance worse than planned*. Leftover are *non-planners*, but they will not be further discussed within the scope of this paper.

[12] See for example, Mintzberg, 1991, 'The Entrepreneurial Organization', in: ed. Mintzberg and Quinn, *The Strategy Process*, Engelwood Cliffs, N.J.: Prentice-Hall, 604-613; and Naffziger and Kuratko, 1991, 'An Investigation into the Prevalence of Planning in Small Business', *Journal of Small Business and Entrepreneurship*, vol. 3, no. 2, 99-109.

[13] Olson and Bokor, 1995, l.c., 37.

[14] Matthews, C.H., and Scott, S.G. (1995) 'Uncertainty and Planning in Small and Entrepreneurial Firms: an empirical assessment', *Journal of Small Business Management*, vol. 33, no. 4, 34 and 40.

[15] Robinson and Pearce, 1988, 'Planned Patterns of Strategic Behavior and Their Relationship to Business-Unit Performance', *Strategic Management Journal*, vol. 14, no. 4, 43-60.

[16] See Crijns, H. and Ooghe, H., 'Entrepreneurial Companies as Job Creators in Belgium: the processes of professionalization of management and institutionalization of ownership', and Hufft, E.M., 'A Comparison of the Ownership and Growth of Family Businesses and Small Firms', *42nd World Conference International Council for Small Business*, Journal of Best Papers, San Francisco, June 1997.

[17] Only originally retrieved significant correlations by one-way ANOVA/ MANOVA which were reinforced by either the sign or the intensity of the Spearman R rank correlation value for ordinal scales were selected for further research on their relative impact on business survival and growth. The adhered methodology is generally accepted and is described in Huizingh, E. (1996) *SPSS voor Windows*, Academic Service - economie en bedrijfskunde, Schoonhoven - Holland, p. 286.

References

Atherton, A. and and Hannon, P. (1995) 'The Business Plan - A 21st Century Dinosaur?,' in: Klandt, H. and Muller-Boling (ed.), *IntEnt '95 Proceedings*, 22.

Atherton, A., and Hannon, P. (1996) 'Building Strategic Awareness Capability - The cognitive tools and methods of thinking of small business owner-managers,' 24. Stockholm: paper presented at the 41st ICSB World Conference.

Attahir, Y. (April 1995) 'Critical Success Factors for Small Business: perceptions of South Pacific Entrepreneurs,' *Journal of Small Business Management*, vol. 33, no. 2, 68-73.

Ballantine, J.W., Frederick, W.C. and Koeller, C.T. (April 1992) 'Characterizing Profitable and Unprofitable Strategies in Small and Large Businesses,' *Journal of Small Business Management*, vol. 30, no. 2, 13-24.

Brown, R. (October 1990) 'Encouraging Enterprise: Britain's Graduate Enterprise Programme,' *Journal of Small Business Management*, vol. 28, no. 4, 71-77.

Cooper, A.C. and Gascon, F.J. 'Entrepreneurs, Processes of Founding, and New-Firm Performance,' in: Sexton, D. and Kasarda, J.D. (1992) The State of the Art of Entrepreneurship, 301-340. Boston: PWS-Kent Publishing Company.

Covin, T.J. (July 1994) 'Perceptions of Family-Owned Firms: the impact of gender and educational level,' *Journal of Small Business Management*, vol. 32, no. 3, 29-39.

Crant, J.M. (June 1996) 'The Proactive Personality Scale as a Predictor of Entrepreneurial Intentions,' *Journal of Small Business Management*, vol. 34, no. 3, 42-49.

Daily, C. and Dalton, D.R. (April 1992) 'Financial Performance of Founder-Managed versus Professionally Managed Small Corporations,' *Journal of Small Business Management*, vol. 30, no. 2, 25-34.

Day, D.L., 'Research Linkages between Entrepreneurship and Strategic Management or General Management,' in: Sexton, D. and Kasarda, J.D. (1992) The State of the Art of Entrepreneurship, 117-163. Boston: PWS-Kent Publishing Company.

Dillman, D.A. (1978) Mail and Telephone Surveys: The Total Design Method. New York: Wiley-Interscience.

Fuller, E. (1993) 'Small Business Trends, Some Implications for Skills and Training into the Next Century,' 20. United Kingdom: Skills and Enterprises Network.

Gibb, A.A. (1995) 'The Role of Education and Training in Small and Medium Enterprise in Europe: creating an agenda for action,' Inter-Ministerial Conference of Education and Employment Ministries of the European Union and Partner States, in: Small and Medium Enterprise Education, 1-35. Italy: Italian Foreign Ministry and European Training Foundation.

Gibb, A.A. and Nelson E. (1996) 'Personal Competencies, Training and Assessment: a challenge for small business trainers,' 26th EFMD European Small Business Seminar, in: Developing Core Competencies, 97-108. Finland: Center for Continuing Education, University of Vaäsa, Vaäsa.

Hornaday, R.W. (October 1990) 'Dropping the E-Words from Small Business Research: an alternative typology,' *Journal of Small Business Management*, vol. 28, no. 4, 22-33.

Kirby, D.A. (October 1990) 'Management Education and Small Business Development: an exploratory study of small firms in the UK,' *Journal of Small Business Management*, vol. 28, no. 4, 78-87.

Kuratko, D.F. (March 1995) 'The Real Challenges are Risk, Stress, Ego, and Motivation,' *Entrepreneurship, Innovation, and Change*, vol. 4, no. 1, 3-10.

Lyles, M.A., Baird, I.S., Orris, B. and Kuratko, D.F. (April 1993) 'Formalized Planning in Small Business: increasing strategic choices,' *Journal of Small Business Management*, vol. 31, no. 2, 38-50.

Matthews, C.H. and Scott, S.G. (October 1995) 'Uncertainty and Planning in Small and Entrepreneurial Firms: an empirical assessment,' *Journal of Small Business Management*, vol. 33, no. 4, 34-52.

Olson, Ph.D. and Bokor, D.W. (January 1995) 'Strategy Process-Content Interaction: effects on growth performance in small, start-up firms,' *Journal of Small Business Management*, vol. 33, no. 1, 34-44.

Rosa, P., Scott, M.G. and Klandt, H., (1996) Educating Entrepreneurs in Modernizing Economies. England/USA: Stirling Management Series, Avebury.

Shrader, C.B., Mulford, C. and Blackburn, V.L. (October 1989) 'Strategic and Operational Planning, Uncertainty, and Performance in Small Firms,' *Journal of Small Business Management*, vol. 27, no. 4, 45- 60.

Van Clouse, G.H. (April 1990) 'A Controlled Experiment Relating Entrepreneurial Education to Students' Start-Up Decisions,' *Journal of Small Business Management*, vol. 28, no. 2, 45-53.

22 University-small Firms Relationships: Strategic Paths of Academic Spin-offs

Emilio Bellini
Guido Capaldo
Mario Raffa
Giuseppe Zollo[1]

Introduction

Start-ups are common in emerging industries, such as personal computers, software, industrial control, biotechnology, and so on. Those sectors are characterized by the presence of many competing and often redundant companies, created under the double opportunities of availability of resources and growing market demand. A wide range of strategic and organizational choices are available for those firms, because traditions, habits, culture, standard process technology and reference examples are almost completely absent (Kao, 1991). In such conditions the entrepreneurs must deal with a high degree of uncertainty both internally and externally. The original culture, vision, skills of the entrepreneur are the unique factors which can turn the original ambiguity, uncertainty and disorder into a successful organization (Filion, 1991).

As most part of ambiguity and uncertainty comes from technological side, the new entrepreneurs with a strong scientific and technological competence are regarded as more appropriate in high-tech sectors. Those competencies are present in all the organizations knowledge-based as research centres, high technology firms and Universities. Consequently, Universities are regarded as actors that could play a major economic role by transforming knowledge in marketable products and services. The most common types of involvement of universities in economic activities are based on the *knowledge transferring*, such as consultant activities, training activities, joint R&D projects and patenting (Bonaccorsi, Piccaluga, 1994). The direct and continuous involvement of universities' personnel in *knowledge transforming*, that is in direct exploitation of scientific and technological knowledge, is rare, even if positive effects for economic environment are high (Berman, 1990).

The *Academic Spin-offs (ASOs)* are regarded as the major type of knowledge transforming activities. According to current definition of Academic Spin-offs (Smilor et al. 1990, Formica and Mitra, 1996) three types of companies are included in such a category:

i)   companies founded by teaching or research staff of universities;
ii)   companies founded by student and graduates to exploit commercially the results of research in which they have been involved at university;
iii)   companies founded to exploit commercially the results of university's researches.

In this paper we define as Academic Spin-offs only companies belonging to the first two types, that is when commercial exploitation of scientific and technological knowledge is realized by university scientists (teachers or researchers), students and graduates. In those cases the Academic Spin-offs follow the model suggested by Richter (1986): in the incubation stage the university scientists develop considerable consulting practices for private companies, and at the same time they manage research teams, that have the character of 'quasi-firm'. It is sufficient the perception of a profitable market occasion to convince the scientists to move from ordinary consulting activities into entrepreneurial activities.

Within this framework the authors have been developed a research on the strategic paths of the Academic Spin-offs. In this paper they present some preliminary findings based on an empirical research on ten Academic Spin-offs operating in Information Technology industry.
The paper presents as follows:

- in the section 2 some remarks on the start up of the Academic Spin-offs;

- in the section 3 the theoretical framework of *competence-based competition* as strategic theory to analyze the dynamics of the Academic Spin-offs;
- in the section 4 the methodology and the sample of the empirical research;
- in the section 5 the findings of the empirical research;
- in the section 6 some preliminary implications of the findings;
- in the section 7 the limits and the open problems of this research.

Key Questions on the Academic Spin-offs

Personal abilities, commitments and individual attitudes are seen to be the critical factor of successful Academic Spin-offs. An increasing number of studies refers to the personal characteristics of the entrepreneur as the key to the success of the firm in the early stages of its life (Miller et al. 1988). Roberts and Hauptman (1986) demonstrated that founders' characteristics were associated with the technological level of the firm's product. Moreover, Roberts (1991) presents a simple model which assumes that new companies are based on the technological knowledge learned by the entrepreneur from the 'mother environment', i.e. former companies, university laboratories, engineering departments.

The core aspect of the firms surveyed in this paper, is the *transforming* of scientific knowledge developed in the Universities, in useful knowledge to realize competitive products for the market.

The key problem in the start-up of the Academic Spin-offs is the difficulty to translate the academic knowledge in managerial and organizational objectives.

This does not imply that the firm's performances should be attributed only to the entrepreneurial characteristics. During the passage from organizational infancy to adulthood the firm undergoes several transformations which reduce the central role of the entrepreneur (Greiner, 1972). Nevertheless, the technical knowledge of the founder-entrepreneur plays a crucial role during the first stage of the firm's life, and the main issues concern the skills and culture of the entrepreneur, together with the availability of professional services and the financial support. During the growth stage, a more complex set of resources is necessary to sustain the firm's activities, and the main issues regard availability of financial resources, organizational weaknesses, availability of specialized suppliers, availability of professional services. Actually, those issues are strictly linked, to the weaknesses of the entrepreneurial culture in the initial stage. In our opinion a political guidance of academic spin-offs should support, together with adequate services and financial support, the formation of an adequate entrepreneurial and managerial culture, that will display positive effects in the maturity stage. The weakness of academic culture as regards the managerial objectives shows its effects during the passage from the designing products activities to building organization ones.

According to this point of view, two key problems arise:

- a problem in the start-up stage linked to the difficulty of the academic entrepreneurs in transforming their know-how in operative objectives;
- a problem in the development stage linked to the difficulty of academic entrepreneurs in shifting their attention from product building (where the technical aspects are predominant) to organization building (where the managerial aspects are predominant).

To face those problems we have to give some answer to the following questions:

i) What is the role played by the culture, education and skills of the academic entrepreneur in sustaining the competitive advantage of small firms?
ii) How do entrepreneurs adjust their know-how in the course of the firms' life?
iii) What is the interrelations between initial know-how and firms development?
iv) What are the limits of spontaneous academic spin-offs;
v) Is it possible a political guidance in order to pass from spontaneous actions to planned ones?

In the next section we develop a model founded on the *competence-based competition* to give a set of possible answers to the previous questions.

A 'Competence-based Competition' Perspective on Academic Spin-offs

An interesting contribution to the analysis of Academic Spin-offs comes from concepts developed within the theoretical framework of competence-based competition, stimulated by articles and books by Gary Hamel and C.K. Prahalad beginning in the late 1980s (Hamel 1989; Prahalad and Hamel 1990; Hamel 1991; Prahalad and Hamel 1993; Hamel and Heene 1994; Sanchez, Heene and Thomas 1996). The ambitious objective of researchers moving within this theoretical framework is to incorporate the dynamic and cognitive aspects of the core competence perspective in a wider theory of strategic management. New emphasis is given to intangible assets, knowledge creation, shared vision, co-ordination activity.

According to the competence-based competition theory the firm is a learning organization that builds and deploys assets, capabilities, skills in order to achieve strategic goals (Hamel, Heene, 1994).

The *assets* are anything tangible or intangible the firm can use in its processes for creating, producing, and/or offering its product to a market. *Capabilities* are repeatable patterns of action in the use of assets to create, produce, and/or offer products to a market. *Competence* is an ability to sustain the co-ordinated deployment of assets in a way that helps a firm achieve its goals.

To define a business activity as a *competence* three conditions are needed (Sanchez, Heene e Thomas, 1996): *intention* in the use of assets, *organization* in co-ordinating a deployment of assets, and *goal attainment*.

Within the competence-based theory the following concepts are relevant for the analysis of the Academic Spin-offs:

i) Competence Building

It is any process by which a firm achieves qualitative changes in its assets, capabilities and skills, including new abilities to co-ordinate and deploy of existing assets. Competence building creates new options for future actions. The birth of a new firm is a process of competence building, as the entrepreneur is developing new abilities in co-ordination of his own skills and is setting-up new assets, capabilities and skills. As competence building defines the firm's power to act, it is important to detect the available assets. As regarding Academic Spin-offs the most important initial asset is the technical competence of the entrepreneur. We expect the more the Academic Spin-offs are involved in competence building activities the more the skills of employees and capabilities will change.

ii) Competence Leveraging

It is the applying of a firm's existing competencies to market opportunities in ways that require only quantitative changes in the firm's assets or capabilities. The competence leveraging is the exercising the existing options for action. It is important to emphasize that the competence leveraging require a very high ability to detect and develop market opportunities. While the competence building process emphasizes technological issues, the competence leveraging process emphasizes market issues. As regarding Academic Spin-offs, the competence leveraging should be regarded as strategy aimed to the growth of firm assets. We expect the more the Academic Spin-offs are involved in competence leveraging activities the more they will increase the market share, the cash flows, the number of employees.

iii) Firm-specific Assets

They are those assets which a firm owns or tightly controls. While large firms could run their business only with specific assets, small firms usually possess an incomplete set of internal resources. We can suppose that when Academic Spin-offs start their business they should develop their initial resources and design a suitable organization to co-ordinate internal and external resources.

iv) Firm-addressable Assets

They are those which a firm does not own or tightly control, but which he is able to address and use. The ability to address external resources is a primary competence for Academic Spin-offs. This ability, which we define as 'networking activity', is mainly liked to competence building process, even if in some cases small firms address external resources with the aim of competence leveraging in order to cut costs and react more rapidly to market opportunities.

v) Causal Ambiguities

It is a property of managerial cognition which affect the evaluation and decision process concerning both the competence building and leveraging and the definition of strategic goals. For Academic Spin-offs the causal ambiguities have two dimensions. The first dimension regards the inherently ambiguous data gathered from the turbulent environment characterizing the innovative economic sectors in which Academic Spin-offs operate. The second dimension regards perceptions of managers, whose interpretations are strongly influenced by their technical orientation. We expect that Academic Spin-offs overestimate technical aspects, while they underestimate marketing issues.

vi) Co-ordination Ability

It is the management process through which firms co-ordinate deployments of assets and capabilities. For Academic Spin-offs, and in general for small innovative firms, the primary task of co-ordination concern the management of human resources and the integration of different skills and technical knowledge.

The 'competence-based' perspective suggests us a general framework to interpret the development of Academic Spin-offs, and in general of small innovative firms. Two dimensions define the *Field of Action of Small Innovative Firms*:

i) the types of prevalent assets (*specific* or *addressable*);
ii) the ways in deployment of assets (for competence *building* or *leveraging*).

Figure 1 illustrates four situations which connect assets and their deployment.

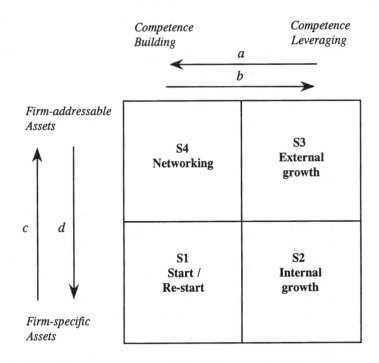

Figure 1 - The Field of Action of Small Innovative Firms

Situation #1, named 'Starting/Restarting' (Competence Building/Firm Specific Assets) characterizes the development of new strategic options through the building of new internal competencies.

Situation #2, named 'Internal Growth', (Competence Leveraging/Firm Specific Assets) defines a growth strategy through the acquisition of new resources similar to the previous ones.

Situation #3, named 'External Growth' (Competence Leveraging /Firm Addressable Assets) defines a growth strategy through relationships with external actors (consultants, technicians, other firms).

Situation #4, named 'Networking' (Competence Building /Firm Addressable Assets) defines a strategy of building new competencies through relationships with external actors.

Our hypothesis is that, because financial, human, technological resources, small innovative firms can not occupy the whole field of action at the same time. Thus the small firm is forced to oscillate between the activities of Competence Building and Competence Leveraging (dynamics a and b in the Fig. 1), and between the deployment of Firm Addressable Assets and Firm Specific Assets (dynamics c and d in the Fig. 1). This dynamics let small firms to redefine their strategic options for action and to effectively deploy its assets.

By observing the sequence of the dynamics followed by a single firm it is possible to reconstruct its strategic path.

Particularly, Academic Spin-offs should start in Situation #1, when the academic entrepreneur redefines the strategic goal of his activity, and then he should move to Situation #2 in order to leverage existing competence to achieve financial results.

The next part of the paper will show ten cases of Academic Spin-offs in order to define the issues concerning their development. Particularly, the paper focuses on the role of cultural environment of universities in shaping the cognition abilities of entrepreneurs.

The Empirical Research: Sample and Methodology

The empirical research has been concerned with: a sample of ten small innovative firms working in the information technology industry acting in Campania Region in Southern Italy. All the firm of the sample were founded by entrepreneurs with an academic experience.

Academic Spin-offs working in the information technology industry were chosen for two reasons:

a)   the software industry displayed in the last decade a high growth rate, and several new firms were founded by technical entrepreneurs, mainly coming from universities' laboratories and technical departments of large companies;

b)   in the last three years, because of the economic recession and the general crisis of the information industry, the information sector went through a difficult period, and the original technical culture of the academic entrepreneurs displayed his weaknesses.

Each firm has been studied by interviewing the management with the aid of a semi-structured questionnaire. The information and data collected during the interviews included the general aspects of the firms' history and the training of the entrepreneurial group, the aspects of organisation, technical and professional expertise, the degree of external interaction, the technological characteristics of the products, development services and processes, the market and the customer profile.

All the interviews were collected in the 1996. Starting from those data the *case studies* were developed in order to define the dynamics of each firm within the *Field of Action* defined in the Fig. 1. The strategic paths of each firm were analyzed according to the following factors (Fig. 2):

i) identifying the critic dynamics from the start up stage (initial characteristics, mother environment, co-ordination ability, product/market combination) until to the period of the empirical research (final characteristics);

ii) analyzing the principal aspects in the intermediate situations (critical event, networking activities, strategic goal attained).

The findings of this analysis are showed in the next section.

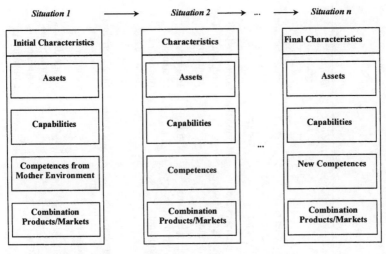

Source: Bellini, Capaldo, Raffa, Zollo, 1997

Figure 2: Methodology of Case Studies

Findings of the Empirical Research

The main issues of the ten firms surveyed are showed in the Tables 1a, 1b, 1c. In the following we report a brief description of each case.

Table 1a: Initial Characteristics of the Ten Case Studies

	Year of Start up	Mother Environment	Initial Knowledge	Skills	Initial No. of Employees	Skills Coordination	Initial Market	Initial Product
Case #1	1979	University Professor	Technical	Technical	1	Entrepreneurs are involved in Software development	Single Regional Customer	Single Software system
Case #2	1979	Three university professors	Academic	Technical	5	Entrepreneurs are involved in Software development	Regional	Software for structural engineering
Case #3	1978	Three technicians with academic experience	Technical	Computer science	32	Entrepreneurs are involved in Software development	National	Integrated Systems (hardware, software and services)
Case #4	1980	University Professor	Technical	Technical	3	Entrepreneurs are involved in Software development	Regional	Single product (software for notary)
Case #5	1976	Entrepreneurs with academic experiences	Technical	Technical	3	Entrepreneurs are involved in Software development	National	Single product (software for insurance companies)

428

Case	Year	Founders						
Case #6	1987	Entrepreneurs with academic experiences	Technical	Technical and Marketing	2	Entrepreneurs are involved in Software development	Regional	Single product (software for big stores)
Case #7	1982	Two electronic engineers with academic experience	Technical	Technical	2	Entrepreneurs are involved in Software development	Regional	Single product (software for accounting)
Case #8	1989	Entrepreneurs with academic experiences	Technical	Technical	2	Entrepreneurs are involved in Software development	Regional	Single product (software for public bodies)
Case #9	1981	Entrepreneurs with academic experiences	Technical	Technical	7	Entrepreneurs are involved in Software development	Regional	Single product (software for small firms)
Case #10	1979	University Professor	Technical	Computer science	3	Entrepreneurs are involved in Software development	Regional	Custom Software

Table 1b: Growth Paths of the Ten Case Studies

	1° Critical Event	2° Critical Event	Technological Networking	Strategic Goals Attained	Initial No. of Employees
Case #1	(1985) Increase of software employees		Personal informal relation with University	Enlargement of product range (software + services)	1
Case #2	(1984) Trade agreement with a large firm		Relationships with large firms Collaboration with external consultants Informal relation with University	Enlargement of product range and market (national)	5
Case #3	(1982) Organizational changes (separation of software and hardware sales activities)	Organizational changes (split of activities in two companies)	Partnerships with large firms	Enlargement of market (European)	32
Case #4	(1981) Organizational changes (introduction of Marketing competencies)		Informal relation with University	Enlargement of product range and market (national)	3

Case #5	(1985) The firm is forced to pass to new hardware technology	(1991) Shifting to new software system (Unix)	Absent	Same Product- Same Market	3
Case #6			Absent	Enlargement of product range (software + services)	2
Case #7	(1985) Shifting to new operative system	(1995) Introduction of marketing competencies	Absent	Same Product- Same Market	2
Case #8			Informal relation with University Collaboration with external consultants	Same Product- Same Market	2
Case #9	(1988) Participating share by a large firm	(1995) Increase of software employees	Informal relation with University Collaboration with external consultants	Enlargement of market (national)	7
Case#10	(1984) The firm becomes official retailer of a large hardware firm	(1986) Increase of employees	Absent	Diversification of product range (hardware sales)	3

431

Table 1c: Some Final Characteristics of the Ten Case Studies

	Competencies	Final No. of Employees	Skills Co-ordination	Combination Product /Market
Case #1	Technical	1	Internal and academic training Creation of Project Teams for Software development	Software (50 per cent) and Services (50 per cent) for Same Market
Case #2	Renewal of Technical and introduction of Marketing	12	Renewal through external consultants Entrepreneur is Project Manager	Services (70 per cent) and Software (30 per cent) for National Market
Case #3	Renewal of Technical	31	External training at large firms Project Manager is selected on the basis of competence	Software (70 per cent) Services (15 per cent), Training (10 per cent) and Sales (5 per cent) for European Market
Case #4	Technical and introduction of Marketing	15	Internal and external training Project Manager is selected on the basis of competence	Training (40 per cent), Software (30 per cent) and Services (30 per cent) for National Market

Case				
Case #5	Technical	Same	8	Same Product-Same Market
Case #6	Technical and Marketing	Internal training Creation of Project Teams for Software development	4	Services (70 per cent) and Software (30 per cent) for Same Market
Case #7	Renewal of Technical and introduction of Marketing	External training Creation of Project Teams for Software development	3	Same Product-Same Market
Case #8	Technical	External training at University Creation of Project Teams for Software development	6	Same Product-Same Market
Case #9	Renewal of Technical	External training Creation of Project Teams for Software development	27	Same Product-for National Market
Case #10	Computer science and Marketing	External training at suppliers	5	Hardware sale (60 per cent) Software (25 per cent) and Services (5 per cent) for Regional Market

In the Case #1 the firm, very weak on marketing capabilities, was forced to diversify on professional services linked to software product (e.g. consulting, maintenance). The assets and capabilities under complete control are unvaried. The competencies do not display qualitative changes, there is not Competence Building activities. After the *critical event* (increase of software employees) the firm is not able to open itself to external environment. The networking activities that are limited to personal informal relationships with University. The weakness of Firm Addressable assets allows only a partial evolution of products/markets combination. The market is still regional, the range of products is enlarged with services.

In the Case #2 the firm shows a more complete strategic path. In a first stage the firm is linked to the academic knowledge of the founders and realises only an enlargement of its geographic field of action. This success is due essentially to the high technical level of the unique product in portfolio. The technical level is very high and the product is included in a trade agreement with a leader firm (IBM). In this first stage the qualitative features of the assets are unchanged, but the number of employees increases. In a second stage of its life the firm succeeds in completing its strategic goal by a differentiation of its products (software + services). At beginning this phenomenon did not derive from a qualitative change in the assets, but it was linked to organizational improvements in the co-ordination skill. Afterwards, the improvement in networking activities with University, large firms and external consultants allows a double qualitative change: a renewal in technical capabilities and the introduction of marketing competencies.

In the Case #3 the firm, born from a large firm, maintains for the whole period of the analysis a strong technical feature. This superior technical ability let the firm be the unique of whole studied sample that operates in international market. From a 'competence-based' perspective, the firm is not able to build new competencies (e.g. marketing). This static behaviour is confirmed by the constancy of number of employees. It is linked to the low level of networking activities, that are limited to relationships with large mother firm.

In the Case #4 the firm maintains, in the first stage of its life, artisanal characteristics. This feature allows it to strengthen its competitive position in the regional market as a specialized firm in software for notary.

434

Afterwards the firm, even through the qualitative characteristics of assets are unchanged, increases its interaction with external environment, especially with University and innovative customers. By the networking ability the firm enlarges its competencies. It introduces steadily a marketing activity. From a 'competence-based' perspective the higher dynamics explain the strategic goal attained, as the double enlargement of product range and markets.

In the Case #5 the firm, born around a single product, shows a very low level in competencies enlargement. In fact only the technical competencies are partially renewed, but this improvement depends on external conditions as change in hardware and software standard. Those elements, with the absence of networking activities, explain the static 'products/markets' combination in a very long period (nineteen years).

In the Case #6 the firm is the only one in the sample analyzed that is born with a double competence in technical and marketing issues. This characteristic explains the reason why, in spite of the absence of networking, the firm was able to enlarge its products range.

In the Case #7 two critical events make a double enlargement of competencies, both technical with the passing to a new operative system and marketing with the introduction of a steady function (3° quadrant). In spite of those enlargements, the absence of networking obstructs the improvement of 'products/markets' combination.

In the Case #9 the firm shows a good level of technical relationship with his the large firm shareholder. This partial opening to external environment allows a competence-leveraging process showed by the increase of number of employees. The initial weakness in marketing competencies is not overcome by the networking with University and the large firm. The non-diversification of product, in spite of the increase in number of employees, confirms that the strategic path is stopped to the third quadrant.

In the Case #10 the firm shows a unique path. The firm shows a change in 'products/markets' combination characterized by a slide to more simple activities that do not require technical competencies (hardware and software sales). This path is linked to the absence of relationships with technical actors, that obstructs the renewal of initial knowledge of academic-founder.

The analysis of ten *case studies* let us identify the strategic path of each Academic Spin-off surveyed within the *Field of Action* defined in the

435

previous § 3 (see Figure 3). Those paths highlight the barriers in building new internal competencies to complete the strategic path.

Only two firms (cases #2 and #4) have been able to realize significant strategic objectives (enlargement both of products range and markets), extending their initial competencies. This success is strictly linked to the attention in networking activities with large firms and Universities.

Three firms (cases #7, #8 and #9) have been able to sustain their growth thanks to the capability in using the assets available in the environment. In those cases the less success (missed enlargement of products range or of markets) is due to their inability in using firm addressable assets in way to obtain qualitative changes in existing stock of assets and capabilities.

A third group of firms includes the most part of cases (#1, #3, #5, #6, #10). Those firms are unable to mange effective relations with external actors. Consequently their growth is based only on quantitative increase of existing assets and capabilities.

The ten cases shows a clear trend. The technical culture usually drives the firms in a niche market, from which they have difficulty to escape. The prevalent destiny of those firms is to survive in the niche market. The small firms can overcome the boundaries of the niche market only if they are able to integrate and to complete their initial knowledge by effective networking relationships. This is the example of cases #2 and #4.

Figure 3 summarizes the paths followed by each of firms analyzed. It confirms the inability of Academic Spin-offs to use networking activity to build new competencies and the difficult to oscillate in order to deploy effectively their assets.

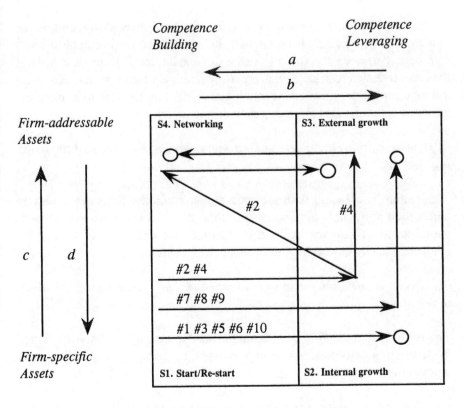

Figure 3: The Field of Action of Small Innovative Firms

First Evidences Coming from the Empirical Research

The results of empirical research allow us to define some guidelines on key questions addressed in the introduction.

i) What is the role played by the culture, education and skills of the academic entrepreneur in sustaining the competitive advantage of small firms?

Concerning the first question regarding the role played by culture of academic entrepreneurs, it seems that the strong technical orientation acts as a barrier to open the firms to external contributions. There is a general idea that technical competencies are a sufficient condition to succeed in an industry rooted on advanced technologies. Only one firm try to expand his previous competencies through a networking activity.

ii) How do entrepreneurs adjust their know-how in the course of the firms' life?

This pattern is coherent with the general result that the firms are unable to adjust their know-how in the course of their life (second question). None of surveyed firms reaches again the situation #1, and tries to renew his competencies by modifying his firm-specific assets.

iii) What is the interrelations between initial know-how and firms development?

The result is that the firm development (third question) is primarily guided by leveraging activities, which deploy existing assets, by expanding them on quantitative way.

iv) What are the limits of spontaneous academic spin-offs ?

The cultural limits of technical entrepreneurs display their effect in long run, affecting the business size and the economic role played by Academic Spin-offs (fourth question). It seems that for academic entrepreneurs it is impossible to revert priorities and to consider the marketing issue, in certain phases of firm's life, as the major one.

v) Is it possible a political guidance in order to pass from spontaneous Academic Spin-offs actions to planned ones?

The last question is the most difficult to answer. We need to stress some key issue on relationship between Universities and Industry.

From a managerial point of view the decisive question, as pointed out by Schimanck (1988, p. 330), 'is how and to what extent political guidance of the technology transfer between universities and firms is possible. What

438

can political actors do to promote the realization and the effectiveness of transfer interactions between university researchers and firms?'.

Policies directed at encouraging and fostering stronger networks and Academic Spin-offs should support the personal commitment of the scientist-entrepreneur by offering several services promoting an increasing involvement of Universities in their economic environment.

The passage from spontaneous Academic Spin-offs actions to planned ones can be organized defining suitable *Policies and Actions* for each of the common steps of establishing a new business (Table 2).

Table 2: Policies and Actions for developing Academic Spin-offs in Less developed Areas

Steps	*Policies*	*Actions*
Defining the business idea	- Permanent Monitoring of New Business Ideas deriving from results of academic researchers and firm's technologists	- Data Bank of 'business ideas' - Brainstorming with academics, students and firm's technicians to develop creativity
	- Permanent Monitoring of Market Opportunities	- Monitoring of market opportunities - Evaluating existent relationships between researchers and firms
Defining the Entrepreneurial Group	- Promotion of Multi-skill Entrepreneurial Groups	- Data Bank of potential new entrepreneurs
	- Training graduates and scientists in Entrepreneurship	- Workshops for permanent diffusion of entrepreneurship culture - Meetings with entrepreneurs
	- Mentoring new entrepreneurs	- Consulting
Defining the Business Plan	- Joint definition of technological, marketing and financial aspects	- Project management - Supporting networking activity - Consulting - Information providing

439

Funding	-	Maximization of public funding for new business	-	Agreements between Universities and Financial and Local Institutions
	-	Activation of innovative financial tools (venture capital, seed capital)	-	Creation of focused structures: e.g. consortia between universities and investors (venture capitalist, merchant banks)
Starting up	-	Developing relationships between new firms and markets	-	Agreements between new firms and services companies
			-	Tutoring new firms
	-	Developing managerial skills	-	Training

In the initial steps (i. Defining the Business Idea; ii. Defining the Entrepreneurial Group) the simultaneous monitoring of technological and marketing opportunities and the promotion of Multi-skill Entrepreneurial Groups are based on mixed knowledge (Technology, Marketing, Finance). We propose two specific actions: data banks on knowledge and research projects developed in local universities and workshops with academics, student and technicians that develop new approaches and creative solutions. In the successive steps (iii. Defining the Business Plan; iv. Funding; v. Starting-up) other actions become decisive: promotion of innovative financial tools, external tutoring and continuous training to sustain the initial competitive advantages. The strategic action seems to be the strengthening of technological networking. In this way the new firm will develop R&D projects to continuous updating and incremental innovation of their products and processes.

More implications regard the management of infrastructures acting in job creation and innovation transfer (e.g. Science and Technology Parks, Business Innovation Centres). Usually those organizations are suitable to realize those actions and play the role of networking companies because they are made by several different actors interested in joining their competencies, such as Universities, Research Centers, Local Authorities and Public Local Financing Agencies, large private firms. In order to act as a networking company those organizations should learn to manage immaterial assets, such as knowledge, values, competencies, relational skills, technological know-how, political relationships with local actors. All those elements should be utilized and combined in specific projects from which each participant could gain competitive advantages, that in the long run generate added value. At the end the effectiveness of a policy for developing Academic Spin-offs is linked to the creation of a new University's culture regarding the utilization of science and technology as a resource for social and economic development.

Limits of the Research, Open Problems and Future Steps

The results showed in this paper represent a first remark on Academic Spin-off issue and more on the direct exploitation of scientific and technological knowledge developed in the Universities.
This problem is very current in Italy as showed by the policies of Government aimed to promote the mobility of university researchers and a more effective integration between Universities, Research Centres and Industry.

The cases analyzed in the empirical research concern only a particular less developed area of Italy. Therefore the results showed can be conditioned by the specific context. In others contexts the same methodological approach could give different results. Consequently in the next step of the research, the same methodology will be applied to a different area to evaluate the incidence of environmental factors and to verify the generalizability of the results.
Moreover it is important to study deeply the influence of cultural factors of mother environment of Academic Spin Off.

To this end we are starting an empirical research on ninety research groups operating in the Universities located in the same area of the ten Academic Spin Off surveyed in this paper. We expect to estimate more precisely all the variables influencing the relationships between research groups and external environment, both local and global.

Notes

[1] The authors work at ODISSEO (Centre for Organization and Technological Innovation), Dept. of Computer Science and Systems, University of Naples Federico II. M. Raffa is the Scientific Director of ODISSEO and Full Professor of Business Economics and Organization; G: Zollo is Associate Professor of Business Management; Guido Capaldo is Researcher in Managerial Engineering at the Faculty of Engineering of the Second

University of Naples, E. Bellini is Doctoral Student in Managerial Engineering. Although the paper is a joint product, in this version sections #2 and #4 were written by G. Capaldo, #3 by G. Zollo, #5 by E. Bellini; the remaing sections are common.

References

Berman E.M., (1990), 'The economic impact of industry-funded University R&D', *Research Policy*, 19, 4, pp. 349-355.

Bonaccorsi A. and Piccaluga A. (1994), 'A theoretical framework for the evaluation of University-Industry relationship', *R&D Management 24, 3, 1994.*

Filion L.J. (1991), *Vision et relations: clefs du succès de l'entrepreneur,* Les éditions de l' entrepreneur, Montrèal.

Formica P. and Mitra J. (1996), 'Cooperation and Competition', *Industry and Higher Education,* June 1996, pp. 151-159.

Greiner L.E. (1972), 'Evolution and Revolution as Organizational Growth', in *Harvard Business Review*, July-Aug.

Hamel G. (1989), 'Strategic Intent', *Harvard Business Review*, vol. 67, pp 63-76.

Hamel G. (1991), 'Competence for Competence and Inter-Partner Learning within International Strategic Alliances', *Strategic Management Journal*, vol. 12. pp. 83-103, 1991.

Hamel G., Heene A. (editors) (1994), *Competence-Based Competition*, New York, Wiley.

Kao J. (1991), *The Entrepreneurial Organization*, Prentice Hall London.

Miller D., Droge C. and Toulose J.M. (1988), 'Strategic process and content as mediators between organizational context and structure', *Academy of Management Journal, 31 (3).* Pp. 544-569.

Prahalad C. K., Hamel G. (1990), 'The Core Competence of the Corporation', *Harvard Business Review*, vol.68 (3), pp-79-93.

Prahalad C. K., Hamel G. (1993), 'Strategy as Strech and Leverage', *Harvard Business Review*, march-april 1993.

Richter M. (1986), 'University Scientists as Entrepreneurs', *Society,* July/August: 73-88.

Roberts E.B., (1991), 'The technological base of the new enterprise', *Research Policy, 29,* pp. 283-298.

Roberts E.B. and Hauptman O. (1986), 'The Process of technology transfer to new biomedical and pharmaceutical firm', *Research Policy, 15* pp. 107-119.

Sanchez R. , Heene A., Thomas H., (edited by) (1996), Dynamics of Competence-Based Competition: theory and practice in the new strategic management, Pergamon, Oxford.

Schimanck U. (1988), The contribution of University research to the technological innovation of the German economy: societal auto-dynamic and political guidance, Research Policy, vol. 17 n. 6 pp. 329-340.

Smilor R.W., Gibson D.V., Dietrich G.B., (1990), 'University Spin-Out Companies: technology start-ups from UT-Austin', Journal of Business Venturing, 5, 63-76.

23 How a Management School Deals with Innovation in Entrepreneurship Education[1]

Dirk De Clercq
Hans Crijns
Hubert Ooghe

Abstract

The main objective of this paper is to describe the process of innovation in entrepreneurship education at the School voor Management (University of Ghent). This process includes an inventory of present and future activities in entrepreneurship at the School voor Management and a literature review on entrepreneurship and entrepreneurship education.

As a result, conditions and possible scenarios, regarding the introduction of entrepreneurship education at the School voor Management at a graduate level, emerge.

Three possibilities are proposed: (1) a Master in Entrepreneurship, (2) a Quarter in Entrepreneurship or (3) an Area of Emphasis in Entrepreneurship.

Introduction

Recently a project 'Innovation in Entrepreneurship Education' at the School voor Management (University of Ghent) has been launched.

The project aim is the development of education that enhances the intellectual, managerial, entrepreneurial and personal development of (graduate) students, in order to improve their capacity to plan, start up and manage new ventures in an international economy.

In order to meet the School's ambition, conditions and scenarios for a new entrepreneurship education program have to be clear.

Because in entrepreneurship education, as in entrepreneurship (and in any other profession), luck is where preparation and opportunity meet !

De Vlerick School voor Management

De Vlerick School voor Management is the management school of the University of Ghent and is the number one business school in Belgium. Its mission is to develop and propagate a management culture based on professionalism, synthesis, entrepreneurship and internationalization.

The School is highly regarded in the region for its top quality teaching, for its focus on practice and relevant business problems, and for its close cooperation with the business world and the government.

The main focus of the business school is on management education and training, research and networking.

Concerning the education and training, De Vlerick School voor Management offers Master Programs on the one hand and Post-experience programs on the other hand.[2]

(1) Four full-time Master programs are offered:
- Master in Business Administration;
- Master in Marketing;
- Master in Finance;
- Master in Tax Management.

The school also runs 2 part-time Executive Master programs:
- Executive Master in Business Administration (Junior Management Program);
- Executive Master in Industrial Engineering.

(2) The post-experience programs are designed for business people having some years of work experience. They are situated in the following areas:
- General Management;
- Management of Small and Medium-sized Enterprises (SME).

Each year a large number of short term programs is being offered in a wide variety of areas. In Table 1 an overview is given of the different departments in De Vlerick School voor Management.

Table 1: Departments in De Vlerick School voor Management

• Strategic Management • General Management and Organizational Behavior • Management Accounting and Control • Accountancy • Financial Management • Financial Services and Insurance • Marketing Management • Human Resources Management	• SME-Management • Growth Management • Information Management • Operational Management • Tax Management • Juridical Management • Environmental Management • Management of Public Organizations

Approach

In order to address the goals of the project, an inventory of the existing and future activities in the field of entrepreneurship at the School has been executed together with a theoretical literature review about entrepreneurship and entrepreneurship education. This literature review provides the theoretical background for the innovation process at the School voor Management.

Finally some possible scenarios in entrepreneurship education at the School voor Management are summarized in order to facilitate the decision making process.

The inventory in the School has been carried by a questionnaire, developed and submitted to the different departments (cfr. Table 1). By means of this questionnaire it was intended to have an overview of the different visions on entrepreneurship and of the existing/future activities in entrepreneurship, in these departments. The questionnaire is represented in Table 2.

Table 2: Questionnaire

- What definition is linked with entrepreneurship in your department?

- What are the existing and future activities in your department in the field of entrepreneurship?

- What learning methods are used and should be used to teach entrepreneurship?

Definitions of Entrepreneurship at the School voor Management

A broad variety of definitions and descriptions of entrepreneurship is existing in the different departments at De Vlerick School voor Management.

In some cases, no specific definition of entrepreneurship was given. This can be explained by a lack of knowledge about the topic or by a lack of interest. Another reason can be the complexity of 'entrepreneurship' or the fact that 'a definition would be unimportant'.

Often entrepreneurship is defined in terms of innovation, creativity and the willingness to take risks. In this case a link is made with the opinion that entrepreneurship is a mental attitude/behavior of an individual. The link between entrepreneurship and intrapreneurship sometimes leads to confusion.

In some cases, entrepreneurship is *only* identified in terms as SME-management, family business, start-ups, growing companies... For this variety in interpretation of entrepreneurship, the following explanations can be found:

- The expertise and knowledge of the staff is situated in different functional areas, that differ from entrepreneurship.
- De Vlerick School voor Management is a 'management' school. The focus is more on management than on entrepreneurship.
- A myriad of definitions exists for entrepreneurs and entrepreneurship.

Entrepreneurship : a Review of the Literature

A review of the literature revealed various streams in defining entrepreneurs. A first stream describes the entrepreneur and his role in the economic world, as opposed to the non-entrepreneur. Most of these authors are researchers in the economic field. They look at the entrepreneur's role in creating new ventures, implementing new technologies, stimulating growth and wealth in the economy.

In this respect an early and important contribution to the description of entrepreneurship is given by Schumpeter. Entrepreneurship is characterized by the existence of new combinations causing discontinuity (Schumpeter, 1936). These new combinations include the introduction of a new product, a new product quality or a new production method; the opening of a new market, a new source for the delivery of raw materials or components; the reorganization of an industry.

Innovation is not always considered as a sufficient condition for entrepreneurship. The existence of outcomes is also an important factor.

Two approaches are developed by Gartner (1990). A first one focuses on the existence of characteristics such as innovation, growth and uniqueness. The second one describes the outcomes of entrepreneurship, as characterized by the realization of profit and the creation of added value.

Entrepreneurship is also defined as an act of innovation that involves adding a new wealth-producing capacity to existing resources (Drucker, 1985).

A second stream in the literature describes the main characteristics that are related to entrepreneurship.

Examples of these concepts are 'fundamental change' (Murray, 1984), 'innovative, flexible, dynamic risk taking, creative' (Stevenson and Gumpert, 1985), 'alertness' (Kirzner, 1985), 'need for achievement' (McClelland, 1961), 'ambition' (Sexton, 1980), etc.

Some authors point out difficulties in defining distinctive characteristics between entrepreneurs and non-entrepreneurs. There may be differences but the nature of these differences is not predictable (Low and McMillan, 1988; Bull and Willard, 1993).

A third group concentrates on success factors for entrepreneurs. These factors may be internal- or external-expertise, information networks and environmental conditions.

447

With regard to expertise, Cooper (1985) uses the term 'incubator organization' to describe the entrepreneurs' place of employment immediately prior to the founding (or take over) of a new venture.

The fundamental mindset in entrepreneurship, according to Stevenson (1985), is that skills and personal networks are the key source of security.

Some research concentrates on entrepreneurship related to the external environment (Birley, 1990). Variables such as environmental conditions, market forces, government policy can be of significant importance. Three environmental forces are described by Knight, Dowling and Brown (1987): new technology, new markets and shifts in government regulation.

Moreover, the presence of role models is considered to be of significant influence. Would-be entrepreneurs see role models primarily at home, at work and in the region (Bygrave, 1994).

Many more authors may be cited. But in our perception, most definitions focus on the entrepreneur as a person (1) who carries out a role in the economic world by creating added value and who bears the risk and responsibility, (2) with a combination of specific personal characteristics (creative, innovative, dynamic, etc.).

We perceive two conditions that seem to be vital in order to become an entrepreneur: the will to (succeed, achieve, etc.) and opportunities for (creating value, innovation, etc.).

Entrepreneurship and Different Types of Businesses and Management

Out of the literature various relationships emerge between entrepreneurship and different types of businesses and different types of management:

- small business and small business management;
- family business;
- growing business;
- start-up of new ventures;
- intrapreneurship;
- ownership.

Although they may be related with entrepreneurship, they should not be considered as synonymous.

Small business and entrepreneurship

All small business owners are not entrepreneurs, and all entrepreneurs are not small business owners.

According to Davidsson (1989) an entrepreneur exploits ideas through forming and expanding a business firm. To qualify a person as an entrepreneur, he has to be oriented towards and actively pursue change.

Twaalfhoven (1985) points out the distinguishing characteristics of a dynamic entrepreneur, in contrast to those of the average small business owner:

Table 3: Small/Medium Business Owners versus Dynamic Entrepreneurs

Small/Medium Business Owner	*Dynamic Entrepreneur*
static	growing
status quo	vision opportunistic
local	global
limited	expanding
internal resources	external resources
self employed	professional team
avoids competition	seeks competition
risk adverse	risk taking and sharing
survival	success

Family business and entrepreneurship

Entrepreneurship sometimes is related to family business and vice versa.

Here again the difficulty in defining family business remains. Family businesses may be family owned, family controlled or owned and managed by a family. Moreover the difference between the persons (as owners and/or managers) and the family is not always very well defined.

According to Carland et al. (1984) a distinction has to be made between the strategies of 'entrepreneurial ventures' and 'family business ventures'.

In a family business, strategic management often emphasizes preferences and needs of the family as opposed to those of the business. When in conflict, the family needs can override those of the company. An example is the family business strategy to remain independent and to provide outlets for family investment and careers for family members.

An entrepreneurial strategist however would opt for the obtaining of the best personnel available, in order to pursue growth and maintain the firm's distinctive competence.

Entrepreneurship and growth

According to some authors, growth seems to be a typical characteristic of entrepreneurial ventures.

Here, the existence of growth is more important than the company size. According to Twaalfhoven (1985), entrepreneurship occurs at all size levels of companies. It is characterized by companies growing rapidly through the size hierarchy, not by those who remain at one particular level.

It is important to have a clear description of the term 'growth'. A distinction can be made between qualitative and quantitative parameters for company growth (Crijns, 1996).

Quantitative growth can be characterized by the company size (turnover, added value, volume), the profitability of the company and the value of the company (shareholder value).

Qualitative objectives are linked with the quantitative objectives, not as an aim in itself but as strategic means for the realization of the growth of the enterprise. The companies' competitive position, product quality and customer service are examples of qualitative objectives.

Company growth is also linked with diversification and 'portfolio entrepreneurship'. 'Portfolio entrepreneurs' are individuals who own and control more than one business. If control of different companies is vested in groups or clusters of such individuals, then analyses of firm start up and growth cannot be adequate if only based on the 'firm' as the unit of analysis: 'a firm is merely a legal unit which can be manipulated by discerning entrepreneurs to maximize their advantage' (Rosa and Scott, 1995).

Entrepreneurship and new ventures

The start-up of a company is considered as an important phase in the whole entrepreneurial process. A lot of attention in the literature is paid to the driving forces to start a business.

For Bygrave (1994), opportunities are the basis of the entrepreneurial process. A distinction should be made between ideas and opportunities. Each idea is not necessarily an opportunity, though an opportunity is always linked to an idea in a certain way.

In this respect entrepreneurship is described as a market driven process. An opportunity is anchored in a product or service that creates value or adds value to the buyer. Opportunities exist as a consequence of the imperfection of the market (changing circumstances, unequal distribution of information, ...). Entrepreneurs have the ability to recognize these imperfections and to take advantage out of it.

Some authors consider the 'entrepreneurial event' as the result of the interaction between social, cultural and personal factors. Negative displacements (being fired, retired, angered, insulted, bored, divorced or widowed) can be the motive for the entrepreneurial event (Shapero and Sokol, 1982). Another reason to start a business is the expectation of gain. That expectation can be reinforced by culture, family, peers and colleagues.

Entrepreneurship and intrapreneurship

A particular stream in the literature deals with intrapreneurship. It states that entrepreneurship also can occur in big companies. In this case, the 'entrepreneurial spirit' of small companies is transferred to big companies.

Intrapreneurship is a method for stimulating and then capitalizing on individuals in an organization who think that something can be done differently and better (Hisrich and Peter, 1995).

There are strong similarities between 'intrapreneurs' and 'entrepreneurs (as strongly contrasted with the characteristics of traditional managers). In the case of intrapreneurs however, the existence of a hierarchical structure within the organization should be taken into account.

Entrepreneurship and ownership

The existence of company ownership by the entrepreneur gives a specific dimension to the management of the firm, through the investment of own financial resources. A distinction can be made between companies with a 'closed' and an 'open' ownership structure (Crijns et al., 1994). A 'closed' ownership structure is connected with a shareholdership that is restricted to the person or the family. When a third party has joined the shareholdership, the shareholdership is called 'open'.

Some authors do not consider ownership as a distinctive characteristic for entrepreneurship. For example, Schumpeter (1936) stated that *a shareholder may be an entrepreneur, but shareholders per se, however are never entrepreneurs, but merely capitalists, who in consideration of their submitting to certain risks, participate in profits.*

Conclusions

Definitions of entrepreneurship and the entrepreneur are divided in three streams : the ones describing the role of the entrepreneur, others describing the characteristics, a third group focusing on success factors.

Summarizing, the entrepreneur can be described as a person (1) who carries out a role in the economic world by creating added value and who bears the risk and responsibility, (2) with a combination of specific personal characteristics (creative, innovative, dynamic, etc).

Two conditions seem to be vital in order to become an entrepreneur : the will to (succeed, achieve, etc.) and opportunities for (creating value, innovation, etc.).

Entrepreneurship can exist in different kinds of businesses, on all levels of company size and in different functions.

In some cases growth should be considered as a relative phenomenon, taking into account diversification i.e. the spread of ownership over different companies.

With regard to the project 'Innovation in Entrepreneurship Education' at the School voor Management (University of Ghent), entrepreneurship should be clearly defined as a learning object, out of theoretical as well as pragmatic reasons.

Based on the undertaken review of the literature and of the School's inventory, a clear focus of the project is needed.

The following criteria should be fulfilled:

- a dynamic and innovative behavior (the 'Schumpterian' attitude) = characteristics
- leadership (general management) and ownership = economic role.

The last criterion is linked with the ownership of company shares. This shareholdership does not need to be controlling, but should be substantial and involve a restricted number of shareholders.

Based on the previous remarks, a model has been developed, situating an entrepreneur in a two-dimensional framework (the terminology is based on Stevenson and Gumpert, 1985 and on Hisrich en Peter, 1995):

Economic Role (ownership and leadership)

yes	Administrator	Entrepreneur
no	Controller	Intrapreneur

no	*yes*

Characteristics (Schumpeterian attitude)

Out of this model, an 'entrepreneur' is opposed to an 'intrapreneur', an 'administrator' and a 'controller' (the names are used as prototypes and are in no way meant to be normative). The entrepreneur is a person characterized by a dynamic and innovative behavior (horizontal dimension) and by the combination of ownership and leadership of the company (vertical dimension). Hence the second dimension in this model is a compression of two elements.

Innovation and creativity as criteria for entrepreneurship lead to the difficulty of the measurement and detection of entrepreneurship. How can entrepreneurship be detected? How to develop education renewal in this respect?

453

On the one hand creativity and innovation are linked with the *contents* of education renewal. On the other hand an important objective for renewal in entrepreneurship education is the stimulation of the 'entrepreneurial attitude' among students. In this case the focus is not so much on *what* is to be taught, but on *how* it is to be taught.

Existing Activities in Entrepreneurship Education at the School voor Management

With regard to the inventory of the existing activities in entrepreneurship education at the School voor Management, an overview is given in Tables 4 to 6, for three levels of education: (1) undergraduate education, (2) graduate education and (3) post-experience education.

Table 4: Undergraduate Education

Target group	Course	Contents	Learning method
all faculties	'Schumpeter-project'	development of an entrepreneurial awareness among university staff and students	- lectures - guest speakers - company visit
all faculties (except economics and engineering)	'Introduction to Management'	- search for and implementation of ideas - development of a business plan	- lectures - cases - guest speakers
faculty of economics	Financial Management	- venture capital	- guest speaker
faculty of economics	Marketing	- market focus	- group project - interviews - presentation
faculty of engineering	Industrial Management	- development of a business plan	- guest speaker

454

Table 5: Graduate Education

Target group	Course	Contents	Learning method
Master in Business Administration	Financial Management	- venture capital	- guest speaker
Master in Business Administration	Human Resources Management	- problems within family businesses	- cases
Master in Business Administration	Special week on Entrepreneurship[1]	- entrepreneurial awareness - start-up and growth of a venture	- cases - guest speakers - simulation game
Master in Finance	Financing	- venture capital - growth financing - acquisition financing - Management Buy Out	- cases - guest speakers
Master in Tax Management	Tax Management	- fiscal aspects of start-ups, growth, acquisitions and succession	- cases

A variety of initiatives in the entrepreneurship field already exists at the School voor Management, but this in a rather implicit way. Regarding the existing learning methods, the School voor Management seems to be strong in the use of cases (though there is a need to develop more Belgian case studies to teach entrepreneurship).

Table 6: Post-experience Education

Target group	Department	Contents	Learning method
SME starters/managers	SME-Management1	- management techniques for small businesses - start-up of a new venture - business plan - SMEs and Internet - women and entrepreneurship	- lectures - cases - guest speakers - workshops - individual coaching - group discussions
Owner-managers of growing companies	Growth Management	- strategic choices - family succession - ethical dimension - growth financing - creativity - acquisitions - stress management	- lectures - cases - guest speakers - workshops - individual coaching - group discussions

Suggestions and Possibilities in Entrepreneurship Education at the School voor Management

The inventory provided also insight in the staff's suggestions for future activities in the field of entrepreneurship education (Table 7 and 8).

Table 7: Undergraduate Education

Target group	Course	Contents	Learning method
all faculties (except economics and engineering)	Introduction to Entrepreneurship	- basic knowledge about entrepreneurship - entrepreneurial awareness - small businesses	- lectures - cases - business plan - guest speakers
faculty economics	elective about Entrepreneurship	- entrepreneurship and new ventures - financing of owner-managed companies - growth management	- lectures - cases - guest speakers - interviews - business plan
faculty engineering	Business Economics	- business plan - new ventures	- lectures - group work

Table 8: Graduate Education

Target group	Course	Contents	Learning method
Master in Business Administration	general	general	- inviting entrepreneurs - dinner with entrepreneurs - selling of products by students - writing of cases - community projects - starting an own venture
Master in Business Administration	Financing	- venture capital - growth phases	- cases - business game
Master in Finance	Financing	- growth phases - investment decisions	- cases
Master in Tax Management	Tax Management	-entrepreneurship	- business game

457

Entrepreneurship Education: Lessons from the Literature Review

Although entrepreneurship is becoming an academic discipline and a field of study, there remains, to this day, considerable disagreement with regard to what constitutes a model entrepreneurship curriculum and what courses should be taught in entrepreneurship programs. Another question that should be solved is the issue of the way of teaching entrepreneurship. A literature review on this subject has been executed in order to provide a theoretical base for the project.

Entrepreneurship program models

Generally a variety of emerging models for an entrepreneurship program can be given. Each model reflects a conceptual view of entrepreneurship education.

According to Hill (1988) three main focuses are possible: the business plan, the business life cycle and the business functions.

A distinction should be made between management and entrepreneurship programs.

The majority of the management programs are functionally oriented. Many management educators teach the functional format as if it were equally applicable to ventures at all levels of development. However, few ventures begin with a functionally differentiated structure in the start-up phase; functional differentiation is something that is created through time (McMullan and Long, 1987).

As a consequence, entrepreneurship education needs to be differentiated more by stage of venture development rather than by department of functional expertise. The knowledge available in the different domains are not irrelevant to new ventures, but should be incorporated within an appropriate developmental framework.

Learning objectives

The learning objectives of entrepreneurship education can vary from the creation of an entrepreneurial awareness among students, through the development of entrepreneurial skills, to the teaching of specific business related knowledge.

The importance of several objectives in entrepreneurship education was measured, based on a survey among 15 leading university entrepreneurship educators (Hills, 1988). The results of this survey show that major importance (on a 7 point-Likert-scale) was given at:

- increasing awareness and understanding of the process involved in initiating and managing a new business enterprise (6.7);
- increasing student awareness of the new venture/smaller company career option (5.5);
- developing a fuller understanding of the interrelationships between the business functional areas (5.5);
- contributing to an appreciation of the special qualities of the entrepreneur (5.1);
- increasing the understanding of the role of new and smaller firms within the economy (3.6).

Learning contents

For this paper a study was made on the topics that are dealt with in entrepreneurship education in 25 leading business schools in the USA. The list of business schools is based on the survey undertaken by *Success Magazine* in 1996 (Exhibit 3). In Table 9 an overview and categorization of the mentioned topics is given.

Learning methods

Concerning the courses offered by leading business schools in the USA (Exhibit 3), a synthesis was made about the learning methods used. A distinction can be made between methods applied inside and outside the class room.

Inside the class room, there are some classical tools which are used to teach entrepreneurship such as: *lectures, readings, workbook exercises and writing a paper.* The use of *cases* seems very common and several procedures are applied in order to enhance the interaction between the teacher and the students and among the students: *class discussion, discussion with experts, guest speakers, individual coaching, role plays, team teaching and team work.*

Table 9: Topics to be Dealt with in Entrepreneurship Education

start-up of ventures	
creativity	*obtaining the required resources*
financing new ventures	*planning new ventures*
identification and evaluation of	*purchasing existing ventures*
opportunities	*risk analysis*
implementation of new ventures	*starting new ventures*
management of new ventures	
new venture marketing	

growth of new ventures and critical moments	
bankruptcy	*management of growth*
financing growing ventures	*mergers and acquisitions*
joint ventures	*selling a venture*
management buy-ins	*transition from start-up to growth*
management buy-outs	

marketing	
brand management	*marketing planning*
commercialisation of products	*marketing strategy*
entrepreneurial marketing	*product development*
marketing of new products	*sales*

financial aspects	
accounting	*financial planning*
cash flow analysis	*financing growing ventures*
creating value	*financing new ventures*
development of budget control system	*valuation of a venture*
financial analysis	*venture capital financing*
financial compensation	

organisation and human resources management	
entrepreneurial career	*organization management*
entrepreneurial teams	*organization structure*
HRM aspects	*staffing*
organization culture	*work roles in organizations*

operational and technological management	
information management	
strategic issues	
corporate strategy	*industry strategy*
entry strategies	

legislation related issues	
franchise management *government contracting* *intellectual property*	*legal aspects* *licensing* *taxation aspects*
innovation	
change management	*innovation management*
small and large companies	
differences between small and large organizations *family businesses*	*intrapreneurship* *small business management*
personal aspects, characteristics and skills of entrepreneurs	
business ethics *development of entrepreneurial competencies* *leadership* *negotiations*	*personal values* *persuasion process* *skills of entrepreneurs*
general issues	
business transactions *international aspects* *management consulting*	*project management* *utilization of resources*

The writing of a business plan is an important method in teaching the principles of entrepreneurship. In this way an integration can be made between the several aspects which are dealt with in the (more theoretically orientated) courses. The writing of a business plan is often combined with a field project in which the students have to write a business plan for a real (new) venture. The start-up of an own venture by the students sometimes is also part of this method.

Other examples of tools that are used to 'teach' entrepreneurship *outside* the class room aim at a close contact between students and real entrepreneurs (who serve as a role mode): *cooperation with an incubator for new ventures, dinner with entrepreneurs, internships (working for an entrepreneurial company) and interviews with entrepreneurs.*

Target groups

A distinction can be made between three types of audiences in entrepreneurship education: entrepreneurs, intrapreneurs and entrepreneurial sympathizers (Block and Stumpf, 1992).

Entrepreneurs are business starters and/or business owners who are self-employed. Intrapreneurs foster opportunity identification and exploitation within the organization they work for. Finally entrepreneurial sympathizers are dealing with entrepreneurs by the nature of their profession (bankers, advisors, etc.).

Conclusions

The objectives of entrepreneurship education can be situated in a broad range, varying from the acquirement of specific knowledge on the start-up and management of new and growing firms, through the identification and stimulation of entrepreneurial skills, to the creation of an awareness of the process involved in the initiation and management of an own company.

A functional approach is not often seen an effective way for teaching entrepreneurship. The integration of the various functional domains however can create an added value to the students. An effective method to practise this integration is the writing of a business plan. Another suggestion that is frequently made, is the build-up of an entrepreneurship curriculum along the various stages of the venture development.

Concerning the used learning methods, there are teaching methods, such as lectures, cases, assigned readings, guest speakers, the writing of a business plan and the start-up of an own venture. Entrepreneurship education should mainly be practically oriented and not be overloaded with theoretical expositions. The learning focus should be definitely on entrepreneurial training as contrasted with the traditional university/business school emphasis on the analysis and knowledge of large amounts of information.

It is interesting to make a comparison between the curriculum and pedagogical methods as found in the literature and in some leading universities on the one hand and at the School voor Management (University of Ghent) on the other hand.

By comparing the teaching contents as revealed in Table 9 with the existing offerings at the School voor Management, it can be concluded that for undergraduate and graduate students, attention has already *partly* been paid to the start-up and development of small ventures, the financing of new and growing ventures and the writing of a business plan.

However there is also a broad range of subjects which are not or insufficiently covered by the actual curriculum, such as the management of growing firms during its different developmental stages, the creation of an entrepreneurial awareness, the dealing with legislation and taxation aspects or the possibility of an entrepreneurial career.

Regarding the existing learning methods at the School voor Management and comparing them with methods used in the leading universities, the School for Management seems to be strong in the field of using cases in the class room (though there is an actual need to develop more 'own (Belgian)' cases to teach entrepreneurship).

It could be useful to organize more activities outside the class room in the future. Specific possibilities could be in the cooperation, working and meeting with real entrepreneurs (e.g. the interviewing of entrepreneurs, the real life projects in owner-managed companies) or the writing of a business plan for an own venture.

Anyhow, a variety of initiatives in the entrepreneurship field already exists at the undergraduate and graduate level in the University of Ghent, but this in a rather implicit way.

There is a clear need for further integration. This coordination could be realized e.g. by a close cooperation of teachers in the different functional domains, by the active participation of entrepreneurs in the curriculum or by the internship of students in entrepreneurial companies.

Conditions and Scenarios for Entrepreneurship Education at the School voor Management

As stated in the project objectives, the primary target group of the innovation project in entrepreneurship education at the School voor Management are the graduate students. In order to facilitate the decision making process, conditions and scenarios for entrepreneurship education at the School voor Management are listed.

Conditions

Based on a literature review, the following conditions, regarding the entrepreneurship programs at the School voor Management, are suggested:

- Innovation in entrepreneurship education at a graduate level can have synergetic effects on undergraduate and postacademic education (vertical integration).
- Horizontal integration is a condition sine qua non and corresponds with the integration between the knowledge of the several functional domains within the School voor Management.
- There should be agreement about the term 'entrepreneurship' as a learning object. A consensus was obtained about the characteristics (innovation) and the economic role (ownership and leadership).
- The whole spectrum of the life cycle of a company should be present in entrepreneurship education: from the start-up, through the several growth stages, to the selling of the company.
- Sufficient attention should be paid to the use of 'entrepreneurial' learning methods. The learning focus may not be restricted to the obtaining of huge amounts of information and techniques.

Scenarios

Concerning the graduate education at the School voor Management, the following scenarios are to be considered:

Master in Entrepreneurship

This option includes two alternatives:

a) one Master-program (with a focus on entrepreneurship)

The introduction of a Master in Entrepreneurship at the School voor Management (University of Ghent) would be unique in Europe and strongly differentiating with regard to other business schools. Of course it should be analyzed if the market demand is big enough for such a program. The recruitment of students should undoubtedly be organized on an international scale.

464

b) a new Master-program, next to other graduate programs

The same comments can be given as for the previous option. However, a new Master-program assumes sufficient diversification with regard to the other graduate programs.

Quarter in Entrepreneurship

This scenario would be offered as an additional program for one-year Master-students or as an optional major for two-year Master-students (from foreign universities).

Two alternatives emerge for this scenario: (a) a complete quarter in entrepreneurship or (b) a summer quarter in entrepreneurship.

Area of emphasis in Entrepreneurship

An area of emphasis in entrepreneurship (either obligatory or facultative) would be introduced in order to provide basic knowledge in entrepreneurship to graduate students. Two alternatives are possible:

a) one module in Entrepreneurship, offered to all graduate programs

This alternative corresponds with the need for integration in entrepreneurship education. The different approaches from the students in different graduate programs could provide added value.

b) different modules in Entrepreneurship, for the specific graduate programs

This alternative offers the possibility to focus on specific aspects of entrepreneurship, corresponding with the interest of the students.

It is to the School voor Management to make a choice; maybe a little luck is needed.

Because - paraphrasing Bygrave - in entrepreneurship education, as in entrepreneurship (and in any other profession), luck is where preparation and opportunity meet!

Exhibit 1:

Overview of the existing research on entrepreneurship related issues at the School voor Management

Department	Contents
Financial Management	- venture capital in Europe and the USA - financing of starting high-tech ventures - added value of venture capital financing - business angels
Growth Management	- strategic dimensions and growth - learning to grow - the entrepreneur as manager - new organization types - marketing to growth - internationalization
SME-Management[1]	- screening (by universities) of technology in SMEs - technology transfer from university to SMEs (feed sector) - bottle-necks for new and growing SMEs (textile sector) - follow-up of alumni of the SME-programs - small businesses and employment
Organizational Behavior	- questionnaire about time management of business owners

Exhibit 2:

Overview of the existing entrepreneurial services at the School voor Management

Department	Contents
Growth Management	- organization of conferences (e.g. EFER) - distribution of the 'Entrepreneur of the Year Ernst & Young Award' - individual coaching
SME-Management[1]	- development of business plans for small businesses - individual coaching - audit of small businesses

466

Exhibit 3:

Success Magazine's list of business schools, active in the field of entrepreneurship

1. University of Arizona, Karl Eller Graduate School of Management
2. Babson College, F.W. Olin Graduate School of Business
3. Ball State University, College of Business
4. Baylor University, Hankamer School of Business
5. Brigham Young University, Marriott School of Management
6. University of California at Los Angeles (UCLA), The Anderson School
7. Carnegie Mellon University, Graduate School of Industrial Administration
8. University of Colorado, the Graduate School of Business Administration
9. Cornell University, Johnson Graduate School of Management
10. DePaul University, Charles H. Kellstadt Graduate School of Business
11. University of Georgia, Terry College of Business
12. Harvard University, Harvard Business School
13. University of Illinois, Chicago, College of Business Administration
14. University of Maryland at College Park, The Maryland Business School
15. University of Nebraska-Lincoln, College of Business Administration
16. New York University (NYU), Leonard N. Stern School of Business
17. Northwestern University, J.L. Kellogg Graduate School of Management
18. University of Pennsylvania, the Wharton School
19. Rensselaer Polytechnic Institute, Lally School of Management and Technology
20. St. Louis University, School of Business and Administration
21. University of St. Thomas, Graduate School of Business
22. San Diego State University, College of Business Administration
23. University of Southern California, School of Business Administration
24. University of South Carolina, College of Business and Administration
25. University of Texas at Austin, Graduate School of Business

Notes

[1] The project 'Innovation in Entrepreneurship Education' is funded by the University of Ghent.
[2] The Master programs are organized by the *School voor Management*, i.e. the university part of De Vlerick School voor Management. The Post-experience programs are offered by the private part of the school, i.e. the *Institute Professor Vlerick*.

References

Alldrich H. (1989), Networking among women entrepreneurs, in: Hagen D., Riuchun C. and Sexton D., *Women owned businesses*, p.103-132.

Benson G.L. (1991), Thoughts of an entrepreneurship chairholder model entrepreneurship curriculum, *Journal of Applied Business Research vol.9(1)*, p.140-146.

Birley S. (1985), The roles of networks in the entrepreneurial process, *Journal of Business Venturing vol. 1(1)*, p.107-117.

Block Z. and Stumpf S.A. (1992), Entrepreneurship education research: experience and challenge, in: *The State of the Art of Entrepreneurship*, Sexton D. and Kasarda J., PWS-Kent Publishing Company, Boston, p. 17-42.

Bull I. en Willard G.E. (1993), Towards a theory of entrepreneurship, *Journal of Business Venturing vol. 8*, p. 183-195.

Bygrave W.D. (1994), *The portable MBA in Entrepreneurship*. John Wiley & Sons, Inc., 468 p.

Carland J.W., Hoy F., Boulton W.R., Carland J.A.C. (1984), *Academy of Management Review 9*, p.354-359.

Cooper A.C. (1985), The role of incubator organizations in the founding of growth oriented firms. *Journal of Business Venturing 1(1)*, p.75-86.

Cooper A.C. and Bruno A. (1977), Success among high technology firms, *Business Horizons vol. 20(2)*, p.16-22.

Crijns H. (1996), Fasen in de groei van middelgrote ondernemersgeleide bedrijven. *Management Jaarboek 1996*, Roularta, p. 385-390.

Crijns H., Ooghe H., Cosaert M. (1994), Transitions of medium-sized family companies, paper presented at the *RENT VIII Conference*, Tampere, Finland, 1994, p. 1-33.

Davidsson P. (1989), Continued entrepreneurship and small firm growth, The Economic Research Institute, Stockholm, 272 p.

Deschoolmeester D. (1996), *Annual Report on the SME-Center*, De Vlerick School voor Management.

Deschoolmeester D., Schamp T. Vandenbroucke A.-M., Leger K. (1997), *The Influence of Management Training on the Entrepreneurial Attitudes and Managerial Techniques of Small Business Starters* (SMEs).

Drucker P.F. (1985), *Innovation and Entrepreneurship*. Harper & Row, New York.

Garavan T.N. and O'Cinneide (1994), Entrepreneurship education and training programmes: a review and evaluation, part 1, *Journal of European Industrial Training, vol.18(8)*, p.3-12.

468

Gartner W.B. (1990), What are we talking about when we talk about entrepreneurship?, *Journal of Business Venturing*, vol. 5, p. 15-28.

Gibb A.A. (1987), Enterprise culture, its meaning and implications for education and training, *Journal of European Industrial Training, vol.11(2)*.

Hills G.E. (1988), Variations in university entrepreneurship education: an empirical study of an evolving field, *Journal of Business Venturing vol.3*, p.109-122.

Hisrich R.D. and Peter M.P. (1995), *Entrepreneurship: starting, developing and managing a new enterprise*, Irwin, 3rd edition, 650 p.

Katz J.A. (1991), The institution and infrastructure of entrepreneurship, *Entrepreneurship Theory and Practice*, Spring 1991, p.85.

Kirzner I.M. (1985), *Discovery and the capitalist process*, University of Chicago Press.

Knight K.E, Dowling M.J., Brown J.B. (1987), Venture survivability: an analysis of the automobile, semiconductor, vacuum tube and airline industries, *Frontiers of Entrepreneurship Research*, p. 138-153.

Leibenstein H. (1968), Entrepreneurship and development, American Economic Review vol. 38, p.2.

Low M.B., MacMillan I.C. (1988)., Entrepreneurship: past research and future challenges, *Journal of Management vol. 14(2)*, p.139-161.

McClelland D.C. (1961), *The achieving society*, Princeton, N.J.: D. Van Nostrand.

McMullan W.E. and Long W.A. (1987), Entrepreneurship education in the nineties, *Journal of Business Venturing vol.2*, p.261-275.

Murray J.A. (1984). A concept of entrepreneurial strategy, *Strategic Management Journal vol. 5*, p.1-13.

Plaschka G. R. and Welsch H.P. (1990), Emerging structures in entrepreneurship education: curricular designs and strategies, paper presented at the *Symposium on the Political and Social Environment of Entrepreneurship*, Entrepreneurship division, Academy of Management, August 12, 1989, George Washington University; and Emerging structures in entrepreneurship education, Entrepreneurship Theory and Practice Spring 1990, p.92.

Rosa P. and Scott M.G. 1995), Some comments on the unit of analysis in entrepreneurship research and growth and start-up, *Recent research in entrepreneurship* (RENT IX), Piacenza, Italy, p. 1-11.

Rothwell R. and Zegveld W. (1982), *Innovation and the small and medium sized firm*, Frances Pinter, London.

Schumpeter J.A. (1936), The theory of economic development, *Harvard University Press*, Cambridge.

Sexton D.L. (1980), Characteristics and role demands of successful entrepreneurs, *Paper presented at the meeting of the Academy of Management, Detroit, 1980*.

Shapero A. and Sokol L. (1982), The social dimensions of entrepreneurship, *Encyclopedia of Entrepreneurship*, p.72-90.

Smilor R. and Gill, Jr., M.D. (1986), *The new business incubator: linking talent, technology, capital and know-how*, Lexington, MA, D.C. Heath & Co.

Stevenson H. (1993), The nature of entrepreneurship, in: Dynamic *Entrepreneurship in Central and Eastern Europe*, Delwell Publishers The Hague, 291p.

Stevenson H. and Gumpert D.E. (1985) *The heart of entrepreneurship*, Harvard Business Review, p.85-94.

Twaalfhoven B.W.M. (1985), The role of the dynamic entrepreneur, in: *Dynamic Entrepreneurship in Central and Eastern Europe*, p.7-12.

Van de Ven A. (1993), The development of an infrastructure for entrepreneurship, *Journal of Business Venturing vol. 8(3)*, p.211-230.

Vesper K.H. and McMullen W. (1988), Entrepreneurship today classes, *Entrepreneurship: theory and practice*, Fall 1988, p.7

Vesper K.H. (1980), *New venture strategies*, Englewood Cliffs, N.J.: Prentice-Hall, Inc.

Vesper K.H. (1985), *Entrepreneurship Education 1985*, Babson College, Wellesley.

24 Training for Entrepreneurship: Playing and Language Games - an Inquiry into the Swedish Education System

Daniel Hjorth
Bengt Johannisson

Abstract

Each and everyone has entrepreneurial experience, namely as children; in play we interactively enacted new realties independent of the arena on which we were operating. These playing activities were guided by passion, not by rational intent. In many respects the adult entrepreneur resembles the child, making ventures emerge as an outcome of experiential action. In child development playing and the building up of a vocabulary are closely related. We suggest that also in this respect there is a parallel between the child and the entrepreneur. We therefore propose here a language-game framework for entrepreneurship.

Jointly with pedagogues the conditions for training for entrepreneurship in the Swedish education system have been researched. The study includes both high school and universities; for the latter a unique comprehensive survey is provided. The findings report a number of activities in order to promote entrepreneurial behavior on all levels in the education system. Not withstanding such achievements, the real breakthrough has not yet come.

There seems to be several obstacles delaying the creation of a more entrepreneurial society (in Sweden) in general and a more entrepreneurial school in particular. The most fundamental barrier, though, is our language. Our language constitutes our ability to recognize and describe the entrepreneurial phenomenon. There is therefore a need for language redesigning including, first, more frequent thinking on entrepreneurship that prompts the vocabularies of passion, intuition, metaphor, and experimentation. Second, in order to recognize the emerging character of entrepreneurship nouns should be replaced by verbs, e.g. organization by organizing. There is also a need for coining new concepts which capture the unique feature of entrepreneurship, e.g. 'creactive' in the sense that entrepreneurship is about creative ideas which also are put into action.

Entrepreneurship as Learning

Entrepreneurship and learning have overlapping features. Entrepreneurship is about learning in the marketplace. On the macrolevel the creation (and the closure) of firms is a major strategy which industries and regions should learn (and unlearn). On the microlevel individual entrepreneurial enterprises, by commercializing innovation, invite potential buyers to learn to use the new products or assume new behaviors. This indicates that training for entrepreneurship cannot be separated from entrepreneurship itself. Such training in turn has to be related to personal strategies being used to adopt an entrepreneurial mode in everyday life. Training for entrepreneurship bridges tacit and formal knowledge (Nonaka and Takeuchi 1995). As pointed out by Vesper (1990) successful entrepreneurs must be able to combine learning by training with learning by experience.

With e.g. Stevenson and Jarillo 1990, Gartner et al. 1992, Frank and Lueger 1995 we perceive entrepreneurship to be an organizing endeavour with the aim of deploying resources according to opportunity. Organizing is obviously associated with human interaction where fluency, and continuous adjustments are necessities. Such interaction is important not only because it facilitates the acquiring of resources and disposing of products. The multiplex dialogue, 'polylog' of personal networking also represents a generic learning strategy for entrepreneurs.

The traditional approach to learning for entrepreneurship assumes that ignorant, unlearned, children should successively be trained to acquire entrepreneurial capabilities. In a recently published study on behalf of the Swedish Ministry of Trade and Industry, we conclude instead that entrepreneurs are 'naturally born' - they all reveal an entrepreneurial disposition in their early socialization process (Johannisson and Madsén

472

1997). Their entrepreneurial behavior includes taking own and spontaneous initiatives, questioning what others take for granted, and inviting others to play. Children's play is in many respects the practice of entrepreneurship in which they share emerging tacit knowledge with fellow children much in the same way as adult entrepreneurs share experience with trusted businesspersons while enacting their ventures. Thus, the challenge for any entrepreneurial education, in our mind all education, is not to reform children's learning modes. It is rather a matter of providing an educational system which enforces these natural capabilities and wards off attacks staged by well-meaning but uninformed meddlesome adults.

Children are then learners by nature, i.e. not only because they have to accept to be educated by us as adults. Learning for children is in its generic forms a social happening whether it is within the dyadic child-parent relationship or within children's play. Children play everywhere independent of the institutional conditions and that play is characterized by an intense dialogue whereby substantive experiences and pure fantasies are combined into an enacted reality. Even children which play alone in such sense-making processes often present plays with several actors. The multiple spoken parts reveal the importance of language in the learning process. Children as well as adult entrepreneurs literally 'make' sense to their environments in an experiential learning process characterized by dialogue and exchange, cf. Gartner et al. 1992, Weick 1995.

In the above-mentioned investigation we saw that one of the most important criticism of the school system was its 'inability' to unlearn children's ability to play. We could say that, in a slightly more abstract sense, as children's ability to keep a playing mode to reality, to have a 'playality' as well as reality in terms of their life worlds. What this means for the individual is here seen as secondary to what it means for the intersubjective, social, and relational aspect of reality. We are aware of the fact that the life-world concept is a concept that signifies the individual. We try to show how this might be a conception inherited from a more subject-focused epistemology. Play is here seen as a social activity, an activity that invites us to see the individual both as potentially spontaneous, intentional, and creative and a discursively produced subject. The participating mode, i.e., intentional or behavioral (reactive), is a question of context and life world.

Words are generic symbols which however may remain symbolic, i.e. may not lead to practice. While the Swedish business climate is considered

473

to be rather harsh, the Swedish educational system superficially communicates a strong belief in entrepreneurial values and behavior. The general curriculum of the Swedish high school and junior college clearly encourages an entrepreneurial mode of behavior.

Table 1: The Curriculum of the Swedish High School/Junior College - a Blueprint for Entrepreneurial Learning

SCHOOL OBJECTIVES	ENTREPRENEURIAL LEARNING
* Develop curiosity, desire for learning	* Alertness, change orientation
* Encourage a personal learning mode	* Own vision guides experiential learning
* Nourish willfulness and cooperation	* Self-confidence and personal networking
* Question assumptions in problem solving	* Take nothing for granted
* Reflect upon own experiences	* Learn by accumulated experiences
* Evaluate own learning	* Reflecting by interacting

Considering that the business climate in Sweden is today rather harsh, our challenge is to identify why the actual culture and the proclaimed objectives of the school are so contradictory. We assume that a weighty explanation is the lack of both recognition of the child's natural capabilities and an appropriate language to communicate entrepreneurship. In the next section we present a theoretical discourse concerning the role of language in organizations in general and in learning settings in particular. Then we discuss the consequent implication that entrepreneurship should be approached as though different in kind from management. By outlining the need for a different kind of language use, even a new vocabulary, a new framework emerges. This is used when reflecting upon experiences from the review of the Swedish education system with respect to how it trains for entrepreneurship.

An Emerging Framework

The notion of entrepreneurship as emergence means shifting the perspective from structure to process, from uncertainty reduction to coping with equivocality. Within a processual ontology, a canon repeated by Heraclitus, Nietzsche, and to some extent Heidegger, the focus is shifted from *being* to *becoming* (e.g., Whitehead 1929, cf. also Schon 1971, Chia 1996). A quote from Nietzsche, albeit we do not intend to give an extensive philosophical reflection here, would be appropriate to illustrate this view: '...all believe, desperately even, in what is being. But Heraclitus will remain eternally right with his assertion that being is an empty fiction...' (in Kaufman 1975).

The need for stability is possible to interpret in many ways. From the perspective of those who envy natural science we, as social scientists, should develop the same usefulness of, e.g., causality as often is the case within the natural sciences. Choosing a perception of the world as 'being' rather than becoming would certainly facilitate a translation of the language game of causality to suit the social sciences (here primarily restricted to management, organization, and entrepreneurship). But also, and this is the main point here, entrepreneurship would be seen as an even more romantic and striking conception if the world was this being. In such a world the breaking of patterns would certainly be a 'job for a hero'. This perspective would invite to a return into trait theories about entrepreneurship, a journey we want to avoid, especially since our destination is an understanding of the terms for entrepreneurial education within the formal education system.

From a linguistic perspective, attention would then, in the traditional 'being' world view, certainly be organized toward nouns rather than verbs, nouns thereby confirming this image of the world. It cannot be stressed enough that it is precisely through the normalized preferred use of nouns that the world has become one of being rather than becoming. The great importance of language games is thus apparent. These games include a textual, a linguistic, and a narrative dimension (the semiotic system: the subject of speech, the spoken subject, and the speaking subject, Kerby 1991). It is not only the 'linguistic turn' (as it is most often called) that influences this need for rethinking learning as tied to language games; also the concrete social conditions which are the concern of most (at least)

European countries today influence the need for creative processes in reshaping society.

We have investigated some of the conditions within the Swedish education system since it is traditionally 'within' that system that young people are taught the language they use in constructing their world views. Formal learning processes are thus the pivotal ground for the ambition to change the inertia being built into everyday language through the use of stalemating metaphors such as the evolutional, the biological, and the dynamic (Foucault 1991: 62). These in turn produce dualisms such as aggressive-adaptive, inert-living, and movement-immobility, just some examples of how an unreflected translation of scienticizing language leeds to unfruitful discourses for learning. These mentioned metaphors alone, very much present within e.g., organization theory, have vast implications for self-perceptions - functionalistically drawn identities - and thus for participation or co-creation potentials.

The process view of reality which embeds the notion of entrepreneurship as social and economic emergence, as organizing, perceives the world as becoming. The simple example of organisations vs. organizing illustrates the language game. We have been teaching (not learning) students theories about organizations so that all they see when it is the time for practice is this noun: the organization. The need for a creative and naturally moving business is thus not met through a search for specific heroes with psychological characteristics (e.g., McClelland 1961, Rotter 1966), but through a shift toward a 'verb-perception': organizing. This leaves the Hollywoodistic glamour image of the entrepreneur far behind, as did the recent development in leadership research (i.e., shift from 'who is' to 'how to do'), and in a sense also challenges the subject-object division from an epistemological perspective.

We are not suggesting that we intend to adopt this view fully in this paper. That would take a much more careful consideration of our own language use. Instead we want to focus on how training for entrepreneurship, or 'entrepreneuring', as there is no verb for this noun, can be approached from a socio-linguistic understanding of the life-world concept play the intersubjective, relational concept of language games.

Tightly intertwined language-learning-world-view form a relational complex. Our world-view comes to us through language, in the discourses we become involved in and in the discourses we intentionally set out to enter (e.g., Foucault 1970 has discussed this). But this 'discovery' as well as intentionality are both concepts that we have learned (or been taught often) through language. These words, as signs in a sign system, are presenting themselves as signifiers, ready-made concepts, that acquire their meaning in an endless chain of signifiers (de Saussure 1974, Kristeva 1991, Lacan 1968). This relational construct of meaning is reproduced in the social realm of life where understanding becomes both a contextual and a relational accomplishment. The need for understanding not only what is learnt (in a more traditional sense) but how one is in fact learning is thus dependent on my way of relating to me as a language-using individual and to the context (discourses and social relations) I find myself in.

As has been fruitfully developed elsewhere (O'Connor 1996, Czarniawska 1997) the narrative approach to knowledge and thus learning, discloses the artificially maintained scientific discourse of knowledge which gives prominence to stereotyped perceptions of not only the textual nature of reality but also to the learning situation. The latter has been invaded by a functionalistic 'division of labor' that places the student and the teacher in a mail-tube model of language where sender and receiver are seen as being at each end of the tube. In such a learning situation the world becomes fixated, the inner-outer metaphor is erected in numerous ways: teacher/student, student/practitioner, school/society, subject/object, and so on. In our effort to abolish these perceptions we present later in this paper some tentative images of a new 'virtuous circle' for a contextual-relational view of learning as a life-long activity *within* the society, not for society.

After this short elaboration on the choice of themes, let us now move on to a further discussion of proposed themes: 1) the life-world concept; 2) playing as a mode of relating to reality; 3) learning processes as a relational concept; and 4) language games as a narrative concept. This discussion does not have the ambition to build a framework or a conceptual wholeness for an understanding of learning and entrepreneuring. Faithful to our own image of learning we instead encourage the reader to make own interpretations and contextualize them, in the places for learning that s/he is co-creating. It is only in this sense that we believe this 'contribution' can be a contribution.

1. The life world:

We can of course not apply any inherited concept and expect it to work. The extension of concepts and meanings into life worlds of individuals is something that occurs along with ideological and political practices. Inasmuch as well as life world as a concept has to be given a meaning within the context of this paper (and its objective), we should also be somewhat self-reflective and make clear that our personal life worlds are included in the description of life world here. Our overall approach of resistance to the concept as it presents itself to us is vital for the emergence of local meanings. The concept was brought into social-philosophical discourse by Habermas and is early tied to the processes of colonization that different value-spheres set in motion as they spread, rather isomorphically, into the individual's life worlds (Habermas 1984; Deetz 1992). Let us only add to this description the more language-focusing conception developed by Wittgenstein and Schütz. The life world holds what they call the dogmatism of the individual's language use. Here they refer to those aspects of language, values, ideologies, and taken-for-grantedness that escape reflection and thus present themselves in thinking and speaking as being natural and neutral.

In the shaping of life worlds not much intentional architecture is used. The life world is more fruitfully understood as a discursive web *within* which we reflect, not as a background *against* which we reflect. It is therefore more important *how* learning processes are created rather than *what* they are about. 'How' is often a reflection of the taken-for-granted aspects of the life world. But all discourse is not discovered (if at all) as we become adults. Many discourses are entered by us (of course as discursive constructs) and we try to learn from them, or let them form us in certain ways, e.g., become a 'researcher'. The importance of a consistency in the educational system is here evident. Little is today done except for the tearing down of the conceptions students carry with them into the university system. Not even that effort is always successful.

Trying to understand discourse that influences you, that is you, the representation you perform of yourself (i.e., yourself as representation), not the least from the initial discussion of this paper, would allow more reflexive learning processes to emerge. Calling students out to play with their own taken-for-grantedness is often the first vital step toward entrepreneuring, toward learning how they learn, and thus toward a more playful mode of relating to reality.

2. *Playing as a mode of relating to reality:*

Winnicott (1971) has developed a framework for understanding what happens when a child 'learns' her/his reality. The question that engaged Winnicott was 'where we spend our time if it is not primarily in the Freudian inner or in the objectivist outer'. He concluded that for understanding these learning processes the *potential space* was the most interesting. This space, as we conceive it, is the in-between that has similarities with the intersubjective and the relational. The spatial connotation of Winnicott's concept is important though as well since it ties the concept to the child's use of space, 'spacing' as it were, and thus grasps both the subject-object dimension of 'intersubjective', and the social dimension of the relational.

The discussion in Winnicott aims to show, among other things, the importance of a safe relation to a mother figure and this relation's constitutional effect on playing. Playing can occur in this relation. For us it is important to reflect on the use of this conception for the understanding of learning and play. We can easily see the need for a new perception of the world, i.e., perceiving the world as becoming rather than being. This perception would reduce the anxiety when facing radical breaks with everything that the latter view sees as urgent. Seeing the world as becoming and myself as part of this, as co-creator, enables the safe (ontological) relation in which individuals feel safe to enter the in-between, the potential space, where playing can occur.

It seems that we are arguing for a parental mission, for those responsible for learning processes here. We would interpret this in the light of the discussion thus far: the reflexive use of one's life world and the life worlds of others, in learning processes, has to start with the establishment of safe relation in which play, i.e., life worlds which are dialogically made visible can occur. This is what makes it possible for children to both take the world for granted and equally naturally try to change it so as to enact new ones.

3. Learning processes as a relational concept:

Our aim is to abandon the view on education as something that can be understood through the metaphor of sender-receiver. This stereotype cuts off relations of trust and keeps the individual's life worlds in the background (thereby conserving their dogmatic nature of influence). Here potential space, and hence play, is impossible.

The most desirable mode of learning is a collective and shared responsibility for the creation of learning processes. The directedness, so to say, that is taken for granted in learning organizes e.g., 'students' attention away from one another and toward someone constructed as teacher. Failure to make play a social activity in the development of a child is thus evident here. In extreme cases this is referred to as autism, in terms of learning we should apply this term: many student come out of the educational system as learning autists. By this we mean that they are not well trained to train themselves or see their colleagues as co-creators of learning processes. Here we find ground for much of the so-called, and quite classical, communication problems of professional life.

4. Language games as a narrative concept:

Also 'science' has built up its stock of narratives to constitute what science is in accordance with certain styles of writing and thinking. These styles were believed to create a safe border between, e.g., the arts and lay-man knowledge which echoed the Platonic split between aesthetics, ethics, and truth. Long before the debate between so-called modernists and postmodernists, that between traditionalists and modernists dealt with similar rhetoric tricks in order to establish such borders. What we attempt to do here is to show how our understanding of entrepreneurship with its own language game can be furthered by applying a narrative approach to knowledge.

The language game of entrepreneurship is formed through several discourses, not the least that of the Austrian school of economics (to which Schumpeter belonged) and Hollywood (to which most of the today's heroes of entrepreneurship belong). We would also stress the mutual dependence between the language games of management, or better, managerialism, and entrepreneurship since these, particularly within the corporate context, have created this need for each other. The latter can be seen as a result of the unrelaxed use of metaphors of dynamics as discussed above. As a very young discourse within our educational systems, there is still much to be done in the shaping of this language game. Awareness of the discursive setup, only briefly hinted in the above-mentioned influencing discourses (e.g., Hollywood) facilitates a more creative play.

With a narrative approach we would say, together with Kerby (1991:5) that: 'In claiming that the self is a product, and implicate, of action, we are thereby removing epistemological priority from the human subject. That is, there simply is no self serving as the originator of meaning, something or someone to whom we might appeal in matters concerning the meaning or truth of his or her utterances as though these were prefigured in some nonlinguistic interiority of consciousness.'

In this perspective storytelling 'in the class-room' would play an important role to bring forth individual life worlds as they narrate them. This opens their understanding of themselves as subjects generated by the narrative. A world view that approaches reality as becoming would neutralize the tendencies to closure that all stories carry. As language is never personal or private, the social aspect of play is guaranteed through this narrative approach, which also contributes constructively to the awareness of the political and ideological aspects of myself and other selves. There is thus a dimension of selfhood which is inherently social. While sites for learning, from which to write and speak, are of course not free from ideologies and values, this is part of the picture - the need for entrepreneuring as oppositional play: 'It is the potential "rule-bound freedom"', of creative deviance, which many contemporary fictions seek to explore in the analogy they draw between games and writing, a qualified liberty which I would like to extend to the gaming communal subject. ... playfulness offers a means of theorizing the creative possibilities available to human subjects within community' (Worthington 1996: 104).

Entrepreneurship Education in Context - the Swedish Case

Trends in Entrepreneurship Education

Since new and small firms have been acknowledged as the major job creators in Sweden, the promotion of business start-ups has become a major concern in public policy: about 40 per cent of those launching new

481

ventures are subsidized by the State. In addition concern has been increasing for the role of the education system in promoting entrepreneurship. Therefore we - a research team consisting of researchers of entrepreneurship and didactics - were commissioned by the Ministry of Trade and Industry to investigate how entrepreneurship might be promoted in the education system. Since the Swedish public sector is highly decentralized, with financially very strong municipalities, the directives prescribed special attention to the local interplay between school and different stakeholders in the community. We were also asked to identify existing barriers to the promotion of entrepreneurship in the education system and to suggest means to overcome these.

As a first step the research team redefined entrepreneurship so as to encompass the relational features presented above, moving from a traditional trait approach to the image of organizing. Also, along with e.g. OECD (CERI 1989), we associate entrepreneurship more with general enterprising behavior than with innovative market exchange and more with evolutionary change than radical. This understanding of entrepreneurship was further elaborated with regard to level of education. Promotion of entrepreneurship in junior high school could mean enforcing spontaneous learning processes inasmuch as the young children were alertly and with confidence exploring their emerging reality. In senior high school the focus could be organizing in the more restricted sense and practising collaborative behavior in projects. Only at the university level would tool kits, with e.g. feasibility plans for launching an own firm, be effective.

Major findings of the investigation relevant to the present discussion include:

- On all levels of high school pedagogical experiments promoting entrepreneurial behavior are going on and are launched mainly by 'education entrepreneurs'. In a study carried out jointly with students at the teachers' college at Växjö University, 188 Swedish education entrepreneurs were identified and surveyed in mail and telephone interviews. Behaviors they have in common with entrepreneurs in the market include a passion for their job, proactive motivation of pupils, project organizing across classroom and school boundaries. In spite of their potential contribution to a more vital school, these school entrepreneurs remain more or less isolated in their local contexts,

482

getting little recognition for their work. This is partially however a self-constructed situation since the education entrepreneurs devote little time to anything but their students and their general networking.

- A number of campaigns promote entrepreneurship, such as 'Young Enterprise' , specialized entrepreneurial senior high schools, programs run as joint ventures with larger corporations, and programs in entrepreneurship.

- In the 1990s academic programs at business and technical schools at Swedish universities have skyrocketed. About 80 different programs and courses, encompassing the majority of Swedish universities, report that they offer entrepreneurship and/or small business management. Yet many of these programs/courses are only about innovation, new venturing or small business management, with little ambition to promote student venturing. While most appreciated by students are projects in businesses, the university staff find student exchange in small classes most stimulating.

Having confirmed the playfulness and enterprising mode of all children, we put the searchlight on different hindrances for the development of a more entrepreneurial Swedish education system. These barriers can be identified, considered, and subsequently coped with by identifying their practical/material, ideological/political, and symbolic/ cultural dimensions. The Swedish education system is under hard pressure because restrictions due to a weak national economy and tight municipal budgets. Huge classes and a minimal supportive staff make the time available for individual guidance and students' initiatives very scarce. Ideological/political barriers include professional norms which favour a hierarchical and closed system which trains the young people to aspire to become nothing but salaried employees. The colleges training teachers for the junior high school in Sweden, with the exception of Växjö, offer no training for entrepreneurship, nor enrol staff with concrete business experience. Symbolic/cultural barriers, finally, include existing values and attitudes to entrepreneurship in the school context. As indicated we consider the current usage of language to be the major source of obstacles to the creation of an entrepreneurial education system. We discuss in the next subsection the drastic need for a reform.

In an intriguing paper Gartner (1993) has invited to research about entrepreneurship and language. Gartner's ambition is to initiate reflection about the generic features of entrepreneurship as a process among academics. Our ambition is, in contrast, to propose a reflective use of language for encouraging entrepreneurship which goes beyond what is usually associated with culture (e.g. people's entrepreneurial attributes and intentions or their attitudes to becoming an owner-managers and establish a family business). We want to propose substantive strategies to inhabit colloquial language with a vocabulary which, if enhanced by the education system, may turn entrepreneurial behavior into that which is taken for granted. More specifically our 'program' for an entrepreneurial vocabulary includes the following features.

1. More frequent use of common words associated with entrepreneurship
2. Use of verbs and not of nouns indicating becoming
3. Promotion of a new vocabulary re-presenting entrepreneurship

1. *Encourage use of common words reflection entrepreneurship:* Since our vocabulary represents our socialized image of reality, a use of language which is inhabited by words which reflect entrepreneurial behavior will create a setting which promotes this entrepreneurial behavior. More frequent everyday use of general words such as 'opportunity', 'initiative', 'responsibility', 'intuition', 'commitment' and 'passion' will direct attention to corresponding behaviors. This reality builds on both what the person says/does her-/himself and what s/he observes and pays attention to in others' behavior. By talking about 'taking' initiative and responsibility we put even more emphasis on the active personal involvement in the creation of the own context.

The use of words usually associated with business in other settings may also enhance the legitimacy, and thereby the practice, of entrepreneurship. However, this is a delicate matter. In e.g. Sweden, the market ideology has become introduced into the public sector in an effort to make it more effective. Administrative units are turned into 'cost centres' or even 'profit centres' and clients are turned into 'customers'. However, this shift in terminology does not seem to have increased the efficiency of the public sector (its employment and value creation seem to have shrunk correspondingly). An alternative to this management approach to the vitalization of the public sector would be to provide an entrepreneurial vocabulary. Ironically enough, in Sweden it seems to be legitimate to be 'enterprising' in the general connotation of work in all societal sectors except that of business. A strategy of making the context of business more entrepreneurial by way of language use may operate as a lever for genuine and substantive entrepreneurial activity.

Some self-reflection concerning ourselves as members of the academic community, itself embedded in the overall educational system, may be clarifying. As pointed our by Chia (1996) academia needs its own entrepreneurs. However, there is then not only a need for more creative and bold thoughts and action in writing but also for a new vocabulary. Typically, academic reports originate in a 'problem statement', continue with a review of previous research (locked into traditions) and the location of the research frontier, and continue with a thorough structuring of available data (analytical bias). It is easy to draw a parallel between this traditional way of doing research and management. The alternative, more entrepreneurial, approach would imply an 'opportunity statement', scanning the research environment for previous experiences useful for analogy and impressionistically implementing a prospective research strategy (cf. Schön 1983).

2. *Give priority to verbs, not to nouns:* Nouns are embedded in an existence of being while verbs are associated with emergence, with entrepreneurship as becoming. Accordingly we associate entrepreneurship with 'organizing' - of e.g. images and resources - not with 'organization'. Enacting new ventures is a process characterized by networking, trust building, and learning. Management and institutions in contrast are described by nouns such as structures, contracts and formal competencies. An intriguing difference between 'entrepreneurship' and 'learning' is that while entrepreneurship appears only as a noun and not as a verb it is the other way around with regards to learning.

The use of verbs itself does not imply an entrepreneurial orientation. Marketing may imply nothing but implementing market plans although it does include promises about dialogue and mutual learning. Buzzwords such as 'benchmarking' may be associated with the constant comparison with exemplary competitors. Yet entrepreneurs are creating their own behavior; even this sometimes means creative imitation.

485

3. *A special entrepreneurial vocabulary:* As we have indicated the management vocabulary being used is not a technical matter but reflects an ideology, by us addressed as managerialism. Using theses words, recontextualizing them into an entrepreneurial setting, is therefore doomed to fail. Some would e.g. argue that while management is about periodic planning and associated implementation and evaluation, entrepreneurship is about shorter learning cycles. However, we believe that a vocabulary independent of management must be developed. Managerialism, as argued, is occupying major institutions and gives a certain bias to the existing vocabulary used to present business activity. Typically the heartland of management, financial planning and accounting, is overrun with detailed terminology while the genuine features of entrepreneurship mainly appear in colloquial language. Obviously there is a need for language development if justice is to be done to entrepreneurship.

Below we give a small contribution to an emerging vocabulary for entrepreneurship (our ambition here is limited by English not being our mother tongue). It may seem pretentious to provide completely new terms, but entrepreneurship is different in kind to what has traditionally been associated with business. These traditions are not only prevailing in the education system but in the Swedish society at large. Our argument is that a renewed vocabulary will not only create a broader understanding and legitimacy of entrepreneurship but also solve some of the concrete problems in the present school system.

Table 2: Contributions to a Dictionary of Entrepreneurship

Proposed concept/word	Comments
Creactive	Entrepreneurship is not just about idea generation, not even a reduction to invention, but implies the enactment of new patterns of behavior in the market. Entrepreneurship is about creativity and action.
Reflaction	While the linear rationality of managerialism proposes that thought and planing should precede action, entrepreneurship as experiential learning calls for own actions and subsequent reflection as they amalgamate with other parties' action into an enacted environment.
Glocal	While managerialism advocates global values, theories, and business activity, entrepreneurs combine such an outlook with local insights including e.g. personal theories and concern for details.
Polylogue	Entrepreneurship as organizing is beyond the dialogue of the dyadic relationship; it calls for versatile networking where new parties are continually invited to contribute.

If the children's playfulness is accepted as just another word for entrepreneurship, and described in 'proper' language which in a creative way bridges between the school world and the life world, will parents become motivated to get involved in school operations. Resources will be generated and projects, also including business, will spontaneously be organized across school borders. Such projecting will thus encourage the establishing of an entrepreneurial school. A virtuous circle emerges.

Entrepreneurship Education - A Linguistic Challenge

For a number of reasons the 'entrepreneurial' objectives of the Swedish education system according to Table 1 remain the proclaimed goal alone,

487

far from the actual practices. A reformed teachers' education would challenge the prevailing traditional teaching mode and more perforated boundaries between the school and the local community would enlarge the resource base for the staff and the playground for the students. Exchange with the business community would also provide mutual learning opportunities, not the least through the creation of a common language. In addition, and perhaps even more important, such exchange between the school and the world of practice will make clearer the limits to the spoken language and thus to formal education. Qualified internships followed up by reflection and discussion in the classroom setting will help the students to create knowledge on their own terms, cf. Nonaka and Takeuchi 1995.

With respect to the university system, Swedish authorities and institutions today (1997) pay lip service to the need for a more entrepreneurial academic setting. As reported, it is quite common that Swedish universities offer courses and even larger programs in entrepreneurship and small business management. Nevertheless, with few exceptions the entrepreneurial teaching activities remain as reserves in the overall academic system. Due to lack of teaching material and the prevailing examination standards, management vocabulary and therefore managerialism still rules. Only cross-breeding with disciplines outside the social and technical sciences, such as philosophy and aesthetics, will make it possible to break out of this mental prison.

As we have argued elsewhere (Hjorth and Johannisson 1997) the shift toward a process view of reality places the implied conflict between the organizing (vs. organization) for stewardship and organization (vs. organizing) for renewal in a new light. Similarly managerialism and entrepreneurialism could be seen as proper labels within the same dichotomy, pointing out the ideological dimension of the juxtapositioning. We use 'organizing' here also as a metonym for learning in a way that leave room for many other interpretations of this broad activity. If these interpretations are going to promote entrepreneurship however there is a need for a vocabulary which can articulate entrepreneurship in such a way that it can challenge the managerial hegemony at our business schools.

Academic training for entrepreneurship must for two reasons be especially concerned with providing a professional language which bridges academic thought and practical action. First, the universities represent a major source for the cultivation of management vocabulary which has to be actively challenged. Second, in Sweden, the universities have been enjoined to include in their everyday practice a third task besides that of research and education: actively transferring their competencies to the different external stakeholders, in particular the business community. While our evaluation of existing internships show that students and entrepreneurs/practitioners do not have any language problems, the efficiency of the educational programs would probably increase considerably if separate vocabularies were bridged already in the academic setting.

We have offered some contributions to the renewal of the colloquial language so as to encompass a vocabulary and grammar which enforce enterprising behavior. The circuit then so to say is closed because young children typically develop both their terminology and grammar during the primary socialization, experiment as much with language as with concrete activities in their playing and living. Just as it is natural for them to practice this experiential and entrepreneurial mode of behavior, we adults routinely tell the children to behave, even stop playing. We can only agree with March (1976) who suggests that we should imitate children rather than censure them, just as to allow ourselves to play around with words when e.g. reading fiction (especially poetry). In order to create an entrepreneurial society in general and entrepreneurial education in particular we must dare to perforate every boundary to the playground.

References

Beck, U. (1992) *Risk Society*. London: SAGE.

Behler, E. (1990) *Irony and the Discourse of Modernity,* Seattle: University of Washington Press.

CERI (1989) *Towards an Enterprising Culture: A Challenge for Education and Training.* Mimeo. Paris: OECD/CERI.

Chia, R. (1996) 'The Problem of Reflexivity in Organizational Research:Towards a Postmodern Science of Organization', *Organization*, Vol. 3, No. 1, pp 31-59.

Czarniawska, B. (1997) *Narrating the Organization.* Chicago: University of Chicago Press.

Deetz, S. (1992) *Democracy in an Age of Corporate Colonization: Developments in Communication and the Politics of Everyday Life.* Albany: State University of New York Press.

Foucault, M. (1970) *The Order of Things.* New York: Random House.

Foucault, M. (1991) In Burchell, G, Gordon, C and Peter Miller (Eds) *The Foucault-effect: Studies in Governmentality.* Chicago: The University of Chicago Press.

Frank, H. and Lueger, M. (1995) Zur Re-Konstruktion von Entwicklungsprozessen. Die *Betriebswirtschaft.* Vol. 55., No. 6., pp 721-742.

Gartner, B. (1993) 'Word Leed to Deeds: Towards an Organizational Emergence Vocabulary.' *Journal of Business Venturing.* Vol. 8, pp 231-239.

Gartner, W. B., Bird, B. J. and Starr, J. A. (1992) Acting As If: Differentiating Entrepreneurial from Organizational Behavior.' *Entrepreneurship Theory and Practice.* Spring 1992, pp 13-31.

Habermas, J. (1984) *The Theory of Communicative Action. Volume 1: Reason and the Rationalization of Society.* Boston: Beacon Press.

Hjorth, D. and Johannisson, B. (1997) 'The Ugly Duckling of Organizing.' Paper presented at the *42 ICSB World Conference*, San Francisco, June.

Johannisson, B. and Madsén, T. (1997) *I entreprenörskapets tecken - en studie av skolning i förnyelse.* Närings- och handelsdepartementet, Ds. 1997:3. Stockholm: Fritzes. (with D. Hjorth, U Ivarsson and A Öien)

Kaufmann, W. A. (ed.) (1975) *Existentialism from Dostoevsky to Sartre.* New York: New American Library.

Kerby, A. P. (1991) *Narrative and the Self.* Indianapolis: Indiana University Press.

Kristeva, J. (1991) *Stranger to Ourselves.* New York: Columbia University.

Lacan, J. (1968). *The Language of the Self.* Baltimore: John Hopkins University Press.

March, J. (1976) *The Technology of Foolishness.* In March, J and Olsen, J P (Eds) *Ambiguity and Choice in Organizations.* Oslo: Universitetsforlaget.

McClelland, D. (1961) *The Achieving Society.* Princeton: D. Van Nostrand.

Nonaka, I. and Takeuchi, H. (1995) *The Knowledge-Creating Company.* New York: Oxford University Press.

490

O'Connor, E. (1996) 'Lines of Authority: Readings of Foundational Texts on the Profession of Management'. *Journal of Management History*,

Rotter, J. R. (1966) 'Generalized Expectancies for Internal Versus External Control of Reinforcement.' *Psychological Monographs*.

Saussure, F. de (1974) *Course in General Linguistics*. London: Fontana.

Schon, D. A. (1971) *Beyond the Sayable State*. New York: Random House.

Schön, D. (1983) *The Reflective Practitioner. How Professionals Think in Action*. New York, N.Y.: Basic Books.

Stevenson, H. H. and Jarillo, C. (1990) 'A Paradigm of Entrepreneurship: Entrepreneurial Management'. *Strategic Management Journal*. Vol 11, Special Issue on Corporate Entrepreneurship. Pp 17-27.

Vesper, K. H. (1990) *New Venture Strategies*. Revised edition. Englewood Cliffs: Prentice Hall.

Weick, K. (1995) *Sensemaking in Organizations*. Sage: Thousand Oaks.

Whitehead, A. N. (1929) 1960 *Process and Reality - An Essay in Cosmology*. New York: Harper and Row and Evanston.

Winnicott, D. W. (1971) *Playing and Reality*. Harmondsworth: Penguin Books.

Worthington, K. L. (1996) *Self as Narrative*. Oxford: Clarendon Press.

25 Applied Technology to the Business Plan's Development Workshop

Rafael Alcaraz
Jorge Ledezma

Introduction

In the 1940s, the Monterrey Institute of Technology (ITESM), in Mexico, began its operations offering professional majors in the areas of administration and engineering. The purpose of this institution was to form specialized people that the businesses in Mexico required. In the 1980s, the ITESM decided to include a series of abilities, conduct, values and characteristics in the proiffesional formation of its students, and one of them was to make the students be entrepreneurs. This required a special formation, a process that could permit the development of professionals with an innovative attitude, able to act in a way that they would create new directions, new ideas, builders of a new society, actors and not part of the audience of life. In other words, that they would become 'agents of change'.

With this in mind, the Entrepreneurial Program is born to give a sign of distinction to the graduates of the ITESM System, being a part of its fundamental mission to form college graduates and postgraduates with levels of excellency in the area of their specialty, giving incentives to the students so that they can develop an innovative and entrepreneurial spirit the vocation of leaders committed with the development of their communities, respect towards human dignity, and an appreciation for the cultural, historical and social values of their community. In order to reach this mission, the ITESM gave the Entrepreneurial Program its fundamental goal: 'To promote and develop the entrepreneurial and innovative spirit in the students of the ITESM.' To be able to reach this goal, since 1978 the Entrepreneurial Program gathered a group of experts, who were in charge of coordinating, establishing and giving way to the program in the 26 campus that the ITESM System has. This same group was in charge of designing an educational model as a base of operation for the program, and in the same way the organizational structure gives the program a solid background.

The practical tool that is used in the educational model of the Entrepreneurial Program is the gestation, development and implantation of a student-made business; a job that, under certain guidelines, constitute the key element in order to reach the development of the entrepreneurial spirit of everyone involved.

The academic area of the educational model is made up of a mandatory course and a degree, both of which are based on the educational package of the Entrepreneurial Program, which has more than 21 basic manuals and support manuals, and there are also more than 65 selected books that can be used for taking a deeper look at the topics that are seen in the various courses that the program has. Every semester new manuals are developed and they become part of the Educational Package of the program; each manual is made better and better every semester, until it is good enough to be published, and this is why to this date, eight books have been published and four more are in the process of being published. These books are put in reach of the community in general and of any person that is interested in developing him or herself in the various areas of the program.

One of the books that has been developed under the guidelines that have been mentioned before, is 'The Successful Entrepreneur'. This book is a supportive guide so that the entrepreneurs can develop a their business plan in a series of steps that go from the creation of an idea to the development of a project or of a company. This permits the evaluation of the technical, economical and marketing of the project to see if it is feasible.

The book gives entrepreneurs a chance to make a planning process (goals, objectives and activities, with the number of physical, human and economical resources, etc.) selecting the right way to go to be able to reach their objectives. This is why the guide is organized in a clear manner and its comprehension is easy to be able to take the entrepreneur, step by step, with concrete examples in the processes that were mentioned earlier.

There is also a complimentary application, for Windows 3.11 or Windows 95, that is oriented towards the development of a business plan.

It contains many aspects, from the way in which a company is explained in general terms to the projection of financial statements. It includes the organizational structure, the market study and the way to plan the production.

This application was developed with the goal of making it easier to create a business plan, giving a chance to the entrepreneur of being able to concentrate in the investigation and not in the complementary aspects like the creation of drawings, diagrams, calculations and formats.

Compared to other support software, this one contains calculation sheets with predefined formats, and in each of the topics there is a brief description of what is to be done in the topic and a space so that the user can write down the specific information regarding his or her topic in that particular topic.

For example, if a person wants to know what a credit is and if it is applicable to the project that he or she is currently developing, the only thing that they have to do is go to the menu, click on the topic Finances and look for the word Credit. Here they will find a definition of credit and a space so that the person can determine whether his or her business will use credits to acquire any goods. There is also another space where the user can place the amount of credit that will be necessary for the business to run smoothly.

On the top left hand corner of every page there are four options to choose to return to the previous page, file, print, or go back to the menu that has been mentioned previously.

A person can print all of the business plan, a chapter or a fraction of any chapter. Besides, the program can be saved in both Microsoft Word and Excel or in one of the two. And it can be saved in the diskette as well as in the hard disk of the computer.

There are also tools where a person can draw a flow chart or the design of a manufacturing plant that the user may have in mind, for example. Here a person may include arrows, circles, squares, etc. These are tools found on the left of the drawing sheet. Also, in the Market section, a business chart can be developed and graphs can be created and mod)fied in the Financial section.

This is a very innovative project, and it can help people who have decided to be entrepreneurs to make their business plan in a faster, more comfortable, and in a more organized manner. These people will have a clearer view of what their business will require and of its advantages and disadvantages.

This Software Version's Characteristics

This version automatizes the majority of the processes involved in the elaboration of a business plan according to the model presented through the book 'The Successful Entrepreneur' (McGraw Hill, 1997), written by Rafael Alcaraz.

In this program we can gather all the relevant information on a new business such as the mission, objectives of each one of the areas, assumptions that have been considered, job descriptions, etc. It also includes the business section providing an interrelated and automatized environment to handle the basic financial tools in a business plan: cash flow, balance sheet, income statement and financial indicators.

Main Menu

Following the presentation window, the main menu will appear. In it there are buttons available for each one of the elaboration stages of the business plan according to the book.

The way to 'surf' through the program is by a system of pages and hypertext. The pages contain information that has to do with the subject that they talk about but you will also see that some of the words are underlined and are blue. Those words are connections to other pages or to terminal windows. To reach these other pages all you have to do is click on the connection that you are interested in and the corresponding page or terminal window will appear.

The terminal windows are not linked to any other page for now, so the only possible option is to go back; this is why they are known as terminal. However, the terminal windows ask that you introduce data for information that the business plan requires.

Sharing Files with Excel and Word

If you wish to dispose of all of the information that you have gathered throughout this program in the Excel or Word applications, when you store the information you can specify that it be done in a file with both Excel and Word formats.

When you use this format two files will be generated with the same name but with .XLS and .DOC formats for Excel and Word, respectively.

Drawing Board

Throughout the program you will find sections where drawings or graphs are included to represent the process flow and a layout plan, for example. The program has a drawing blackboard with specialized tools for the elaboration of the previously mentioned graphs. On the left side of the drawing blackboard, there is a vertical tool bar that makes the creation of graphs easier. The role that they play is of pre-fabricated pieces that can be put together in the blackboard to form graphs.

To select one of these tools, simply click on it. Then on the upper left hand side of the drawing area, the selected element will appear and you can move it around by dragging it until it is in the required position. Other drawings that have been made previously in other programs (Paintbrush, for example) can also be used in the format of map bits in Windows (BMP.) You can open them in the drawing blackboard and then transfer them to the corresponding section of the business plan.

It is important to mention that there can be no modifications done to the open file inside the drawing blackboard. To open a file select the File menu, and the Open command. The way the dialogue box opens files is similar to opening files in the business plan. You can go to this section if you wish to obtain more details. After you have built your graph or if you have opened a BMP file, you can transfer it to the graphic section of the terminal window from where you took the drawing blackboard.

Designing Organization Charts

The program has a tool to design organization charts regarding your business. Click on the area where an organization chart is shown in the terminal window or in the Organization chart button in order for the tool to appear. When the tool appears, you will note that it looks like the drawing blackboard only that in this case, the tool is oriented towards designing organization charts. To put a level on the organization chart click on the category button, then drag the category until it is in the desired position. Then, to write the name of the level, click twice on the category and write the desired name there. After putting the necessary levels you can join them two by two using the line button. All you have to do is click on one of the levels that you want to join and then click on the other level.

Gantt Graphs

Gantt graphs are a way of representing a sequence of operations in time. It is useful for planning the activities when the business project that has been created is materialized. In a similar manner to the organizational chart designs and the drawing blackboard, click on any area where the graph is to be placed to make the Gantt Graph maker. Then write the name of the operation stage, the starting date and the number of days that the stage will last.

Financial Section

Throughout the program you will be asked to give specific quantities according to the terminal window in which you are found. All of these quantities are then used to elaborate the four financial tools that the book uses for its business plan: Cash flow, balance sheet, income statement and financial indicators. Its management is very simple. You only have to go to the terminal windows and wherever you find a blank space that specifies what should be introduced: a cost, expense, income, etc., write down the corresponding amount and it will automatically be reflected in the corresponding financial tool.

Probably the most complicated part is when categories or accounts that have not been specified in the standard category and account groups found in the program have to be added. In these cases you will have to define the category type, the account to which it belongs, the subordinate categories, etc. It is possible to add categories or accounts in the financial system to be able to adapt it to the individuality of your business plan. When this is possible there is a button that says 'Personalize' in the terminal window.

The program contains a series of categories that are known in the book as 'base'. However, as it was mentioned earlier, it is possible to add more categories to the system.

The system manages two kinds of categories: Superior categories and subordinate categories. The superior categories can contain zero, one or more than one subordinate category. When a superior category has subordinate categories, an amount cannot be introduced directly, instead it is calculated automatically from the subordinate category.

Each subordinate category can operate on that calculation independently. The available operations are: addition, subtraction, division, multiplication and percentages.

To create a superior category follow these steps:
1.- Write the name of the category.
2.- Select the type of category.
3.- Press Enter.

To create a subordinate level follow these steps:
1.- Write the name of the category.
2.- Press the level button.
3.- Select the operation.
4.- Press Enter.

Once you have finished adding, eliminating or editing all the necessary data, press the OK button so that the changes can be reflected in the rest of the program.

The program has a series of accounts that the book mentions as base. However, as it was mentioned before, it is possible to add more accounts to the system.

498

To create a new account follow these steps:
1.- Write the name of the account.
2.- Select the type of account.
3.- Press Enter.

Financial Behavior

This is a tool that permits a monthly and a manipulation throughout the financial projections period, of every amount reflected in the cash flow. To use this tool click twice in the space to introduce quantities found in any terminal window. A behavioral tool will appear. There are two ways of changing the quantity of a certain month: dragging the node or writing down the quantity. To drag the quantity click on the month that you wish to change, move the mouse up or down until you reach the desired value and click again to set the amount. To write down the amount click twice on the month that you wish to modify, write down the desired quantity and press enter.

Command Buttons

The command buttons permit you to carry out certain general functions in all of the pages. There are four buttons: Back, File, Print and Go to start. Back: Takes you back to the previous page. File: Opens or saves the business plan in the disk. Print: Prints the information from the chapter or from all of the business plan. Go to start: Takes you back to the main menu.

File Management

After gathering all of the information of your business plan in the file, click the File command in any of the program's pages and then select the Save business plan option. In the file list all of the files that are found in the current directory and that coincide with the type of file specified in the types of files list are shown. You can click on one of them if you wish to write on it or you can write its name in the box that says File name. You can erase the extension and the program will automatically place a pre-defined extension .EMP. If you wish to save the file in another disk, the disk units list all of the disks (hard or flexible) that can be accessed from your computer. Click on the expansion button to see the list and then click on the desired disk unit. The directory list and the file list are automatically actualized when you change the disk unit. Under the unit list the directory structure is shown. If you wish to store the file in a directory that is not the current one, then use this list to change the directory.

Opening a File with the Business Plan Information

To open a file that was previously saved in the hard disk or in a floppy disk, use the file command button from any one of the program's pages and the select the Open business plan option. A dialogue box will appear where you can select one of the files. In the file list all of the files that are found in the current directory and that coincide with the type of file specified in the type of file list will be shown. Click on any one of them to open it. In the disk unit list all of the disks are shown (hard, flexible and CD-ROM disks) that you computer can access. Click on the expansion button to see the list and the click on the required disk unit. The directory list and the file list are automatically brought up to date when the disk unit is modified. Under the unit list is the directory structure. If the file that you are looking for is not found in the current directory, then use this list to go to another directory.

Printing the Business Plan Information

You can print all of the business plan, one of its chapters or one of its subjects. Use the Print command button that is found in any of the pages. A dialogue box will appear. It has three options: Print all of the chapter, Only some of the subjects in the chapter or All of the business plan. If you choose All of the chapter, the chapter that you are in will be printed. If you choose Only some of the subjects in the chapter then you will have to choose, from the list of topics, the ones that you need to print. To select them, simply click on them. Click on the OK button to begin printing.

500

Conclusions

In the future it will be more and more usual to find technological support that will make entrepreneurial development easier. For example, during the following year the ITESM will give access to a series of technological support elements for its Entrepreneurial Program, which are:

- Web pages with access to selected cases and articles.
- Web pages with links to data bases and for contacting other entrepreneurs.
- A CD for obtaining information and with self-learning modules.
- Groupwares have been formed for the analysis of business opportunities, sharing technical, financial and market information and the development of business plans by establishing strategic alliances.
- Spaces for collaborative learning.
- Etc.

But all of this will be a concept of analysis and presentation of future congresses.

Reference

Alcaraz R., (1995) *El Emprendedor de Éxito (Guía de Planes de Negocios)*, Editorial McGraw-Hill, Interamericana Editores.

Appendices

Appendix to Chapter 17

Appendix 1

Related Programs at the University of Strathclyde

The Center for Enterprise Education

Based within Strathclyde's Faculty of Education at Jordanhill, this Center is a resource for schools throughout Scotland. The Center operates the Scottish Schools Enterprise Program, through which one teacher from every school in Scotland is trained to deliver modules relating to business and enterprise skills. It offers teachers access to an Enterprise Resource Center containing learning materials collected from sources internationally. It undertakes research in Enterprise education and has produced a number of learning packs for use in Primary Enterprise programs. The Center runs a regular 'Enterprise Week' for schools.

The Center's work is contributing significantly to the Scotland-Wide initiative currently being stimulated by Scottish Enterprise to change culture, attitudes and aspirations towards entrepreneurship.

Young Enterprise Scotland

4,000 school pupils annually take part in the Young Enterprise program, which operates in secondary schools throughout Scotland. This is a voluntary activity whereby teams of pupils form companies which trade for a short period, thereby learning about the business process. Local business people give their time without charge to mentor the pupils.

Strathclyde University's Business School has been involved with this program for many years, its Faculty Officer is Vice Chairman of the Glasgow Area Board and organises the administration of the annual examinations which are taken by 2,500 Achievers each year. Furthermore, it is interesting to note that 30 per cent of students taking the Strathclyde Initiative's 'New Venture Creation' class were Young Enterprise Achievers.

Related classes in individual departments

For many years certain departments within the University have offered elective classes relating to business start-up to students in their final year. These have originated as a result of the interests of individual academics, or in some circumstances, at the suggestion of business contacts of Heads of Departments. These classes have been instrumental in encouraging and supporting a number of students in starting successful businesses. Departments involved include:

- Bio-science and Biotechnology
- Design Manufacturing and Engineering Management
- Marketing
- Physics and Applied Physics
- Scottish Hotel School
- Technology and Business Studies
- Strathclyde Graduate Business School (MBA - elective class)

University careers service

The Strathclyde Careers Service (which was awarded a Charter Mark for its service to students) is keen to support initiatives which encourage students to plan their 'portfolio career'. Its Director has been instrumental in organizing short courses and workshops for graduates who wish to consider business start-up. She is developing linkages with dynamic SMEs to allow students to gain vacation work experience and also to develop programs which increase the number of graduates who consider careers within SMEs.

Outreach

The University offers, through a University company, Scottish Management Projects Ltd., a Continuing Professional Development Certificate in Entrepreneurial Studies which is tailored to the needs of SME owner/managers wishing to develop their businesses.

In addition, through the normal consultancy routes, the University continues to be active in supporting growing businesses through the application of the expertise of academic staff in a very broad range of specialisms.

Spin-outs, Science Park and Strathclyde University Incubator

The University's Business Ventures Group, as well as the University's Research and Consultancy Services Department, actively support academic staff in commercializing the results of their research. A number of Strathclyde spin-outs are showing particular promise at this time.

The University operates, jointly with Glasgow University, the West of Scotland Science Park, which provides an excellent environment for science-based companies and houses a number of Strathclyde spin-outs.

The University's Incubator Center, on campus in central Glasgow, was established in 1990 and places emphasis on young technology-based businesses. It provides in-house support for companies in the two most-needed areas - marketing and financial issues. 73 companies have developed to date through the Incubator, of which only four have been liquidated.

Fraser of Allander Institute

The Institute is internationally known for its regional economic modeling, particularly of the Scottish Economy. More recently, its teams have taken particular interest in identifying ways to asses the implications of innovation and entrepreneurship for economic development. Recent studies include:

- Research into the determinants of entrepreneurial choice within the UK
- A major study of the innovation process within manufacturing firms in the UK, Ireland and Germany.

The development of this work is now a priority within the Institute and provides a linkage between the work of the Strathclyde Entrepreneurship Initiative and policymakers.

ETRAC Emerging Technologies Research and Assessment Center

ETRAC is a self-financing Research Center whose expertise is in the strategic management of technological innovation.

'ETRAC brings together a dynamic mix of leading-edge theory and real-world practice.'

Head of Technology Policy and Innovation Division, Department of Trade and Industry.

The main work of the Center is focused on how wealth is created from public-sector research. Thus the Center acts as advisor and undertakes research for policy-makers but also works with departments and research groups within universities, stimulating strategic orientation and enhancing the potential for technology transfer. ETRAC may also partner with financial institutions to advise public sector bodies on enterprise in new technology-based firms.

Appendix 2

Strathclyde Entrepreneurship Education Forum Program 1996/7

The Strathclyde Entrepreneurship Education Forum, organized by the Strathclyde Entrepreneurship Initiative, has the objective to provide a regular Meeting Forum for those responsible for, and interested in entrepreneurship education.

The interchange of best practice and experience is stimulated by meetings, presentations, structured discussion and workshop sessions. In this way the Forum operates as an informal support group, nurturing awareness of and attitudes towards entrepreneurship and associated educational issues.

Launch Meeting - Tuesday 10th December, 1996.

The Significance of Entrepreneurship Education to the University of Strathclyde.

505

Professor John Arbuthnott, Principal, University of Strathclyde.
Dr Mike Yendell, Director, Strathclyde Entrepreneurship Initiative.

How a Young Strathclyde Science Graduate Grew a Multi-million Pound International Business Since 1993.
David Wares, Managing Director, Display Products Technology

Tuesday 21 January, 1997

The Impact of Today's Educational System on the Development of Entrepreneurial Skills.
Are our students more entrepreneurial then they used to be?
What impact are the schools enterprise programs having?

Bob Adams, General Manager, New Ventures, Scottish Enterprise.
Brian Twiddle, Director, Center for Enterprise Education, Jordanhill
Nicola Crofts, Strathclyde Undergraduate, Participant in Young Enterprise Scotland.

Friday 21 February, 1997

Graduate Entrepreneurs' Reflections
'What we wish we had learned when we were at Strathclyde!'

Colin Grant, Managing Director, BioLogic Remediation Works.
Tom Hunter, Managing Director, Sports Division, Scottish Entrepreneur of the Year.

Tuesday 11 March, 1997

Entrepreneurship Education at Rensselaer Polytechnic Institute, USA

Professor Susan Sanderson, Center for Technological Entrepreneurship,
Rensselaer Polytechnic Institute, Troy, New York State.

Tuesday 15 April, 1997

Career Development and Entrepreneurship - Graduate Aspirations and the Changing Graduate Jobs Market.

Alasdair McKenzie, Director, Yellowbrick Training & Development Ltd.
Professor Dave Mckay, Managing Director, JVC Manufacturing Ltd.
Douglas Stewart. President, University of Strathclyde Students' Association.

Thursday, 8 May, 1997

The Biotechnology Enterprise Program - a Collaborative Program between Strathclyde, Glasgow and Paisley Universities.

Professor Iain Hunter, University of Strathclyde.
Dr Maggie Sheen, University of Strathclyde
Alison McCaig, Life Technologies Ltd.

Wednesday 18 June, 1997

An Entrepreneurship Program Linking Business & Engineering Undergraduates.
The University of Limerick Experience.

Patricia Fleming*, Program Leader, Entrepreneurship Faculty, Department of Management, University of Limerick.*

Appendix 3

External Inputs to the Entrepreneurship Initiative Program

- *Numerous Entrepreneurial Businesses in Scotland.* Identifying entrepreneurs who can participate in class sessions is crucial, and provides a rich source of role models and case studies local to, and hence meaningful to, Strathclyde students.

507

- *The Entrepreneurial Exchange.* A membership organization allowing Scottish entrepreneurs to network effectively, this is an excellent source of contacts for staff and students alike. In 1996, at the Exchange's Annual Dinner, now Glasgow's major business dinner, their Entrepreneur of the Year Award was presented to a Strathclyde graduate, Tom Hunter, founder of the Sports Division sportswear retail chain which has a £250M turnover.

- *Glasgow Chamber of Commerce,* Scotland's largest, with 2000 members. Itself an entrepreneurial organization, the Chamber gives support to the Entrepreneurship Initiative.

- *Glasgow Quality Forum.* The Director of the Initiative was instrumental in the development of the Forum, which has 200 member companies, all of whom are committed to quality in business.

- *The West of Scotland Environment Business Forum.* Chaired by the Director of the Initiative, helps companies gain business benefits through improved environmental performance.

- *Scottish Environmental Industries Association.* A new trade association for companies providing environmental goods and services, already having 60 members, many of whom are young entrepreneurial companies. The Director was actively involved with its formation

- *Glasgow Opportunities* provides support to start-up and growing small businesses. It also houses the Glasgow Business Shop, and the Glasgow Branch of the Princes Scottish Youth Business Trust. Students wishing to develop start-up small businesses are signposted to Glasgow Opportunities, just five minutes walk from the main Campus, and receive hands-on assistance.

- *Scottish Enterprise (SE),* who stimulate entrepreneurial activities throughout Scotland and developed the Scottish Business Birth-rate Strategy and provided start-up funds for the Initiative.

- *Glasgow Development Agency (GDA)*, who actively support entrepreneurs locally and have strong interests in knowledge-based entrepreneurship. Funding was secured from GDA for the Alumni Market Research and also to start the Entrepreneurship Education Forum.

- *Lanarkshire Development Agency (LDA)*, who are recognized as having been most successful of the Scottish LECs in supporting high growth start-ups. Funding was secured from LDA for the first purchases within the Resource Center and also for the Alumni Seminars series.

- *Strathclyde European Partnership*, which manages distribution of EU regional funding and puts particular emphasis on the creation and growth of knowledge-based businesses.

- *LINC Scotland.* Scotland's Business Angels Organization.

Appendix to Chapter 19

Index of Entrepreneurship Centers, Competitive Analysis Breakdown

School	Curriculum	Faculty	Student Programs
University of Arizona, The Karl Eller Center	Integrative Classes. Associate offered in 1997 for technical college students.	5 Regular Faculty, 6 business adjunct professors. Play tutorial/mentoring role.	Business Plans Competition, Enterprise Magazine.
Babson College's Center for Entrepreneurial Studies	8 Undergraduate courses, 12 Graduate, Joint majors.	4 Endowed Professorship Chairs, Professor for Free Enterprise.	Mentor Program, Entrepreneurial Exchange, Entrepreneurial Review.
Ball State University, Midwest Entrepreneurial Education Center	6 Undergraduate courses, 3 Graduate courses.		Fast Trac$_{TM}$ I, II.
Baylor University, John F. Baugh Center for Entrepreneurship	Undergraduates complete secondary core and 15 hrs., Graduates -lock - stop core and 9 hrs.		Student Club, Mentor Club Venture News, International Exchange, Student run companies.
Bringham Young University, Center for Entrepreneurship	U/G courses.	3 Entrepreneurs in Residence, Teaching Faculty from all areas in business school (7 are endowed).	Student Entrepreneur of Year/Business Plan competitions, Mentoring.
California State University, Hayward, CSUH Center for Entrepreneurship	U/G courses. U includes practicum for a growth firm. G includes strategic growth plan.	4 Professors involved w/the center Dr. Singson/E of Year for N. Ca.	Internship programs, Students in Free Enterprise(serves as incubator for student ventures).
University of California, Lester Center	Strict division of duties between research and teaching units, 1 - U course, G required internship.		Partners for Entrepreneurial Research, Berkeley Solutions Group.
University of California, Los Angeles, Harold Price Center for Entrepreneurial Studies	15 Graduate School courses. Variety of electives from R&D policy to High Tech Marketing.	Bill Cockrum, Bill Yost voted #1 and #11 entrepreneurship professors by *Business Week Magazine* 15 F/Pt staff.	Mentor Program, Venture Capital Roundtable, Conferences, Career Placement, Competitions.

Community Outreach	Research	Resources	Awards and National Recognition
Dialogue/Guest Speakers, Forums, Start up/ regeneration of 200 Arizona business.	Finaova Business/Academic Dialogue papers edited and published in JAI Press Series.	Supported by H.N. & Frances C. Berger Foundation.	
Entrepreneurial Exchange, National Foundation for Teaching Entre - preneurship, Institutes.	Numerous research, publications and books by variety of authors at Babson.	7 Scholarships.	#1 program by US. News & World Report-5 consecutive years, #1 by *Success Magazine.*
Fast Trac$_{TM}$ I, II.	Dr. Donald F. Kuratko has published over 100 articles, and written seven books.		National model program, Top 10 and 3 by Kauffman Foundation, Ernst & Young, and *Inc. Magazine*
Innovation Evaluation program, Fast Trac, Business Research Center, Institute for Family Business.	SBA On - line, Business Plan Manual, Business Plan Checklist.	5 Scholarships, Center spun off from private enterprise.	Selected as National model by USASBE.
Panel Presentation, Sponsor of Utah Valley Forum, Enterprise Mentors, local incubator.	Primary focus on writing case studies, participation in forums.	Funding form Entrepreneur Founders (90+), 6 Scholarships.	
Sponsors National Innovation Workshop, Feasibility studies, for federally funded technologies.	Focus on technology seminars, assists emerging high tech firms.		Voted one of the top entrepreneurship programs in country by *Success Magazine*, 1995
Works with two laboratories to develop successful technology transfer stratagems, Web site.		Advice from 3 Boards, 2 student Fellowships, 2 - 4 funded internships, 8 - 10 summer intern fellowships.	
Management Development for Entrepreneurs, (200 participants) Seminars for Head Start directors.	Center for Research in Entrepreneurship, Business Development and Innovation.	Board of Advisors oversees finances.	Ranked #4 in nation by *US. News & World Report.*

Index of Entrepreneurship Centers, Competitive Analysis Breakdown

School	Curriculum	Faculty	Student Programs
Carnegie Mellon University, The Donald H. Jones Center for Entrepreneurship	Continuing Education courses, Undergraduate, major emphasis is at graduate level (8).	2 Full Time Profs. 6 Adjuncts, all faculty have experience in entrepreneurship.	Entrepreneurship clubs, contests, projects for local companies.
University of Colorado at Boulder, The Center for Entrepreneurship	4 Undergraduate, 5 graduate.	7 tenure track, 2 adjunct faculty, topics guest entrepreneurs.	Summer internships, Entrepreneurship Organization, focus group consulting.
Cornell University, The Entrepreneurship and Personal Enterprise Program	Educate 750+ students a year. Multi - disciplinary program.	Faculty from seven of Cornell's colleges.	Entrepreneurship Organization, business plan and consulting competition.
The Council for Entrepreneurial Development	Special interest roundtable.	7 Full time Staff.	
DePaul University, DePaul University Entrepreneurship Program	MBA Concentration - 11 courses, Undergraduate - 9 courses.		Small Business Institute, Student Internships, Annual CEM conference, Creative ideas competition.
Harvard University, Graduate School of Business Administration Entrepreneurship Programs	No specific degree.	16 Full time divide time between teaching, research and coursed development.	Plan Contest, Entrepreneurial Learning Program, Student field studies.

512

Community Outreach	Research	Resources	Awards and National Recognition
Seminars, conferences, and programs with affiliated organization in Pittsburgh.	Research is supported on interdisciplinary basis with other faculty members and Ph.D. students.	Advisory Council, financial support for student projects, entrepreneurship library, some scholarships.	
Summer internships, Entrepreneurship Organization, focus group consulting.	Summer internships, Entrepreneurship Organization, focus group consulting.	18 Scholarships, Research Grants.	
Forums, training for area entrepreneurs, pilot site for Kauffman Foundation sales training program.	Entrepreneurial Update, Several published articles.	Internship Stipend program.	
Annual Conferences, Fast Trac, Youth programs, interns.	CED Connections, Membership Directory, Web site, Venture Capital Shortage study.	Governed by 15 member operating Board of Directors.	Selected as one of 3 National Finalists and inducted into Entrepreneur of the Year Institute.
Private Enterprise Symposium, works with area economic development with research and training.	Focused on Economic Development, various books.	#2 Nationally in Vesper's Entrepreneurship Education Survey, Top 25 programs by *Success Magazine* and *Business Week.*	
Field Studies, provides outreach to broader based community, Executive Education Program.			

Index of Entrepreneurship Centers, Competitive Analysis Breakdown

School	Curriculum	Faculty	Student Programs
University of Illinois at Chicago, Institute for Entrepreneurship Studies	MBA concentration, Undergraduate certification.	One Chair, 6 Full time, 4 Tenure Track, 5 part time professors.	Student Entrepreneurship Organization, Collegiate Entrepreneurs of America.
The University of Iowa, John Pappajohn Entrepreneurial Center	21 Graduate/ 21 undergraduate courses, Technological Entrepreneurship Certificate.	13 Faculty, 4 part time from related departments, 9 adjuncts from the business community.	Student internships, Consortium of 15 community colleges to assist in outreach programs.
Kennesaw State University, Department of Management & Entrepreneurship	7 Graduate, Undergraduate courses, Division of Continuing Education.	11 Faculty, 1 adjunct.	International business plan competition, Small Business Development Center.
University of Louisville, College of Business and Publication	1 Undergraduate course, 10 Graduate courses.	2 Full Time Faculty with business experience.	2 Full Time Faculty with business experience.
University of Maryland, The Michael D. Digman Center for Entrepreneurship	1 Undergraduate course (full curriculum planned for 1997 - 1998), 9 graduate courses.		Entrepreneur club, speaker series, internships and placement assistance, group field projects.
University of Nebraska, Lincoln Nebraska Center for Entrepreneurship	4 Undergraduate courses, 3 graduate.	6 Faculty.	Internships, Study Tour, Students in Free Enterprise.

Community Outreach	Research	Resources	Awards and National Recognition
Neighborhood Consulting Connected to UIC incubator, Family business council.	Leads annual research symposium with AMA, focused on marketing.		Top 20 - 25 Program: *Success* and *Business Week Magazine*, 1994 & 1996.
Coordinates Fast Trac training in Iowa, partners with *INC. Magazine* to present 5 Executive seminars.	Venturing - the JPEC newsletter.		Voted top 35 programs by *Success Magazine*, 1996.
Family Enterprise Center, Center for Excellence in Organizations, Corporate Governance Center.	Much research in progress.		
Fast Trac$_{TM}$ I & II, The Family Business Center offers training seminars and individual consulting.	All faculty have published research.	The CBPA sponsors annual grants to encourage other faculty to establish research.	
Business plan reviews, special seminars , speeches and economic development activity.	Quarterly newsletter, Special section, *Venture Capital Mid - Atlantic.*		Top 25 Success Magazine, 1994 - 96, Top 15 US. News and World Report, 1996.
Entrepreneurs of the Future Camp, Pan Pacific conference, Global Conference on Creative Entrepreneurship.	Numerous articles in *Journal of Small Business Management.*	Housed in Management Department.	

Index of Entrepreneurship Centers, Competitive Analysis Breakdown

School	Curriculum	Faculty	Student Activities
New York University, The Berkeley Center for Entrepreneurship	2 Undergraduate, 9 Graduate.		Internships, Student consulting, Entrepreneurial Training retreat, Business Plan competition.
Oklahoma State University, The Entrepreneurship Center	2 Undergraduate, 4 Graduate courses, program only 2 years old.		
University of Oregon, Lunquist Center for Entrepreneurship	5 Undergraduate, 6 Graduate (offered as area in 1996).	5 instructors for Graduate, 10 additional professors.	New Venture Network, New Venture competition, Entrepreneur group, Internships.
University of Pacific, Pacific Center for Entrepreneurship	Undergraduate and Graduate(10) courses.		Internships, student consulting, student run business, outreach activities to local school systems.
University of Pennsylvania, WHARTON Entrepreneurial Center	Oldest center is U.S., Enrollment over 700/yr.	4 standing faculty, 13 adjuncts, visiting scholars program, linkages with developing countries.	
Rensselaer Polytechnic Institute, (CENVT)	4 undergraduate and 9 graduate courses.	5 faculty, 3 clinical faculty.	Intern, EntrePrep, Entrepreneurship Council, Business Plan Competition.

Outreach	Research	Resources	Awards and National Recognition
Entrepreneurial Careers in Family owned businesses, Conferences, Venturing forum.	Berkeley center working papers, Co - sponsor of 'Effectiveness of Entrepreneurship Ed.'.	Price Institute Fellowships, (MBA students), grant from Ira Rennert to support research and teaching.	Top 25, *Success Magazine* 1994 - 96.
Working w/OK government and business to develop a strategy to encourage enterprise.		$10 MM Dept. of Defense grant to support virtual factories who supply to Defense Logistics Agency.	
Association of OR entrepreneurs, forums, Opportunity planning teams (in conjunction with graduate students.		Lundquist Entrepreneurial scholarship.	Named as one of the up and coming schools by *Success Magazine*, 1995.
Entrepreneurship and educational programs, Institute for family business.		Funded by an anonymous grant of $3M.	
Incubator facility, venture capital fund, executive programs.	Small Business Development Center, Journal of Business Venturing, International Research.	Privately financed.	
Incubator program, focus on technology.	Dr. Pier Abetti, 1995 finalist for the Kauffman Foundation Educator of the Year.	Established to create bridge between university, entre - preneurs, incubator and Tech Park.	

Index of Entrepreneurship Centers, Competitive Analysis Breakdown

School	Curriculum	Faculty	Student Activities
St. Cloud State University, Center for Entrepreneurship	Planned for Fall of 1997.		
St. Louis University, Jefferson Smurfit Center for Entrepreneurial Studies	4 Undergraduate and 4 Graduate courses.		Association of College Entrepreneurs, Small Business Institute.
University of St. Thomas, Center for Entrepreneurship	6 Undergraduate, 10 Graduate Courses, linked with Center for Family Business.	1 full - time faculty, 6 adjunct, 30 part time SBDC consultants, 15 part time Fast Trac.	Entrepreneurship club, Master Venture Organization, newsletter.
University of Southern California, The Entrepreneur Program	4 Undergraduate courses, 3 Graduate courses.	Team teaching, 7 faculty.	
Syracuse University, The Michael J. Falcone Center for Entrepreneurship	7 Undergraduate Courses, Minors program to students outside College of Business.	2 Co - Directors.	
The University of Texas at Austin, Center for Commercialization and Enterprise			

Outreach	Research	Resources	Awards and National Recognition
Family firm forum, Gateway research conference, Tots to teens education programs.	Published in many journals including Advances in Entrepreneurship and Journal of Small Business.		Ranked #6 Graduate Program and #1 faculty in the country by *Success Magazine.*
St. Paul Ecumenical Alliance of Congregations, Strategic Alliance Conference Series.	Director, 1994 finalist for the Kauffman Foundation Educator of the Year.	Institute for Frachise Mgt. Small Business Dev. Center, Small Business Institute, FastTrac.	National Model Program Award, Kaufmann Found. Entrepreneur of Year Finalist, Success Magazine.
Business Expansion Network, Family and Closely Held Business Program.	Articles in Journals of Business Venturing.	Advisory council of 30 members.	
SBA case study program.	Research grants.	Center initiated in 1996. Will be able to fund between $20,000 and $30,000 a year for research.	
Austin Technology Incubator, The Capital Network, Center for Technological innovation.	Leading edge theory development, applied research activities.		

Index of Entrepreneurship Centers, Competitive Analysis Breakdown

School	Curriculum	Faculty	Student Activities
Thunderbird University, International Center of Entrepreneurial Studies	Masters in International Management, 9 credit hours.	.	
University of Wisconsin, Madison The Enterprise Center	3 Undergraduate Courses, 8 Graduate Courses.	3 full professors.	U/G Entrepreneur Club, Speakers, Student run companies, Student internships, venture investment programs, student placement.
Xavier University, Xavier Entrepreneurial Center	14 Undergraduate Courses, 9 Graduate Courses.		Roundtable luncheons, Case competition, U Entrepreneurship club.
	Outreach	**Research**	**Resources**
Thunderbird University, International Center of Entrepreneurial Studies	Limited outreach.	Case studies in field.	Lack of resources keeps the center limited to internal purposes.
University of Wisconsin, Madison The Enterprise Center	U.S. and International outreach, conferences, enterprise forum, technology market assessment service.	The Enterprise Newsletter, Research articles in academic and professional journals.	
Xavier University, Xavier Entrepreneurial Center	Incubator, Greater Cincinnati Venture Association, Consulting Services.	Not part of mission.	Dr. Sandy Eustis, Director, won Entrepreneurship Supporter of the Year at Ernst & Young LLP's competition.

Breakdown of Unique Programs and Activities

School	Student Activities	Outreach
Babson College's Center for Entrepreneurial Studies	*MBA students act as consultants to companies for a year. *MBA Students work on semester long project - based assignments. * IMIP: MBA students complete projects for companies in Europe, Latin America, Asia, and the United States.	*Babson Entrepreneurial Exchange sponsors a variety of conferences, seminars, workshops, forums, and guest speakers.
Center for Entrepreneurship Bringham Young University	*3 practicing 'Entrepreneurs in Residence' mentor students who are operating or starting business. Internship program. *3 Students with Russian Language Skills are being sent to Belarus to assist local Entrepreneurs.	*Panel presentations for community. *Sponsor of Utah Valley.Entrepreneurial Forum. *Supports local city - sponsored incubator.
The John F. Baugh Center for Entrepreneurship, Baylor University	*Student - run companies. International Exchange Programs. *Students are interns in Fast Trac.	*Innovation Evaluation Program. *Fast Trac. *Business Resource Center (Small business development center, import/export assistance, workshops and seminars). *Institute for Family Business (family business forums, retreat program, seminars and workshops).
Harold Price Center for Entrepreneurial Studies, The Anderson School at UCLA	*Mentor program, *Noon speaker series, EA Thinktank, Venture Fellows program offers selected students with hands on experience with venture capital management. *Student Investment Fund provides students with real money to invest in stock and bond market.	*UCLA Ventures program provides business feasibility analysis, management consulting services, and business plan presentation to UCLA engineering and research staff.

Centers In BSU's Market

School	Curriculum	Faculty	Student Activities
Xavier University, Xavier Entrepreneurial Center	14 Undergraduate courses, 9 Graduate Courses.	7 adjunct professors.	Roundtable luncheons, Case competition, U Entrepreneurship club.
University of Illinois at Chicago, Institute for Entrepreneurship Studies	MBA concentration, Undergraduate certification.	One Chair, 6 Full time, 4 Tenure Track, 5 part time professors.	Student Entrepreneurship Organization, Collegiate Entrepreneurs of America.
University of Louisville, College of Business and Publication	1 Undergraduate course, 10 Graduate courses.	2 Full Time Faculty with business experience.	Paine Weber Business Plan competition.
DePaul University, DePaul University Entrepreneurship Program	MBA Concentration - 11 courses, Undergraduate - 9 courses.		Small Business Institute, Student Internships, Annual CEM conference, Creative ideas competition.

Outreach	Research	Resources	Awards and National Recognition
Incubator, Greater Cincinnati Venture Association, Consulting services.	Not part of mission.	Dr. Sandy Eustis, Director, won Entrepreneurship Supporter of the Year at Ernst & Young LLP's competition.	Raises all funds through its own activities.
Neighborhood Consulting Connected to UIC incubator, Family business council.	Leads annual research symposium with AMA, focused on marketing.		
Fast Trac$_{TM}$ I & II, The Family Business Center offers training seminars and individual consulting.	All faculty have published research.	The CBPA sponsors annual grants to encourage other faculty to establish research.	
Private Enterprise Symposium, works with area economic development with research and training.	Focused on Economic Development, various books.	Entrepreneurial Strategy, Text and cases; Training and Education of Entrepreneurs.	#2 Nationally in Vesper's Entrepreneurship Education Survey, Top 25 programs by *Success Magazine* and *Business Week.*